The Peri-Urban Interface

We dedicate this book to the memory of Anders Närman (b.1947), colleague, friend, and co-author of Chapter 12, who died suddenly on 15 November 2004. His natural ability to blend scholarship, activism and engagement with state and society wherever he worked in Sweden, Africa and Sri Lanka should inspire us all.

The Peri-Urban Interface

Approaches to Sustainable Natural and Human Resource Use

Edited by
Duncan McGregor, David Simon
and Donald Thompson

London • Sterling, VA

First published by Earthscan in the UK and USA in 2006

ISBN 13: 978-1-84407-188-3 paperback
ISBN 10: 1-84407-188-X   paperback
ISBN 13: 978-1-84407-187-6 hardback
ISBN 10: 1-84407-187-1   hardback

Typesetting by FiSH Books, London
Printed and bound in the UK by Cromwell Press Ltd, Trowbridge
Cover design by Ruth Bateson

For a full list of publications please contact:

Earthscan
8–12 Camden High Street
London, NW1 0JH, UK
Tel: +44 (0)20 7387 8558
Fax: +44 (0)20 7387 8998
Email: earthinfo@earthscan.co.uk
Web: **www.earthscan.co.uk**

22883 Quicksilver Drive, Sterling, VA 20166-2012, USA

Earthscan is an imprint of James and James (Science Publishers) Ltd and
publishes in association with the International Institute for Environment and
Development

A catalogue record for this book is available from the British Library

Library of Congress Cataloging-in-Publication Data has been applied for.

Printed on elemental chlorine-free paper

Contents

List of Figures and Tables

Figures

Tables

List of Contributors

Edlam Aberra is a PhD student in geography at Queen Mary, University of London, UK. Her doctoral thesis investigates the sustainability of the livelihoods of pastoralists settled in urban and peri-urban spaces in the Borana pastoral region of southern Ethiopia. Her interests have been in sustainable livelihoods, gender, peri-urban livelihoods and the urban settlement of pastoralists.

Abdullah Adam-Bradford is an agricultural sociologist with research interests in smallholder farming systems, urban and peri-urban agriculture, appropriate technology, ecological sanitation and community mobilization. Currently, he is undertaking doctoral studies at the Centre for Developing Areas Research, University of London, UK, working on environmental sanitation issues in peri-urban Kumasi, Ghana.

Alhaji Adepetu is a senior member of the School of Geography and Planning at the University of Jos, Nigeria. He has carried out research among the irrigated vegetable producers on the Jos Plateau since the 1970s, and is particularly interested in how they market their produce.

Adriana Allen is a senior lecturer at the Development Planning Unit (DPU), University College London, UK, and the director of the DPU Environmental Planning and Management Programme. Since 1998, she has been involved in a number of research projects that explored different aspects of the peri-urban environmental problematic and responses to it in Argentina, Brazil, Colombia, Egypt, India, Mexico, Ghana, Tanzania and Venezuela.

Rachel Berger has worked for the Intermediate Technology Development Group (ITDG, from July 2005 'Practical Action'), UK, since 2001 and is currently international coordinator of the programme on reducing vulnerability. Following a career in town planning, landscape architecture and environmental consultancy, Rachel completed a Master's degree at Birmingham University's International Development Department in 2000. Special interests include pastoralism as a livelihood system, the promotion of agro-ecological approaches to food production and the impact of climate change on development. She has published on a wide range of topics, including a book on rainforest loss in Malaysia, and an article on conflict over natural resources among pastoralists in northern Kenya.

Prakash Bhat is the director of the Dharwad office of the BAIF Research Foundation Development (Bharatiya Agro Industries Foundation), the largest natural resource non-governmental organization (NGO) in India. He trained as a veterinary surgeon and is now involved in several externally funded research and development projects in the Hubli-Dharwad area.

Tony Binns has been Ron Lister Professor of Geography in the University of Otago, Dunedin, New Zealand, since October 2004. Prior to this, he was based at the University of Sussex, Brighton, UK. Tony has worked in the field of development studies for over 30 years, with particular experience in Africa, where he has had a longstanding interest in food production systems, rural change and community-based development.

Tanya A. S. Bowyer-Bower is a lecturer in geography at Kings College London, UK, and a researcher in the Environment, Politics and Development Research Group. She has focused on issues of environment and development, mostly in Eastern and Southern Africa, since the early 1980s and specializes in drylands.

Robert M. Brook has taught agriculture and rural development in the School of Agricultural and Forest Sciences, University of Wales, Bangor, since 1993. He has managed a number of research projects funded by the UK Department for International Development (DFID) on the peri-urban interface in Hubli-Dharwad, and has participated in others based in Kumasi, Ghana, and in China and Vietnam.

Nimal Dangalle is Dean, Faculty of Graduate Studies and professor of geography at the University of Kelaniya, Sri Lanka. His main fields of interest include development theory, population and regional and urban development. He has made contributions to recognized journals, both local and overseas, on many occasions. Recently he has been involved in a research project on regional development in southern Sri Lanka in collaboration with the late Professor Anders Närman of the Göteborg University, Sweden.

Julio Dávila is a senior lecturer in the Development Planning Unit (DPU), University College London, UK. He has been involved in three large research projects on the peri-urban interface since 1998, and was co-editor with Robert Brook of *The Peri-Urban Interface: A Tale of Two Cities* (School of Agricultural and Forest Sciences, University of Wales, Bangor and Development Planning Unit, University College London, 2000). He has published extensively on urban and environmental planning and management, including articles, three co-edited books and a biography of a mayor of Bogotá, Colombia. He co-founded the journal *Environment and Urbanization* in 1989. He is a trustee of the London-based charity Children of the Andes.

Rocio A. Diaz-Chavez was born in Mexico City and holds a BSc in biology and ecology from the Universidad Autonoma Metropolitana-Iztapalapa, Mexico. She has worked as an academic and an environmental consultant in Mexico and abroad, and has collaborated as a consultant in projects with the United Nations Development Programme (UNDP), the World Bank and the Inter-

American Development Bank (IADB). Her PhD at the Environmental Assessment Unit of the University of Wales, Aberystwyth, was funded by Consejo Nacional de Ciencia y Tecnologia (CONACYT) and Secretaria de Educación Pública (SEP) in Mexico.

Ian Douglas began work in the tropics in North Queensland, Australia, while doing his PhD. In 1966, through the Centre for South-East Asian Studies at Hull University, UK, he began a long association with that region. Originally concerned with humid tropical geomorphology, he became involved with urban environmental issues, publishing *The Urban Environment* in 1983 (Edward Arnold, London). For the Scientific Committee on Problems of the Environment (SCOPE), he has worked on the effects of urbanization on earth surface processes, on peri-urban environmental change, and on the ecological planning and management of cities. He has been at the University of Manchester since 1979.

Jasper Dung is a lecturer at the School of Geography and Planning, University of Jos, Nigeria. Following a Master's degree from the University of Northern Iowa, he is currently undertaking PhD research at the University of Oklahoma. He has been engaged in DFID-funded research on vegetable marketing in Plateau State, Nigeria. Other research interests include soils, geographical information systems (GIS) and remote sensing.

Sampson Edusah is currently at the Bureau of Integrated Rural Development at Kwame Nkrumah University of Science and Technology, Kumasi, Ghana, where he has served a term as director. He has a PhD from Bradford University, UK, and has research interests in rural development and land-use planning in Ghana.

Katherine Gough is associate professor at the Institute of Geography, University of Copenhagen, Denmark. Her main research area is urban issues in developing countries. Starting from a focus on low-income housing she has expanded her research interests to include urban land and housing markets, urban governance and civil society, home-based enterprises, urban youth, and rural–urban linkages. Her main research areas are West Africa (Ghana) and Latin America (Colombia/Brazil), though she has recently also begun to work in South-East Asia (Vietnam).

Frances Harris is senior lecturer in environment and natural resource management at Kingston University, Kingston-upon-Thames, UK. She has worked in Kano, Jigawa and Plateau states of Nigeria, as well as other countries in West Africa. Her research focuses on soil fertility management strategies of smallholder farmers.

Michael K. Kinyanjui has worked for the Intermediate Technology Development Group (ITDG, from July 2005 'Practical Action'), UK, since 2001 and is projects officer in ITDG's Improving Access to Infrastructure

Services programme. Michael is currently undertaking his Master's in urban management at the University of Nairobi, Kenya. He has special interests in urban development, with a key focus on improving participatory urban governance for urban poverty reduction.

Kenneth Lynch is a senior lecturer in geography at Kingston University, Kingston-upon-Thames, UK, where he has lectured in geography and development since 1993. He has published articles on food issues in rural and urban locations in Africa and a book on *Rural–Urban Interaction in Developing Countries* (Routledge, London, 2004). In 2004 he was awarded a National Teaching Fellowship.

Roy Maconachie recently completed his PhD at the Department of Geography, University of Sussex, Brighton, UK. For his doctoral work, he spent one year in northern Nigeria conducting fieldwork on land degradation. He was recently awarded a Leverhulme Early Career Fellowship and is currently based at the Institute of Development Studies at Sussex.

Duncan McGregor is senior lecturer in geography at the Centre for Developing Areas Research, Royal Holloway, University of London, UK. His research interests include tropical land management in general, and soil erosion and land degradation in particular. Ongoing work includes research into land-use change and watershed management strategies in peri-urban Kumasi, Ghana; land degradation and environmental change in the Caribbean; and land-use change in semi-arid West Pokot, Kenya. He has also published on the effects of deforestation on land-use systems in Amazonia.

Madhumita Mukherjee is the deputy director of Fisheries (Microbiology and Parasitology), Government of West Bengal. He has MSc and PhD qualifications in parasitology, with post-doctoral work in microbiology. He has taught at the University of Calcutta and Jadavpur University, India, as well as the Central Institute of Fisheries Education, India, and has administrative responsibility for the Aquatic Resource Health Management Centre of the West Bengal Department of Fisheries.

Michelle Mycoo is a geographer and land-use planner in the Planning and Development Programme, Department of Surveying and Land Information, University of the West Indies, Trinidad. She has published on integrated coastal planning and management, land tenure, gated communities, urban infrastructure provision and water demand management. One current area of research focus is sustainable livelihoods, funded by the UK Department for International Development (DFID). She has been researching the mainstreaming of land-use planning in hazard mitigation, funded by the award of a US Fulbright Fellowship in 2003.

The late **Anders Närman** was an associate professor of human and economic geography, Göteborg University, Sweden. He lectured primarily on various aspects of development issues. A main part of his research was on education, as well as on conflicts and regional development. The location of his research was Kenya, Uganda, Tanzania and Sri Lanka.

Anil Nitturkar is a technical officer working for the BAIF Institute for Rural Development – Karnataka (BIRD-K), which is the local manifestation of the Bharatiya Agro Industries Foundation (BAIF) within Karnataka State, southern India. He is an agricultural graduate with expertise in livestock.

Kwasi Nsiah-Gyabaah is director of Sunyani Polytechnic, Brong Ahafo Province, Ghana. He holds a PhD from Wye College, University of London, UK, has wide-ranging research interests in rural development planning and natural resource management, and has been a local collaborator on a number of UK Department for International Development (DFID)-funded programmes.

Margaret Pasquini is a research officer at the Centre for Arid Zone Studies at the University of Wales, Bangor. She carried out her PhD research (based at Durham University) on the Jos Plateau, Nigeria, studying soil fertility management strategies among the irrigated vegetable producers.

Nigel Poole is a senior lecturer at Imperial College London, UK, and works on the role of agricultural and other natural resource markets and enterprise in economic development. He has researched in Latin America (including 11 years working with indigenous communities in Paraguay), the Mediterranean Basin, sub-Saharan Africa, and South and South-East Asia. Recent research has been published in the journals *Food Policy*, *Development Policy Review* and *Environmental Conservation*.

James Quashie-Sam is senior lecturer and a former director of the Institute for Renewable Natural Resources, Kwame Nkrumah University of Science and Technology, Kumasi, Ghana. He has research interests in agroforestry and remote sensing/geographical information systems (GIS), with recent funding from Canadian and UK agencies, including the UK Department for International Development (DFID).

Kiran C. Shindhe has a postgraduate degree in mechanical engineering and is currently employed as assistant professor in the Department of Mechanical Engineering at SDM College of Engineering in India. He has been involved in peri-urban research since 1997. His focus has been on land-use studies in the peri-urban context, and the changes in natural resources and livelihoods due to urbanization and urban infrastructure.

David Simon is professor of development geography at Royal Holloway, University of London, UK. His particular research interests include development theory and policy; the development–environment interface; urbanization and urban–rural interaction; transport; and geopolitics. He has extensive research experience in sub-Saharan Africa and tropical Asia. He is also editor of *Fifty Key Thinkers in Development* (Routledge, 2005).

Lucy Stevens has worked for the Intermediate Technology Development Group (ITDG, from July 2005 'Practical Action'), UK, since 2002 and is currently international coordinator of the programme on Improving Access to Infrastructure Services. She has a particular interest in urban poverty and development. Her DPhil from the University of Oxford, UK, focused on tracking the impact of upgrading developments in four informal settlements in Gauteng Province, South Africa. This research was conducted in collaboration with the South African NGO Community Agency for Social Enquiry. At ITDG, Lucy manages a number of international programmes in urban areas, which take an integrated approach using the sustainable livelihoods framework.

Donald Thompson is departmental skills and information technology (IT) training officer in geography at the Centre for Developing Areas Research, Royal Holloway, University of London, UK. His main research interests lie in soil erosion and land degradation, fluvial processes, hydrology and water quality. He also has interests in water harvesting technologies. Recent work has included a UK Department for International Development (DFID)-funded project in Kumasi, Ghana, concerned with watershed management and water quality issues in the peri-urban zone; and land degradation and soil erosion in southern Spain. He has also co-led Earthwatch expeditions to the Indian Himalayas.

Paul Yankson is currently professor and head of the Department of Geography and Resources Development, University of Ghana, Legon, Ghana. His area of specialization is urban and regional; he has carried out research in these areas and has published in both local and international journals. His current research interest is decentralization and poverty reduction in Ghana. He holds a BA in geography from the University of Ghana, an MA in urban planning from McGill University, Montreal, Canada, and a PhD in planning studies from the University of Nottingham, UK.

Acknowledgements

We acknowledge the assistance of the Natural Resources Systems Programme of the UK Department of International Development (DFID), who provided funds for the production and distribution of the book to developing areas institutions; to the Scientific Committee on Problems of the Environment (SCOPE) Peri-urban Environmental Change Project (PU-ECH), which made funds available for the attendance of an overseas participant in the conference from which this book is drawn. Our thanks are due to Jenny Kynaston, Department of Geography, Royal Holloway, UK, who redrew and produced all the figures for the book (with the exception of Figure 5.1, for which thanks to Claire Ivison, Department of Geography, Kingston University, UK), and to our departmental secretaries, Anne Ballard, Tricia Eldridge and Melanie Price, who drafted the tables.

List of Acronyms and Abbreviations

ADP	aerial digital photography
AFD	Action for Development (Ethiopia)
AGRITEX	Agricultural Extension Services (Harare)
AMA	Accra Metropolitan Area (Ghana)
APC	African, Caribbean and Pacific
ASG	Atomic Speed Group (Tanzania)
BAIF	Bharatiya Agro Industries Foundation (India)
BIRD-K	BAIF Institute for Rural Development – Karnataka (India)
BOD	biological oxygen demand
BOOT	build–own–operate–transfer
CBS	clan-based support
C/D	city/delegation
CEDEP	Centre for the Development of People (Kumasi, Ghana)
CLF	community level facilitator
CMR	Colombo Metropolitan Region (Sri Lanka)
C/N ratio	carbon/nitrogen ratio
COD	combined oxygen demand
CONACYT	Consejo Nacional de Ciencia y Tecnologia
CSD	United Nations Commission for Sustainable Development
CSZ	Close-Settled Zone
CWSA	Community Water and Sanitation Agency (Ghana)
DAP	di-ammonium phosphate (fertilizer)
DF	Federal District (of Mexico City)
DFID	UK Department for International Development
DHHCS	Department of Health, Housing and Community Services (Harare)
DO	dissolved oxygen
DPU	Development Planning Unit (of University College London)
DSD	district secretariat division (Sri Lanka)
DSIVP	dry season irrigated vegetable production
DTPW	Department of Town Planning and Works (Harare)
EC	European Commission
EC	European Community
EMR	extended metropolitan region
EPA	Environmental Protection Agency (Ghana)
ESAP	economic structural adjustment programme

EU	European Union
FAO	United Nations Food and Agriculture Organization
FDC	Finance and Development Committee (Harare)
FPG	fish production group
GDF	Gobierno del Distrito Federal (Mexico)
GDP	gross domestic product
GIS	geographical information system
GND	*Grama Niladhari* division (Sri Lanka)
GNI	gross national income
GWC	Ghana Water Company
ha	hectare
HDMC	Hubli-Dharwad Municipal Corporation (India)
HIDROCAPITAL	Caracas public-sector regional water supply company (Venezuela)
IADB	Inter-American Development Bank
ICSU	International Council for Science
ICT	information and communications technology
IDRC	International Development Research Center
IDS	Index of Sustainable Development (in Spanish)
IGIP	Ingenieurgesellschaft fuer Internationale Planungsaufgaben
IHDP	International Human Dimensions Programme
IMC	Indian major corp
IMECA	Metropolitan Index of Air Quality (Mexico)
INE	Instituto Nacional de Ecologia
INEGI	National Institute of Statistics, Geography and Informatics of Mexico
IT	information technology
ITDG	Intermediate Technology Development Group
ITTU	Intermediate Technology Transfer Unit (Ghana)
IWMI	International Water Management Institute
JFPM	Joint Forest Planning and Management Programme (India)
JSS	junior secondary school (Ghana)
KBS	kinship-based support
kg	kilogram
km	kilometre
KMA	Kumasi Metropolitan Assembly (Ghana)
KVIP	Kumasi ventilated improved pit latrine
LAP	Land Administration Project (Ghana)
LPG	liquid petroleum gas
m	metre
mg	milligram
MIS	market information system
ml	millilitre
mm	millimetre
MOLAND	Monitoring Land Use/Cover Dynamics project

MOST	Ministry of Surface Transport (India)
MPN	most probable number
n	population sample
NCDC	National Co-operative Development Corporation (West Bengal)
NGO	non-governmental organization
NHDL	Nandi Highway Developers (India)
NPK	nitrogen-phosphorus-potassium (fertilizer)
NRB	Natural Resources Board (Harare)
NRSP	Natural Resources Systems Programme (of DFID)
OECD	Organisation for Economic Co-operation and Development
PADP	Plateau Agriculture Development Programme (Nigeria)
PAR	Participatory Action Research
PRA	Participatory Rural Appraisal
PRSP	poverty reduction strategy paper
PS	*Pradeshiya Sabha* (Sri Lanka)
PU-ECH	Peri-Urban Environmental Change Project (of SCOPE)
PUI	peri-urban interface
SCOPE	Scientific Committee on Problems of the Environment
SEP	Secretaria de Educación Pública
SHEP	Self-Help Electricity Programme (Ghana)
SIMUS	Sequential Interactive Model for Urban Sustainability
SLHTP	St Lucia Heritage Tourism Programme
SMA	Secretaria de Medico Ambiente
SMS	short messaging service
SO_2	sulphur dioxide
SORDU	Southern Rangelands Development Unit (Ethiopia)
SSA	sub-Saharan Africa
SSP	single super phosphate (fertilizer)
UC	unit committee (Ghana)
UCL	University College London
UDA	Urban Development Authority (Sri Lanka)
UN	United Nations
UNCED	United Nations Conference on Environment and Development
UNCHS	United Nations Centre for Human Settlements (Habitat) (*now* UN-Habitat)
UNDP	United Nations Development Programme
UNEP	United Nations Environment Programme
UNESCO	United Nations Educational, Scientific and Cultural Organization
UN-Habitat	United Nations Human Settlements Programme (*formerly* UNCHS (Habitat))
UNRISD	United Nations Research Institute for Social Development
VFC	village forest committee

WATSAN	water and sanitation (committee) (Ghana)
WMF	Watershed Management Framework
WSS	water supply and sanitation
WTO	World Trade Organization
WWF	World Wide Fund for Nature

Part 1

The Search for Peri-Urban Resource Sustainability

Contemporary Perspectives on the Peri-Urban Zones of Cities in Developing Areas

David Simon, Duncan McGregor and Donald Thompson

Introduction

This book brings together a range of conceptual and empirical studies representing the state of the art in contemporary analysis of peri-urban areas in several regions of the global South. The origins of this collection lie in a session on this theme that we organized at the annual conference of the Royal Geographical Society (with the Institute of British Geographers) in London from 5–6 September 2003. The response to our call for papers produced lively presentations and discussions, seeking to explore the relationships between local specificities and contingencies, and the generalizability of peri-urban processes of change. These concerns are reflected prominently in Part 1 of this volume, where we examine definitional and conceptual issues, the approaches adopted by various donor and research-commissioning agencies, and comparative assessments across different situations. Inevitably, a few papers at the original session were unavailable for publication, while a few initially offered but ultimately not presented at the conference have been included as chapters.

In revising the drafts for publication, we encouraged authors to explain the nature of the peri-urban zone or interface (PUI) in their specific contexts, particularly for the case studies, in order to help illuminate the extent of similarities or differences. We pick up these issues both in the definitional discussion below and in Chapter 20; but first we examine the origins and nature of the construct of the peri-urban.

We make no claim for complete geographical coverage and are conscious, for instance, that China, the world's most populous state and where the rate and dramatic nature of urban and peri-urban change are frequently featured in the news media, is not represented. Peri-urbanization there is also rather different from the contexts covered here, being very large scale and often heavily industrialized (Webster, 2002; Webster and Muller, 2002; Webster et al, 2003). In other respects, elements of the extended metropolitan region (EMR) phenomenon outlined below apply to parts of China too. We considered commissioning a chapter on China; however, in view of space considerations and the difficulties of integrating such different material, we resolved instead to draw attention here to the importance of the very different peri-urban processes in that country. Central Asia is also not covered; moreover, very little is known about the nature of peri-urbanization there. Some of the discussion and examples from the literature cited below reflect the predominance of African and South Asian case studies in this book; but they nevertheless illustrate wider generic issues.

Between urban and rural: Distinctiveness or hybridity?

The terms 'urban' and 'rural' are still often used colloquially in traditional, mutually exclusive terms, and most people have clear mental conceptions of some ideal-type landscape corresponding to each. However, this simple dichotomy has long ceased to have much meaning in practice or for policy-making purposes in many parts of the global South, not least sub-Saharan Africa. This is because rapid urban population growth and expansion of the built-up area, technological change, global economic restructuring and the impact of externally driven macro-economic adjustment policies have combined to alter the interface between 'urban' and 'rural' quite profoundly in many places.

Nowhere is there a neat dividing line where the city meets the savanna, bushveld, forest or desert. In a manner reminiscent of colonial suburbanization under conditions of land speculation, cities have spread rapidly but not uniformly. There has been no circular outward ripple. Instead, the process has been differentiated according to combinations of the following factors:

- the size and structure of the existing city;
- the composition of the urban and migrant populations in terms of age, sex, family and household structure (including multi-local households), ethnic, cultural and religious diversity, educational and income levels, urban experience, and so forth;
- extensive oscillating or circular migration, with multi-local households often spanning rural areas and different categories of urban centre;
- physical terrain and environmental barriers beyond the existing built-up area;
- the orientation, accessibility and affordability of transport networks;
- land tenure systems, land values and land uses surrounding the city;
- occasionally substantial differences between administrative/political and *de facto* urban boundaries, which may give rise to contestations over jurisdiction between urban and non-urban local authorities and/or between traditional and state authorities.

As a result, today there are different types of transition zones between city and countryside – between what is unambiguously 'urban' and supposedly typically 'rural'. Some may resemble relatively uniform sprawl, others honeycomb structures or spines of growth along specific corridors. These transition zones – generally known as peri-urban areas in English – vary in width and nature, and are subject to rapid change with increasing urban pressures. Many indigenous villages, previously located in rural areas a considerable distance from the city, have experienced in-migration, growth and changes in population composition, land use and economic base. As a generalization, the closer the city comes, the more pronounced is the transition from 'rural' to 'urban' characteristics. Eventually, these settlements become part of the built-up urban area, which then comprises a complex mixture of formal houses, shanties and rural huts and other dwellings. Although the dwellings may be rebuilt in more urban styles over time, these areas often retain distinct identities and even traditional chieftaincy structures. As indicated earlier, this could bring traditional and state authorities into conflict. Furthermore, these areas may fall within combinations of urban and/or rural local authority boundaries. Subsequent boundary changes to reflect the results of rapid urban growth could then change their administrative status.

It is interesting to note how the term 'peri-urban' – now well-established in the English lexicon – is expressed in different languages and cultural contexts. For instance, the nearest equivalent in Dutch is *halfstedig* (semiurban), in German *urban-ländlichen Zonen* (urban–rural zones) and in Afrikaans *buitestedelik* (outer city or beyond the city). Yet, these differences are modest in comparison to the fact that, in many indigenous languages in the global South, the concept is entirely unknown. Naturally, this presents substantial problems for researching a concept or construct that local people frequently do not recognize, and a salutary warning against assuming the universal relevance of academic or planning constructs. Even where the term does have an equivalent, as in the examples above, the linguistic differences may play a significant role in framing ideas, research and analysis. Definitional issues are no less important and are discussed later in this chapter.

In East Asia and parts of South-East Asia, a new form of EMR has emerged as a process labelled *desakota* (city village) (Ginsberg et al, 1991). While various factors contribute in each case, in general this process primarily reflects the phenomenal economic buoyancy of the Pacific Asian region – apart from the relatively short interruption of the 'Asian crisis' from mid 1997 – and the rise of newly industrialized countries, with often 'hi-tech' production now spilling out of the heavily congested metropolitan cores to cheaper, more accessible areas beyond. Hence, many previously rural areas now have farmland interspersed with small factory units and larger enterprises; all are essentially parts of the urban economy. However, this process has very different characteristics from conventional metropolitanization in that many villages and small urban centres retain much of their previous distinctiveness and some rural activities, while simultaneously being integrally 'plugged in' to manufacturing or processing for the new industries and world economy. Land-extensive tourist and leisure facilities (for example, golf courses and theme parks) catering to urban and international clienteles are also concentrated in such zones (not only in East Asia). The *desakota* phenomenon is thus helping to force a redefinition of traditional conceptions of urban–rural distinctions and relations (Ginsberg et al, 1991; Parnwell and Wongsuphasawat, 1997; Wang, 1997; Douglass, 1998; Kelly, 1998). As Dávila explains in Chapter 4, a similar phenomenon characterizes Latin America's large metropolises, which – because of the particular forms of their close integration with the world economy as identified 20 years ago by Armstrong and McGee (1985) – have also evolved into 'urban archipelagos' with diffuse boundaries and weakened official planning controls.

However, to date, nothing directly comparable has emerged in the very different geo-economic and socio-cultural conditions pertaining in Africa. Although probably more akin to the US beltway and 'edge city' phenomenon (Garreau, 1991), the extended metropolitanization occurring in the Johannesburg–Pretoria region of South Africa's Gauteng Province warrants study in this context. Nevertheless, with the possible exception of parts of South Africa, the African continent remains very largely in the periphery of the increasingly globalized world system, except as a source of natural resources. There are still relatively few export-oriented industrialization or producer services geared towards regional or global markets, although Africa's role as an international 'pleasure periphery' has grown. Indeed, Briggs and Mwamfupe (2000) found little evidence of outer suburban retail malls, office parks or hi-tech industrial nodes in Dar es Salaam, and also suggest that metropolitan polycentricity may have less relevance to Africa than to other regions on account of its global economic peripherality. Polycentricity is itself usually a feature of relatively advanced physical, functional and/or administrative decentralization, something that is occurring more widely in Africa as a result of urban size and congestion (Jaglin and Dubresson, 1993; Briggs and Mwamfupe, 1999). Briggs and Mwamfupe's (1999) conclusion, with which we concur, provides further circumstantial evidence that Asian-style EMRs are not a feature of African metropolises at present (with the possible South African exception mentioned above) since EMRs are quintessentially polycentric, and tend to arise through peri-urban and rural transformation beyond the outskirts of already large and polycentric conurbations. Of course, the question as to whether EMRs might arise in future is difficult to answer; but any such development would almost certainly depend on a significant prior change in the continent's present geo-economic peripherality.

The situation in South Asia is diverse, with increasing export industrial production in Sri Lanka and parts of India, for example; but no literature yet exists on whether Mumbai or other major metropolises fit the EMR model. This book includes a case study of part of Colombo's PUI; but the city as a whole does not constitute an EMR. Even in the very different context of west-central Nepal, on South Asia's outer periphery, Blaikie et al's (2002, p1257) re-study some 23 years after their initial research reveals the often profound nature of 'peri-urban development which has transformed a small village (with a weekly market and six tea stalls under three large banyan trees), into a town (with 60 shops and five banks)'.

The objective of this introductory chapter is to provide a context for the book as a whole through an overview and assessment of recent conceptualizations of PUIs in their wider geopolitical and geo-economic contexts. It then outlines the chapters that follow. Accordingly, the next section examines the growing importance of, and research into, interactions between urban areas and their surrounding peri-urban and rural areas. Thereafter, the nature of peri-urban areas as interfaces between urban and rural areas is explored. The final section comprises a chapter-by-chapter outline of the book's contents.

Beyond the built-up city: The peri-urban interface (PUI) and urban footprints

Many fast-growing large cities across the global South are surrounded by dense and generally impoverished shantytowns or other forms of informal and/or irregular housing, characterized by inadequate infrastructure, service provision and security of shelter. These often spread into previously rural and peri-urban land, commonly enveloping or merging with existing villages of varying age, size, and physical and functional structure. This process creates complex zones in terms of land tenure, security of tenure, land use, access to services, and other measures of social, economic and political integration. These complexities – and the associated tensions and conflicts – therefore pose formidable challenges to planners, governments, non-governmental organizations (NGOs) and the residents alike in terms of enhancing security of tenure, upgrading settlements, service provision, integration with the urban areas and associated governance issues, and forward planning. This explains the recent increase in internationally funded research into, and concern with, peri-urban areas.

On the other hand, changing international divisions of labour are producing new areas of rapid industrialization and economic development within or beyond existing metropolitan boundaries (for example, the EMR phenomenon cited earlier) in some parts of the world. These are accompanied by rising incomes and improved quality of life for some groups of inhabitants, but often at the expense of the immiseration of others in both these new cores and peripheries. However, new local styles, resistances and hybrid forms are emerging to give new forms of diversity at different levels. Hence, significant forces of *divergence* are also at work; the notion of progressive unidirectional *convergence* is too simplistic (Armstrong and McGee, 1985; Simon, 1992; Potter, 1993). Nevertheless, despite the vast literature on individual city growth and management in various parts of the global South, remarkably little attention has been devoted to the urban fringe or peri-urban areas; indeed, the term is absent from the indexes of many books.

The Peri-Urban Interface: A Tale of Two Cities (Brook and Dávila, 2000), a publication arising directly from the UK government's Department for International Development's (DFID's) peri-urban interface research programme in Kumasi and Hubli-Dharwad, India, represents probably the only book-length treatment of peri-urban dynamics. Similarly, little if any attention is devoted to peri-urban zones in the many journal articles and individual chapters on African cities within more general edited books.

Interestingly, a major research programme at the Nordic Africa Institute in Uppsala, Sweden, on the nature and role of small towns in Africa did focus explicitly on aspects of rural–urban interaction (Baker, 1990; Pedersen, 1991; Baker and Pedersen, 1992); but the issue of peri-urban areas and their dynamics received little attention, perhaps because the rate and scale of growth and change has been more limited than in large conurbations.

Following much discussion and definitional debate in both the global North and South during the 1970s (Mortimore, 1975), intellectual interest in peri-urban areas declined. They then received little explicit attention in the literature as a whole, except for limited mention of their rapid transformation by urban sprawl, some rethinking of their position within the rural–urban dichotomy referred to earlier, and the value for integrated urban planning of considering urban regions rather than merely the built-up or administrative areas of individual cities.

However, since the 1980s, the importance of peri-urban areas as a source of urban food supply has been underlined by the growing body of research on urban agriculture (especially in Africa, from which the following examples are drawn), even though much of this literature concentrates largely on urban areas themselves and the 'peri-urban' has been treated in different ways (Guyer, 1987; Sanyal, 1987; Rakodi, 1988; Freeman, 1991; Gefu, 1992; Smit and Nasr, 1992; Memon and Lee-Smith, 1993). A notable exception in Africa is Marshall and Roesch's (1993) study of land tenure and food production in the *zonas verdes* (green zones) surrounding Nampula in Mozambique, which examines how many predominantly female producer co-operatives gained access to high-quality land to supply the urban market successfully before the wave of land privatization during the 1990s. Briggs and Mwamfupe (1999, pp269–272; 2000) argue that research into expanding urban agriculture and its promotion, and research into subsistence versus commercial production priorities there, have been largely responsible for the resurgence of interest in peri-urban zones across Africa since the early 1990s. More recently, attention has also embraced the emergence of formal and informal land markets and the related land-use changes in peri-urban areas.

Maxwell et al (1999) highlight the differences in processes between four peri-urban sites around the Ghanaian capital, Accra. Depending on specific combinations of circumstances, these areas have variously experienced one or more of the following processes: land loss to housing; economic transformation away from agriculture; agricultural intensification and commercialization; environmental degradation; and agricultural decline without replacement by alternative economic activities.

Although the terminology and approach of livelihoods strategies, including diversification and risk spreading rather than merely survival strategies, have rarely been applied to such published work on peri-urban areas, they have been adopted within some ongoing donor-sponsored research (see Brook and Dávila, 2000; Mbiba and Huchzermeyer, 2002; while Rakodi's 2002 edited book demonstrates applications of the approach to *urban* areas on behalf of the DFID). As the livelihoods framework recognizes, many people's livelihoods strategies embrace urban, peri-urban and/or rural areas (Diyamett et al, 2001).

This provides another reminder of the contextual meanings and significance of these terms.

More generally, the growing debate during the early 1990s about urban sustainability helped to concentrate attention on the impacts of cities beyond their boundaries. William Rees introduced the now-popular term the 'urban ecological footprint' to capture these relationships in terms of the importance of thinking about sustainable cities as parts of wider sustainable systems (Rees, 1992). This concept refers to the impact of an urban area on the environment, ecology and natural resources often well beyond its boundaries in terms of 'appropriated carrying capacity'. This involves both source and sink functions regarding which resources (including people as migrants and commuters; construction materials; fuelwood and other energy sources; food and water) are supplied to cities while urban manufactured products, services, effluents and wastes from them are sold, dumped or diffused elsewhere. The precise balances of positive and negative impacts, and their spatial extent, vary over time and between locations (Drakakis-Smith, 1995; Mitlin and Satterthwaite, 1996; Pugh, 1996; Satterthwaite, 1997; Simon, 1999; Yankson and Gough, 1999). However, by virtue of their spatial contiguity, peri-urban zones commonly (but not invariably) experience some of the most substantial impacts.

In turn, these issues have now been linked to the stated objectives of several multilateral and bilateral donor organizations, including DFID, to reduce or eliminate poverty (Burnell, 1998; Brook and Dávila, 2000; Mbiba and Huchzermeyer, 2002; Rakodi with Lloyd-Jones, 2002), although the peri-urban has been defined or conceptualized in very diverse ways, if at all. Since the majority of rural–urban migrants in most parts of the global South nowadays are relatively and/or absolutely poor, they have a great impact upon overall levels and intensities of urban poverty, already often exacerbated by structural adjustment and liberalization policies. Moreover, the difficulties of finding and/or affording accommodation within the existing city means that for some considerable time already, a substantial proportion of predominantly poor urban dwellers have resorted to the urban fringe or peri-urban areas to buy, rent or construct their own shelter. All of these factors have combined to create a very dynamic and important peri-urban transitional or interface zone between city and countryside, between the urban and rural. This raises obvious definitional difficulties, to which we now turn.

Defining the peri-urban

The DFID has funded a research programme on the PUI as one of the 'production systems' within its multimillion pound Natural Resources Systems Programme (NRSP), 1995–2005. The natural resource focus gave the NRSP a strong rural orientation; but the PUI programme represented a conscious strategy to generate new knowledge on the dynamics of change and to ascertain what may be distinctive with regard to urbanization's implications for natural resource use and the environment. The NRSP defined the PUI as follows:

> *The peri-urban interface is characterised by strong urban influences, easy access to markets, services and other inputs, ready supplies of labour, but relative shortages of land and risks from pollution and urban growth.* (Phillips et al, 1999, p5)

It can be divided into two zones, to paraphrase Phillips et al, 1999, pp5–6:

- *a zone of direct impact – which experiences the immediate impacts of land demands from urban growth, pollution and the like;*
- *a wider market-related zone of influence – recognizable in terms of the handling of agricultural and natural resource products.*

There has been some divergence of view and even duplication of research and review effort in terms of the PUI between different arms of the DFID and other agencies (Mbiba and Huchzermeyer, 2002, pp118–119). However, the above definition forms a useful starting point for the main section of this chapter, although we do not make such a clear-cut subdivision within the peri-urban area, preferring instead the notion of an approximate continuum. It is also worth pointing out that even within the NRSP's PUI programme, different definitions have been adopted by the parallel streams of research on Hubli-Dharwad in India and Kumasi in Ghana. For the former, the definition used has been loosely 'the area comprised within the Hubli-Dharwad city region, but outside the core urban area and encompassing the villages connected to Hubli and Dharwad by city bus services' (Brook and Dávila, 2000, pp25–26). Phillips et al (1999) suggest a radius of about 40km around Kumasi as approximating the PUI. In contrast, the original baseline study for Kumasi differed significantly and avoided setting such spatial limits on account of their brief value in a situation of rapid growth and because various activities and processes would straddle any such arbitrary boundary. Instead, the villages selected for study were included by virtue of having bush/fallow agriculture, but which are also experiencing competition for land with non-agricultural uses (Brook and Dávila 2000, pp13, 25–26). Our own approach is broadly compatible with this latter, but goes rather further. Accordingly, it appears that no single definition will fit all circumstances and situations unless couched in broad and functional terms, rather than attempting to set discrete spatial limits.

Hence, our emphasis now is on conceptual distinctions and a process orientation. This is more appropriate for examining the continuum between the poles of urban and rural, and understanding the dynamics of change as they affect particular parts of the peri-urban zone, as well as shifts in the position of the zone as a whole. Theoretically, a peri-urban zone may change in width and the steepness of what we might call its rural–urban gradient over quite short periods of time, depending on the nature of pressures within the growing metropolis and of migration towards it. Similarly, there is little conceptual value in seeking to discern empirical regularities – for example, whether particular city size classes have similar peri-urban features – because of the divergent rates of change around cities of similar size, but located in regions of different degrees of economic dynamism, and the likely influence of socio-cultural and environmental differences in creating diverse situations in cities of comparable size.

In other words, it is unhelpful to expect or to search for uniform processes in different circumstances. Similarity of urban structure (including size) at one point in time is not a good predictor of similarity in underlying processes and the dynamics of change.

The effect of *desakota* and other emerging forms of metropolitanization is to enable some profoundly urban and post-industrial features and activities within rural areas where other conditions are conducive. Conversely, increasing poverty, widespread urban agriculture and livestock rearing are increasing the 'ruralization' of many towns and cities. Therefore, it is increasingly difficult to think of the extremes of the continuum as truly 'urban' and 'rural' in the traditional sense. We need greater flexibility of concept. In practice, the extent of peri-urban zones varies for the reasons just indicated, although 30–50km beyond the urban edge is a reasonable generalization for large cities; major metropolises may have even wider zones (Webster, 2002; Webster and Muller, 2002; Webster et al, 2003).

As a generalization, there is commonly a gradient between more 'urban' and more 'rural' segments within a peri-urban zone. This gradient slopes away from the city but is not of uniform steepness either across the entire zone or in all directions. Indeed, there may well be islands of 'urbanity' in the outer (more rural) segment if pre-existing settlements of considerable size and distinctive economic mix have recently come to be within the zone. In time, these may be absorbed into the expanding city, as has already happened to many proximate villages and other settlements. Conversely, but more unusually, zones or pockets of more rural character may persist within the growing urban area on account of particular environmental, political, institutional or social and cultural factors.

For many purposes, it is important to consider the peri-urban zone as an extension of the city rather than as an entirely separate area. This is because the city region functions in a more or less integrated way in terms not only of its ecological footprint but also of its economic and demographic processes. For instance, agricultural markets provided by rapidly growing urban populations may stimulate commercial production in peri-urban and closer rural areas (see the Nampula, Mozambique, example cited earlier), while recreational landscapes in the PUI may cater to urban and international clienteles. In practice, there are often obstacles to adopting such an integrated functional perspective, let alone to implementing integrated policies. Several reasons for this can be distinguished:

- Urban and previously rural peri-urban areas commonly fall under separate administrative jurisdictions, with different resources, capacities and political leanings. In many metropolises, the municipal or metropolitan council boundaries have been expanded to take account of rapid urban growth – for example, Greater Harare and Nairobi during the 1970s.

However, this has often divided the peri-urban zone, either immediately or after a further period of urban growth, with the inner segment falling within the town and townlands, and the outer segment then falling within one or more peri-urban or rural jurisdictions. Sometimes, however, as in China, the expanded metropolitan boundaries may still encompass the entire peri-urban zone.

- Responsibility for the provision and maintenance of infrastructure and services may lie with different government departments or agencies at central, regional and local government levels.
- Following from the above, census or other urban statistical databases seldom cover the entire area. Compiling inclusive data sets is therefore time consuming and difficult, especially if they have different base years or geographical extents and accuracy of coverage.
- There is no tradition of holistic planning so that most officials adhere to narrow conceptual and procedural guidelines. Traditional bureaucratic procedures invariably discouraged integration across sectors, agencies and areas; this is beginning to change only slowly and unevenly in the face of demonstrable failures of existing practices and the examples being demonstrated by externally funded initiatives.
- In terms of ecological footprints, it is often in the interests of urban officials and planners not to have to engage with, and bear responsibility for, waste disposal and environmental quality 'downstream' beyond the jurisdiction of the local authority. They may therefore seek to avoid such integrated city–region initiatives.
- Villages and rural areas becoming more closely associated with, and enmeshed in, the city's sphere of influence in its peri-urban zone often have distinct histories and identities which the inhabitants are keen to safeguard, even if their lives become more integrated within the urban economy and society over time. An analytical concept used in geography and planning, the term 'peri-urban' or 'urban fringe' is also alien to the vast majority of local people. Instead, village membership is often retained as the main source of community identity, even long after settlements have been enveloped by the expanding city.

Conversely, the peri-urban zone should also be considered as part of the adjacent rural area for purposes of a holistic approach to rural research and development since there are two-way influences and interactions.

Overview of the book's contents

For the sake of coherence, this book is divided into four complementary sections. Part 1, 'The search for peri-urban resource sustainability', comprises four chapters, of which this is the first. Chapters 2 to 4 comprise broad overviews that set the scene for subsequent sections. In Chapter 2, Ian Douglas reviews the approach and work of SCOPE, one of the largest and longest running international research programmes on environmental problems with regard to the PUI. This programme has been responsible for much awareness-raising on relevant issues, including the relationship between environment and society. In Chapter 3, drawing on recently completed comparative research projects, Adriana Allen assesses the most common and pressing environmental problems in the PUIs of large metropolises in different regions of the South. Finally, in Chapter 4, Julio Dávila adopts a similar approach, but with the emphasis on policies adopted to address such problems. He distinguishes policies with explicit spatial elements from those where the spatial impact, if at all discernible, is indirect.

Part 2, 'Production systems at the peri-urban interface', is devoted to studies of particular peri-urban production systems, most of which reflect opportunities presented by growing urban demand. In Chapter 5, Frances Harris, Margaret Pasquini, Jasper Dung and Alhaji Adepetu examine the social and environmental impacts of irrigated dry season vegetable cultivation in the PUI of Jos, Nigeria. Despite concerns about soil fertility, water resource management and disease control, agriculture in Jos's PUI is thriving and now supplies markets countrywide. This is followed, in Chapter 6, by Kenneth Lynch and Nigel Poole's assessment of the use and impact of horticultural marketing information around Tanzania's capital, Dar es Salaam, during the period of market liberalization. This encompasses the nature and dissemination of market information, and the potential impact of information and communications technologies (ICT) in reducing and mediating farmers' total risk and honing their marketing strategies. The chapter is informed by a case study of the wonderfully named Atomic Speed Group, the members of which produce well together but lack a collective marketing strategy or even appropriate skills and information. In Chapter 7, Robert Brook, Prakash Bhat and Anil Nitturkar report on the rapid growth and profitability of stall-fed (that is, zero-grazing) dairying in the PUI of Hubli-Dharwad in India's Karnataka state. This study and that reported in Chapter 13 report on research undertaken as part of the DFID NRSP's PUI programme, in which Hubli-Dharwad formed the South Asian focus in parallel with Kumasi, Ghana, in sub-Saharan Africa (see Chapters 16 and 19). Although the distribution of gains from dairying around Hubli-Dharwad is uneven, this development has enabled even poor people to improve the sustainability of their livelihoods and quality of life. Similarly, Madhumita Mukherjee's study of peri-urban fish culture using urban waste in Chapter 8 reflects the scope to help meet urban protein requirements through exploiting a non-traditional adaptation of a traditional livelihood activity. Careful design of fish ponds and systematic use of the associated banks and dykes points the way to holistic and sustainable land use, and to augmented livelihood and leisure opportunities. As Edlam Aberra demonstrates in Chapter 9, the harsh realities in southern Ethiopia are driving livestock-destitute pastoralists to settle increasingly permanently in the PUI of Yabello, where they are forced to adopt diverse livelihoods strategies that have hitherto proven unsustainable. Finally, Chapter 10 by Michelle Mycoo comprises an overview of livelihoods strategies in the settlement of Anse La Raye on the small Caribbean island of St Lucia. This highlights that 'peri-urbanness' exists at very different geographical scales, from EMRs to centres that are considered large only in their very local context.

Part 3, 'Planning and development of the peri-urban zone', shifts attention to issues of peri-urban planning and management. In Chapter 11, Tanya Bowyer-Bower draws on her field research in Harare, Zimbabwe, to explore the conceptual and practical policy challenges of achieving sustainability in the PUI in a situation where the urban authorities have persisted with restrictive policing against cultivation, despite the worsening economic and food security situation during recent years. In Chapter 12, in the very different context of Gampaha, the northernmost of the three districts constituting Sri Lanka's Colombo Metropolitan Region, Nimal Dangalle and the late Anders Närman assess the social, economic and environmental costs of peri-urbanization. The rate and scale of land conversion from agricultural to residential, commercial and industrial uses in the face of demographic densification and transformation will intensify with the promotion of three official growth centres in the district. Chapter 13 examines the implications of the construction of a national highway bypass around the twin cities of Hubli-Dharwad in India's Karnataka state on livelihoods in the peri-urban area. Kiran Shindhe concludes that the poor, who have fewer lands, are most affected by the loss of livelihoods. On the basis of the research experience, he suggests a set of policies to assist the poor, in particular, and to minimize the overall effects of major bypass construction. Chapter 14 provides a longitudinal perspective on both planned and unplanned peri-urban change. Katherine Gough and Paul Yankson revisited five peri-urban communities around Accra, Ghana, some eight years after their initial research and here they explore their findings by means of 'stories' that encapsulate the dominant dynamic in each. In Chapter 15, Tony Binns and Roy Maconachie draw on the considerable body of existing work on the historically dynamic Close-Settled Zone (CSZ) surrounding Kano in northern Nigeria as a context to their recent research assessing the sustainability of current human–environment relationships. Examining competition for land, soil fertility and erosion, changing tree cover and fuelwood use, and water quality along a transect of settlements through the zone against the backdrop of deepening economic crisis, they conclude that sustainable livelihoods are increasingly under pressure and add to the growing literature highlighting the need to move beyond the stale polarities of the Malthusian versus Boserupian debate over people–environment relationships.

Finally, Part 4, 'Strategies for sustainable development', seeks to chart some possible ways forward in the complex and dynamic circumstances prevailing in the PUI. In Chapter 16, Abdullah Adam-Bradford, Duncan McGregor and David Simon indicate the considerable potential of house-hold-scale community-based waste recycling in poor peri-urban communities. Their study of Kumasi, Ghana, assesses how different appropriate technologies can be utilized to help residents compost the high proportion of organic waste in their household refuse in order to tackle the waste disposal problem, to create a healthier living environment and, in particular, to promote higher agricultural yields for their own kitchen gardens or plots or to create an income stream through compost sales. In Chapter 17, Rocio Diaz-Chavez presents her research into the value of a set of peri-urban sustainability indicators, with an application to Mexico City. Linked to current international initiatives, this is designed to provide a geographical information systems (GIS)-based toolkit to facilitate regular monitoring and policy-making by planners, local authorities and other stakeholders. A different approach is provided in Chapter 18 by Lucy Stevens, Rachel Berger and Michael Kinyanjui, who survey the experiences of their NGO, the Intermediate Technology Development Group (ITDG) in Nakuru, Kenya, with several community-based initiatives to tackle the prevailing economic, social and environmental problems in this environmentally important area abutting the famous Lake Nakuru National Park in the Rift Valley. They see social mobilization to empower the poor as a key starting point, while a process of participatory technology development enables improvements in livelihoods – both of these through increased financial and social capital. The final substantive chapter, by Duncan McGregor, David Simon, Donald Thompson, James Quashie-Sam, Sampson Edusah and Kwasi Nsiah-Gyabaah, presents an innovative co-management approach to the complex and dynamic situation in Kumasi's PUI. This water management framework was a key output from a DFID-funded action research project that sought to demonstrate how much residents could do to improve their own living conditions, and to empower them to interact with and draw upon official and other actors in managing the changing conditions cooperatively. Chapter 20 by Duncan McGregor, David Simon and Donald Thompson then offers some concluding editorial reflections on the contents of the book and the contribution that this collection makes to advancing understanding and appropriate policies to promote sustainable resource use and livelihoods in the PUI.

Acknowledgements

Previous versions of some of the arguments in this chapter have appeared as 'Veränderungen von urban-ländlichen Zonen in afrikanischen Städten' by David Simon in the German journal *Peripherie* (2001) vol 81/82, pp138–162; and David Simon, Duncan McGregor and Kwasi Nsiah-Gyabaah (2004) 'The changing urban–rural interface of African cities: Definitional issues and an application to Kumasi, Ghana', *Environment and Urbanization*, vol 16, no 2, pp235–247. This work formed an output from a project funded by the UK Department for International Development (DFID) for the benefit of developing countries. The views expressed are not necessarily those of DFID.

References

Armstrong, W. and McGee, T. G. (1985) *Theatres of Accumulation; Studies in Latin American and Asian Urbanization*, Methuen, London

Baker, J. (ed) (1990) *Small Town Africa: Studies in Rural–Urban Interaction*, Nordiska Afrikainstitutet, Uppsala

Baker, J. and Pedersen, P. O. (eds) (1992) *The Rural–Urban Interface in Africa: Expansion and Adaptation*, Nordiska Afrikainstitutet, Uppsala

Blaikie, P. M., Cameron, J. and Seddon, D. (2002) 'Understanding 20 years of change in west-central Nepal: Continuity and change in lives and ideas', *World*

Development, vol 30, no 7, pp1255–1270

Briggs, J. and Mwamfupe, D. (1999) 'The changing nature of the peri-urban zone in Africa: Evidence from Dar-es-Salaam, Tanzania', *Scottish Geographical Journal*, vol 115, no 4, pp269–282

Briggs, J. and Mwamfupe, D. (2000) 'Peri-urban development in an era of structural adjustment in Africa: The city of Dar es Salaam, Tanzania', *Urban Studies*, vol 37, no 4, pp797–809

Brook, R. M. and Dávila, J. D. (eds) (2000) *The Peri-Urban Interface: A Tale of Two Cities*, School of Agricultural and Forest Sciences, and Development Planning Unit, University College London, Bangor and London

Burnell, P. (1998) 'Britain's new government, new White Paper, new aid? Eliminating world poverty: A challenge for the 21st century', *Third World Quarterly*, vol 19, no 4, pp787–802

Diyamett, B., Diyamett, M., James, J. and Malaba, R. (2001) 'The case of Nimo and its region, northern Tanzania', *Rural–Urban Interactions and Livelihood Series, Working Paper 1*, IIED, London

Douglass, M. (1998) 'A regional network strategy for reciprocal rural–urban linkages: An agenda for policy research with reference to Indonesia,' *Third World Planning Review*, vol 20, no 1, pp1–33

Drakakis-Smith, D. (1995) 'Third world cities: Sustainable urban development 1', *Urban Studies*, vol 32, nos 4–5, pp659–677

Freeman, D. B. (1991) *A City of Farmers: Informal Urban Agriculture in the Open Spaces of Nairobi*, McGill University Press, Montréal

Garreau, J. (1991) *Edge City: Life on the New Frontier*, Doubleday/Anchor Books, New York

Gefu, J. O. (1992) 'Part-time farming as an urban survival strategy: A Nigerian case study', in Baker, J. and Pedersen, P. O. (eds) *The Rural–Urban Interface in Africa: Expansion and Adaptation*, Nordiska Afrikainstitutet, Uppsala

Ginsberg, N., Koppel, B. and McGee, T. (eds) (1991) *The Extended Metropolis: Settlement Transition in Asia*, Hawaii University Press, Honolulu

Guyer, J. I. (ed) (1987) *Feeding Africa's Cities: Studies in Regional Social History*, Manchester University Press, Manchester

Jaglin, S. and Dubresson, A. (1993) *Pouvoirs et Cités d'Afrique Noire: Décentralisations en Gestion*, Karthala, Paris

Kelly, P. F. (1998) 'The politics of urban–rural relations: Land use conversions in the Philippines', *Environment and Urbanization*, vol 10, no 1, pp35–54

Marshall, J. and Roesch, O. (1993) 'The "green zones" agricultural co-operatives of Nampula city: A new phase in the Mozambican co-operative movement?', *Journal of Southern African Studies*, vol 19, no 2, pp240–272

Maxwell, D. W., Larbi, O., Lamptey, G. M., Zakariah, S. and Armar-Klemesu, M. (1999) 'Farming in the shadow of the city: Changes in land rights and livelihoods in peri-urban Accra', *Third World Planning Review*, vol 21, no 4, pp373–391

Mbiba, B. and Huchzermeyer, M. (2002) 'Contentious development: Peri-urban studies in sub-Saharan Africa', *Progress in Development Studies*, vol 2, no 2, pp113–131

Memon, P. A. and Lee-Smith, D. (1993) 'Urban agriculture in Kenya', *Canadian Journal of African Studies*, vol 27, no 1, pp25–42

Mitlin, D. and Satterthwaite, D. (1996) 'Sustainable development and cities', in Pugh, C. (ed) *Sustainability, the Environment and Urbanization*, Earthscan, London

Mortimore, M. (1975) 'Peri-urban pressures', in Moss, R. P. and Rathbone, J. (eds) *The Population Factor in African Studies*, University of London Press, London

Parnwell, M. J. and Wongsuphasawat, L. (1997) 'Between the global and the local: Extended metropolitanisation and industrial decision making in Thailand,' *Third World Planning Review*, vol 19, no 2, pp119–138

Pedersen, P. O. (ed) (1991) 'The role of small and intermediate urban centres in planning in Africa', Special issue of *African Urban Quarterly*, vol 6, nos 3 and 4

Phillips, D., Williams, K., Andrews, G., Clarke, J., Carter, M., Kinsman, P., Smith, D., Willis, K., Bradbury, I., Wu, K. and Hillyer, A. (1999) *Literature Review on Peri-Urban Natural Resource Conceptualisation and Management Approaches*, Final Technical Report, DFID Natural Resources Systems Programme (NRSP), Project R6949, University of Nottingham and University of Liverpool

Potter, R. B. (1993) 'Urbanisation in the Caribbean and trends of global convergence-divergence', *Geographical Journal*, vol 159, no 1, pp1–21

Pugh, C. (ed) (1996) *Sustainability, the Environment and Urbanization*, Earthscan, London

Rakodi, C. (1988) 'Urban agriculture: Research questions and Zambian evidence', *Journal of Modern African Studies*, vol 26, pp495–515

Rakodi, C. with Lloyd-Jones, T. (eds) (2002) *Urban Livelihoods: A People-Centred Approach to Reducing Poverty*, Earthscan, London

Rees, W. E. (1992) 'Ecological footprints and appropriated carrying capacity: What urban economics leaves out', *Environment and Urbanization*, vol 4, no 2, pp121–130

Sanyal, B. (1987) 'Urban cultivation amidst modernization: How should we interpret it?', *Journal of Planning Education and Research*, vol 6, pp197–207

Satterthwaite, D. (1997) 'Sustainable cities or cities that contribute to sustainable development?', *Urban Studies*, vol 34, no 10, pp1667–1997

Simon, D. (1992) *Cities, Capital and Development: African Cities in the World Economy*, Belhaven, London

Simon, D. (1999) 'Rethinking cities, sustainability and development in Africa', in Kalipeni, E. and Zeleza, P. T. (eds) *Public Quarrels and Sacred Spaces: African Cultural and Economic Landscapes*, Africa World Press, Trenton, New Jersey

Smit, J. and Nasr, J. (1992) 'Urban agriculture for sustainable cities: Using wastes and idle land and water bodies as resources', *Environment and Urbanization*, vol 4, no 2, pp141–152

Wang, M. Y. L. (1997) 'The disappearing rural–urban boundary: Rural socioeconomic transformation in the Shenyang-Dalian region of China', *Third World Planning Review*, vol 19, no 3, pp229–250

Webster, D. (2002) 'On the edge: Shaping the future of peri-urban East Asia', Stanford University Asia/Pacific Research Center Discussion Paper, Stanford University

Webster, D., Cai, J., Muller, L. and Luo, B. (2003) 'Emerging third stage peri-urbanization: Functional specialization in the Hangzhou peri-urban region', Stanford University Asia/Pacific Research Center Discussion Paper, Stanford University

Webster, D. and Muller, L. (2002) 'Challenges of peri-urbanization in the lower Yangtze region: The case of Hangzhou-Ninbo Corridor', Stanford University Asia/Pacific Research Center Discussion Paper, Stanford University

Yankson, P. and Gough, K. (1999) 'The environmental impact of rapid urbanisation in the peri-urban area of Accra', *Danish Journal of Geography*, vol 99, no 1, pp89–100

2

Peri-Urban Ecosystems and Societies: Transitional Zones and Contrasting Values

Ian Douglas

Introduction

Peri-urban areas are the transition zone, or interaction zone, where urban and rural activities are juxtaposed, and landscape features are subject to rapid modifications, induced by human activities. These critical areas of land cover change, leading to transformations in the hydrological, ecological, geo-morphological and socio-economic systems, are often neglected by both rural and urban administrations. However, as cities develop, much of their growth is located in such areas. Many peri-urban activities move outwards as the city grows; other activities and land uses become incorporated within the urban fabric. Peri-urban areas are mosaics of temporary, new residents and activities mingled with longstanding land uses, including farms, villages, quarries and forest patches.

Peri-urban areas receive two flows of migrants creating wide variations in wealth and social status: urban people seeking a more rural lifestyle or cheaper accommodation, and poorer rural people searching for work and better chances for their children. The peri-urban areas of many cities have both high value middle-class properties and poor in-migrant squatter settlements a few hundred metres apart. Located among these uses will be market gardening, sand and gravel workings and brick clay pits, oil refineries, petrochemical plants, power stations, tanneries, airports and divided highways.

Peri-urban areas thus come to be valued in different ways by diverse groups. These values vary between continents, nations and regions. They include:

- *for the poor:* places where it is easier to build shelters and to occupy land for agriculture;
- *for industry:* sources of materials essential for urban life: water, brick-clays, sand and gravel, limestone, fuelwood and timber;

- *for the middle class:* a place for houses in a rural setting, with golf courses and other recreational facilities;
- *for local government:* sites for landfills, waste dumps, peripheral freeways, airports or noisy and toxic industries;
- *for conservationists:* the site of valuable protected areas, forested hills, preserved woodlands, important wetlands or mangroves, and major coastal ecosystems;
- *for education and human well-being:* the place of first contact that urban people have with major areas of natural vegetation and biodiversity.

The task of this chapter is to attempt a developing areas perspective of our scientific understanding of these diverse peri-urban environments, indicating the key issues of peri-urban areas seen by scholars in Latin America, Africa and Asia. It reports evidence collected in the Peri-Urban Environmental Change Project (PU-ECH) of the Scientific Committee on Problems of the Environment (SCOPE) of the International Council for Science (ICSU). Established by ICSU in 1969, SCOPE undertakes assessments of what we know about key, emerging environmental issues and identifies the most important research priorities for future work on those issues. Forty national academies of science (including The Royal Society), 26 scientific unions (including the International Geographical Union) and several other ICSU interdisciplinary bodies, such as the International Human Dimensions Programme (IHDP), are members of SCOPE. Their representatives elect the SCOPE Executive and approve SCOPE projects. The projects range from the impacts of military development of nuclear sites to endocrine disruptors. They are usually undertaken in partnership with scientific unions, other ICSU committees or bodies, such as the United Nations Educational, Scientific and Cultural Organization (UNESCO) and the United Nations Environment Programme (UNEP). Projects are put forward by members, by the Executive or by United Nations (UN) bodies. On approval by the United Nations General Assembly, a project scientific advisory committee, normally with a member from each continent, is appointed. The PU-ECH scientific committee has members from Argentina, Canada, China, Italy, the UK, Zambia and UNESCO. It has held meetings in Argentina, China, Lebanon, Nigeria and Zambia, which between them have brought together some 200 scientists from 65 different countries. The sections of this chapter relate to the seven themes of PU-ECH. Contributions from the meetings are identified by the participant's name and the meeting (for example, PU-ECH Abuja).

The need for an applied science view

Managing peri-urban areas requires an integrated view of all the activities and land uses occurring within them. Much research, however, tends to be thematic, focusing on individual important sectors of activity – sectors which inevitably impinge on other activities, such as the effects of atmospheric pollutants on peri-urban agricultural crops. If the perspective of ecosystem dynamics is adopted and human interventions are seen as perturbations of ecosystems, peri-urban environmental change becomes part of the global biogeochemical cycling supporting all life. What makes the peri-urban environment so interesting is the complexity of political, economic and social drivers impacting locally on those biogeochemical cycles and the resulting outcomes for the health, well-being and economic survival of people in peri-urban communities. Ecosystem dynamics can be used to link decisions and actions by one agency to outcomes and consequences for communities and individuals. In this way, we can allocate responsibilities, identify environmental injustices and assess the consequences, both on-site and off-site of planned future peri-urban changes.

Integrated management of a contested space, where the off-site impacts of land uses and activities are at least as important as those within the changing land unit, thus becomes a challenge to all the environmental, geographical and planning disciplines. It is as complex as delivering Local Agenda 21 since it involves reconciling the diverse special interests of different sectors and communities to achieve agreed shared goals by developing understanding between politicians, business, officials, civil society organizations and the public. The first step in this is to achieve a shared awareness of the different interests and concerns in peri-urban environments. This begins by understanding the nature and rate of land-use/land cover change.

The nature and rates of land cover/land-use change in developing area peri-urban zones

The poor and the middle class affect peri-urban land use differently. Low-density middle-class urban sprawl – the occupation of former rural land by low-rise developments – is becoming a major issue in developing countries. With probably 300 million middle-class people each in India and China, peri-urban housing estates are occupying farm land and increasing food prices for rich and poor alike. Particularly spectacular urban spread occurs in the Pearl River Delta (Li and Yeh, 2004) and around Shanghai and Beijing, the built-up area of the latter expanding by 25 per cent between 1992 and 2002 (Li et al, 2005).

The European Commission (EC) Monitoring Land Use/Cover Dynamics (MOLAND) project on urban and regional land-use change has been applied to several cities in Africa. Defining the urban system as the portion of land covered with continuous artificial surfaces, including a buffer of the same area around them, MOLAND develops indicators of change in areas of peri-urban agriculture and natural vegetation (Barredo and Demichelli, 2003). Using information ranging from early maps to the detail of IKONOS and specially flown aerial digital photography (ADP), the evolution and outward shift of peri-urban areas can be established. Good ground-truthing is particularly important. For example, work in Kumasi, Ghana, found that digital methods tended to classify sand extraction (quarrying) areas – a common peri-urban land use around the city – as built environment, thus exaggerating the land area occupied by settlements (Pender et al, 1999). Peri-urban expansion has been modelled by examining how individual grid cells of land around cities will respond to the factors driving change, such as land attributes, land prices and proximity to commuter highways (Cifaldi et al, 2004). At the PU-ECH Abuja meeting, C. L. Odimuko emphasized the need for a national land information system in Nigeria with organized and standardized data on secure tenure, title, deeds and structures, and the Honorable Levi Oguike explained the use of spatial information systems for tracking urban growth, in-migration, spread of housing and illegal occupation of land.

Peri-urban land cover/land-use changes and their origins in processes of migration, poverty and providing basic human needs

Migration forced by war, civil conflict or environmental degradation often increases peri-urban populations. The prolonged civil war in Mozambique caused approximately 6 million people to move to peri-urban areas where resource degradation is now an increasing problem. More than 70 per cent of these people are 'ultra-poor', unable to afford the minimum daily nutritional intake of food. This situation occurs in many African cities, where the urban poor often devote 60–70 per cent of their incomes to purchasing food (Tanya Bowyer-Bower, PU-ECH Shenzhen). In the Maila Saba peri-urban settlement of Nairobi, 68 per cent of the households in this informal settlement practise some kind of farming and can earn up to US$6.5 per week. They have no security of tenure and rely on being able to break into the dilapidated town sewer pipe to divert water to their plots at least once a week (Sammy Ngoke, PU-ECH Shenzhen). Some municipal officials consider urban agriculture to be a backward step (Eduardo Spiaggi, PU-ECH Rosario). Tenure regularization on peri-urban land and policies linking peri-urban agriculture to food security are needed (Shingirayi Mushamba, PU-ECH Lusaka).

Despite its contribution to supplying immediate food needs, the effectiveness of urban agriculture is being questioned (Lynch et al, 2001) (see Table 2.1). Many women food producers suffer stress and poor health due to their insecurity, risk of eviction and pollution of crops (Rain, 1997). Large numbers of people grow their own food around Amman, Jordan; but they use so much fertilizer that adjacent aquifers are affected. Poor home gardeners suffer from severe water shortages and are unable to buy extra water or to purchase storage tanks for rainwater harvesting (Khamis Raddad, SCOPE Beirut).

Consequences of land cover/land-use changes as induced by materials flows for shelter, manufacturing, infrastructure and transportation: Accumulation of the urban 'stock'

Cities have always exploited the local forests, clays, sands, gravels and rocks of their immediate hinterland to build shelter and infrastructure. While timber is

Table 2.1 *The benefits and problems of peri-urban agriculture*

Benefits	Problems
Vital or supplementary food source	Seasonal water shortages for irrigation
Ensuring availability of fresh vegetables	Health impacts of contaminated waste
Food waste provides livestock feed	Air pollution impacts on crop yields
Environmental benefits (for example, flood basins; carbon sequestration; urban heat island modification)	Contamination of crop foliage
	Pollution of aquifers by contaminated irrigation water
Employment for the jobless	Irrigation water malaria risks
Survival strategy for low-income residents	Insecurity of agricultural land tenure
Use of urban wastes as fertilizers	Potential conflict with other land uses
	Often administratively an 'illegal' or inappropriate land use
	Real impact on overall urban food supply may be limited
	Relative advantages of peri-urban or rural production unclear

Source: adapted from Lynch et al, 2001; Agrawal et al, 2003; Afrane et al, 2004

now traded globally, materials for brick and concrete manufacture continue to be sourced close to cities, often at the expense of important land uses, especially peri-urban agriculture and horticulture, as around Aligarh City, India (Singh and Asgher, 2005). Clay working and brick manufacture degrade both land and the environment, forcing farmers to shift their land from agricultural to non-agricultural uses. Around Aligarh, farmers and agricultural workers are now contractors, labourers or drivers, or even brick kiln owners. Development and prosperity in these villages have increased; but the government and environmentalists are concerned about the serious impacts of brick kilns on land and the environment. Alternative materials, such as saline and alkaline soils, red soils and fly ash mixed with inferior-quality clay, could be used instead of fertile agricultural soils.

Around the Argentine city of Mar del Plata, much land has been disturbed by clay extraction for brick-making, with illegal clay working in many places. Use of the holes left behind as landfills leads to many problems, particularly groundwater pollution. In many places above the fractured ortho-quartzite bedrock, seepage from the landfill has caused severe nitrate contamination, affecting many wells beneath the city (Luis del Rio, PU-ECH Rosario).

Many consequences of minerals extraction arose in discussion at PU-ECH Beirut. Deep quarries some 30km west of Cairo and former phosphate mines outside Amman, Jordan, are used for landfill. Although quarrying on Mount Lebanon is now banned, little rehabilitation of the extensive unregulated quarrying that took place during the Lebanese war has transpired. Coastal land reclamation is occurring in Lebanon at many sites, from Beirut northwards to Tabarja. Widespread beach mining – the illegal extraction of sand from the foreshore – in Lebanon affects coastal erosion. Beach ownership is now a politically significant peri-urban issue, with access to many parts of the coast being cut off by fences and claims of private ownership.

Air and water pollution and soil and land contamination in peri-urban areas, and their health and ecosystem impacts

Peri-urban ecosystems involve great modifications of natural biogeochemical flows. Chemical transformations associated with manufacturing, food processing and urban building lead to the release of heavy metals, plant nutrients and organic compounds to the atmosphere and to soil and water bodies that in excessive concentrations may cause harm to living organisms. Poor sanitation and drainage compound these problems. Many peri-urban residents cope with high local pollution levels every day of their lives.

Around Karachi, Pakistan, water supplies and waste management cannot cope with haphazard urban growth, especially in peripheral squatter settlements. However, the Orangi township has overcome some of the issues through a series of public–private partnerships developed after complex social factors, including lack of initiative, local politics and disputed payments to tanker contractors, led to water riots. Tanks built by the military force, the Pakistan Rangers, filled by commercial contractors (Ahmed and Sohail, 2003) and managed by the mosque and neighbourhood local elder committees, are regarded by local people as a temporary arrangement until the sustainable long-term solution of a piped supply arrives.

Throughout the world, some municipal sewer systems are overloaded, others have combined sewers with storm overflows to rivers, while some lack maintenance and leak and others are deliberately broken to extract irrigation water, exposing farmers to dysentery and cholera risks from faecal bacteria and worm infestation (Bradford et al, 2003). Nevertheless, urban wastewater is used for agriculture in Kumasi, Ghana, through collaboration with local communities to control impacts on watercourses by careful latrine siting. Industrial effluents pose bigger problems, with instances of textile dyes being thrown directly into channels and municipal trucks dumping sewage, which then flows directly into channels (Kwasi Nsiah-Gyabaah, Duncan McGregor and David Simon, PU-ECH Abuja).

Air pollution affects different crops in various ways (Agrawal et al, 2003; Wahid et al, 2001). The Mung bean, for example, is sensitive to sulphur dioxide (SO_2) which may cause a 56.5 per cent reduction in yield. SO_2 is a primary pollutant, but secondary pollutants and particulates also need to be considered, especially the heavy metals that fall on crops as aerial deposition and which can affect food safety (Fiona Marshall, PU-ECH Shenzhen). Copper and SO_2 pollution from the Mulfira, Zambia, smelter affects soils, vegetation and probably human health in areas immediately downwind (Everisto Kapungwe and John Volk, PU-ECH Lusaka). Acid rain has seriously affected forests and crops around Guangzhou, China (Jin Lahua, PU-ECH Shezhen).

Peri-urban communities around Kumasi, Ghana, successfully experimented with household-composting strategies to improve sanitation and provide organic fertilizer (Kwasi Nsiah-Gyabaah, Duncan McGregor and David Simon, PU-ECH Abuja; see also Chapter 16 in this volume). Such fertilizers (and bio-fuels) can cost less than landfill, provided the health risks to waste handlers, farmers and consumers are managed (Cornish et al, 1999). Mitigation methods include minimizing heavy metals in compost by separating urban market waste from industrial waste; reducing or eliminating gastrointestinal infection transmission risks by thermophilic composting; extended storage and/or drying; applying untreated excreta two months before sowing cereal crops, although farm workers are still exposed to worm eggs; care in waste and compost handling (Vasquez et al, 2002). Nevertheless, the off-site impacts of both compost and waste nutrients on soils and water bodies need attention.

Impacts of water use and hydrological and aquatic ecosystem transformation, and their consequences

Many peri-urban people depend on easily contaminated shallow wells whose water levels and quality reflect the land-use transformations around them. Groundwater levels around Beijing fell 15m to 25m between 1950 and 2000. A ten-year surge in vegetable and livestock production involving annual fertilizer applications of up to 1000kg per hectare led to 170 square kilometres of Beijing municipality having excessive groundwater nitrate concentrations (Wolf et al, 2003). The changing diet of the wealthier urban population thus feeds back into the urban and peri-urban water supply. Similar water pollution issues arise throughout developing peri-urban areas. Poor sanitation and a fissure rock substrate cause springs in the peri-urban South Lunzu township in Blantyre, Malawi, to have between 730 and 9500 faecal coliforms per 100ml, while wells average 11,000 and the Lunzu River 18,500 compared with the township borehole average of 30 (Lobila Palamuleni, PU-ECH Lusaka). The European Union (EU) limit of 2000 faecal coliforms per 100ml for bathing water indicates the seriousness of this contamination.

Peri-urban flooding, inadequate storm-water drainage and poor waste management (Parkinson, 2003) increase health hazards such as mosquito breeding grounds. Poor storm drainage leads householders to use sandbags to protect their properties, pushing runoff water on to other people's land (as observed at Mandevu, Lusaka during PU-ECH fieldwork).

The rapid deterioration of aquatic life in many Asian, African and South American urban rivers is well illustrated by endocrine disruptors from pharmaceuticals that pass through the urban sanitation and drainage system to rivers and into the food chain, causing changes in the sexual balance of fishes and possibly creating hazards for people who eat such fish (Alejandro Oliva, PU-ECH Rosario). Such complex chains of causality linking human behaviour to environmental change and then, in turn, affecting human health emphasize the need to understand the dynamics of peri-urban ecosystems and to endeavour to maintain and restore many natural ecosystem attributes close to cities.

Ecology and biodiversity of urban areas: Resilience and response, particularly in stressed environments

Invasive species introduced by urban activities affect the ecosystem services provided by peri-urban green spaces, including local climate modification, reducing air pollution, sequestering carbon dioxide and storm runoff reduction (Li et al, 2005). However, invasive species frequently increase the biodiversity of peri-urban areas. Salma Talhouke (PU-ECH Beirut) found 441 species in 26 plots in densely populated coastal Lebanon, where abandoned agricultural land was richer in biodiversity than other land.

From Beijing to São Paulo, peri-urban green belts face challenges from new recreation provision and transportation infrastructure. China opened its first golf course in 1984, but had 200 by 2004 and plans for 1000 more. Tree planting is also expanding, urban forestry providing both economic and environmental benefits for developing area cities (Su and Profous, 1993). Beijing is creating three large-scale tree belts by 2006, including a 240 square kilometre green belt between the third and fourth ring roads. The São Paulo City Green Belt Biosphere Reserve (Rodrigo Victor and Joaquim de Britto Costa Neto, PU-ECH Rosario) contains varied habitats, from coastal and inland moist forests to mangroves, *cerrado* (savanna), wetlands and urban areas (Victor et al, 2004).

Abandoned peri-urban industrial land offers a diversity of ecological habitats often having apparently natural vegetation. Derelict land restoration is a growing issue in tropical countries. Even rudimentary restoration of tropical formerly mined land increases bird numbers and diversity (Passell, 2000); is better than abandoned mine sites; and brings local community benefits, reducing dust, providing recreation and, eventually, facilitating reuse for agriculture or urban development. Derelict land restoration in Hong Kong shows heavy metals, and landfill gases affecting plant regrowth and soil subsidence risks over restored but improperly managed landfills (Wong Ming, PU-ECH Shenzhen).

The expansion of cities exposes both humans and wildlife to new pathogens and vectors. Hantavirus pulmonary syndrome, Lassa fever, cryptosporidiosis, Nipah virus disease, bird 'flu and plague affect people; but livestock pathogens transferred to wildlife reduce biodiversity. This peri-urban disease emergence encompasses subtle, complex and often overlooked threats (Daszak et al, 2000), requiring careful investigation of linkages between people, nature and biogeochemical fluxes.

Political and institutional factors in peri-urban environmental change

Political ecology helps in analysing economically, ecologically and politically vulnerable peri-urban squatter and slum settlements where landlessness and land scarcity are as critical for residents as access to clean, safe water and sanitation (Moffat and Finnis, 2005). Inequity in environmental quality, shelter and access to both natural and social resources (such as education and healthcare) is rooted in social and political factors, as shown by the struggles and delays poor people face in getting water and avoiding pollution and flooding. Municipal authorities often receive the votes of the poor, but either place their needs below those of more powerful elites or ignore them altogether (Burra et al, 2003).

Private-sector involvement in urban service provision produces further inequality by restricting former users' access to resources such as waste. Under public-sector management, once in the street or in municipal bins, solid waste belongs to municipal authorities. They are responsible for waste collection and disposal. In India, 'rag picking' of recyclable materials and animal grazing on waste continues. However, waste at private-sector dump sites is more strictly controlled. Who gets access to waste is largely a political decision; but it should consider both financial and social policy objectives (Nunan, 2000). Political power also plays the key role shaping vulnerabilities to geophysical hazards in peri-urban areas (Pelling, 1999).

Top-down construction of 'community' groups in which leaders and members are self-selected from established elites often undermines peri-urban grassroots participation in decision-making. New 'community leaders', closely associated with local government, often put local political elites in control of local community organizations and thereby retain their control of environmental rehabilitation projects. Even in recognized peri-urban community organizations, marginalized vulnerable individuals may be excluded from the decision-making networks of relatively high socio-economic status, house-owning business people.

The global drivers of peri-urban change, including structural adjustment, alter prevailing economic, social and political conditions, producing land-use changes in and around African cities. In Dar es Salaam, this has meant infill and increased density, rather than further linear expansion along roads, and limited spatial growth to the south. Greater public transport competition and more private transport have improved access. Rapid capital accumulation, from trade liberalization and rent acquisition by some individuals, has extended investment in peri-urban areas, but with an emphasis on short-term returns rather than larger scale production (Briggs and Mwamfupe, 2001).

Conclusions

Careful analysis is required to ascertain the complex social, economic and political controls of peri-urban life and environmental change. Often the influence of the rich and powerful is only part of the picture. Subtle intra-group dynamics among the deprived and powerless can be significant in deciding if projects, whether locally inspired or externally supported, succeed and become sustainable. PU-ECH is recognizing how these complexities relate to the different uses and values of peri-urban areas. Some of the recommendations made at the different meetings are summarized as follows:

For the poor:

- formal inclusion of peri-urban agriculture in the planning process;
- sustainable use of wetlands used for urban and peri-urban agriculture;
- increasing (community) knowledge of peri-urban soil fertility and contamination;
- safe use and application of compost;
- safe agricultural production with water-quality control and certification.

For industry:

- the benefits of rehabilitating mining land;
- acquiring detailed field data on contaminant levels in soils, water and plants and understanding of contaminant movement through soils and water into plants and the food chain.

For the middle class:

- examine the peri-urban environment as an interface between the consumer system and the natural environment;
- promote legislation to control speculative industrial, residential and commercial land development.

For local government:

- cost savings by organic waste management;
- use of advanced tools, such as geographical information systems (GIS), for city development/planning;
- assess ways of alleviating the health-related impacts of air and water pollution and soil and land contamination;
- security of land tenure and participatory land-use planning.

For conservationists:

- development of policies for establishing urban biosphere reserves;
- evaluation of the status of urban ecosystems;
- use behavioural studies of people's attitudes and expectations regarding areas of natural vegetation to inform policy development.

For education and human well-being:

- recognizing peri-urban areas as a key environmental science issue, with a specific focus on the critical gender issues relating to land use;
- link science to policy-makers at all levels to develop policy changes and new management structures.

Clearly, being multifunctional areas of land-use competition, peri-urban areas experience direct impacts, such as new construction, land-use changes and resource exploitation, together with indirect effects through land degradation, waste disposal, air pollution and water quality deterioration. Much of the science of how individual ecological and human components and activities in peri-urban areas work is well documented. PU-ECH is taking a holistic view of this transition zone to see how problem solving, improving the quality of people's lives, managing the biogeochemical consequences of change and maintaining ecosystems and biodiversity can work together. It is aiming to produce outputs for both the scientific community and the major stakeholders. Results are already being communicated to UN bodies. Many participants at PU-ECH meetings are active members of local or international bodies which promote better management of peri-urban areas. By working at different scales and on many fronts, PU-ECH is aiming to disseminate its findings widely and to intervene where it can be most effective. It is thus both a scientific and an advocacy project that may help in exchanging and stimulating ideas on integrated peri-urban environmental management.

References

Afrane, Y. A., Klinkenberg, E., Drechsel, P., Owusu-Daaku, K., Garrns, R. and Kruppa, T. (2004) 'Does irrigated urban agriculture influence the transmission of malaria in the city of Kumasi, Ghana?', *Acta Tropica*, vol 89, pp125–134

Agrawal, M., Singh, B., Rajput, M., Marshall, F. and Bell, J. N. B. (2003) 'Effect of air pollution on peri-urban agriculture: A case study', *Environmental Pollution*, vol 126, pp323–329

Ahmed, N. and Sohail, M. (2003) 'Alternate water supply arrangements in peri-urban localities: *Awami* (people's) tanks in Orangi township, Karachi', *Environment and Urbanization*, vol 15, no 2, pp33–42

Barredo, J. I. and Demicheli, L. (2003) 'Urban sustainability in developing countries' megacities: Modelling and predicting future urban growth in Lagos', *Cities*, vol 20, pp297–310

Bradford, A., Brook, R. and Hunshal, C. S. (2003) 'Wastewater irrigation in Hubli-Dharwad, India: Implications for health and livelihoods', *Environment and Urbanization*, vol 15, no 2, pp157–170

Briggs, J. and Mwamfupe, D. (2001) 'Peri-urban development in an era of structural adjustment in Africa: The city of Dar es Salaam, Tanzania', *Sage Urban Studies Abstracts*, vol 29, pp1–3

Burra, S., Patel, S. and Kerr, T. (2003) 'Community-designed, built and managed toilet blocks in Indian cities', *Environment and Urbanization*, vol 15, no 2, pp11–32

Cifaldi, R., Allan, J. D., Duh, J. D. and Brown, D. G. (2004) 'Spatial patterns in land cover of exurbanizing watersheds in Southeastern Michigan', *Landscape and Urban Planning*, vol 66, pp107–123

Cornish, G. A., Mensah, E. and Ghesquire, P. (1999) *Water Quality and Peri-Urban Irrigation: An Assessment of Surface Water Quality for Irrigation and Its Implications for Human Health in the Peri-Urban Zone of Kumasi, Ghana*, Report OD/TN 95, HR, Wallingford

Daszak, P., Cunningham, A. A. and Hyatt, A. D. (2000) 'Emerging infectious diseases of wildlife threats to biodiversity and human health', *Science*, vol 287, pp443–449

Li, F., Wang, R., Paulussen, J. and Liu, X. (2005) 'Comprehensive planning of urban greening based on ecoprinciples: A case study in Beijing, China', *Landscape and Urban Planning,* vol 72, no 4, pp325–336

Li, X. and Yeh, A. G.-O. (2004) 'Analyzing spatial restructuring of land use patterns in a fast growing region using remote sensing and GIS', *Landscape and Urban Planning*, vol 69, pp335–354

Lynch, K., Binns, T. and Olofin, E. A. (2001) 'Urban agriculture under threat: The land security question in Kano, Nigeria', *Cities*, vol 18, pp159–171

Moffat, T. and Finnis, E. (2005) 'Considering social and material resources: The political ecology of a peri-urban squatter community settlement in Nepal', *Habitat International*, vol 29, no 3, pp453–468

Nunan, F. (2000) 'Urban organic waste markets: responding to change in Hubli-Dharwad, India', *Habitat International*, vol 24, pp347–360

Parkinson, J. (2003) 'Drainage and stormwater management strategies for low-income urban communities', *Environment and Urbanization*, vol 15, no 2, pp115–126

Passell, H. D. (2000) 'Recovery of bird species in minimally restored Indonesian tin strip mines', *Restoration Ecology*, vol 8, pp112–118

Pelling, M. (1999) 'The political ecology of flood hazard in urban Guyana', *Geoforum*, vol 30, pp249–261

Pender, J., Mills, A. P., de Souza, G., Quashie-Sam, J. and Boateng, K. (1999) 'Geographical information systems for the management of natural resources in a peri-urban environment: The case of Kumasi', *Proceedings of the Fourth AFRICAGIS Conference 1999*, Accra, Ghana

Rain, D. (1997) 'The women of Kano: Internalized stress and the conditions of reproduction, Northern Nigeria', *GeoJournal*, vol 43, pp175–187

Singh, A. L. and Asgher, M. S. (2005) 'Impact of brick kilns on land use/landcover changes around Aligarh city, India', *Habitat International*, vol 29, no 3, pp591–602

Su, M. and Profous, G. (1993) 'Urban forestry in Beijing', *Unasylva*, vol 44, pp13–18

Vasquez, R., Cofie, O. O., Dreschel, P. and Mena-Bonsu, I. F. (2002) 'Linking urban agriculture with urban management: A challenge for policy makers and planners', in Brebbia, C. A., Martin-Duque, J. F. and Wadhwa, L. C. (eds) *The Sustainable City II: Urban Regeneration and Sustainability*, WIT Press, Southampton

Victor, R. A. B. M., Costa Neto, J. De B., Ab'Sáber, A. N., Serrano, O., Domingos, M., Pires, B. C. C., Amazonas, M. and Victor, M. A. M. (2004) 'Application of the biosphere reserve concept to urban areas: The case of São Paulo City Green Belt Biosphere Reserve, Brazil – São Paulo Forest Institute: A case study for UNESCO', *Annals New York Academy of Sciences*, vol 1023, pp237–281

Wahid, A., Milne, E., Shamsi, S. R. A., Ashmore, M. R. and Marshall, F. M. (2001) 'Effects of oxidants on soybean growth and yield in the Pakistan Punjab', *Environmental Pollution*, vol 113, pp271–280

Wolf, J., van Wijk, M. S., Cheng, X., Hu, Y., van Diepen, C. A., Jongbloed, A. W., van Keulen, H., Lu, C. H. and Roetter, R. (2003) 'Urban and peri-urban agricultural production in Beijing municipality and its impact on water quality', *Environment and Urbanization*, vol 15, no 2, pp141–156

3

Understanding Environmental Change in the Context of Rural–Urban Interactions

Adriana Allen

Beyond conventional dichotomies

The purpose of this chapter is to provide an overview of the problems and opportunities of the peri-urban interface (PUI) with regard to the broader concerns of environmental sustainability and the environmental conditions affecting the livelihoods and quality of life of the peri-urban poor. In doing so, rather than focusing on a single case study, the chapter draws on the findings from several research projects conducted by the author since 1998, in collaboration with colleagues from the Development Planning Unit (DPU) and from other institutions in the UK and partner countries. In addition to two international comparative studies funded by the Department for International Development (DFID), these include three projects supported by DFID Natural Resources Systems Programme (NRSP), which focused on the urban-region of Hubli-Dharwad, India, and aimed to enhance the management of natural resources and the livelihoods of the poor in the PUI. Common to all of these initiatives was a concern with understanding how to act upon two main sets of environmental challenges affecting the PUI.

The first group of challenges refers to the environmental conditions of the PUI as the living and working environment of a large and varied number of people. Despite its heterogeneous and rapidly changing social composition, very often the PUI constitutes the habitat of lower income groups, ranging from those engaged in urban-based livelihoods living in informal settlements on the periphery of the city, to small and marginal farmers affected by dynamic processes of land use and market change. The poor in the PUI are particularly vulnerable to the impacts and negative externalities of nearby rural and urban systems, and are often affected by the 'worst of both worlds' (Birley and Lock, 1998). These impacts include health risks and physical hazards related to the occupation of inappropriate sites, lack of access to basic water and sanitation, and poor housing conditions. At the same time, environmental changes impact upon their livelihood strategies, decreasing or increasing their access to different types of assets, including natural resources.

The second set of challenges refers to the sustainability of the natural resource base of peri-urban ecosystems in relation to the pressures imposed by the city region upon renewable and non-renewable resources and environmental services. In this sense, the environmental sustainability of adjacent urban and rural areas affects and is affected by the flows of commodities, capital, natural resources, people and pollution taking place in the PUI.

The need to consider these two sets of challenges in an interconnected way has been stressed in the principles and goals laid out in the United Nations Conference on Environment and Development (UNCED) Agenda 21, signed by over 100 governments in 1992 in Rio (see also Chapter 4 in this volume). Four years later, the Habitat Agenda and its political statement – the Istanbul Declaration – endorsed and expanded on Agenda 21, calling for effective action to provide adequate shelter for all and sustainable human settlements in an urbanizing world. Agenda 21 and the Habitat Agenda are two milestones of a significant shift in perspective during the 1990s in recognizing environmental concerns as an integral part of social and economic development processes. This shift also shed new light on the role of the urbanization process in development and its wide impact beyond the city limits.

Implicitly, these two agendas set the stage to bridge the so-called 'green' and 'brown' perspectives on urbanization: environment and development. On the one hand, the green agenda calls for the need to pay attention to the long-term environmental problems resulting from development impacts, such as rainforest depletion, global warming and biodiversity loss. On the other hand, the brown agenda emphasizes the need to focus on specific problems associated with the deterioration of local environmental conditions. However, a problem remains in considering both agendas separately – that is, in focusing attention either on local environmental problems which have immediate and evident impacts on people's health and quality of life, or in looking at sustainability issues exclusively from the perspective of the natural resources base. One of the main reasons for this prevailing dichotomy lies in the difference between the 'defence of nature and ecology' approach that has traditionally characterized the green agenda and the 'people, rights and places' approach of the brown agenda (Allen and You, 2002).

The recognition that both agendas are, by definition, interlinked has led to a renewed debate on the environmental problems and opportunities arising from rural–urban interactions. While this concern is not entirely new, the contemporary processes shaping these interactions are giving place to new phenomena and rendering the traditional conceptions of 'urban' and 'rural' increasingly inadequate to capture the environmental processes of change that characterize the PUI. The central argument of this chapter is that in order to understand the specific environmental challenges arising from rural–urban interactions and particularly manifested in the PUI, it is necessary to overcome the rural–urban and green–brown dichotomies and to recognize the specificity of the PUI.

The next section of this chapter provides a working definition for analysing the environmental conditions of the PUI, outlining some of factors that need to be looked at for a better understanding of the broader pressures giving rise to environmental change in this context. The following section characterizes the problems and opportunities that emerge in the PUI from the use of natural resources and environmental services. The final main section draws a number of conclusions from the previous analysis, aimed at informing planned interventions in the PUI.

Bringing the peri-urban interface (PUI) into focus

Although there is no consensus on the conceptual definition of the PUI, development professionals and institutions increasingly recognize the fact that rural and urban features tend to coexist more and more within cities and beyond their limits. The working definition adopted here conceptualizes the PUI as a distinct ecological and socio-economic system under uncertain institutional arrangements. This definition is not based on physical features (distance to urban areas, density or infrastructure), but refers to a gradient between the urban and rural poles that can only be apprehended by examining the dynamics of rural–urban interaction affecting the PUI (Simon et al, 2004).

The socio-economic heterogeneity and complex institutional setting of the PUI have been highlighted by several authors (for example, Tacoli, 1998, 2003; Mattingly, 1999; Allen, 2003). In addition, the PUI can be characterized in ecological terms as a mosaic of 'natural' ecosystems, 'agro-ecosystems' and 'urban' ecosystems, affected by material and energy flows demanded by urban and rural areas (Morello, 1995). All ecosystems can be classified energetically by applying the ratio between production (P) (energy absorbed or transformed) and consumption (C) (loss of energy). In natural ecosystems the ratio P/C is equal to 1, as these are typically subject to low levels of disturbance. Agro-ecosystems, such as crop areas or tree plantations, are characterized by a ratio P/C higher than 1, where the energy resulting from the ecosystem's photosynthesis is exported and consumed beyond its limits. Urban areas are by definition 'consumer ecosystems', where P/C is lower than 1, as their biomass is relatively insignificant and the energy consumed tends to be imported from adjacent or distant 'elsewheres'.

The PUI is the context where many of the changes in urban–rural flows materialize, leading to problems and opportunities not only for peri-urban communities, but also for the sustainable development of adjacent rural and urban systems. For instance, Douglass's (1989) study of land-use changes in the metropolis of Jakarta shows how the loss and degradation of prime agricultural land, deforestation and water pollution in peri-urban areas were, in fact, the outcomes of combined rapid urbanization and the expansion of rural land use in coastal, upland and forest areas at the regional level and along the Jakarta–Bandung corridor. The breaking down of supportive reciprocal relations between cities and their hinterlands tends to aggravate unsustainable patterns of natural resources use and the transference of environmental problems to distant regions. The concept of an 'urban ecological footprint' helps to explain how the relationships between cities and their hinterlands change over time and the environmental costs associated with these changes (Rees, 1992). Increasingly, through trade and flows of environmental goods and services, cities tend to draw on the material resources and ecological productivity of vast and scattered hinterlands. However, bulky and low-value commodities, such as building materials, are usually drawn from close by, which explains the proliferation of extractive activities of high environmental impact in the PUI. The same applies to the disposal of urban wastes, as it is often too expensive to transport wastes long distances, making the PUI their prime location. The expansion of the urban ecological footprint has important implications for the PUI, both in terms of increasing pressures over its carrying capacity and in terms of missed opportunities, as when food is imported from distant regions rather than supplied from the city's hinterland.

Figure 3.1 represents the various scales and sources of change likely to have an environmental impact on the PUI. This suggests that the use of peri-urban environmental resources and ecological services might be driven by local pressures (for example, the competition between residential and agricultural land uses), by sub-national and national conditions (for example, the promotion of dispersed industrialization) or by international pressures, such as falling prices of export crops, increasing the migration of impoverished farmers from rural areas to the PUI in search of alternative livelihoods. These pressures often result in a number of environmental problems and opportunities related to three main processes of environmental change: land-use changes, changes in the use of renewable and non-renewable resources and changes in the generation of waste and the use of the absorptive sink capacity.

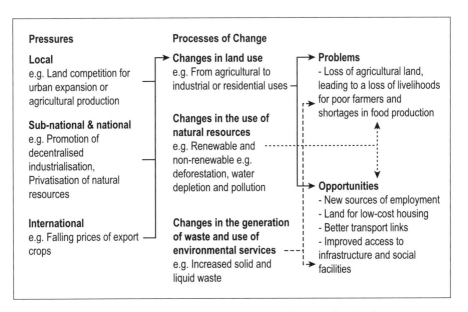

Figure 3.1 Processes of change in the peri-urban interface (PUI)

The extent to which the peri-urban poor are negatively or positively affected by these changes depends on their livelihood sources, which are usually more heavily reliant on natural resources than those of wealthier, more urban-based groups. But it is not just the absolute availability of natural resources in relation to population and its density that helps to explain the emergence of environmental problems and opportunities for the peri-urban poor, but the conditions regulating their access to and control over such resources (Tacoli, 2003). This demands a detailed consideration of land tenure systems and of the regulatory framework which might safeguard or threaten their needs and interests, as well as a consideration of their social and political capital to act individually and collectively and its effects on the management of natural resources and services.

Common barriers identified or perceived in the formation of social capital in urban and peri-urban areas include the heterogeneity and high mobility of the population; the breakdown of traditional networks; adversity; relative poverty and, therefore, a lower ability to pursue community struggles collectively; and exploitation (Rakodi, 2002). While some of these assumptions can be verified in reality, they can also help to perpetuate the idealization of rural characteristics against often negatively typified urban features.

A comparative analysis of the political capability of peri-urban dwellers to deal with water-related problems in two villages in Hubli-Dharwad sheds light in this respect (Thoday, 2003). The study focused on the villages of Mugad and Kelgeri, falling respectively within the *Gram Panchayat* and municipal jurisdictions, which in India represent the rural and urban local government structures. Both villages were initially included in an NRSP-funded participatory action-planning project aimed at facilitating the development of local action plans to enhance livelihoods and natural resources management in the peri-urban context around Hubli-Dharwad. Kelgeri was soon dropped from the project because, in the words of one local non-governmental organization (NGO) facilitating the action planning process, the village was subject to 'an uncomfortable transition, from being a peri-urban settlement to being urban with some remaining rural characteristics' (Thoday, 2003, p18). By contrast, Mugad was depicted as enjoying 'a lot of trust, [which] makes it more rural in character' (Thoday, 2003, p9).

Thoday's study revealed that while local institutions in Mugad appeared to have greater political capacity than in Kelgeri to attract and collect funds and make local changes, formal political processes were highly internalized and dominated by a strong patron–client relationship, which extended to other areas of social interaction and conflict among villagers. In contrast, in Kelgeri, villagers showed a greater understanding of the political processes being shaped by agents outside the bounded location of the village, and also of the need to pursue change through other channels than those exclusively managed and influenced by local social structures. This highlights the complexity and diversity of the collective and individual processes of social and political action deployed in the PUI context.

Environmental processes of change in the PUI

This section explores the processes of environmental change commonly affecting the PUI and the problems and opportunities which arise from them with regard to two main concerns: the sustainable management of environmental resources and services at the regional level, and the quality of life of the most disadvantaged groups working and living in the PUI.

Changes in land use

A distinctive characteristic of the PUI is that land is often under intensive pressure due to different processes of use conversion and increased commercialization. These are not only a result of urban sprawl but also of the loss of farming land in rural areas due to the process of 'de-agrarianization' or even to the abandonment of customary practices of land allocation, as illustrated by several studies in East and West Africa (Lupala, 2001; Bah et al, 2003). Other factors include in-migration of the poor from rural areas; the urban poor moving towards the outskirts where rents and land prices are lower; the better-off building new houses in less congested areas; loss of agricultural land due to the physical expansion of the city (usually along major transport routes), with farming land engulfed in the urban fabric; speculation and land-use changes prompted by industrial location policies or by the development of special and large-scale infrastructures.

Thus, PUI land-use changes might respond to the relatively 'spontaneous' strategies of the poor (both from rural and urban areas) to access land in proximity to diversified livelihood opportunities, to market forces, or to public policies aimed at restraining urban sprawl, dispersing industrial development or locating special physical infrastructure with high potential environmental impacts away from densely populated areas (Dávila, 2003). As a result, the PUI is often characterized by a 'patchwork' of different developments, including residential settlements interspersed with vacant land (often held for speculative purposes) and agricultural land shifting from subsistence to commercial uses. Although the variety of processes at play makes it difficult to generalize, an overview of the main environmental consequences likely to be associated with peri-urban land-use changes is appropriate:

- *Urban expansion at the expense of high environmental costs, due to replacement of soil and vegetation with human-made impermeable surfaces, and the routeing of rainwater along drains and sewers altering natural hydrological networks.* Urban development can reduce land pressures in rural areas that are becoming too densely populated and provide economies of scale in the provision of better services and health conditions for more dwellers. However, access to the advantages offered by cities often remains unevenly distributed in social and physical terms. In addition, uncontrolled urban expansion characterized by low-density development and vacant or derelict land imposes several disadvantages, such as higher infrastructure costs, a wasteful use of land resources and increasing energy consumption and air pollution due to the greater impact of motorized transport.

- *Increasing pressure over biophysical support reflected, for example, in the lessening or cessation of essential ecological functions, such as nutrient recycling or the absorption of pollutants.* Due to the price and amount of land required, the availability of natural resources and pollution and safety considerations, the PUI is often the preferred location for infrastructural developments, such as airports, reservoirs and dams, power stations, drinking water and sewage treatment plants, dumping sites and military installations, all of which impose high environmental impacts on the surrounding environment. For instance, power stations require intensive water abstraction for steam generation and for cooling turbines, while the high temperature and large amounts of waste water discharged to water bodies reduce the ecological value of water resources through thermal pollution, unless prior cooling occurs.
- *Disruption of traditional natural management systems and shifts in agricultural practices leading to loss and degradation of agricultural land and increased use of pesticides.* Horticultural production relies more heavily on proximity to transport networks and urban markets than traditional or plantation crops. In the case of Kenya, peri-urban horticulture for export has grown rapidly since the mid-1970s to become one of the top three foreign exchange earners in 2001 (Walls, 2004). This trend had significant environmental implications and also affected foreign exchange as the rise of horticultural production led to a significant increase in pesticide imports and use (Lowery, 1997). While the shift to higher value crops might be initially perceived as an opportunity for peri-urban farmers, in practice, this process may displace smallholders who rely on farming but lack the resources to adopt more capital-intensive methods or lack sufficient land to use as collateral for credit.

An immediate conclusion from the above is that the driving forces behind peri-urban land-use changes need to be understood in the light of the complex set of rural–urban interactions and with specific consideration to the sources, problems and opportunities outlined by Figure 3.1. Second, changes in peri-urban land use often result in a combination of environmental consequences raised by the brown and green agendas. Third, in the short and medium term, the processes described above often impact disproportionately upon the poor. In the long term, they also have multiple effects on the sustainability of adjacent urban and rural areas.

Use of renewable and non-renewable resources

Renewable resources, such as water and biomass fuel supplies, are essential for the existence of any system – urban, rural or peri-urban. Environmental problems arise when they are exploited beyond their regenerative capacity. By contrast, non-renewable resources, such as fossil fuels and other mineral resources, are depleted with stock use and consumption, which poses the need to address their finite nature through the reduction and rationalization of wasteful consumption and increasing reuse and recycling.

Use of renewable and non-renewable energy

For many urban and peri-urban dwellers in the developing world, a large share of energy needs is still met by biomass fuels – particularly in and around smaller cities in Africa and Asia. However, urban sprawl and the increasing ease of access to fossil fuels lead to a disregard for the exploitation of renewable regional resources and alternative energy sources. There is a strong relationship between land-use patterns, overall transport demand and motor vehicle use, which results in greater air pollution and traffic congestion. Energy-intensive urban and peri-urban land use has dramatic ecological impacts, not only because of the depletion of non-renewable resources, but also because it is associated with the causation of severe global environmental problems such as climate change, acid rain and increased risk of radiation release or accidental oil spills. In addition, many peri-urban areas are severely constrained by electricity shortages because the provision of power grid energy beyond a certain radius tends to be expensive and unreliable. This constrains the provision of electricity to dispersed populations.

The loss of forested land or woody biomass is another typical process affecting the PUI. The sources of this problem are varied, including the impact of air pollution, forest clearing by illegal settlers or displaced farmers in search of arable land for cash crops, or simply due to fuelwood collection. Access to fuelwood varies significantly even among peri-urban dwellers. For instance, wealthier households in peri-urban Hubli-Dharwad use tractors or bullock carts to collect fuelwood only a few times a year, sometimes with the help of paid labourers, while landless labourers spend, on average, between four and ten hours a week collecting fuelwood (Brook and Dávila, 2000).

During a participatory action planning project conducted in Hubli-Dharwad in 2001, improved access to forests was prioritized in three out of the five peri-urban villages covered (Mugad, Channapur and Kotur) as an issue highly relevant to the poor, particularly women, the landless and artisans who produce pots and baskets. For the first and last groups, this is a means to access non-timber forest produce and to improve the availability of fodder, while for artisans it provides access to raw materials. Although relevant to all peri-urban dwellers (including landowners), increased access to firewood was especially significant to women and artisans. In those villages with forest lands, this led to the organization of village forest committees (VFCs) under the government Joint Forest Planning and Management Programme (JFPM), while agro-forestry was promoted where no forest lands existed (Brook et al, 2001).

Use of water resources

The PUI is often the location of water supply facilities, such as reservoirs, and the area where underground water sources are replenished due to the higher infiltration capacity of the system in comparison with urban areas. In and around cities, water is commonly in short supply and under increasing competition among different users. Urban growth leads to increasing demand for industrial and domestic uses that conflict with agricultural demands, often intensified by shifting irrigation practices. Very often, this pre-empts resources that were previously used by peri-urban dwellers or were essential to the health of valuable ecosystems.

A comparative study conducted on the governance of water supply and sanitation (WSS) in the peri-urban context of five metropolitan areas revealed a significant gap in access to WSS between urban and peri-urban dwellers, with the latter suffering significant conditions of deprivation, often invisible under aggregated statistics (Allen et al, 2004). In three of the case studies examined (Mexico District Federal; Chennai, India; and Caracas, Venezuela), peri-urban dwellers face a paradoxical situation, suffering from water depriva-tion while living in jurisdictions which are net exporters of water to other metropolitan localities. Given the general inadequacy of service provision in the peri-urban context, most households spend a significant percentage of their income to obtain water, which among the poor often represents about 10 to 15 per cent. In addition, only medium- and high-income groups often rely on central sewerage systems and septic tanks. As a result, these areas are affected by a number of water- and sanitation-related diseases, including diar-rhoea, intestinal worms, typhoid, cholera and dysentery, with the poor being most exposed and disadvantaged. Failure by the public and private sectors to improve WSS often means that peri-urban dwellers, particularly the poor, are left to their own devices to access these essential services. Furthermore, as their needs and practices are often ignored by the public sector, policy changes aimed at improving the efficiency of the formal WSS system frequently do little to improve their access to these services and often even constitute an obstacle. An exception to this trend can be found in the case of Caracas, where WSS is the responsibility of HIDROCAPITAL, a public-sector regional water supply company. A new process of decentralization and recent political reforms promote the participation of the peri-urban poor in the WSS system, who can now negotiate through Technical Water Fora. These have helped to improve coverage of services and strengthened social capital (Allen et al, 2004).

In the peri-urban context, the qualitative and quantitative aspects of the 'water and sanitation challenge' present particular characteristics which often remain 'invisible' or undifferentiated. These characteristics refer to the specific forms of deprivation affecting the peri-urban poor, but also to the crucial role that peri-urban ecosystems play in supplying water for, and in absorbing and assimilating, liquid wastes and effluents from broader adjacent urban and rural areas.

Extraction of mineral aggregates and production of building materials

Due to its comparative locational advantage in terms of accessibility, produc-tion and transport cost and time, the PUI is the prime area subjected to extraction activities for construction materials. Occupation of fertile agricul-tural land, soil erosion and pollution of local water resources are commonly cited problems associated with aggregate resource exploitation in the PUI (Phillips et al, 1999). Some of these processes can be observed in the case of

Hubli-Dharwad. As agriculture becomes unviable in many peri-urban villages in comparison to more profitable land transactions for housing, or due to scarce and more expensive labour, small farmers increasingly seek means to alternate their livelihoods and lease their land to building contractors for brick-making, with the consequent loss of top soil. Quarrying has also been intensified in peri-urban areas, in particular due to the demand for stone grit for the construction of a four-lane highway (Brook et al, 2001).

Construction materials also have indirect environmental impacts due to the intensive use of fuels required in the production of processed materials such as cement and bricks. However, the production of building materials constitutes a livelihood opportunity for a significant number of people in peri-urban areas, and the displacement of sources of construction materials further away from urban areas can have a knock-on effect on their costs, depriving people from their earning source and demanding more energy for the transport of building materials. More research is needed, particularly in relation to the short- and long-term trade-offs between peri-urban livelihoods and natural resources.

Changes in waste generation

Because of the availability of open space and good accessibility from urban areas, the PUI is often the 'backyard' for urban waste disposal, often surpassing the absorptive capacity of these areas and imposing severe impacts on the health of the ecosystems and human population. The environmental impacts of liquid and solid wastes depend on their sources; composition; volume; whether they are informally dumped into rivers and vacant land, or burned or disposed of in official dumps or landfills; and how well such sites are prepared and maintained. Solid and liquid waste disposal in the PUI requires specific management approaches given the combination of different pollutants from multiple sources (domestic, industrial and agricultural). While in urban areas, it is often a requirement that waste liquids are treated before being discharged into the environment; this is seldom the case in the PUI, and even when regulations are in place their enforcement is usually weak. In spite of the fact that many waste treatment facilities are located in the PUI, capital resources invested in environmental quality monitoring and management facilities are often fewer than in core urban areas (Phillips et al, 1999).

An issue gaining prominence in both green and brown agenda circles is the link between urban waste and sustainable agriculture and food production. Recycling and reuse of organic waste generated by cities, including compost and appropriately treated sewerage, is increasingly feasible and desirable and a traditional practice in many peri-urban areas of the south. In Hubli-Dharwad, peri-urban farmers have been buying auctioned municipal solid waste since 1937, although the quality of composted municipal waste has declined over the time due to increasing amounts of inorganic matter. Similarly, the availability of sewage irrigation throughout the year provides significant opportunities for horticultural production in several peri-urban villages (Brook et al, 2001).

The potential for nutrient recycling from organic city waste for agriculture is significant. Nevertheless, there are only a few success stories that capitalize on this opportunity. It is estimated that in Kumasi, only up to 10 per cent of the major plant nutrients entering the city are effectively reclaimed (Drechsel et al, 2002). Recycling nutrients from urban areas towards rural agriculture could potentially reduce on-farm soil nutrient mining and land degradation and also enhance the lifespan of urban landfills. The International Water Management Institute is applying this approach in several municipalities in Ghana. The initial stages of the project confirmed the existence of sufficient organic waste of appropriate quality for composting, a significant compost demand, as well as options for successful community involvement in the operation of compost stations. The main challenges to be addressed relate to economic viability, marketability and distribution, as farmers' ability to pay for compost is still several times lower than operational production costs and additional transport costs set municipal compost out of reach for rural farmers (Drechsel et al, 2002). The key to closing the loop in the nutrient cycle depends on changes in a wide range of policies, practices and attitudes towards waste, in general, and to the comprehensive analysis of costs and benefits of the entire food production and nutrient cycle. Household and community-based composting is another valuable strategy element (see Chapter 16 in this volume).

Conclusions

An environmental conceptualization of the peri-urban interface and of the broader rural–urban interactions that give rise to specific processes of change in the PUI has several implications for devising planned interventions.

First, the environmental perspective opens a new understanding and valorization of the processes of change taking place in the PUI, requiring the articulation of social, economic and biophysical aspects. For instance, the processes of private appropriation of land, either through real state speculation or through the direct marginalization of certain groups, reinforce unequal conditions of environmental quality within society. In this way, areas subjected to environmental hazards often become home to lower income groups, while those areas of high environmental quality constitute the epicentre of speculative mechanisms, reducing or 'freezing' the capacity of these areas for the productive accumulation by indigenous inhabitants or eliminating valuable ecological functions performed by natural systems.

Second, comprehension of the PUI cannot simply be based on the extrapolation of urban and rural features, but requires the analysis of the nature and quality of rural–urban interactions. Given that such interactions vary greatly from context to context, generalizations are difficult and, to a certain extent, unhelpful. The PUI is not only subject to the influence of nearby urban systems, but is influenced (or created and sustained) by different types of urban–rural linkages, which may be represented by different types of flows operating at different scales (Douglass, 1998). This has implications not only for problem identification, but also for the opportunities arising from them, as exemplified in the win–win scenario that can result, for instance, from the promotion of nutrient recycling between urban, peri-urban and rural areas, bringing benefits to municipalities and farmers alike.

Environmental planning and management of the PUI require the articulation of the green and brown agendas. The analysis here has shown that most processes of peri-urban environmental change refer to a combination of the issues addressed by both agendas. This implies that peri-urban environmental problems cannot be addressed solely from the perspective of the sustainability of the natural resource base, or from localized effects in some peri-urban villages. More attention needs to be paid to synergies and trade-offs of planned interventions at the regional and local levels.

However, while a regional perspective is needed to understand broader trends and the extent to which rural–urban interactions are mutually beneficial or negative, this should not prevent a localized examination of the distribution of benefits and burdens among peri-urban dwellers. 'Peri-urban interfaces' must be disaggregated and livelihood strategies must be researched if planned interventions are to benefit the poor. This includes the consideration of their existing patterns of participation in the public sphere and perceptions of how change could be brought about. It also involves examination of the perceptions, attitudes and approaches to change of external support agencies. While focusing on strengthening the collective organization of the peri-urban poor, it is essential to make their needs and aspirations 'visible' to the different agencies intervening in this context. However, an isolationist approach might fail to articulate their demands with those of other interests groups and, therefore, prevent the emergence of interdependent coalitions between the poor and the non-poor, as well as between internal and external political processes. This points to the need to examine the political capacity of peri-urban groups both individually and collectively and its effects on resource management.

Acknowledgements

This chapter draws on two previous papers produced by the author. Allen et al (1999) provides a detailed examination and exemplification of the environmental processes of change examined in this chapter. Allen (2003) outlines different approaches to environmental planning and management in the peri-urban interface.

References

Allen, A. (2003) 'Environmental planning and management of the peri-urban interface (PUI): Perspectives on an emerging field', *Environment and Urbanization*, vol 15, no 1, pp135–147

Allen, A. with Da Silva, N. and Corubolo, E. (1999) 'Environmental problems and opportunities of the peri-urban interface and their impact upon the poor', Research paper, Strategic Environmental Planning and Management for the Peri-Urban Interface project, Development Planning Unit, London, www.ucl.ac.uk/dpu/pui

Allen, A., Dávila, J. and Hofmann, P. (2004) 'Governance and access to water and sanitation in the metropolitan fringe: An overview of five case studies', Paper presented at N-Aerus Annual Conference on Urban Governance, Diversity and Social Action in Cities of the South, Barcelona, Spain, 15–16 September

Allen, A. and You, N. (2002) *Sustainable Urbanisation: Bridging the Green and Brown Agenda*, Development Planning Unit/UN-Habitat/DFID, London

Bah, M., Cissé, S., Diyamet, B., Diallo, G., Lerise, M., Okali, D., Okpara E., Olawoye, J. and Tacoli, C. (2003) 'Changing rural–urban linkages in Mali, Nigeria and Tanzania', *Environment and Urbanization*, vol 15, no 1, April, pp13–24

Birley, M. H. and Lock, K. (1998) 'Health and peri-urban natural resource production', *Environment and Urbanization*, vol 10, no 1, pp89–106

Brook, R. M. and Dávila, J. D. (eds) (2000) *The Peri-Urban Interface: A Tale of Two Cities*, School of Agricultural and Forest Sciences, University of Wales and Development Planning Unit, University College London, www.ucl.ac.uk/dpu/pui

Brook, R., Purushothaman, S. and Hunshal, C. (eds) (2001) *Changing Frontiers: The Peri-Urban Interface, Hubli-Dharwad, India*, Books for Change, Bangalore

Dávila, J (2003) 'Enfoques de intervención en la interfase periurbana', *Cuadernos del CENDES*, vol 20, no 53, pp17–32

Douglass, M. (1989) 'The environmental sustainability of development: Coordination, incentives and political will in land use planning for the Jakarta metropolis', *Third World Planning Review*, vol 11, no 2, pp211–238

Douglass, M. (1998) 'A regional network strategy for reciprocal rural-urban linkages', *Third World Planning Review*, vol 20, no 1, pp1–33

Drechsel, P., Cofie, O. and Danso, G. (2002) 'Closing the rural–urban nutrient cycle?', in Allen, A. and Dávila, J. (eds) 'Mind the gap: Bridging the rural–urban divide', *Insights*, no 41, Institute of Development Studies, www.id21. org/insights/insights41/index.html

Lowery, N. (1997) 'TED case studies: Kenya pesticides and exports', Paper prepared for the American University, Washington, DC, December, www.gurukul.ucc.american.edu/ted/kenpest.htm

Lupala, A. (2001) 'Land management in the peri-urban zone of Dar es Salaam', Paper presented at the International Conference on Rural–Urban Encounters: Managing the Environment of the Peri-Urban Interface, Development Planning Unit, London, 9–10 November

Mattingly, M. (1999) 'Institutional structures and processes for environmental planning and management of the peri-urban interface', Paper produced for the research project Strategic Environmental Planning and Management for the Peri-Urban Interface, Development Planning Unit, University College, London, www.ucl.ac.uk/dpu/pui

Morello, J. (1995) *Manejo de Agrosistemas Peri-Urbanos*, Centro de Investigaciones Ambientales, FAUD, UNMdP, Mar del Plata

Phillips, D., Williams, K., Andrews, G., Clarke, J., Carter, M., Kinsman, P., Smith, D., Willis, K., Bradbury, I., Wu, K. and Hillyer, A. (1999) 'Literature review on peri-urban natural resource conceptualisation and management approaches', in Final Technical Report, *Peri-Urban Production Systems Research, Natural Resources Systems Programme (NRSP)*, DFID, London, March, mimeo

Rakodi, C. (ed) (2002) *Urban Livelihoods: A People Centred Approach to Reducing Poverty*, Earthscan, London

Rees, W. (1992) 'Ecological footprints and appropriated carrying capacity: What urban economics leaves out', *Environment and Urbanization*, vol 4, no 2, pp121–130

Simon, D., McGregor, D. and Nsiah-Gyabaah, K. (2004) 'The changing urban–rural interface of African cities', *Environment and Urbanization*, vol 16, no 2, October, pp235–247

Tacoli, C. (1998) 'Rural–urban interactions: A guide to the literature', *Environment and*

Urbanization, vol 10, no 1, pp147–166

Tacoli, C. (2003) 'The links between urban and rural development', *Environment and Urbanization*, vol 15, no 1, pp3–12

Thoday, K. (2003) 'Political capacity and its effects on resource management', Annex to Technical Report, DFID project R8084, *Enhancing Livelihoods and NR Management in Peri-Urban Villages near Hubli-Dharwad*, DFID, London, mimeo

Walls, M. (2004) *Fact Sheets: Facts and Figures on Urban and Rural Change*, Unpublished report for DFID, Development Planning Unit, University College, London, August, mimeo

4

Falling between Stools? Policies, Strategies and the Peri-Urban Interface

Julio Dávila

Introduction

This chapter presents an exploration of the possible direct and indirect environmental impacts of current policies and strategies on the peri-urban interface (PUI). Here, the terms 'policies and strategies' refer to guiding principles formulated by public agencies operating at the national, regional or local level, usually arising from a political process, to inform specific planning and management interventions with intended or unintended environmental, social and economic effects on a given locality or sets of localities. For purposes of this review, the effects of these interventions on the PUI are perceived as changes in its natural resource endowment and in the type and volume of flows (of people, goods and waste) between urban and rural areas. The environmental focus of this chapter does not deny that there are other crucial dimensions in peri-urban processes, such as social and economic change, particularly in the way that they affect the poor. These are covered in, among others, Brook and Dávila (2000) and Allen and Dávila (2002).

Most interventions that might be regarded as explicitly focused on the PUI take as their starting point a physical definition, such as the 'urban periphery' or 'green belt'. This is because such interventions are either initiated or guided largely by one or more government tiers that are generally obliged to implement their actions within an administrative boundary. Although the state no longer has an undisputed monopoly in planning urban (and peri-urban) development (Healey, 1997; Safier, 2002), by and large, it still plays a major role in providing guidance over spatial development. In the urban and peri-urban arenas, new practices are constantly emerging where the state is, at best, acting as facilitator to other agents (such as community-based organizations or the private sector) and, at worst, seeks to exclude or obstruct the actions of less powerful groups seeking to assert their rights, as well as small-scale informal producers and service providers. In what is sometimes referred to as 'insurgent practices', groups acting mostly at the local level (though increasingly connected to other groups across national boundaries through fora and the

Internet) are gradually challenging what Santos (2002) calls 'hegemonic globalization'. These practices often seek to subvert existing power relations and the administrative apparatus that embodies them. This chapter focuses on more conventional interventions where the state retains a non-negligible role.

Few cases of metropolitan intervention (and, therefore, interventions directly or indirectly affecting the PUI) might be seen as 'pure' instances of metropolitan environmental planning and management (Mattingly, 1999). Institutions with an overall responsibility for the environment with a remit that cuts across administrative boundaries are rare. With few exceptions, most documented environmental interventions in a metropolitan context appear, instead, to be components of other forms of interventions, most of which take space as their starting point (Atkinson et al, 1999; Adell, 1999; Phillips et al, 1999; Allen and Dávila, 2002).

This chapter distinguishes between two broad kinds of interventions: those relatively rare actions with an explicit spatial dimension which directly or indirectly affect developments in the PUI; and sectoral policies that generally lack an explicit spatial dimension but the application of which has (intended or unintended) effects on the environment of the PUI. Although the boundaries between these two types are sometimes blurred, this chapter argues that non-spatial policies tend to have the more profound environmental impact on the PUI.

Policies with an explicit spatial focus

Cities and regions of poorer countries marked by rapid urbanization, uncontrolled urban expansion, lack of basic infrastructure, and loss and degradation of agricultural land and of valuable ecological sites, appear to have particularly acute problems. In richer countries and countries with a slower process of urbanization, the use of renewable and non-renewable resources, and the generation of waste and pollution affecting the PUI, would appear to be more pressing issues (Allen et al, 1999).

Because a specific concern with the PUI is either relatively recent or rarely made explicit in governments' policy interventions, the challenge is to identify elements of individual interventions that might directly or indirectly impinge upon the PUI. Environmental interventions at a metropolitan or peri-urban scale are rare. Urban and regional policy interventions with an explicit environmental dimension are, by and large, restricted to individual sectors (such as water supply and forests), often constrained by strict territorial boundaries, and tend to be shaped by a combination of ready-made responses to problems as perceived by experts and the clientelist demands of their political masters (Dávila and Atkinson, 1999). One can identify a range of different policy foci, such as land-use changes; use and protection of renewable and non-renewable resources; pollution and waste generation; spatial integration and environmental equity; and institutional reforms with a spatial dimension, such as decentralization to lower tiers of government.

Guided by the aim to protect valuable agricultural land, traditional top-down policy formulations narrowly focusing on an exclusively physical dimension have tended to fail. The New Communities Programme launched by Egypt's President Sadat during the mid-1970s was an ambitious programme of construction of nearly 20 new satellite towns in the desert with the aim of decongesting Cairo, protecting valuable peri-urban arable land around it and laying claim to vast areas of desert (Shetawy, 2004). However, 30 years later, Cairo (now a metropolis of 14 million people) continues to expand at high densities on peri-urban agricultural and desert land, while the new towns have attracted only a fraction of the projected population and offer built environments unfamiliar to many Egyptians.

Other policy concerns that have preoccupied planners and policy-makers include renewable and non-renewable resources such as water supply, energy, deforestation and mineral extraction. With the exception of water, explicit policies dealing with most of these from the point of view of urban or metropolitan – including peri-urban – environmental management are relatively rare. This is largely because line ministries or watershed management agencies, rather than local governments, usually deal with such concerns, so they are rarely integrated within urban or regional planning efforts.

Given its importance as the most vital basic human need, a considerable proportion of infrastructure expenditure in many cities goes into appropriating and treating water. A smaller proportion goes into post-use treatment. The volume of water required to supply large concentrations of people can have considerable environmental consequences for a city and its surrounding peri-urban and nearby rural hinterland. Mismatches between political boundaries and watersheds can lead to conflict. In Mexico City and Chennai, India, peri-urban residents often complain that water from their aquifers is exported to other localities while they face serious deficits (Citizens Alliance for Sustainable Living, 2003; Torregrosa et al, 2003). In Manizales, Colombia, the city's partially privatized water supply agency purchased a peri-urban forested area to protect water sources for future requirements; the fact that the land is located within the boundaries of the neighbouring municipality of Villamaría, with which it forms a conurbation, added to existing tensions between the two municipalities centred on environmental issues (Velásquez and Pacheco, 1999). As with other similar interventions by its richer and more populated neighbour, the municipality of Villamaría complained that it was not consulted. The mediating role of non-governmental organizations (NGOs), academic groups and professionals helped ease tensions and coordinate actions between the two.

With greater or lesser degrees of success, local and regional plans have often sought to protect natural resources such as woodfuel, minerals (especially those used as sources of building materials) and valuable environmental services such as lakes and forests. An innovative and multifaceted approach to reconcile conflicting social, environmental and economic demands arising from the conflicting interests of urban expansion and the preservation of agricultural land was tried in peri-urban Accra, Ghana.

With an increasing amount of land required for residential development, the International Development Research Centre's (IDRC's) Cities Feeding People Programme during the 1990s identified the need for policy guidance on the extraction of non-renewable rural and peri-urban resources, such as construction materials, arguing that such activities should be licensed and subject to taxes to avoid the high costs of reclaiming environmentally degraded land. The aims of spatial integration, coordination and environmental equity were fostered through the commercialization and intensification of agricultural production, coupled with attempts to upgrade peri-urban farmers' skills and their access to credit and water for irrigation. Faced with the certainty of land conversion in peri-urban Accra, the programme sought to support those who rely on agriculture for their livelihoods and are worst affected when agricultural land is lost (Maxwell et al, 1998).

Pollution affecting the PUI and originating largely in urban-based activities is an issue of growing importance (Allen and You, 2002), with the added complication that institutional responsibilities are seldom clearly defined. This may be due to rapidly changing situations, a secular tendency by government agencies to operate sectorally or within narrowly defined remits, or, perhaps more likely, to the fact that much pollution and waste are disposed of outside the administrative boundaries where they are generated.

The Chilean city of Concepción provides an interesting case where such problems were confronted successfully. Vaguely defined responsibilities among different government agencies gradually led to the environmental deterioration of seven lakes located in the city's peri-urban area. Causes included unplanned use of land, inadequate disposal of storm water and a lack of environmental awareness (Gilbert et al, 1996). With assistance from the United Nations Centre for Human Settlements' (UNCHS) Sustainable Cities Programme, problems were identified through a participatory exercise aimed at producing an urban environmental profile for the city that identified major development trends, their related demands on the resource base and resulting conflicts. This inter-sectoral approach and the appointment of a coordinator led to improvements in water quality, regularization of land use along the lakes' shorelines and increased environmental awareness. The national army collaborated in clean-up activities with residents of the informal settlements along the shoreline; a housing developer constructed a public park on one of the lake shores; and sewerage services were upgraded by the local water authority. Most of the funds for a programme costing over US$430,000 were raised locally, with the leverage of a UNCHS grant of US$20,000.

Insofar as decentralization has the potential to increase government responsiveness to local needs (Faguet, 2004), an effective decentralization programme could impact directly upon urban and peri-urban natural resource management. Appropriate examples include protecting environmental services such as local forests or parks used by local residents, and allowing local government to grant maintenance contracts of roads and water supply systems to local enterprises and organized communities, thus encouraging greater local control and job creation. Local decision-making capacity and spaces for social interaction can also help to reduce inter-ethnic or class tensions and promote a more integrated use of scarce resources, as the case of Colombo, Sri Lanka, shows (Dayaratne and Samarawickrama, 2003; see also Chapter 12 in this volume). Conversely, in some contexts local authorities may be too weak or ill equipped to face additional burdens, thus generating additional tensions both locally and between peri-urban localities and the metropolitan core.

Unintended negative environmental (and also social) consequences of decentralization may arise when, in the context of rapid urban growth, demand for land by large developers often takes them within the jurisdiction of small peripheral municipalities that lack the resources to counteract the power of the large organized private sector. In metropolitan regions of Latin America such as Buenos Aires, São Paulo, Bogotá and Belo Horizonte, this has led to the mushrooming of low-density, high-income 'gated communities' which tend to increase spatial fragmentation and social exclusion, while fostering the private appropriation and intensive use of natural resources and environmental services such as land, water and landscape. Insofar as these large-scale developments often involve peri-urban agricultural land conversion, they may also have serious consequences for the livelihoods of small-scale farmers or farmer tenants who used to cultivate the land and are now displaced and possibly landless.

Over the past few decades, large metropolitan regions in Latin America and elsewhere have abandoned what were historically compact urban forms to become more like 'urban archipelagos' (Aguilar and Ward, 2003; Ciccolella, 2003) – networks of low-density developments with diffuse boundaries akin to the extended metropolitan regions (EMRs) of Asia discussed in Chapter 1. These new developments are very intensive in their use of non-renewable resources such as land and energy, with the added dimension that, in the face of the recent ideological push for a retreat of the state and the weakening of the instruments at its disposal, much of the state's influence over physical planning in peripheral areas of metropolitan regions has been increasingly surrendered to the power of planning and marketing of large developers behind the 'gated communities' (Pirez, 2002).

In many contexts, the weakening or even dismantling of large coordinating bodies such as metropolitan governments has made the task of coordinating and controlling physical expansion much harder. In Brazil, metropolitan governments were associated with centralized, autocratic military rule; their abolition after a return to democracy in the 1980s led to a significant fragmentation of metropolitan regions into separate and often uncoordinated municipal governments. Some authors who, without denying the advantages of such large coordinating bodies, argue that they lack the flexibility to recognize complexity and difference within a metropolis, advocate more nimble bottom-up approaches where citizens can come together through co-operative and representative bodies for specific tasks (Nel.lo, 2003). This is a crucial political issue that must be resolved in locally appropriate terms without resorting to universal recipes. Allied to the issue of an adequate governance structure for metropolitan regions, there is a need for greater understanding of the reasons why spatial policies have proven largely ineffectual in promoting more environmentally sustainable forms of metropolitan development. This also calls for a greater understanding of the effects of non-spatial policies upon the peri-urban environment, as explored in the following section.

Sectoral policies with no explicit spatial focus

As has been discussed in the context of regional development (Simon, 1990), there is a range of government policies and strategies which, although lacking an explicit spatial or environmental focus, has intended or unintended environmental consequences on the PUI. Such policies are mainly of a sectoral nature, although in this category one must also include macro-economic policies indirectly exerting an influence upon the nature and volume of flows (of goods, people, services and waste) between urban and rural areas. Literature explicitly dealing with the environmental effects of this range of policies is scarce, so what follows is a preliminary attempt to think through the possible environmental impacts that these might have on the PUI.

Sectoral policies often have environmental consequences at the local level, most of which are unintended. Awareness about this is growing, partly as a result of pressures from local environmentalists and partly also due to the effect of high-profile global events such as the 1992 United Nations Conference on Environment and Development (UNCED) in Rio de Janeiro, particularly the Local Agenda 21 guidelines that emerged from it, and subsequent international events (Allen and You, 2002). Some governments have put in place programmes not merely in order to raise awareness about this link, but also as attempts to control the unintended impact of such policies. In some cases, local governments actively seek to coordinate policies across sectors, and they do so within a strategic framework.

Not all sectoral policies or strategies have the same environmental impact on the PUI. Despite the difficulties in establishing causality, some play a greater role than others. Such is the case, for example, of transport, energy and agriculture. This is because these sectors have a set of direct or indirect links to the environment, the resources found in the PUI or the poor who either live in it or depend on it for a living. National policies such as privatization and deregulation that impinge upon a range of infrastructure sectors (for example, water, energy and transport) may also have important peri-urban effects, particularly when they lead to higher levels of social exclusion and fragmentation. Pirez (2002) discusses three forms of fragmentation in the management of public services in Greater Buenos Aires during the 1990s: an institutional fragmentation between state and private institutions with little or no coordination between government tiers; a technical fragmentation dictated by the different expansion needs of different basic services; and spatial fragmentation, with standards of service varying considerably across the metropolitan area.

Similarly, liberalization, financial deregulation and credit policies coupled with official practices that restrict building supply in the metropolitan core – and, in some countries such as Ghana, the Philippines, Sri Lanka and India, large volumes of cash remittances from temporary workers abroad – can inflate land prices and lead to legal or unauthorized construction in the PUI. These processes have severe consequences not only on the use of land, but also on the indiscriminate extraction of building materials and the destruction of valuable ecological sites (Maxwell et al, 1998).

Trade policies are also likely to have an effect, particularly upon the use of certain resources and upon movements of people, goods and waste, though again causal links are difficult to prove (Harris, 2004; Stevens et al, 2004). Similarly, the new *de facto* national plans represented by the Poverty Reduction Strategy Papers (PRSPs) demanded from highly indebted poor countries as a borrowing conditionality by aid agencies tend to omit an explicit environmental dimension, concentrating instead on institutional reforms to strengthen market mechanisms, facilitate integration within the world economy and provide social safety nets where needed. In practice, as the case of Uganda shows, PRSP funding has helped to weaken local governance structures (Craig and Porter, 2003), thus reducing local accountability and regulation of environmental processes.

Local transport policies are usually designed to increase the accessibility of a given population. They set the framework for enlarging or improving the supply of roads or railways and related infrastructure, as well as for enhancing and extending public transport networks. Concern with the potential impact of such policies on the environment is fairly recent, and in some national contexts this dimension is still rarely present. In a developing country context, where increased individual accessibility is still the main concern of policy-makers, politicians and users alike, this is likely to take precedence over environmental concerns.

Transport policies are likely either to seek to increase the accessibility of peri-urban areas to a growing number of local residents (mostly middle- or lower middle-income groups who are politically vocal) or to connect the city with neighbouring cities. The main environmental impact of such policies on the PUI relates to the direct or indirect destruction of protected habitats, natural parks, forests or waterways. They may also destroy scarce agricultural land either directly through the construction process or by improving accessibility to it and hastening the process of land conversion to urban uses.

Relevant policies towards agriculture include diverse issues. These range from macro-economic concerns such as import liberalization, domestic pricing of commodities and livestock products, farmer subsidies and other incentives, to policies with a more direct impact on the use of peri-urban land, such as land tenure reform, incentives for urban and organic agriculture, and national rural land-use planning guidelines. Urban farming, by contrast, has conventionally been discouraged in official policies (see Chapter 11 in this volume); yet, it is estimated that some 800 million people around the world regularly farm in urban areas (Mougeot, 1999). But the tide appears to be turning. In Cuba, severe food shortages resulting from the US trade embargo and the collapse of Soviet subsidies led to the fast growth of urban and peri-urban organic farming by small private farmers. Subsequent state recognition and support led to training in integrated pest management and other organic techniques, new forms of land tenure, co-operatives for credit and service, and farmers' markets selling directly to consumers. A crucial factor in the success of this scheme was a new-found flexibility and willingness to negotiate on the part of government officials, as well as allowing a range of farm sizes and land tenure arrangements to suit different locations and forms of social organization (Bourque, 2002). Similarly, official support to farmers' markets selling directly to consumers has tended to benefit both small-scale farmers and consumers. In the Indian state of Tamil Nadu, for example, markets have enabled farmers to diversify their production in response to buyers' needs and, thus, to increase their incomes, with expanded social networks and more balanced gender relations as unintended consequences (Rengasamy et al, 2003).

Strategies to liberalize internal markets while promoting agricultural exports rest on the belief that export-oriented agriculture requires efficient economic linkages connecting producers with external markets. However, spatial proximity to a market may play a much more limited role in improving a farmer's access to the inputs and services needed to enhance productivity than access to land, capital and labour (Dalal-Clayton et al, 1999). Market-led development strategies often fail to differentiate between different groups in society and therefore fail to protect the weakest and most needy while often benefiting the already well-off who can take advantage of market opportunities. This is especially important for poorer farmers in the PUI as their needs may call for official responses ranging from securing rights of access to land to more flexible regulatory frameworks that recognize the multiplicity of farming and non-farming economic activities performed by what are often multi-local households.

The implementation of policies that impinge upon the use of renewable and non-renewable natural resources in the PUI is likely to have an effect on physical development and on the livelihoods of people living in these areas. Examples include policies to protect natural or man-made forests near to major towns. An important issue here is an understanding that for the rural and for many of the peri-urban, poor secure access to a resource base may lie at the basis of their survival. In the case of forests, for example, these often provide the poor in the PUI with woodfuel for cooking (Soussan, 1998). The case of Karnataka State in India (see below) illustrates the difficulties involved in such policies. Similarly, in large cities such as Mexico City, ecologically valuable peri-urban areas such as forests and riverbanks are sources of recreation for the urban poor so that their degradation or loss is more likely to affect these groups than wealthier and more mobile households who can seek out these environmental services further afield (Wiggins and Holt, 2000). Equally important are policy environments where (peri-)urban crop farmers can make use of domestic waste as a source of organic matter (see Chapter 16 in this volume), though attempts to improve composting methods and reduce costs might, in practice, exclude smaller farmers and promote illicit practices, as the cases of Bamako and Ouagadougou suggest (Eaton and Hilhorst, 2003).

In India, the Karnataka State policy promoting the use of liquefied petroleum gas (LPG) in Hubli-Dharwad arose partly from a concern about the use of firewood from nearby forests by the poor (Shepherd et al, 1998). Although LPG has substituted for fuelwood in much of the urban area, the use of fuelwood from forests still remains prevalent in peri-urban and rural areas, and has led to serious forest depletion around Hubli-Dharwad. As a consequence, the state forestry department has switched from a role of energy supply to one of forest conservation. Conflicts have arisen between local people and the forestry department, which wants to reforest common areas with eucalyptus trees. Reforested areas are also prone to further deforestation, as in the case of Aminbhavi village (Patil and Nidagundi, 1999). Other pressures on the forest fringe arise from extensive use of firewood to heat milk and encroachment by poor cultivators. Despite the promulgation of the 1980 Forest Conservation Act, which orders prior approval from central government for non-forest activity within forest areas, this policy has proved difficult to enforce in practice.

Conclusions

This chapter has reviewed a range of policies and strategies that impact directly or indirectly upon the PUI. Since a specific concern with the PUI from the perspective of environmental sustainability does not figure in the agenda of most development interventions by governments, the private sector, NGOs or international aid agencies, the review has sought to examine a broader canvas of interventions at a national, regional and local level.

The chapter distinguishes between policies with an explicit spatial dimension and those of a sectoral nature, generally lacking an explicit spatial focus, whose application has usually unintended effects on the environment in the PUI. Among spatial policies, those targeting the use of land around the urban area were found to be most prevalent. This is facilitated by the existence in most national contexts of well-established institutions (such as planning agencies) and legal tools geared to regulating changes in the use of land. Such tools have been used in a variety of contexts, usually with limited results, although, as some cases suggest, they have been more effective where citizen involvement has been successfully enlisted.

Other policies with an explicit spatial dimension can also help to steer developments in the PUI towards attaining goals of greater equity and sustainability. Apart from those seeking to protect natural resources and to minimize the production and flow of pollutants into the PUI, the review has identified policies which explicitly seek greater spatial integration and environmental equity, as in Colombo.

But while spatial policies can achieve a certain measure of localized success, there is a need to identify and measure the effects of non-spatial policies, particularly as these are often designed by central government with little regard for the specific needs of individual localities. Thus, national transport policies that favour the use of the private car and penalize public transport are likely to promote sprawl, as has been amply documented in the richer countries. Local governments can seek to counteract this but may end up taking on a high fiscal burden. Moreover, in many developing country contexts, governments at all levels tend to be more preoccupied with increasing accessibility than with curbing fossil fuel emissions or reducing sprawl.

Although this chapter has identified a lack of policies directed towards the PUI *per se,* it does not advocate the creation of policies specifically for it. This would most likely involve an additional layer of agents in charge of formulating, implementing and monitoring policies specifically designed for it, with the potential for creating additional fiscal and regulatory burdens for firms and citizens, not to mention the added complexities embodied in the constantly shifting nature of the PUI. It calls, instead, for a greater awareness of the effects of sectoral policies on spatially localized groups, particularly those who are more vulnerable or disadvantaged economically, socially and environmentally.

Finally, the review has said little of the agents involved in formulating, implementing and monitoring these policies and strategies. Although a significant omission (resulting from space limitations), it is not meant to deny their relevance. The state's motivations, goals and relationship with other actors, particularly those who might benefit or be negatively affected by their actions, are very important policy matters. Centralized and hierarchical decision-making structures are unlikely to be responsive to the rapid shifts often experienced in the PUI, while more localized, horizontal structures favouring 'co-production' arrangements between state agencies and organized groups of citizens where both make resource contributions (Joshi and Moore, 2002) are likely to generate more equitable and sustainable development outcomes.

Acknowledgements

An earlier version of this chapter was produced as part of the research project entitled Strategic Environmental Planning and Management for the Peri-Urban Interface run by the Development Planning Unit, University College London, between 1998 and 2001 with funding from the UK Government's Department for International Development (DFID). The author acknowledges invaluable inputs by Jessica Budds and Alicia Minaya to the first version. For a discussion of the project's working definition and downloadable outputs, see www.ucl.ac.uk/dpu/pui.

References

Adell, G. (1999) 'Theories and models of the peri-urban interface: A changing conceptual landscape', Paper prepared for the Strategic Environmental Planning and Management for the Peri-Urban Interface (SEPMFPUI) project, Development Planning Unit, University College London, www.ucl.ac.uk/dpu/pui/research/previous/epm/g_adell.htm

Aguilar, A. G. and Ward, P. (2003) 'Globalization, regional development, and megacity expansion in Latin America: Analyzing Mexico City's peri-urban hinterland', *Cities*, vol 20, no 1, pp3–21

Allen, A. with Da Silva, N. A. and Corubolo, E. (1999) 'Environmental problems and opportunities of the peri-urban interface and their impact upon the poor', SEPMFPUI project paper, Development Planning Unit, University College London, www.ucl.ac.uk/dpu/pui/research/previous/epm/allen.htm

Allen, A. and Dávila, J. (eds) (2002) 'Mind the gap: Bridging the rural–urban divide', *Insights No 41*, Institute of Development Studies, Brighton, www.id21.org/insights/insights41/index.html

Allen, A. and You, N. (eds) (2002) *Sustainable Urbanisation: Bridging the Gap between the Green and Brown Agendas*, UN-Habitat, DFID and Development Planning Unit, London

Atkinson, A., Dávila, J., Fernandes E. and Mattingly, M. (eds) (1999) *The Challenge of Environmental Management in Urban Areas*, Ashgate, London

Bourque, M. (2002) 'Cities going organic: Does it work?' in Allen, A. and Dávila, J. (eds) 'Mind the gap: Bridging the rural–urban divide', *Insights No 41*, Institute of Development Studies, Brighton, UK, www.id21.org/insights/insights41/index.html

Brook, R. M. and Dávila, J. D. (eds) (2000) The *Peri-Urban Interface: A Tale of Two Cities*, School of Agricultural and Forest Sciences, University of Wales and Development Planning Unit, University College London

Ciccolella, P. (2003) 'La metrópolis postsocial: Buenos Aires, ciudad-rehén de la economía global', Proceedings of the conference *El Desafío de las Áreas Metropolitanas en un Mundo Globalizado: Una Mirada a Europa y América Latina*, Barcelona, Spain, 4–6 June

Citizens Alliance for Sustainable Living (2003) 'Characterization of the impact of water and sanitation system management regimes on living conditions of poor and on the environment in the two peri-urban sample localities in Chennai', in *Service Provision Governance in the Peri-urban Interface of Metropolitan Areas Project*, Development Planning Unit, University College London

Craig, D. and Porter, D. (2003) 'Poverty reduction strategy papers: A new convergence', *World Development*, vol 31, no 1, pp53–69

Dalal-Clayton, B., Dent, D. and Dubois, O. (eds) (1999) *Local Strategic Planning and Sustainable Rural Livelihoods: Lessons Learned and the Way Forward. An Overview*, Unpublished draft report for the UK DFID, London

Dávila, J. D. and Atkinson, A. (1999) 'Organisation and politics in urban environmental management', in Atkinson, A., Dávila, J. D., Fernandes, E. and Mattingly, M. (eds) *The Challenge of Environmental Management in Urban Areas*, Ashgate, London, pp193–202

Dayaratne, R. and Samarawickrama, R. (2003) 'Empowering communities in the peri-urban areas of Colombo', *Environment and Urbanization*, vol 15, no 1, pp101–110

Eaton, D. and Hilhorst, T. (2003) 'Opportunities for managing solid waste flows in the peri-urban interface of Bamako and Ouagadougou', *Environment and Urbanization*, vol 15, no 1, pp53–63

Faguet, J.-P. (2004) 'Does decentralization increase government responsiveness to local needs? Evidence from Bolivia', *Journal of Public Economics*, vol 88, pp867–893

Gilbert, R., Stevenson, D., Girardet, H. and Stren, R. (1996) *Making Cities Work: The Role of Local Authorities in the Urban Environment*, Earthscan, London

Harris, N. (2004) 'The impact of the reform of international trade on urban and rural change', Development Planning Unit, University College London, Unpublished paper prepared for DFID, London

Healey, P. (1997) 'The revival of strategic spatial planning in Europe', in Healey, P., Khakee, A., Motte, A. and Needham, B. (eds) *Making Strategic Spatial Plans: Innovation in Europe*, University College London Press, London, pp3–19

Joshi, A. and Moore, M. (2002) 'Organisations that reach the poor: Why co-production matters', Paper presented at the Making Services Work for Poor People World Development Report 2003/04 Workshop, Eynsham Hall, Oxford, 4–5 November

Mattingly, M. (1999) 'Management of the urban environment', in Atkinson, A., Dávila, J. D., Fernandes, E. and Mattingly, M. (eds) *The Challenge of Environmental Management in Urban Areas*, Ashgate, London, pp105–113

Maxwell, D., Larbi, W. O., Lamptey, G. M., Zakariah, S. and Armar-Klemesu, M. (1998) 'Farming in the shadow of the city: Changes in land rights and livelihoods in peri-urban Accra', *Cities Feeding People Report 23*, International Development Research Center (IDRC), Canada

Mougeot, L. (1999) 'Urban agriculture: Definition, presence, potential and risks. Main policy challenges', *Cities Feeding People Report No 31*, IDRC, Canada

Nel.lo, O. (2003) 'Las grandes ciudades en Europa y América Latina: Dinámica, retos y gobernación', Proceedings of the conference *El Desafío de las Áreas Metropolitanas en un Mundo Globalizado: Una Mirada a Europa y América Latina*, Barcelona, Spain, 4–6 June

Patil, A. and Nidagundi, S. (1999) 'Changes occurring in the peri-urban interface of Hubli-Dharwad, India: Review of policy and effects on livelihoods in four villages', SEPMFPUI project paper, Development Planning Unit, University College London

Phillips, D., Williams, K., Andrews, G., Clarke, J., Carter, M., Kinsman, P., Smith, D., Willis, K., Bradbury, I., Wu, K. and Hillyer, A. (1999) 'Literature review on peri-urban natural resource conceptualisation and management approaches', in Final Technical Report, *Peri-Urban Production Systems Research, Natural Resources Systems Programme*, University of Nottingham and University of Liverpool, Nottingham and Liverpool

Pirez, P. (2002) 'Buenos Aires: Fragmentation and privatization of the metropolitan city', *Environment and Urbanization*, vol 14, no 1, pp145–158

Rengasamy, S., Devavaram, J., Marirajan, T., Ramavel, N., Rajadurai, K., Karunanidhi, M., Rajendra Prasad, N. and Erskine, A. (2003) 'Farmers' markets in Tamil Nadu; Increasing options for rural producers, improving access for urban consumers', *Environment and Urbanization*, vol 15, no 1, pp25–33

Safier, M. (2002) 'On estimating "room for manoeuvre"', *City*, vol 6, no 1, pp117–132

Santos, B. de S. (ed) (2002) *Democratizar a Democracia: Os Caminhos da Democracia Participativa*, Civilização Brasileira, Rio de Janeiro

Shepherd, A., Williams, K., Hiremath, G. K., Nidagundi, S. R., Patil, D., Subhas, M. S., Hunshal, C. S., Mullah, H. S. S., Khan, J., Nunan, F., Shindhe, K., Joshi, S. G. and Sumangala, P. R. (1998) 'Baseline study and introductory workshop for Hubli-Dharwad city-region, Karnataka, India' in unpublished Final Technical Report (vol 1) *Peri-Urban Production Systems Research, Natural Resources Systems Programme*, University of Birmingham, University of Nottingham and University of Wales at Bangor

Shetawy, A. (2004) *The Politics of Physical Planning Practice: The Case of Industrial Areas in Tenth of Ramadan City, Egypt*, PhD thesis, University College London

Simon, D. (1990) 'The question of regions', in Simon, D. (ed) *Third World Regional Development: A Reappraisal*, Paul Chapman, London, pp3–38

Soussan, J. (1998) 'Water/irrigation and sustainable rural livelihoods', in Carney, D. (ed) *Sustainable Rural Livelihoods: What Contribution Can We Make?*, DFID, London, pp181–195

Stevens, C., Anderson, E. and Kennan, J. (2004) 'The impact of the reform of international trade on urban and rural change', Institute of Development Studies, Sussex, Unpublished paper prepared for DFID, London

Torregrosa y Armentia, M. L., Arteaga, C. and Kloster, K. (2003) 'WSS practices and living conditions in the peri-urban interface of Metropolitan Mexico City: The cases of San Bartolomé Xicomulco and San Salvador Cuauhtenco, Milpa Alta', in unpublished report *Service Provision Governance in the Peri-Urban Interface of Metropolitan Areas Project,* Development Planning Unit, University College London

Velásquez, L. S. and Pacheco, M. (1999) 'Research-management as an approach to solving environmental conflicts in metropolitan areas: A case study of the Manizales-Villamaría conurbation, Colombia', in Atkinson, A., Dávila, J. D., Fernandes, E. and Mattingly, M. (eds) *The Challenge of Environmental Management in Urban Areas*, Ashgate, London, pp275–286

Wiggins, S. and Holt, G. (2000) 'Researchable constraints to the use of forest and tree resources by poor urban and peri-urban households in developing countries', Unpublished report to DFID's Renewable Natural Resources Knowledge Strategy, Department of Agricultural and Food Economics, University of Reading, UK

Part 2

Production Systems at the Peri-Urban Interface

5

The Environmental and Social Impacts of Peri-Urban Irrigated Vegetable Production around Jos, Nigeria

Frances Harris, Margaret Pasquini, Jasper Dung and Alhaji Adepetu

Introduction

The Jos Plateau, located in central northern Nigeria, is a unique region in West Africa, with a temperate climate and an abundance of freshwater supplies that have allowed it to become a centre for the production of temperate vegetables through irrigated agriculture. This chapter takes a historical perspective to consider how human–environment interactions have led to economic opportunities, which have, in turn, shaped the environment in this peri-urban area. The chapter focuses on dry season irrigated vegetable production (DSIVP) and draws on the results of a survey of farmers at four sites of production in the Jos peri-urban area. The four sites form a north–south trajectory along the centre of the plateau, with contrasting proximity to urban areas and access to markets. The aim is to determine the factors affecting irrigated vegetable production at each location and to identify constraints for the future. Using the sustainable rural livelihoods framework (Scoones, 1998), we discuss social and environmental changes in the Jos peri-urban interface and the sustainability of livelihoods associated with DSIVP.

The peri-urban interface (PUI) is most simply described as the transitional zone between the city and the countryside. However, this physical space is more than an interface between two different types of landscape. The PUI is a dynamic place as the urban area expands and takes over and dominates more of the rural area. Physically, the PUI is constantly moving outwards as the urban area expands. This expansion is not equal in all directions around an urban area: instead, urban expansion often occurs first along main arterial roads and then spreads to the interstices. Furthermore, expansion may either be due to industries positioning themselves on the outskirts of towns, the development of housing on the edges of urban areas, or a combination of both.

The activities at the PUI have environmental consequences for the land.

Those who are aware of imminent loss of farmland to urban expansion may change their attitude to natural resource management. Certainly, the incentive to conserve soil fertility for the long term is reduced; in fact, landowners may feel that they can 'mine' their soils, whether for soil fertility or, indeed, clay for building bricks for housing, prior to its conversion to urban uses. However, some landowners may see the benefit of owning small parcels of agricultural land in or near urban areas to provide high-value crops, such as vegetables, which are not easy to transport long distances and can be sold in urban markets. Hence, urban and peri-urban vegetable production is commonplace in Africa.

In addition to being a physical space, the PUI is also an area of socio-economic interactions. As Unwin (1989) stated, people, not places, create flows between rural and urban areas. The PUI is characterized by trans-portation and movement through the region. From an agricultural point of view, these flows are urban waste (manure and also household waste) used to fertilize agricultural land and the movement of agricultural products to urban areas. Major urban markets can be supplemented by markets located on the outskirts of urban areas or at junctions of major roads. Thus, the PUI can be the home of many networks of exchange and interaction of people, trade and resources. In addition to these physical processes of exchange, the PUI can also be a centre for the flow of information (Douglass, 1998). These social networks are supported by the physical infrastructure of a network of roads and markets which form key focal points within the PUI.

Labour may be exchanged between rural and urban areas as those with specific skills travel to where they are most valued. It is important to note that within households, there can be those engaged in traditionally rural activities, while other members commute into and out of urban areas, either to work or to trade. Thus, the PUI is exploited differently by different people within 'multi-spatial' households (Tacoli, 1998; Rigg, 1997).

The Jos PUI is situated on the Jos Plateau, which is unique in Nigeria in having a more temperate climate. Its fairly central location and mild climate, as well as relatively low incidence of malaria, make it an ideal place to live; as a result, many organizations have set up their headquarters on the plateau. This expatriate and relatively wealthy population provided the original market for vegetables produced through DSIVP. The largest urban area on the Jos Plateau is the city of Jos itself. However, there have always been other towns, such as Bukuru, which is now expanding so that the two cities are growing towards each other, and there are buildings and industry all along the main road that links the two. Many people commute between the two cities. Further south, the urban areas on the plateau are more dispersed and more readily identified as discrete towns. Barakin Ladi is a former tin mining settlement which has now become a centre for DSIVP and hosts a large weekly market. The Jos PUI is therefore a large area dominated by the large urban settlements of Jos and Bukuru, but extending to other towns on the Jos Plateau and into rural areas where local economies are geared towards linking into the networks and markets.

This chapter aims to highlight how environmental, social and economic characteristics of the Jos PUI contributed to the development of DSIVP, and how DSIVP has shaped the development of the PUI.

Historical context

The city of Jos is in a highland area formed of volcanic and granitic materials that are rich in minerals, particularly tin. The undulating landscape is interspersed with granitic outcrops and traversed by many streams. Tin mining around Jos began on a small-scale basis as individuals created small tunnels and brought tin to the surface or panned for tin in streams. Commercial mining began during the early part of the 20th century, benefiting from the establishment of a railway in 1915. Production of tin reached its peak in 1943 and gradually declined until the late 1950s, when it started to fall rapidly (Alexander, 1985) due to a decline in the value of tin on the world market.

At its height, tin mining was the major economic activity of the area, attracting large companies to invest in equipment and develop the infrastructure necessary to support the mining economy (Alexander, 1985). In addition to the rail link established in 1915, rural areas around Jos benefited from the development of a good road network, power supply to all the mining areas and even an airport. Tin mining companies required large amounts of labour, so many people immigrated to the area, and the landscape is dotted with mining settlements (*barakin*), where mining companies housed expatriate and local staff.

The area is traversed by many streams and rivers, and these were dammed to provide large amounts of water for the tin mining process. Commercial open-cast tin mining involved digging deep holes as overburden was removed. Once the layers of tin were reached, water was used to scour tin from the subsoil, and the slurry was pumped up to ground level and run through a series of sluices to separate the tin from other debris. The water then ran into settling ponds, where silt and mud settled out, leaving a shallow pond or paddock of freshwater. The process of tin mining created a scarred landscape of heaps of mine spoil, deep and dangerous ponds, dams (some of which ruptured when later abandoned) and shallow ponds above and below dams where water collected before and after use in the mining process.

When world tin processing collapsed during the late 1950s, mining companies first diminished operations and then abandoned them altogether, showing little regard for contractual clauses to restore mine land and leaving the landscape scarred. Land is still under lease to mining companies; but there is little mining activity. Mine land reclamation programmes to restore the landscape have been undertaken; but only a small percentage of the land is covered by these (Alexander, 1996). Mine spoil was levelled, and planting of trees, usually eucalyptus, has resulted in some re-vegetated areas, although the soil is bare between the trees. The overall effect of this on soil quality has actually been to decrease the fertility of already poor soils even further as the plantation soils have become more acid and nutrient deficient. This means that at the end of the forest cycle, many are likely to have lower fertility than the original reclaimed soils (Alexander and Kidd, 2000).

The decline of mining left a large population without employment. Locals were able to resume farming on land not affected by mining; however, the immigrant population of Hausas from northern Nigeria was in need of a new livelihood. Hausas were familiar with the techniques of *fadama* farming. *Fadama* farming is practised during the cool dry season in northern Nigeria on grey hydromorphic soils along riverbeds, which are seasonally flooded. The heavy soils retain water after the floods, when farmers plant vegetables. Water from the receding river channel is used to irrigate the vegetables until they mature. In the Jos peri-urban area, the landscape left from mining provided some of the prerequisites for irrigated vegetable production (water and soil), although soil quality on mine heaps was poor. Many Hausas who had moved to the plateau to work in the tin mines now combined traditional *fadama* farming skills from the north with the abundant freshwater supplies to develop a DSIVP system. Initial DSIVP was along the banks of streams and rivers, where land was less disturbed. This land is seasonally flooded, so that along the Delimi, for example, the river level rises by 3m or more and deposits silt (and rubbish) on the fields each rainy season. Many farmers are involved in levelling and terracing land. Some farmers dam streams or dig small wells to gain access to water for longer periods in the dry season. As DSIVP has become more widely practised, it has spread to upland areas and to areas that are further from Jos and more remote. It is common to see farmers linking longer lengths of water pipes and several pumps to enable them to cultivate irrigated land further from water sources.

Initially, temperate vegetables were produced for the expatriate community in Jos. DSIVP has expanded rapidly since the petroleum boom of the 1970s (Porter, 1992) and now supplies markets beyond the Jos PUI, such as Abuja, Onitsha, Enugu and Port Harcourt. DSIVP has now expanded to become a major economic activity on the Jos Plateau, covering all the former tin mining areas. Such expansion has not been without its problems. Agricultural production requires agricultural inputs and extension to maintain soil fertility and to control pests and diseases. As more and more people take up DSIVP, there are environmental concerns regarding the use of urban waste, water and associated pollution problems. There are also social concerns. Conflict can arise as traditional users of land and freshwater sources now find DSIVP expanding and limiting access to these resources. The success of the immigrant Hausa community has also encouraged local indigenous people to acquire land and skills in DSIVP.

Methodology

Research was carried out at four sites of DSIVP in the Jos PUI. These were located along a north–south transect of the plateau, extending from the north to the centre of the plateau and passing the major town of Jos (the state capital), as well as smaller towns of Bukuru and Barakin Ladi (see Figure 5.1). The sites were chosen for their contrasting characteristics and, in some cases, a history of research at the site. The characteristic features of each location were observed and reported in the course of several visits and are outlined in Table 5.1. The Delimi location has been a site of research for many years due to its proximity to Jos University. A first survey was conducted in the 1980s by

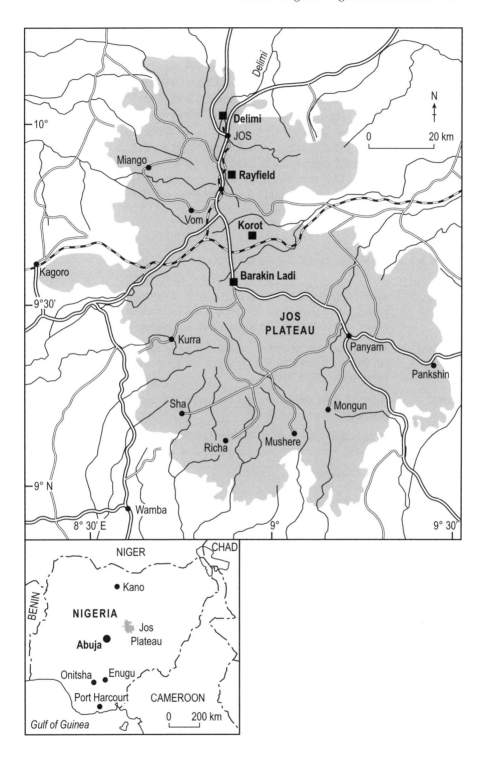

Figure 5.1 The location of four survey sites on the Jos Plateau, Nigeria

Adepetu (Adepetu, 1985) and this was updated in 1990 (Phillips-Howard et al, 1990).

When DSIVP began at Delimi, it was on the outskirts of Jos town; however, as the city of Jos expanded, the Delmi area became surrounded by urban activity. Both the Delimi and Barakin Ladi sites are close to urban areas and associated markets. Initially, farmers in Delimi served the expatriate and wealthy market of Jos; but now they are linked to more markets and some of their produce goes much further afield. Rayfield is further from urban areas; however, it is situated near a main road linking Jos and Bukuru. Therefore, farmers are able to link into the PUI to access inputs (particularly chicken waste from intensive poultry farms) and to sell their produce. Korot is the most remote site, located away from main roads.

Table 5.1 *The four sites of the dry season irrigated vegetable production (DSIVP) survey*

Delimi (n = 52)	An urban farming area, located on the banks of the Delimi River on the northern edge of Jos. Sixty-seven per cent of the land is fadama land. One side of the river is owned by Jos University. Farmers have been working here for about 60 years.
Rayfield (n = 49)	A peri-urban site, located on upland and mine spoil heaps. Water comes from streams and a dam. This is a very open and wind-swept location. Farmers have been here for about 20 years.
Korot (n = 50)	A remote, rural site. Farmers get their water from a stream and farm along the riverbanks.
Barakin Ladi (n = 50)	A peri-urban area close to Barakin Ladi town. Farmers work an undulating landscape formed from mining paddocks and upland terrain. They obtain water from mine ponds or a stream.

At each site, approximately 50 farmers were surveyed by trained enumerators using a questionnaire, while working on their farms. Farmers were also interviewed in detail in Delimi, Rayfield and Barakin Ladi on soil fertility management practices, pest control and general farming problems.

Results and discussion

Social issues

The local indigenous population is predominantly Berom, although there are many other groups, most notably Anaguta, Ngas, Taroh, Igwe, Jarawa and Ron. The ethnicity of farmers surveyed at each site is shown in Table 5.2. The Hausa population has emigrated from the north of Nigeria, although many have been resident in the Jos PUI for generations. Traditionally, nomadic Fulani pastoralists roam the area with herds of cattle. As competition for land has increased, many Fulani have either become sedentary and taken up farming alongside their pastoralist activities, or greatly reduced the range of their grazing circuit, staying closer to a base at all times of the year. As stated earlier, Hausa farmers brought the skills of irrigated vegetable production to the Jos PUI. At the time of this research, they remained the largest group involved in farming, making up to 64 per cent of all the farmers surveyed. At Delimi and Rayfield, more than 70 per cent of DSIVP farmers surveyed were Hausa, with almost no Berom farmers, whereas at Barakin Ladi and Korot, 40 per cent were Berom (see Table 5.2). However, Berom farmers are taking up DSIVP (22 per cent of all farmers surveyed); but this is only seen at Korot and Barakin Ladi, two sites with higher percentages of people from Plateau State involved in DSIVP. Relatively few Fulani and other local tribes are involved in DSIVP; but their low percentages may be due to their relatively lower presence in the population of the Jos Plateau as a whole. In comparison with the other sites, Delimi has good representation from other tribes. This may be due to the fact that, with its more urban location, it attracts many people from within Jos town.

Table 5.2 *Farmers' and labourers' ethnicity, origin, and land tenure (percentage)*

	Delimi	Rayfield	Korot	Barakin Ladi
Ethnicity				
Berom	2	6	40	40
Hausa	73	78	60	44
Fulani	11.5	8	0	14
Other	13.5	8	0	2
Origin				
Local	31	6	24	41.5
Plateau	9.5	8	20	15
Out of state	59.5	86	56	43.5
Labour source				
Plateau	31	37	68	46
Out of state	50	60	40	30
Land Tenure				
Purchase	15	2	12	34
Hire	71	90	46	36
Inherited	13	8	41	30
Pledged	2			

Note: Labour source percentages do not add up to 100 as some farmers do not hire labour while others hire from more than one source.

Farmers were also asked their place of birth (see Table 5.2) to ascertain how many were long-term residents in the Jos PUI and how many had been attracted to the area during their lifetimes. Barakin Ladi had the highest percentage of locally born people working at the site. Rayfield had very few locally born or even Plateau State residents working at the site. Eighty-five per cent of those surveyed came from outside the state, and most of those were from the north. A more detailed analysis of the origin (place of birth) of DSIVP farmers shows that many farmers come from a few places. Kazaure, Kano and Jigawa are mentioned as birthplace by a high proportion of farmers surveyed. There may be some overlap between the three, as Jigawa State was created from territory formerly in Kano and Borno states, and Kazaure has been in Kano State and is now in Jigawa State. However, 16 per cent of farmers stated that they were from Kazaure, 23 per cent from Kano and 12 per cent from Jigawa. Together, these three places were the birthplace of 53 per cent of the farmers surveyed. It would appear that there is a network within places such as Kazaure, which enables people to enter the DSIVP industry in Jos.

DSIVP is very labour intensive, and almost all farmers (90 per cent) hire labourers to assist them during the season. Farmers may hire local people, import seasonal labour or employ a mixture of both, and they may hire them for short periods when agricultural activities are at a peak (for example, during harvest) or for the whole season. At the time of the research, many seasonal labourers were Hausas from the north of the country, and this fits in with their practice of seeking short-term work to earn money during the dry season (*cin rani*), returning to their farmland for the rain-fed farming season. At Delimi and Rayfield, seasonal migrant labourers from outside the state were hired by 50 per cent or more farmers. Most came from Kano, Katsina and Jigawa states. Korot has the highest percentage of people coming from the Plateau State working as labourers.

Table 5.2 shows that, overall, many farmers do not actually own the land they are farming for DSIVP. Therefore, the tribal affiliation of farmers at each site is also reflected in the land tenure at each site. The highest percentage of ownership (by purchase or inheritance) is 64 per cent in Barakin Ladi, where there is a roughly equal distribution between purchased, hired and inherited land. Only 10 per cent of farmers at Rayfield and 28 per cent at Delimi own their land. The high level of hiring land at Delimi may be due to the fact that one of the riverbanks is owned by the university, which rents land to farmers. At Rayfield, 90 per cent of farmers hire their land. Hausas are immigrants to the plateau and even those who have lived there for many generations may not have the opportunity to inherit land. There is evidence now of Berom farmers specifically working alongside Hausa farmers to learn their skills. There is also an increasing trend in Berom farmers working land, and only agreeing to host Hausas as labourers, rather than allowing them to rent and manage vegetable plots themselves (Porter et al, 2003). As more landowning indigenes take up DSIVP, this trend may increase.

Environmental issues

The DSIVP farming system in the Jos PUI benefits from some environmental opportunities associated with its location; but this also presents some environmental challenges. As stated above, the PUI is an area of exchange and networking, and this has particular implications for agriculture in the PUI. Proximity to urban areas means that there are large amounts of urban waste (household waste, night soil and dirty water), which may be used to fertilize soils. Furthermore, proximity to urban areas and daily markets can encourage farmers to produce more market-oriented products, such as perishable vegetables. The proximity of the market removes problems of long-distance transport and damage during storage and travel. Rapid sale of crops allows farmers to reinvest earnings in other farming inputs, such as more seeds, labour and fertilizers (Porter et al, 2003).

As with any farming system, whether in a peri-urban or rural area, maintenance of soil fertility is crucial to its sustainability. In this farming system, farmers engage in rain-fed cultivation of subsistence crops during the rainy season, and then irrigated vegetable production in the dry season, so that the land is cropped continually. In order to sustain this, farmers need to have adequate supplies of soil nutrients and organic matter to maintain the fertility of their soils. In DSIVP in the Jos PUI, all farmers use inorganic fertilizer, purchasing as much as they can acquire, according to both availability and price (see Table 5.3). Virtually all farmers use compound fertilizer (nitrogen-phosphorus-potassium, or NPK) and seem to do this in preference to purchasing specific nutrients, such as nitrogen (in urea) and phosphorus as single super phosphate (SSP) or di-ammonium phosphate (DAP). Organic material is also used (see Table 5.3). Livestock manure is more commonly used in Barakin Ladi and Korot, further from the urban areas, where there are more livestock. Urban and household waste, either burned to ash (Pasquini and Harris, 2005) or fresh, is used by most farmers. Although Rayfield and Korot are more remote from urban waste sources, they use more urban waste and ash than Delimi and Barakin Ladi. Surprisingly, Delimi, the site surrounded by urban areas, uses less urban ash than manure. This is due to the fact that it is difficult for tipper trucks or pick-ups to access the vegetable growing area at Delimi; therefore, farmers cannot get it delivered close enough to their fields. Farmers at the more remote sites of Korot and Barakin Ladi use more manure than those closer to Jos. A very high percentage of farmers at Rayfield use chicken manure. This may be due to the proximity of a commercial poultry unit, from which farmers can arrange to have pick-up trips of poultry manure delivered to their fields.

Table 5.3 *Use of soil fertility amendments at four DSIVP sites on the Jos Plateau (percentage)*

	Delimi	Rayfield	Korot	Barakin Ladi
Inorganic fertilizer use				
NPK	96	98	100	100
Urea	90	90	54	52
Phosphorus	19	52	–	24
Organic fertilizer use				
Chicken manure	46	90	54	60
Livestock manure	25	29	70	74
Urban ash	56	70	68	46
Fresh urban waste	–	–	28	24
Household waste	8	18	–	–

The environmental concerns associated with DSIVP are discussed in detail elsewhere (Porter et al, 2003), but are summarized here. Some of the environmental concerns are particularly associated with the location of DSIVP within the PUI, such as the risk of spread of disease due to the use of urban waste to fertilize soil. Farmers usually set light to piles of urban waste prior to applying it to their soils in order to remove some of the rubbish in the waste (such as paper or plastic bags) and also to 'sterilize' the waste. This actually releases unpleasant smoke and does not necessarily heat the waste to temperatures sufficient to sterilize the waste. Following burning, farmers sort through the waste by hand to remove other debris such as glass prior to applying it to their soil.

Farmers complained that there was a shortage of freshwater, particularly towards the end of the dry season. There is little regulation of water off-take, and as more farmers purchase pumps to enlarge the area that they can cultivate, pressures on water availability are likely to increase. This could be exacerbated by the fact that in more built-up environments, people also make demands on water supply to meet normal household needs, as well as irrigation.

Farmers crop their vegetables intensively in the dry season. Most vegetable plots contain mixtures of crops (for example, lettuce, spinach and carrots in the same bed); however, tomatoes and potatoes tend to be grown as sole crops. This mono-cropping, combined with the irrigation method – where water flows between vegetable plots – means that any outbreak of disease could spread rapidly to affect the whole area. Interviews with farmers showed that farmers were not able to identify specific diseases and made it clear that there was little knowledge of the best way to use agrochemicals, particularly pesticides (Porter et al, 2003). Rather than an informed and targeted approach, farmers were using whatever they could get and applying it without reference to instructions. This is dangerous to those handling the chemicals, and also because farmers may contaminate freshwater supplies with agrochemicals. This could have a large impact if it were to occur in a densely populated peri-urban area.

Farmers' concerns

Farmers were also asked to identify the key constraints they faced in their DSIVP (see Table 5.4). Predictably, financial constraints were mentioned most frequently. This is because the DSIVP farming system is becoming increasingly commercialized in terms of inputs. Farmers pay for fertilizers and agrochemicals to control diseases, and now that all farmers use petrol-fired pumps to get water to their crops, they must either hire or purchase pumps, tubes and the fuel to keep them going. Formerly, farmers could obtain urban waste or manure free; but, increasingly, they must pay for this, as well as the transport costs to get it to their land. Some farmers still sell at the farm gate; but they must also pay transport costs to take material from their land to market. Although DSIVP can be lucrative, it also requires considerable cash investment at the start of the farming season to pay for land preparation, seeds, field for water pumps and labour. This is one reason why farmers intercrop fast-growing products such as spinach between slower growing crops, which enables them to obtain some harvest and, therefore, revenue earlier in the season.

Table 5.4 *Key constraints identified by farmers (percentage) at four DSIVP sites on the Jos Plateau*

	Delimi	Rayfield	Korot	Barakin Ladi
Finance	67	86	74	70
Fuel	63	59	44	14
Fertilizer	46	61	38	44
Pump	35	31	12	14
Water shortage	–	–	22	14
Labour	–	31	–	–

A concern towards the latter part of the season is water shortage. Some farmers have their own pumps; others share pumps and hoses between two to three farmers. All farmers rely on streams, ponds and reservoirs for their irrigation water, and there is no formal system to regulate water off-take. Farmers irrigate their land, on average, twice a week. As the dry season progresses, the water in mine ponds or streams is diminished; in some cases, farmers are left without water when the crop has yet to mature. This was a serious problem in Korot, where irrigation relied on a stream, and was also a concern in Barakin Ladi, but less of a problem in Delimi and Rayfield.

Interestingly, other constraints mentioned included difficulty in obtaining seeds of good quality at reasonable prices and at the right time. Many of the seeds are imported from Holland. Farmers also expressed a desire for more government support of DSIVP farmers. Farmers in Barakin Ladi complained that as the agricultural development programme depot was located in Jos, it was too far to go to purchase inputs; instead, they purchased from local markets. However, only the agricultural development programme supplied seeds and fertilizer at subsidized prices. Farmers at Rayfield complained that they suffered from a shortage of labour, possibly because this is a difficult location to get to without transport, and possibly also due to farms in Rayfield being much larger than at the other sites.

Marketing

The building materials market is the major market for vegetable produce in the Jos PUI, located in Bukuru on the road towards Jos. Other urban markets include *Farin Gada*, a daily market in the north of Jos and Barakin Ladi. There are also markets located outside of towns, at road junctions. Many farmers send produce to distant large markets, such as at Enugu, Onitsha, Abuja and Port Harcourt, major Nigerian cities to the south and south-east of the Jos Plateau. The location of the DSIVP site within the PUI appears to affect farmers' ability to access different markets (see Table 5.5). Farmers at Delimi are located fairly centrally. Vehicular access to their farmland is difficult compared to access to the other sites. They chose to sell most of their produce at markets within Jos, either on farm, at their nearest market (*Farin Gada*, within walking distance) or at the building materials market. Just over 10 per cent of produce is sold to the more distant towns listed above. These farmers appear not to be integrated within the marketing chains that supply the larger markets of more distant towns. In contrast, farmers at Rayfield and Korot were unable to sell much produce from their farm gate. Instead, most farmers at Korot took produce to the building materials market, although others went to closer markets at Bukuru and Foron. Farmers at Korot were much more likely to send produce to distant markets. Perhaps, having to arrange a truck for transport, it is as easy to send it further distances rather than transport it to Jos and then have middlemen (*dilali*) organize further transport. Farmers at Barakin Ladi were able to sell more produce from their farm or at the local market in Barakin Ladi. However, about half took produce to the building materials market, and about the same sold produce to distant towns (see Table 5.5).

Table 5.5 *Market outlets for each of the four DSIVP sites*

	Delimi	Rayfield	Korot	Barakin Ladi
On farm	27	2	10	40
Building materials market	52	63	95	52
Farin Gada market, Jos	86	6	–	–
Bukuru	–	–	34	28
Barakin Ladi	–	–	–	20
Foron	–	–	48	–
Maraba junction	–	45	–	–
Major towns far away	13	4	44	48

Conclusions

The development of the Jos PUI has been shaped, first, by its physical environment and, second, through opportunistic development of livelihoods by the immigrant Hausa population. Human–environment interactions have created, and then recreated, landscapes in response to natural resource-based economic activities. A seemingly degraded landscape after mining has been reclaimed through DSIVP to provide livelihoods for many. The local population has seized opportunities as they have arisen within a dynamic and changing PUI. Thus, this case study provides an example of a responsive society adapting to environmental change as large immigrant communities have made their mark on the environment and the economy.

Over the years, the forces of livelihood change on the Jos Plateau have been the rise of tin mining, the in-migration of populations as labour to support the mining industry, expanding urban centres, the collapse of tin mining, and the development of DSIVP. The scarred landscape of mine spoil, ponds and paddocks left by the mining companies presented opportunities to the Hausa immigrants. Through careful management of the soil (Phillips-Howard and Lyon, 1994; Pasquini, 2002) they have built up soil fertility using all available inputs, creating natural capital on which to base their livelihoods. Through the creation of employment opportunities that attracted people to the region, tin mining also brought the labour pool, particularly those with knowledge of DSIVP techniques, to the plateau. The arrival of the Hausa, with their knowledge, skills and networks to further seasonal labour sources, provided social capital as well. One of the legacies of tin mining was the physical infrastructure of roads, rail and markets from which the vegetable growers now benefit. Thus, inadvertently, tin mining produced both physical and human capital for these new livelihoods. The livelihoods also benefit from the social capital of marketing chains with both local dealers and distant traders from the south being involved. Most financial capital for DSIVP has come from farmers' own sources or informal credit from family, friends, traders or chemical dealers; but it is also provided through loans for irrigation pumps available from a World Bank-funded project through the Plateau Agriculture Development Programme (PADP), which also supports farmers through extension activities and selling seeds and fertilizers at their depot in Jos.

These livelihoods are interlinked with peri-urban sources of inputs, international trade in seeds, distant sources of seasonal labour, and both local and distant markets. Two key questions are: how important has the peri-urban location been in creating these livelihoods and how sustainable are these livelihoods based on DSIVP?

The role of the PUI

This peri-urban agriculture has made use of urban waste, labour and the infrastructure of roads and markets to expand and develop, so that what began as a small industry supplying the needs of a small, local expatriate community has now expanded to become a large industry that supplies markets across Nigeria. Undoubtedly, this industry is only possible due to the combination of climate and freshwater supplies which exists on the Jos Plateau. However, without the initial demand for vegetables based in Jos, the immigrant farmers would not have had a market to justify applying their skills. As a result of its physical location and focal point for exchange, the PUI has been an area of economic importance. It is the site of investment as land is bought and developed, jobs are created and economic links to wider and more distant markets are established. The roads and markets have been the means of expanding the market for vegetables and, therefore, of creating the demand, which has led more farmers to take up DSIVP in this area.

The sustainability of livelihoods based on DSIVP

As outlined above, there are considerable environmental concerns associated with DSIVP. Maintenance of soil fertility, conservation of both sufficient quantities and quality of freshwater, and control of the spread of disease (among the urban population, and also disease within the crops) are all issues which should be given priority if this industry is to continue. Addressing these issues will require a combination of technology and agricultural extension. A clear programme of support for farmers could achieve this.

However, another aspect of the sustainability of this farming system concerns the ethnic tensions in the area. The role of the immigrant Hausa community in developing this industry must be noted. Not only did they bring the techniques, they are still the main vegetable producers. Through their networks (social capital) and practices of *cin rani*, the Hausas provide a large amount of the labour force. DSIVP is useful to those from the north as it provides a means of earning income in their dry season. Thus, DSIVP fills a cultural and financial need within their community. Interestingly, DSIVP bridges a transfer of knowledge, skills and labour from the Hausa in the north of Nigeria, via the plateau, to markets in the south of Nigeria.

The 'indigenization' of DSIVP is interesting in two ways. First, it shows a transfer of skills from one group to another and, second, it indicates that DSIVP is seen as a worthwhile activity that attracts people who traditionally have secured their livelihoods from other means. However, the ethnic divide within DSIVP is a grave concern. Local residents own the vital asset: land. Yet, immigrants have brought the capability of developing the asset with their DSIVP skills, knowledge and labour. Ethnic tensions are always simmering under the surface in Nigeria, and this includes Plateau State, where major riots occurred several times over the few years prior to this study. Since this study, there have been more widespread and serious ethnic riots on the Jos Plateau, sparked, in part, by the crisis of 11 September 2001. Since this survey, the number of Hausa farmers involved in DSIVP has declined due to the ethnic conflict between Berom and Hausa. The continuing 'indigenization' of DSIVP may further ethnic tensions as locals and 'immigrants' (even those whose families have lived there for generations) compete for access to land, water, agricultural supplies and support. Compared to the technical concerns for environmental sustainability, this is a much bigger challenge to overcome and threatens the sustainability of the DSIVP farming system in the Jos PUI.

Acknowledgements

This research was supported by a British Council Higher Education Link programme between the Department of Geography and Planning, University of Jos, and the Department of Geography, University of Durham. Further small grant funding was received from the UK Department for International Development (DFID). We appreciate the support of staff and field assistants based at the University of Jos, and the comments of reviewers and Fergus Lyon on early drafts of the chapter.

References

Adepetu, A. A. (1985) *Farmers and their Farms on Four Fadamas on the Jos Plateau*, Jos Plateau Environmental Resources Development Programme, Interim Report No 2, University of Durham, Durham

Alexander, M. J. (1985) *An Historical Introduction to the Reclamation of Mineland on the Jos Plateau*, Jos Plateau Environmental Resources Development Programme, Interim Report No 4, University of Durham, Durham

Alexander, M. J. (1996) 'The effectiveness of small-scale irrigated agriculture in the reclamation of mine land soils on the Jos Plateau of Nigeria', *Land Degradation and Development*, vol 7, pp77–85

Alexander, M. J. and Kidd, A. D. (2000) 'Farmers' capability and institutional incapacity in reclaiming disturbed land on the Jos Plateau, Nigeria', *Journal of Environmental Management*, vol 59, pp141–155

Douglass, M. (1998) 'A regional network strategy for reciprocal rural–urban linkages: An agenda for policy research with reference to Indonesia', *Third World Planning Review*, vol 20, pp1–33

Pasquini, M. W. (2002) *Soil Fertility Management Strategies in Irrigated Peri-Urban Agriculture around Jos, Nigeria: An Interdisciplinary Approach*, PhD thesis, University of Durham, Durham

Pasquini, M. W. and Harris, F. (2005) 'Efficient use of resources: Urban waste ash and soil fertility on the Jos Plateau, Nigeria', *Area*, vol 37, no 1, pp17–29

Phillips-Howard, K. D., Adepetu, A. A. and Kidd, A. D. (1990) *Aspects of Change in Fadama Farming along the Delimi River, Jos L. G. C. (1982–1990)*, Jos Plateau Environmental Resources Development Programme, Interim Report No 18, University of Durham, Durham

Phillips-Howard, K. and Lyon, F. (1994) 'Agricultural intensification and the threat to soil fertility in Africa: Evidence from the Jos Plateau, Nigeria', *Geographical Journal*, vol 160, no 3, pp252–265

Porter, G. (1992) *Food Marketing and Urban Food Supply on the Jos Plateau: A Comparison of Large and Small Producer Strategies Under 'SAP'*, Jos Plateau Environmental Resources Development Programme, Interim Report No 29, University of Durham, Durham

Porter, G., Harris, F., Lyon, F., Dung, J. and Adepetu, A. A. (2003) 'Markets, ethnicity and environment in a vulnerable landscape: The case of small-scale vegetable production on the Jos Plateau, Nigeria, 1991–2001', *Geographical Journal*, vol 169, no 4, pp370–381

Rigg, J. (1997) *Southeast Asia*, Routledge, London

Scoones, I. (1998) *Sustainable Rural Livelihoods: A Framework for Analysis*, Working paper No 72, Institute of Development Studies, Brighton

Tacoli, C. (1998) 'Rural–urban linkages and sustainable rural livelihoods', in Carney, D. (ed) *Sustainable Rural Livelihoods*, DFID, London, pp67–80

Unwin, T. (1989) 'Urban–rural interaction in developing countries: A theoretical perspective', in Potter, R. and Unwin, T. (eds) *The Geography of Urban–Rural Interaction in Developing Countries, Essays for Alan B. Mountjoy*, Routledge, London

6

Horticulture and Market Information at the Peri-Urban Interface: Agricultural Marketing in Tanzania

Kenneth Lynch and Nigel Poole

Introduction

Agricultural market liberalization in sub-Saharan Africa

Since the 1980s, market liberalization has had a major impact upon the agricultural economies of sub-Saharan African (SSA) countries. On the whole, this has taken the form of rolling back the centralized marketing systems inherited from the colonial period and maintained under independent government.

One aspect that emerges from research on these issues is that markets hold a different place in African societies than in others. For example, Siddle and Swindell (1990, p87) argued that:

> *While other societies develop rituals of formal exchange to high degrees of sophistication and leaven them with informal social activity, it is a particular skill of African societies to shape their elaborate informal exchange mechanisms by a minimum number of formal procedures.*

They go on to suggest that the development of rural markets historically has taken place 'spontaneously' and that the manner of their operation can seem 'outmoded' and 'anachronistic'. They do, however, make a strong case for the fact that extensive rural market systems pre-dated the arrival of European colonialism. There is other evidence that the spontaneous development of markets is, in fact, a highly rational response to particular circumstances. For example, Siddle and Swindell (1990) point out that the establishment of some market places in rural areas is to avoid interference of urban authorities. Other writers have provided accounts for the complexities involved in rural marketing systems:

> *Whereas daily marketing activities at crossroads or on the edge of the marketplace can develop into sizeable gatherings from little more than a handful of individuals waiting in casual consumer sales, the selling of large quantities of local produce depends on the knowledge of its regular availability being shared with potential buyers* (Hollier, 1990, p60).

In addition, the exchange of wholesale agricultural commodities such as foods does not necessarily take place at rural markets. Many cities rely on the production of food in their hinterland stretching from the peri-urban interface (PUI) to distant rural areas (Iaquinta and Drescher, 2001). As areas become involved in the production of goods that are sold on to markets, so the issue of market knowledge becomes vital to successful marketing.

Several economic analysts argue persuasively that markets are the neglected engines of economic development. For example, Kaynak (1986) contends that much development theory focuses on the role of production at the expense of markets. In African economies, where as much as 70 per cent of the working population may depend directly on agricultural production, agricultural markets are crucial economic activities and their potential for linking the different parts of the economy is often overlooked. In particular, commercial agricultural production is carried out largely for urban markets, such as the one illustrated in Figure 6.1. Urban markets offer an important means through which small-scale producers in rural and peri-urban areas can enhance their livelihood opportunities (Mutizwa-Mangiza, 1999). Research on food-related issues at the PUI, like research on such issues in rural areas, has thus far focused largely on issues of production, particularly relating to cultivation and natural resource management (Poole and Lynch, 2003).

There is a need to improve understanding of the mechanisms by which smallholder producers and other food market participants in SSA overcome the informational constraints in fruit and vegetable market systems. These systems are based largely on rural or peri-urban production and urban consumption and are therefore a key component of rural–urban interaction (Lynch, 2004). The provision of market information is only one of a number of constraints to agricultural development; others include the provision of extension services and credit. This chapter addresses the importance of marketing information to small-scale food producers, drawing on research in Tanzania, with comparison from a parallel project in Ghana, to provide tentative notions that may usefully inform future research or interventions. The research reported here therefore explores the exchange of market information between producers and traders in Tanzania. In particular, informal and formal institutions in the horticultural market system and the extent to which they influence the flows of market information are investigated.

Figure 6.1 Urban consumers select from a variety of fresh vegetables, Dar es Salaam

What information?

Market information is usually regarded as data on prices and quantities exchanged, duly processed and made available to market participants. The primary functions of market information services are to collect, process and analyse such market data systematically and continuously, and to ensure delivery of information on a timely basis to all market participants (Schubert, 1993; Poon, 1994).

Shepherd has distinguished *market* information, which consists of data on prices and quantities, from *marketing* information – 'a much wider concept, which is likely to include details on potential market channels, payment requirements, packaging, quality and a whole host of information required by a producer to make a successful sale, *including market information*' (Shepherd, 1997, p5). Galtier and Egg (1998) argue that the role of publicly owned marketing information agencies is likely to be limited to local interventions targeted at local objectives. They suggest that these may be specific informational needs or appropriate institutional developments to reduce informational and other transaction costs. For example, Poole et al (1998) explore the potential of contracts for making transactions to increase the trust between participants in the case of Ghana. Lee (1993) suggests that there may be a role also for 'marketing extension workers' where organizational resources permit.

From a public policy perspective, flows of information within informal trading networks are second best to free and open flows of information in the 'public domain'. At best, information flows within networks of relatively small traders fragment markets with differential access to information, creating situations of monopolistic competition. At worst, networks controlled by dominant traders tend towards oligopoly. However, the transmission of relevant market and marketing information through these networks is often more effective (for network members) than dissemination through official market information systems (MISs).

Informal information sources for producers

Compared to traders, smallholders are usually poorly linked to markets and information sources. Information networks are particularly important to producers: even in the agricultural markets of advanced economies, farmers tend to be passive marketers, reliant on informal sources and 'word of mouth' (Poole et al, 1998). Constraints are due to geographical distance and physical access, but also to time constraints and attitudinal considerations. In addition to neighbours and friends, traders often assume significance as suppliers of information to smallholders (see Figure 6.2). However, market power considerations arise from the informational asymmetries and abuses of trust.

There have been experiments in bringing the private sector into public market information systems – for example, through sponsorship of radio broadcasts or bulletins (FAO, 1999). It is possible that private-sector organizations could take over national MISs, though it is unclear as yet how this might be financed. The difficulty may be to provide a system which is of direct benefit to the target information users and which is economically viable and self-sustaining.

In some areas with good environmental conditions for horticultural production there is sufficient trading for the local authority to invest in market infrastructure such as a market building (see Figure 6.3). However, this also

Figure 6.2 Wholesalers discuss marketing information in Soni periodic market, Tanga Region

results in charging for the facilities, which can be unpopular with both farmers and traders. The development of such institutions in marketing is closely intertwined with theories of collective action, which explore how individuals cooperate to manage resources in particular types of institutional arrangements.

Agriculture in Tanzania

Tanzania has consistently ranked among the world's poorest economies. Recently, the World Bank (2003) estimated the gross national income (GNI) per capita at US$290 in 2003, an increase from US$250 in 1999, but leaving the country firmly in their low-income country classification. Agriculture is the main economic sector, accounting for 17 per cent of the full-time employment, 45 per cent of gross domestic product (GDP) and 53 per cent of the value of exports (United Republic of Tanzania, 1994). However, the level of technology is relatively low, with little use of irrigation, fertilizers, credit and improved seeds. The agricultural systems, however, are highly varied, with highly capitalized production mixed with low-technology, small-scale production.

Horticultural themes in Tanzania

Horticultural crops are produced throughout Tanzania, mainly on a small scale, with vegetables accounting for an estimated 318,000ha in the 1988/1989 growing season and fruit for 1,650,000ha. The main regions are the coastal

Figure 6.3 Mgeta rural wholesale market: Evidence of local authority support for rural trading or opportunity to raise taxation?

belt, the central plateau, the Lake zone and the highlands. This is mainly due to the coincidence of favourable growing conditions, high population densities (providing a concentration of consumers) and relative proximity to large urban markets (FAO, 1994). Figure 6.4 illustrates the steep gradients on which some producers work in order to meet the market needs in locations with high population densities and good market links. One of the major problems for producers and traders alike is the seasonal peaks and troughs in the market (Lynch, 1992). This clearly illustrates that the influence of the urban markets extends considerable distances into the rural areas. The local economy illustrated in Figure 6.4 is strongly influenced by its links to the city, fulfilling many of the criteria of the peri-urban (van Donge, 1992).

Fruit and vegetables have been neglected in research in Tanzania and around the world relative to staple foods, although the sector accounts for half of non-staple food production in Tanzania (see Table 6.1 for available literature). In some of the key production areas, such as parts of Morogoro and Tanga regions, fruit and vegetables can represent the dominant crops. This section collates available information with a view to evaluating the post-harvest aspect of the fruit and vegetable supply chain and, in particular, the role of market information in the marketing of these commodities. Their strategic importance is increasing as interest grows in exploring the potential to develop horticultural production into a major export sector (Minster Agriculture Ltd, 1988; Amka Trust, 1997). Interviews with traders and exporters suggest that improvement of national markets in horticultural commodities is a step towards being able to export.

Figure 6.4 Vegetable production on steep slopes near Morogoro; strong links to the market encourage farmers to make considerable efforts to produce for the urban markets

Table 6.1 *Summary of horticultural issues in the literature*

Theme	Sources
Considerable variety and innovation among producers and traders in spite of difficulties	(Lynch, 1992)
Marketing an important engine for general national development	(Kaynak, 1986)
Potential for horticulture production immense and opportunities for export significant	(Minster Agriculture Ltd, 1988)
Limited supply of quality and affordable inputs, poor marketing infrastructure and insufficient market information	(Mbelwa, 1994)
The horticultural sector in Africa is important to the nutritional status of the population	(Mascarenhas, 1984)
Ujamaa Village Act gave land entitlement to the male head of household	(SAF, 1996)
Ujamaa Village Act also subordinated women to their husbands, especially in relation to marketing	(Platteau, 1996)
Problem of high perishability of commodities and market unable to bear storage	(Jones, 1987)
Major problem for producers and traders alike is the seasonal peaks and troughs in the market	(Lynch, 1992)

Constraints

Industry reviews have identified the main constraints on fruit and vegetable production as limited supply of good-quality seeds, the high costs of agro-chemicals, and poor marketing infrastructure and insufficient market information among traders and producers (cf Mbelwa, 1994). Many such reviews have recommended studies to ensure that a more comprehensive understanding is gained of the industry. However, one consultancy report, while presenting a comprehensive study of the industry, devoted only one short paragraph in its 90 pages to the issue of market information (Kiriwaggulu et al, 1996).

Bryceson (1993) noted the strategic importance of food marketing to the Tanzanian economy and the fact that traders have been seen by Tanzanians as pariahs for decades because of the pressures on consumers and producers and their feelings that the traders must be partly to blame. She suggested that this contradiction could partly explain why food production in the country has remained primarily a subsistence activity and why surplus production for sale has been difficult to encourage. Hyden (1980) suggested that the difficulties in encouraging smallholders to produce for markets during the early independence period arose from a fundamental mismatch between the motivation of the state and the markets, on the one hand, and the peasant farmers, on the other. Much of the activity in relation to horticultural production and marketing is not necessarily motivated by a purely economic logic. Lynch (2004), for example, reported producer and trader respondents engaged in markets for social and cultural reasons, such as maintaining contact with relatives, friends or another market participant with whom they may have a dispute.

Bryceson (1993) reports that in Tanzania, like Ghana, despite the apparent disorganization and under-capitalization of the private markets, informal food marketing networks have proved capable of ensuring supplies to large urban areas under adverse circumstances and have constantly enabled farmers to adapt to urban consumer demands. This suggests that informal networks of information and trade were able to overcome considerable difficulty to ensure that rural producers and urban consumers were able to secure their livelihoods.

The studies on agriculture in Tanzania raise a number of research issues. These include the role of women, access to and control over productive resources, and informational constraints. For example, at the end of the 1980s, horticultural traders and most horticultural farmers felt that radio broadcasts of market information did not meet their needs (Lynch, 1992; Marketing Development Bureau, 1993).

Timing and location of study

Data collection took place between August 1998 and July 1999, and included a producer survey, a trader survey, a producer group case study and in-depth interviews. The research methods were eclectic, employing qualitative methodologies in order to capture the complex and particular characteristics and incentive structures of relational contracting, and to include case studies and key informant interviews.

Five villages in two areas were identified for the focus of the horticultural producer survey. These villages were selected on the basis that they have the appropriate environmental circumstances for horticultural production, but have poor market links. All villages are geographically close to cities; nevertheless, due to poor infrastructure, those centres and the main trunk routes were not easily accessible. In Dodoma Region, the survey villages were Mbabala A (Dodoma Urban District) and Mvumi Mission (Dodoma Rural District). In Morogoro Region, the villages surveyed were Malui, Ulaya Kibaoni and Ngole, all in Kilosa District. In-depth interviews were also carried out in the Atomic Speed Group (ASG) near Mantumbulu village, Dodoma Region, as a relatively rare example of a producer group comprising young, progressive farmers.

Although the survey locations are all rural and are located at varying distances from a city, a strong urban influence extends outwards to these areas because of the particular production advantages that they offer. Although they may be geographically distant, they could arguably be defined as peri-urban to varying degrees because of the importance of the city to their society and economy.

Results

During 1998, 107 interviews of small-scale producers were carried out in the above-mentioned five villages. This provided sets of both qualitative and quantitative data. It should be noted that the 1998/1999 growing season had particularly heavy rains during mid-1998, followed by the failure of the short rains (*vuli*), which badly affected the regions under study (FAO, 1999). It is to be expected that this poor season prior to the data collection may have affected the results reported by respondents.

Almost half the interviewees were less than 35 years old. This is, therefore, a young cohort relative to the general farming population. The majority of farmers interviewed had a minimum primary education. This suggests that these producers had higher than average abilities to make use of technology and to collect, manage and apply information relating to production and marketing activities.

Just under half of the respondents were in households of five or fewer members. However, the group discussions and interviews suggest that households in the villages studied do not have easily identified boundaries, with interdependencies among branches of the families and links with parents and siblings committing respondents to working away from their farm, but also benefiting from reciprocal exchanges of labour and land.

The majority of respondents interviewed were the male heads of household, reflecting the male domination of commercial production of fruit and vegetables. Women produce fruits and vegetables on a small scale and tend to sell only to traders who come to their farms or at local retail and at periodic markets on a very small scale. There is considerable suspicion between the genders on the question of marketing of crops and who benefits from the sale. The men market the produce and do not expect to disclose the details. The women sell produce but are expected to disclose the details and give the money to their husbands. Female respondents avoid full disclosure, if possible, in order to keep some money back from their sales to pay for items such as food, clothing for children and medicines. The result is that market information exchange within the household is far from transparent.

Crop selection

Tomatoes and maize dominate the production activities in the five villages surveyed, accounting for 72 and 70 per cent respectively. The importance of maize, along with rice paddy (28 per cent), sorghum/millet (25 per cent) and sweet potatoes (22 per cent) demonstrates the importance of subsistence production to the farmers interviewed.

Market information

All the respondents reported having sold crops to traders but information reported on crop prices suggests that there is a wide range of abilities in taking advantage of the marketing seasons. Only 21 per cent of the respondents kept records, suggesting relatively low business awareness. However, when questioned further, only 18 per cent reported that they did not know how to keep records. Alternative reasons included that it is a tedious exercise or it is not important.

Market risk

Farmers identified a number of key risks, particularly instability of prices and the small market. Thirty-one per cent of farmers had experienced a problem in their transactions during the previous season. A one-in-three chance of encountering payment problems is a high level of risk. This may be linked to the low level of repeat trading or 'clientization', an indication of a mature and stable market. Only 14 per cent of farmers sold to the same traders last time as the previous time, a situation ascribed by our respondents to a low level of trust between the farmers and the traders. However, the scale of trading is relatively small and traders do not return regularly, as happens in well-established production areas, such as Mikuyuni in Morogoro Region. There is anecdotal evidence of traders not paying, delaying payment or not paying in full for crops – particularly where credit has been granted by the farmers.

Influence on production decisions

In relation to production decisions, respondents' reports suggest that much of the production is driven more by reduction of production risks than by profit maximization. For example, in one village the respondents in a group discussion reported that tomatoes were planted because they do well in the soil, because of tradition, because they are used in the house and because they provide a good income.

Marketing strategies

Forty per cent of farmers decide their marketing strategy based on the previous season's experience, 44 per cent on the information provided by the traders and 1 per cent based on information provided by family and friends. Around 50 to 60 per cent of the respondents indicated that the quality of their marketing information was good or very good (see Figure 6.5). However, this leaves a significant proportion of the respondents feeling that their information is poor.

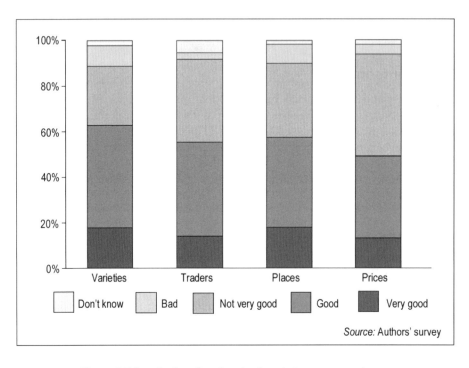

Figure 6.5 Perceived quality of market knowledge among producers

Figure 6.6 shows the sources of key categories of market information, demonstrating that extension officers are an important source of production information, such as varieties; but when it comes to marketing information, fellow farmers and traders are the key sources.

The male head of household dominates the activities involving traders and the market (see Figure 6.7). This ties in with the evidence that the men were

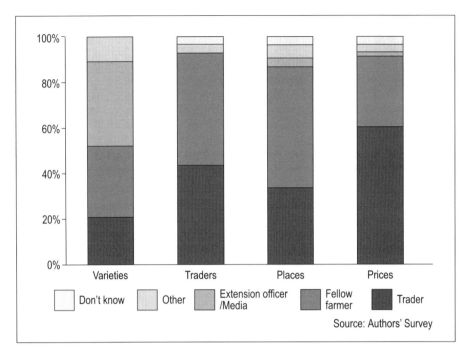

Figure 6.6 Sources of categories of market knowledge among producers

mainly responsible for market-oriented activities. However, where women have control over their own plots of land, they sell the produce themselves. Other household responsibilities and the response women receive from the traders and others in the market place can make this difficult. The three bars on the right in Figure 6.7 illustrate the roles played by women and other members of the household in the production process. This is in line with the orthodoxy that women, along with children, play a key role in contributing agricultural labour throughout Africa. However, the five bars to the left show that men dominate the activities involved in seeking information and knowledge relating to new varieties, the availability of traders and information about prices.

Atomic Speed Group (ASG): Case study of a successful production group

In 1992, a local man and an in-migrant from Iringa began to work to clear and prepare a relatively difficult piece of land close to a reservoir near a village called Mantumbulu, about 20km from Dodoma. This involved moving earth from other parts of the valley to fill in gullies and level the land for production. They constructed a tank and connected it to the reservoir. Gradually, their

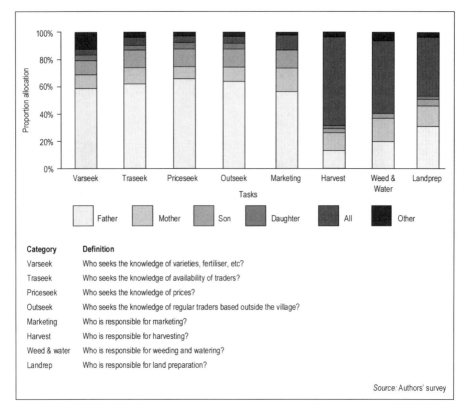

Figure 6.7 Farming responsibilities among members of the household

production began to take off and other farmers, mainly younger men, came to join them. They formed the ASG, which focuses on maintaining the water system and purchasing fertilizers; but they are very successful horticultural producers, cultivating a wide range of products. There is no written constitution, but there are agreed rules to protect the water and the land.

The marketing pattern varies according to levels of supply in the Dodoma and other markets. When the supply is scarce, few traders come to Mantumbulu seeking produce. Therefore, farmers sometimes have to go to Dodoma market with a sample of their produce and try to persuade the traders to come and buy from them. They rarely trade with the same traders regularly. Market uncertainty relates to the fact that they are arriving in a market that the traders know very well but they do not know the prevailing prices. In addition, ASG members reported that they may agree a price in principle but the traders will usually try to bargain the price down again using various ploys, particularly if the farmer's position is weakened – for example, if the crop is already ripe and harvested.

The farmers rarely collaborate on selling. When questioned about this, they saw no need. They plant at different times, so they harvest at different times and therefore coordinated marketing is difficult. They are very unclear on what alternative strategies they could adopt in relation to crop marketing. They perceive the market as high risk – they do not know what market demand is or how many buyers there are, so they are always taking a chance in producing commercially.

The material benefits of membership of this group are clear to the members. They reported that as a result of their success in this project, they have all been able to buy bicycles and put tin roofs on their houses. A number of the younger farmers associated with the group had previously migrated unsuccessfully to cities. They felt that they could learn from the more established members of the group. One young farmer had been able to sit close by when traders had come to negotiate the purchase of produce and felt that he had learned how to do this for himself.

Despite interviewing a number of the farmers, including the founding members, the way in which the group operates remains unclear. It appears to be far from democratic. The longer-established producers have a greater say in decision-making and they dominate the many younger members of the group. The main focus of any 'collective' decision-making appears to be the operation of the irrigation system. Discussions with various members of the group yielded a set of concerns regarding pests, marketing problems, commitments to social or familial responsibilities, the high costs of inputs and poor communication.

Discussion

Producer groups

Both the time and money costs of obtaining market information are usually borne by the individual producer; these can be relatively high. The example of the ASG group shows how important innovative and successful farmers have been to the development of a successful horticulture production project. However, the in-depth interviews suggest that the organization of the group, while effective, is not democratic and inclusive. While, on the outside, this may appear unfair, it may well be part of the reason for its current success. There may be some benefits from a level of producer organization.

Given the problems cited by farmers in the survey villages, any strategy of intervention in Tanzania may be better focused on innovative trading – whether traders, farmer-traders or farmers. Winarto (1994, p154) suggests that information passes down channels structured by prevailing social or cultural relations: 'Understanding new knowledge spreads must be situated within a comprehension of the social dynamics and networks of different kinds of farmers'. This may explain why ASG farmers are the same age or younger than the founder members – their knowledge would, perhaps, not be as acceptable to older farmers in the area.

Market risk

Risk is clearly a major factor in farmer decision-making in relation to participation in produce markets. In order to improve circumstances for the key stakeholders, it is important to assess and provide a basis for minimizing the risks, both perceived and real, of entering the market. It suits nobody involved if the prices are unstable or the market is too small, two of the key market risks identified by the farmer respondents.

Other key problems of Tanzanian horticultural markets identified by this research include a lack of data on market changes and poor understanding of market variations. Available information is considered of little relevance. Second, as in many SSA countries, interurban and rural–urban transport and communications in Tanzania can be very difficult, making market integration difficult. Finally, a major concern was the burden of taxation, which is perceived to be very heavy, with market levies charged in markets themselves, at district or regional boundaries and at urban wholesale and retail markets.

An effective system of marketing information collection and management is required. Whatever form this takes must be clearly targeted at producers and monitored to test effectiveness. Evidence from Ghana suggests that there may be potential for the development of farmers' groups to try to organize themselves to overcome the weakness of their situation vis-à-vis traders and other groups in society (Poole et al, 2003).

The objective of this chapter has been to make a more precise study than hitherto of informational constraints and potential solutions, rather than all marketing challenges. The results lead us to hypothesize that improved information flows to smallholder vegetable producers can be brought about through two mechanisms – namely, the development of longer-term contractual relationships to align the incentives faced by different market participants for the private provision of information, and improving the coordination functions of local (rather than national) government.

Potential delivery systems for appropriate information

Appropriate information

The Tanzanian field data support the views that informal networks tend to serve as the significant sources of information for smallholders, and that existing public-sector systems do not deliver the type of information that farmers require.

While price information matters, farmers want to know about alternative market outlets, new market opportunities and information that informs demand-led production strategies. The potential for, and capacity of, farmers to link production and marketing strategies is an important dimension in enhancing the commercial acumen of smallholders. Evidence from Tanzania also confirmed the importance of information as an input to farmers' overall production and marketing strategies.

In summary, marketing information as an input to a commercial strategy for vegetable production is important. Market price information for vegetables can also serve strategic purposes, but has, at best, limited value as a tactical bargaining tool.

Information acquisition and delivery systems

A solution to the problem of timely dissemination of price information involves a public–private partnership. Table 6.2 provides a conceptual model of informational needs. Information collected by public officials should be delivered through the private sector in a brief but regular daily *agrinews* programme on local language radio services, such as Radio Brong Ahafo in the case of Ghana (Poole et al, 1998). A recorded expert commentary about market dynamics by market traders or officials would furnish the immediate market context.

Table 6.2 *A taxonomy of vertical coordination and information needs*

Form of coordination	Contractual mechanism	Level of product or commodity specification	Information types	Information delivery systems
External coordination	Spot markets	Low	Market	Public
Intermediate forms	Contracting market specification production Management resource providing relational contracts	High	Market and marketing	Public and private
Internal coordination	Firm integration through mergers and acquisitions	Intra-firm	Intra-firm	Intra-firm

Price information should be recorded both centrally and locally. Daily market information will have value in alerting farmers to the actual state of the market and may serve the secondary purpose of improving farmers' price negotiation. However, the main benefits will be the medium- and long-term accumulation in producing areas with 'market knowledge', an increase in demand-oriented production and heightened levels of business acumen among commercially oriented smallholders.

The cost of dissemination is a relevant consideration. However, there may be potential for sponsored partnership between commercial agricultural service firms (such as banks, other credit organizations and input suppliers) and local commercial radio stations.

The future: Enhancing private networks through information and communications technology (ICT)

Information acquisition and delivery systems are already being affected by technological change (Zongo, 2001). In Ghana, we examined a community-based satellite phone for agricultural marketing purposes that was proving versatile and highly popular despite relatively high call charges. However, mobile phones based on cellular technology are currently the most cost-effective technology for connecting rural areas to urban-based information networks. With cellular technology largely limited to urban areas and trunk routes, it will be very important to communication in peri-urban areas (Lynch et al, 2001). Private information and communications technology (ICT) expansion in SSA and other developing regions is currently very rapid, and the timescale for the impact of ICT on many rural smallholders is likely to be over- rather than underestimated (Lynch, 2004). Future information delivery systems must take into account initiatives such as a dial-in telephone service, text messaging (short messaging service, or SMS) access and, eventually, the Internet in order to access the recorded information, whether national, regional or local. Table 6.3 sets out the characteristics of the various information delivery systems on offer. Whatever form ICT access assumes, the new wireless technologies must be taken into account.

Table 6.3 *Informational characteristics of different technologies*

Technology	Distribution	Communication	Information types	Value for 'high-specification' products?	Public or private delivery?
Bulletin boards, newspapers, radio, state-owned commercial television	Mass dissemination	Database to population impersonal, static	Market	Low	Public
Fax, email, Internet	Limited access	Individual/population to database/person, potentially personal, static or potentially interactive	Market and marketing	Medium	Private and public
Email, telephones (landline, mobile, satellite)	Individual dependent	Person-to-person, personal interactive	Marketing	High	Private

Source: authors, except 'Information types', which is adapted from Shepherd, 1997

The private provision of telecommunications systems is a commercial opportunity for ICT firms; but is likely to be patchy. The role of better 'public' ICT is a matter for further consideration, as are the appropriate policy mechanisms to stimulate private demand for telecommunications services. Collective acquisition of ICT by rural communities has a potentially significant role. Public provision may be necessary to serve the poorest and where private incentives are weakest, such as for better market integration in Tanzania.

Enhancing livelihoods

Our research approach has been to learn lessons from (albeit imperfectly) functioning market systems, and the proposals have the potential to reduce informational constraints for all smallholders. In theory, the removal of information constraints by partnerships between the public sector (data collection) and private initiatives (information dissemination) will be of greatest assistance to the most disadvantaged, other things being equal. Often, however, other things are highly unequal! Smallholders will still constitute a heterogeneous community regarding their ability to access information, and almost certainly they will be heterogeneous in their ability to respond to better information and new opportunities. Where information is not the limiting constraint, and where the poorest households experience multiple disadvantages, other constraints such as undercapitalization (in the 'sustainable livelihoods' sense) and geographical remoteness may require specific interventions.

Thus, while better provision of better information enhances the potential for all producers, it is difficult not to conclude that market-mediated mechanisms are likely to be of limited direct benefit to the poorest households in practice. As a result, better market information is only a partial solution to the poverty question. The policies aimed at the poorest may need to improve access not to primary production, but to secondary markets, such as employment opportunities.

References

Amka Trust (1997) *People and Profit – Promoting Fair Trade*, Amka Trust, Dar es Salaam

Bryceson, D. F. (1993) *Liberalizing Tanzania's Food Trade: Public and Private Faces of Urban Marketing Policy 1939–1988*, United Nations Research Institute for Social Development with James Currey, London

FAO (United Nations Food and Agriculture Organization) (1994) *United Republic of Tanzania Irrigated Horticulture Development Project: Preparation Report*, FAO, Rome

FAO (1999) *Special Report: FAO/WFP Crop and Food Supply Assessment Mission to Tanzania*, FAO and the World Food Programme, Rome

Galtier, F. and Egg, J. (1998) 'From price reporting systems to variable geometry oriented market information services', Paper presented at the 57th European Association of Agricultural Economists Seminar, Wageningen, 23–26 September

Hollier, G. (1990) 'Rural distribution channels in West Africa,' in Findlay, A. M.,

Paddison, R. and Dawson, J. A. (eds) *Retailing Environments in Developing Countries,* Routledge, London, pp52–65

Hyden, G. (1980) *Beyond Ujamaa in Tanzania – Underdevelopment and an Uncaptured Peasantry,* Heinemann, London

Iaquinta, D. and Drescher, A. (2001) 'More than the spatial fringe: An application of the periurban typology to planning and management of natural resources', Paper presented to conference on Rural–Urban Encounters: Managing the Environment of the Peri-Urban Interface, Development Planning Unit, University of London, London, 9–10 November

Jones, J. V. S. (1987) 'Food security and economic development in Tanzania: Past problems and proposals for a new strategy', Paper presented to the International Conference on the Arusha Declaration, Arusha, December 1986

Kaynak, E. (1986) *Marketing and Economic Development,* Praeger Publishers, Newark, New Jersey

Kiriwaggulu, J. B. A., Mbelwa, R. and Mashamba, F. (1996) *Marketing Arrangements for Horticultural Produce in Tanzania,* Marketing Development Bureau, Ministry of Agriculture, Dar es Salaam

Lee, C. Y. (1993) 'Agricultural marketing extension', in Abbott, J. C. (ed) *Agricultural and Food Marketing in Developing Countries,* CAB International, Wallingford, Oxon, pp262–267

Lynch, K. (1992) *The Production, Distribution and Marketing of Fruit and Vegetables for the Urban Market of Dar es Salaam, Tanzania,* PhD thesis, University of Glasgow, Glasgow

Lynch, K. (2004) *Rural Urban Interaction in the Developing World,* Routledge, London

Lynch, K., Poole, N. and Ashimogo, G. (2001) 'ICT technology for overcoming market information constraints in East Africa', Paper prepared for the Crop Post Harvest Programme of the Department for International Development, Kingston University, London

Marketing Development Bureau (1993) *The Horticultural Wholesale Trade in Tanzania,* Ministry of Agriculture, Dar es Salaam

Mascarenhas A. (1984) 'Fruits and vegetables in Tanzania's food profile', Paper presented to Workshop on Food Self-Sufficiency in Sub-Saharan Africa, Dar es Salaam, 7–9 May

Mbelwa, R. B. J. (1994) *1993/1994 Industry Review of Horticulture,* R3/94, Marketing Development Bureau, Ministry of Agriculture, Dar es Salaam

Minster Agriculture Ltd (1988) *Sector Study for the Development of Selected Horticultural Crops in Tanzania, Final Report,* Tanzania Investment Bank, Dar es Salaam

Mutizwa-Mangiza, N. (1999) 'Strengthening rural–urban linkages', *Habitat Debate,* vol 5, no 1, pp1–6

Platteau, J.-P. (1996) 'The evolutionary theory of land rights as applied to sub-Saharan Africa: A critical assessment', *Development and Change,* vol 27, no 1, pp29–86

Poole, N. D., Del Campo Gomis, F. J., Juliá Igual, J. F. and Vidal Giménez, F. (1998) 'Formal contracts in fresh produce markets', *Food Policy,* vol 23, no 2, pp131–142

Poole, N. D. and Lynch, K. D. (2003) 'Agricultural market knowledge: Appropriate delivery systems for a private and public good?', *Journal of Agricultural Education and Extension,* vol 9, no 3, pp117–126

Poole, N. D., Seini, A. W. and Heh, V. (2003) 'Improving agrifood marketing in developing economies: contracts in Ghanaian vegetable markets', *Development in Practice,* vol 13, no 5, pp551–557

Poon, B. (1994) *FAO-Agrimarket Guide,* FAO, Rome

SAF (Stoas Agriprojects Foundation) (1996) *Gender Issues in Smallholder Farmers' Response to Structural Adjustment: The Case Study of Kipera Village, Morogoro,* Unpublished report, SAF, Dar es Salaam

Schubert, B. (1993) 'Agricultural market information services', in Abbott, J. C. (ed) *Agricultural and Food Marketing in Developing Countries*, CAB International, Wallingford, Oxon, pp268–272

Shepherd, A. W. (1997) *Market Information Services*, AGS Bulletin, FAO, Rome

Siddle, D. and Swindell, K. (1990) *Rural Change in Tropical Africa: From Colonies to Nation States*, Blackwell, Oxford

United Republic of Tanzania (1994) *Statistical Abstract: 1992*, Bureau of Statistics, Dar es Salaam

van Donge, J. K. (1992) 'Agricultural decline in Tanzania: The case of the Uluguru Moutains', *African Affairs*, vol 91, no 362, pp73–94

Winarto, Y. (1994) 'Encouraging knowledge exchange: Integrated pest management in Indonesia', in Scoones, I., Thompson, J. and Chambers, R. (eds) *Beyond Farmer First: Rural People's Knowledge, Agricultural Research and Extension Practice*, Intermediate Technology Publications, London, pp150–155

World Bank (2003) *World Development Report 2004: Making Services Work for Poor People*, World Bank, New York, http://econ.worldbank.org/wdr/wdr2004, accessed 5 November 2004

Zongo, G. (2001) *Information and Communication Technologies for Development in Africa: Trends and Overview*, International Development Research Centre/Acacia Communities and Information Society in Africa, Dakar

7

Livelihoods from Dairying Enterprises for the Landless in the Peri-Urban Interface around Hubli-Dharwad, India

Robert M. Brook, Prakash Bhat and Anil Nitturkar

Introduction

This study took place in Hubli-Dharwad, a twin city located in northern Karnataka State, India (see Figure 7.1), approximately equidistant between Pune and Bangalore, and on the main road and railway linking those cities. The population at the 2001 census was 736,000, with Hubli being the larger of the two components of the twin city. It is the third largest urban agglomeration in Karnataka State (after Bangalore and Mysore). Dharwad is an administrative and academic centre, while Hubli is a railway junction and commercial centre. There is little heavy industry as the electrical and water infrastructure is rather inadequate, and most industry is related to processing agricultural produce. The centres of Hubli and Dharwad are 20km apart, although the area between them is being rapidly built up. Administratively, Hubli-Dharwad falls under the jurisdiction of the Hubli-Dharwad Municipal Corporation (HDMC), one tier of government down from the Karnataka state administration and established as an administrative entity in 1962. The area outside HDMC is administered by the *zilla panchayat*, or district council, also one tier down from the state administration. These administrations display no cognisance of the concept of a peri-urban space or rural–urban interactions: any particular location is treated as if being either urban or rural. Yet, as this chapter demonstrates, such interactions are much in evidence and can serve to enable the poor to rise out of poverty. The characteristics of Hubli-Dharwad are more fully described in Brook and Dávila (2000).

Hubli-Dharwad is located in an agricultural area with a long-term mean annual rainfall of approximately 800mm, which falls predominantly in the monsoon season from June to October. However, since the mid-1990s recurrent droughts have been a significant constraint to agricultural production. To the west lie soils that are predominantly inceptisols, moderately fertile but with low moisture-holding capacity, hitherto mostly used for growing rain-fed rice.

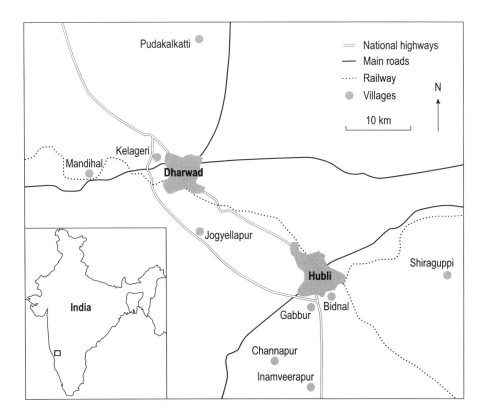

Figure 7.1 Hubli-Dharwad and the location of villages studied

Due to the recent droughts and degradation of small-scale irrigation infrastructure, other cereals such as maize and sorghum are now in the ascendancy. On the east lies the Deccan Plateau, dominated by heavy, cracking clay soils (vertisols) on which cotton, sorghum and wheat predominate. Livestock are very important in the agricultural economy of the region, bullocks still being the main form of draught power, and the river buffalo, *Bubalus bubalis*, used for milking. In this area, buffalo are never used as draught animals. In the monsoon, those livestock which are not exclusively stall fed are grazed on common land or field margins, and in the dry season, crop residues are used for fodder.

Milk and other dairy products are important dietary components in India. Per capita milk production in India has increased from 51kg per capita per annum in 1983 to 77kg in 2003 (Delgado et al, 1999; FAOSTAT, 2004), and is estimated to increase to 135kg by 2020 (Delgado et al, 1999). The main dairying animal is the river buffalo, preferred to the dairy cow because of the better taste and higher fat content of the milk, even though yields are lower. In 2003, of the 87 million tonnes of milk produced in India, 55 per cent was attributable to buffalo, 42 per cent to cattle and 3 per cent to goats (FAOSTAT, 2004).

Selling milk to cities is an important component of the livelihood portfolios of many peri-urban farmers (Vijayalakshmi et al, 1995). Therefore, it is reasonable to expect that as cities expand, greater opportunities emerge for dairy farmers to sell their products. This study sets out to determine whether this was so for Hubli-Dharwad and to answer the following questions:

- Has dairy production changed in importance as a livelihood option over time (testing whether there is a temporal effect of urbanization)?
- Do dairying activities vary with distance from the urban area (testing whether there are spatial effects)?
- What are the effects of natural resource endowment, particularly size of landholding, on the ability to capitalize upon this form of income generation?

In India, the size of landholding is frequently used as a proxy for wealth as in rural areas the landless and small landholders have to work for larger landowners and are low-paid agricultural labourers (Mehta and Shah, 2003). It might be expected that access to urban markets would perturb this general pattern, creating what are, in effect, 'gradients' along which labour, produce and finance, for example, might flow. The concept of the peri-urban gradient has been explored elsewhere. Simon et al (2004) expressed this in terms of a peri-urban continuum, characterizing it as a gradient in factors such as complexity of markets for land, conversion of land from agricultural to residential, occupations and infrastructure, with distance from the urban area being an important explanatory variable. Interestingly, with one exception, farming systems in the villages studied displayed little adaptation to the proximity of a large urban market. Kundu et al (2003) also described gradients away from Indian urban centres of decreasing per capita income, farm size, household size, literacy and school enrolment, while increasing gradients were observed for infant mortality and other indicators of poor health status. However, there have been no studies of gradients in farming systems as such.

This study was a component of a research project funded by the UK Department for International Development (DFID), which, in turn, was part of the peri-urban interface system within the Natural Resources System Programme (NRSP). Its specific objective was to characterize the effects of the processes of urbanization upon land use, agricultural production, livelihoods and markets. The project is reported more fully in Bhat et al (2003).

Methodology

Livestock systems in eight villages at various distances from Hubli-Dharwad were studied (see Figure 7.1). Although the space between the cities was originally agricultural with distinct villages, by the time of this study there had been considerable building development and individual villages were no longer discernible. Cultivation still exists; but farmers often live in nearby suburbs. Thus, the between-city space represented more a low-density urban zone rather than a peri-urban one, and rural–urban interactions would have been difficult to identify. A questionnaire survey was conducted with livestock owners to determine the status of livestock enterprise in those villages. There were 302 respondents, selected according to the following criteria:

- Livestock enterprises would be expected to vary according to the area of land farmed by households. Therefore, the families in the village were stratified by categorizing them as big (> 2ha), small (1–2ha) or marginal farmers (< 1 ha) and landless (no agricultural land), based on the land-holding of the family.
- A list of 15 to 20 names of families of each category was selected randomly from village census lists with the help of key informants, such as the village accountant, secretary or village head, who were aware of the size of each family's landholding. The number of respondents in each category was decided on the basis of proportion of families of that category in the village. Families having livestock of any type at the time of the survey or previously were included in the study. Families who never had livestock at any time were excluded from the sample.
- The first available eight to ten respondents from each category were interviewed. It is recognized that this introduced a bias due to availability; but this approach was applied consistently across villages.
- The questionnaire was conducted by visiting each house and interviewing the head of the family or the key informant from the family.

Although the survey was very comprehensive, results here will be restricted to four factors: number of buffalo per household in 1990 and 2000; disposal of milk (sale or household consumption); sale price; and sources of feed. These were considered to be the factors most indicative of the influence of urbanization. Farmers were not asked for their recollection of milk sales ten years previously as it was considered that this would be difficult to recall with any accuracy, whereas livestock numbers are well remembered. The issue of accuracy of recollections is an issue with any study involving timelines; but they do indicate trends (Engle et al, 1999; Silver and Krosnick, 2001).

Spatial effects were determined by analysing the three sample villages that fell within the HDMC boundary and were classed administratively as being urban ('near' villages), and five more distant villages, located between 11–18km away from the centre of either Dharwad or Hubli ('far' villages) (see Figure 7.1). As this design was unbalanced, a general linear model was used for conducting analyses of variance.

Results

There were highly significant effects of both distance and time upon numbers of buffalo per household (see Figure 7.2). In 1990, there were almost twice as many buffalo per household in near villages (2.12) compared to far villages (1.19; $p = 0.002$), and by 2000, the respective numbers were 3.32 and 1.47 ($p < 0.001$), near villages having more than double the numbers of the average far village household. Over the ten-year interval, households in near villages increased their herds by 56 per cent, while in far villages the increase was only 23 per cent.

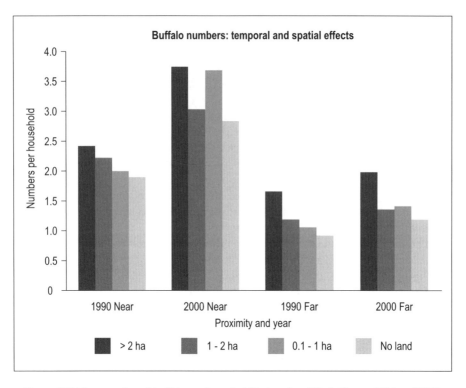

Figure 7.2 Mean number of buffalo per household in 'near' and 'far' villages, 1990 and 2000

In the far villages, size of landholding was a significant predictor of herd size, big landholders (> 2ha) having significantly more buffalo than the other three categories in both 1990 ($p = 0.031$) and 2000 ($p = 0.034$). In near villages, although there was an apparent relationship during 1990 between size of landholding and numbers of buffalo, this effect was not statistically significant. By 2000, there was not even an apparent relationship between landholding and herd size. Over the decade, the marginal farmer category had increased their herd size from 2 to 3.67 animals (84 per cent increase), and the landless category had increased their herd size by 49 per cent.

When patterns of household consumption of milk in 2000 were considered, there was a highly significant effect of both distance from the city and size of landholding (see Figure 7.3) ($p < 0.001$). The average large landholding household consumed 3.23 litres per day in a near village, compared to 1.86 litres for a large landholding household in a far village. The respective consumption figures for landless households were 1 litre and 0.5 litres.

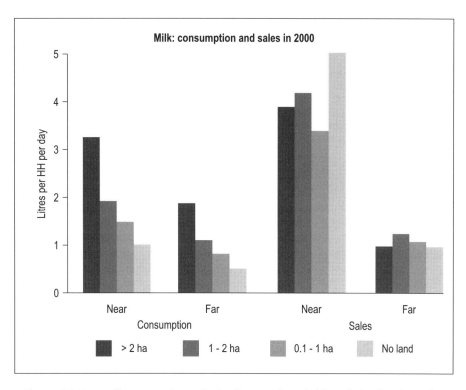

Figure 7.3 Mean milk consumption and sales (litres per household per day) in 'near' and 'far' villages

A large difference in the sale of milk was evident due to distance from the city ($p < 0.001$), the average household in a near village selling 4.09 litres per day compared to 1.05 litres in far villages. However, there was no effect of size of landholding upon quantity of milk sold.

The price received for fresh milk varied from 9.7 rupees to 7.7 rupees per litre (US$1 = approximately 4.5 Indian rupees in 2000), with direct distance from the centre of the nearest city being a significant predictor ($p = 0.024$). When price was regressed against distance (see Figure 7.4), a linear relationship proved to be the best fit, showing that distance explained 67 per cent of the variation in price, which decreased by 0.13 rupees per litre for each kilometre further away from the urban area. There are two reasons for this. Where middlemen are involved with marketing, they reduce the price paid for milk with increasing distance from market. Furthermore, those farmers close to the urban area who directly market their milk obtain a premium based on freshness of the product.

Buffalo are generally grazed when there is the opportunity. During the crop-growing season, they are closely supervised and confined to commons and field margins, as well as forests where accessible. During other seasons, fields lying in summer fallow are used; but the extent of this varies with degree

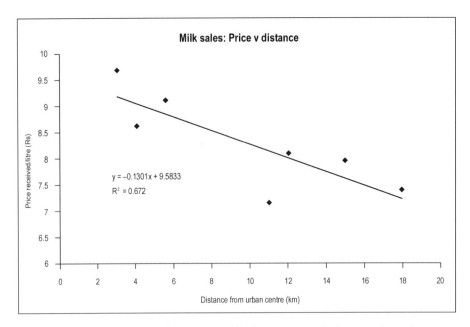

Figure 7.4 Linear regression of price received (Indian rupees per litre) against linear distance from centre of nearest urban area (Hubli or Dharwad)

of urbanization. In near-urban villages, summer fallow ranged from < 2 per cent of village area in Bidnal (now virtually a suburb of Hubli) to 65 per cent in Gabbur and Kelageri, whereas in more distant villages it ranged from 6 per cent to 80 per cent of village area.

Buffalo were stall fed when grazing was not possible due to lack of available grazing land or when there was no grazing left at the end of the season. Table 7.1 shows sources of fodder utilized for stall feeding.

Table 7.1 *Sources of feed other than grazing*

Village proximity	Green fodder[1] Households using (%)	Quantity (tonnes per year)	Dry fodder[2] Households using (%)	Quantity (tonnes per year)	Concentrates[3] Households using (%)	Quantity (tonnes per year)
Near	49	15.7	93	8.9	59	3.3[4]
Far	47	1.5	91	6.9	37	1.2

Notes: [1] Fresh maize and sorghum haulm, grass
[2] Conserved maize, sorghum and legume haulms, wheat and rice straw
[3] Sorghum, maize and pulse grains, groundnut shells and rice bran
[4] Mostly landless farmers

Green fodder consisted of cut grass and crop residues available during the growing season. About half of the households in both near and far villages used green fodder at some stage; but near villages used ten times as much as far villages. Practically all households reported using dry fodder, mostly during the dry season, with higher but not significantly different quantities being consumed in near than in far villages. There was also a greater use of concentrates in near compared to far villages, both in terms of quantity and number of farmers using them. Most of these farmers were landless.

Discussion

The results showed that the dairying sector is dynamic and is responding to opportunities offered by the urban area. Farmers were clearly investing in buffalo as specialized dairy animals, particularly so in villages near to the urban centres where access to the markets is better (see Mulla and Tuson, 2003, for a description of the milk marketing system around Hubli-Dharwad). The main pattern is that intensification was greater in the near-urban villages and that this occurred irrespective of size of landholding. It is of great interest that the highest degree of intensification was in the marginal landholding sector, followed by the landless sector. As these households have little or no grazing land of their own, they either have to buy in fodder and feed, or seek out grazing for their stock on others' land or common land.

Grazing and fodder supplies for livestock varied greatly between villages. In the most urbanized village, Bidnal, there was no reported grazing, but a considerable amount of 'cut-and-carry' fodder (predominantly sorghum haulm, but also forage maize and hybrid Napier grass) was fed to stalled animals. The main dry fodders used in Bidnal were dry sorghum haulm and blended concentrates. Dairying in this suburb was almost entirely a zero-grazing urban activity.

Interestingly, in the other two villages falling within HDMC, Gabbur and Kelageri, both of which still retained a large proportion of agricultural land and where dairying was also intensifying, the dominant source of food for livestock was natural grazing. The proportion of land used for late monsoon second cropping was low, so these summer fallows were used for grazing of the dairy herds. Many respondents reported that the grazing took place on land belonging to 'others', which is necessary for landless livestock owners. This was supplemented to some extent by dry feeds, predominantly rice husks and conserved sorghum and maize haulm, but in much lower quantities than reported for Bidnal. These findings accord with those of Devendra and Thomas (2002), that crop residues form the major feed source for livestock, rather than grains grown specifically for animal feed, as is common in industrialized nations.

On average, a household in a near village earned 13,513 rupees per annum from milk sales, while the much lower corresponding figure for distant villages was 3026 rupees. This lower income reflected not only the lower price received, but also the smaller quantities sold. Farmers in more distant villages were more dependent upon the formal milk marketing system, which paid lower prices than when milk was marketed directly. Milk sales played an important role in household livelihood strategies in villages near the city. Data collected as part of the survey (but not presented here) showed that in the three villages within HDMC (Gabbur, Bidnal and Kelageri), 95 per cent of the marketing was done door to door in the urban area. Vijayalakshmi et al (1995) also found that vendors selling into the informal sector in Bangalore received 12.5 per cent higher prices on average compared to farmers selling into the formal market. This may again be partly ascribed to the perceived 'freshness' factor, while noting also that formal market milk is regarded as inferior because cow and buffalo milk are blended. It should be mentioned, however, that in this study, no account was made of the effects of dilution of milk with water upon prices received.

Clearly, an animal that can be stall fed and, perhaps, grazed on field bunds and in fields outside the cropping season, if available, is a viable livelihood option for a landless family. For landless families in the three villages lying within the HDMC boundary, the annual quantity of milk marketed was 1818 litres, bringing an average income of 16,543 rupees (sold at an average price of 9.1 rupees per litre). In Bidnal, where these enterprises were effectively urban dairies, the mean number of buffalo per landless household was 4 in 2000 and the mean quantity of milk sold was 4000 litres. One landless family had six buffalo, and one family with less than 1ha of land had ten buffalo. Hubli-Dharwad is not self-sufficient in milk, and much has to be imported from districts to the north (NABARD, 2000, p35). In response to this ready market, dairies around the periphery of the city are intensifying as resources to buy new animals permit. Subsequent work conducted in Gabbur by the authors re-inforces this finding. An informal savings and credit scheme was established, enabling 22 households (out of a total village population of 80 households) to buy additional beasts (15 buffalo and 7 cows, usually pregnant) during 2003–2004. This represents a significant intensification, indicating a strong desire to strengthen the dairying enterprise.

It should be noted that there may be nutritional implications arising from the need of marginal landholders and landless families to maximize their household income in order to escape from poverty. It can be seen from Figure 7.3 that although milk production from these groups in near-urban villages was similar to that from larger landowners, a much greater proportion of milk was sold; consequently, less was consumed in the home.

In rural areas, marginal landholders and the landless usually work as labourers for larger landowners or migrate to urban areas for unskilled manual employment. Other studies have found that casual agricultural labourers are the largest group, and cultivators are the second largest group among the chronically poor. This phenomenon is particularly accentuated in agro-ecologically less favoured areas, including dry land areas characterized by frequent crop failures (Mehta and Shah, 2003). In seasons with average rainfall, Hubli-Dharwad is considered to be semi-arid; but over the past several seasons there have been consecutive crop failures, which have deepened the plight of marginal farmers and the landless (anecdotal evidence gathered by Robert Brook, July 2004).

In contrast, this study presents clear evidence that dairying is intensifying in near-urban areas and that it offers an acceptable escape from poverty, particularly for marginal farmers and the landless. Moreover, even though it means buying in fodder, these households will, nevertheless, readily expand their enterprises further if the opportunity presents itself.

Acknowledgements

This chapter is an output from a research project (R7867) funded by the UK Department for International Development (DFID) for the benefit of developing countries. The views expressed are not necessarily those of the DFID.

References

Bhat, P., Nitturkar, A. and Mulla, J. (2003) 'Livestock: Promising livelihood opportunities for the peri-urban poor', in Brook, R. M., Purushothaman, S. and Hunshal, C. S. (eds) *Changing Frontiers – The Peri-Urban Interface, Hubli-Dharwad, India*, Books for Change, Bangalore, India, pp97–120

Brook, R. M. and Dávila, J. D. (eds) (2000) *The Peri-Urban Interface: A Tale of Two Cities*, School of Agricultural and Forest Sciences, University of Wales and Development Planning Unit, University College London, London

Delgado, C., Rosegrant, M., Steinfeld, H., Ehui, S. and Courbois, C. (1999) *Livestock to 2020: The Next Food Revolution*, Food, Agriculture and the Environment Discussion Paper 28, International Food Policy Research Institute, Washington, DC

Devendra, C. and Thomas, D. (2002) 'Crop-animal interactions in mixed farming systems in Asia', *Agricultural Systems*, vol 71, pp27–40

Engle, P. L., Menon, P. and Haddad, L. (1999) 'Care and nutrition: Concepts and measurement', *World Development*, vol 27, pp1309–1337

FAOSTAT (2004) www.faostat.fao.org/faostat/collections?subset=agriculture, accessed 27 August 2004

Kundu, A., Sarangi, N. and Dash, B. P. (2003) *Rural Non-Farm Employment: An Analysis of Rural–Urban Interdependencies*, Working Paper 196, Overseas Development Institute, London

Mehta, A. K. and Shah A. (2003) 'Chronic poverty in India: Incidence, causes and policies', *World Development*, vol 31, pp491–511

Mulla, J. and Tuson, J. C. (2003) 'Marketing systems for agricultural produce in the peri-urban interface', in Brook, R. M., Purushothaman, S. and Hunshal, C. S. (eds) *Changing Frontiers – The Peri-Urban Interface, Hubli-Dharwad, India*, Books for Change, Bangalore, India, pp80–96

NABARD (National Bank for Agriculture and Rural Development) (2000) *Potential Link Plan 2001–2002: Dharwad, Karnataka*, NABARD Regional Office, Bangalore

Silver, M. D. and Krosnick, J. A. (2001) *Optimizing Survey Measurement Accuracy by Matching Question Design to Respondent Memory Organization*, 2001 Federal Committee on Statistical Methodology Conference, US, accessed from http://www.fcsm.gov/01papers/krosnick.pdf

Simon, D., McGregor, D. and Nsiah-Gyabaah, K. (2004) 'The changing urban–rural interface of African cities: Definitional issues and an application to Kumasi, Ghana', *Environment and Urbanization*, vol 16, no 2, pp235–247

Vijayalakshmi, S., Sitaramaswamy, J. and de Boer, J. (1995) 'Rationalization of milk procurement, processing and marketing in Southern India', *Agricultural Systems*, vol 48, pp297–314

8

Waste-Fed Fisheries in Peri-Urban Kolkata

Madhumita Mukherjee

Introduction

Within the past few years there has been a worldwide resurgence of interest in regional authorities, reflecting increased recognition that it is impossible to effectively manage water resources without considering management strategies. With the increase in urban population and expansion of industries, the volume of wastewater produced is increasing rapidly and its composition is also becoming more and more complex. The use of wastewater for aquaculture has also increased during recent decades.

Aquaculture has become an important source of animal protein and income in many parts of the developing world. Asia dominates the world in aquaculture production, with its proportion of world aquaculture production quoted as being as high as 91 per cent (Kongkeo, 2001). Kongkeo also reports that 'In South Asia, fish for food, mainly freshwater species, dominate production, with over 94 per cent of total fish production in 1997.'

The integration of fish within other food production systems is common as an important additional source of animal protein or income. Guttman (1999), for example, claims that small-scale rice field fisheries in the lower Mekong River basin of Cambodia provide up to 75 per cent of the animal protein requirements of poor rural households. Duck production is often closely associated with Asian wetland rice farming. As reported by Cagauan and Nerona (1986) and Cagauan et al (2000), integrated rice, duck and fish farming is now common in Asia, with the duck manure serving as organic fertilizer for plankton, on which the fish feed. *Azolla*, an aquatic floating fern, is also widely used as a nitrogen fixer and as food for ducks and fish alike (Cagauan and Nerona, 1986; Cagauan et al, 2000).

The use of animal manure as fertilizer inputs in Chinese fish farming is reported by Chen et al (1995), who undertook a survey of over 1000 ponds in 101 villages in 8 Chinese provinces. Their results show that 78 per cent of ponds were recorded as having received 'manure of any kind (including night soil, or human waste)'. Chen et al (1995) do not, however, elaborate on the significance of, or prevalence of, the use of night soil.

The use of human wastes is clearly an important consideration; yet in a volume of some 471 pages long, reporting the proceedings of a United Nations Food and Agriculture Organization (FAO)-sponsored international conference on aquaculture (Subasinghe et al, 2001), the use of sewage is only noted in one paper and then only briefly (Funge-Smith and Phillips, 2001). Funge-Smith and Phillips (2001, p131) note that the use of effluents such as sewage raises moral and public health issues – for example, the transmission of disease and the accumulation of toxic compounds. These authors also raise technology issues regarding systems that re-circulate water, pertinent to the use of human wastes, including the present limited knowledge of component interactions and the poorly understood interaction of pathogens and benign microbes. Funge-Smith and Phillips (2001, p135) also state that the composition of discharged water is an important factor in environmental sustainability, but that research is needed in areas such as the biological treatment of wastewaters and methods for the disposal of sludge, as well as the design of feeds which facilitate more efficient waste treatment (for example, faeces treatment).

However, Raschid-Sally et al (2004) note that in a survey of aquaculture in and around 30 cities in Vietnam, 19 use wastewater for aquaculture. More than half of the annual estimated fish production comes from urban and peri-urban Hanoi, where wastewater is extensively used. The authors report that according to doctors interviewed, 'little information was available in Vietnam about health risks associated with sewage-fed aquaculture', which implies that the use of sewage is common.

It is against this background that this chapter examines the use of wastewater in fish farming in the wetlands of peri-urban Kolkata.

Kolkata is a metropolis of 14 million inhabitants. The vast low-lying area to the eastern fringe of the city is popularly known as East Kolkata Wetlands. The wetlands are 'interdistributary' marshes in the delta of the River Ganga. The lakes formed were the spill reservoirs of the tidal channel of the River Bidyadhari that flowed into the Bay of Bengal through the River Matla. With the decay of the Bidyadhari during the early 1930s, a storm-water channel was excavated by Calcutta Municipal Corporation to drain the sewage water of the city and was connected to the Bay of Bengal. Later, to facilitate efficient drainage, the parallel Dry Weather Flow canal was constructed. The entire domestic sewage of the city of Kolkata (currently estimated as 1394.42 million litres per day – that is, 283.2 million gallons per day) runs through the system of principal and ancillary channels passing through East Kolkata Wetlands. These flows are utilized in sewage-treated fisheries for pisciculture. The wetlands purify the sewage water through natural processes of oxidation, radiation and biological breaking down of the organic waste. Out of an estimated area of about 8100ha of wetlands, sewage-fed fisheries (around 280 in number) currently cover about 3900ha, of which approximately 700ha are seasonal. Productivity is showing an increasing trend, and the average production is estimated by the author as around 3.44 tonnes per hectare per annum, an annual total of around 13,000 tonnes. The East Kolkata Wetlands were designated as a Ramsar site in 2002.

Fish farming in the Kolkata peri-urban wetlands

The predominant objective of most wastewater-use systems lies in nutrient recycling. In India, night soil and wastewater reuse in agriculture is a traditional practice that has been followed in irrigation for centuries (Saha et al, 1958; Jana, 1998). West Bengal is the pioneering state, the use of municipal wastewater to fertilize ponds beginning in Kolkata during the 1930s, and it is now perhaps the largest wastewater-fed aquaculture system in the world (Nair, 1944; Jhingran, 1991).

The Kolkata peri-urban area, especially where wastewater fish farming is practised, supports the livelihood of a large number of people through waste recycling and natural resource use. A survey conducted by Mukherjee and Maity (2002) revealed that 15,700 households comprising 70,750 individuals depended on wetland-based activities in East Kolkata. It is uniquely privileged in having a built-in tradition using urban waste in fisheries and agriculture. The city sewage undergoes bio-treatment through production of profitable protein and environmental purification along with employment generation.

It has been realized that the familiar practice of waste recycling shows a pathway towards a sustainable development of cities and should be replicated in other developing world countries (Ghosh, 1990). The tradition of this waste recycling in peri-urban Kolkata is now in danger and under threat of encroachment by urbanization and the annexing of prime areas for real estate business. The wetland ecosystem of Kolkata is a delicate, complex and under-studied area, which requires immediate attention for the overall well-being of the city. It is hoped that this fact will make the developers and the politicians more concerned about wetland conservation.

Three main production systems of this area are sewage-fed aquaculture, waste-fed horticulture and irrigated rice production. The raw sewage is stabilized and biologically treated through fish culture since it is fed into ponds set aside for aquaculture (*bherys*) or applied to fields as a nutrient boost for agriculture. The average water quality parameters of a typical wastewater-fed pond in East Kolkata are set out in Table 8.1, the presence of heavy metals is shown in Table 8.2 and the results of microbial analysis are noted in Table 8.3.

Table 8.1 *Water quality parameters of a typical wastewater-fed pond in East Kolkata*

Parameters	Wastewater
1 pH	7.2–8.2
2 Odour	Offensive
3 Dissolved oxygen (DO)	3–5mg per litre
4 Total alkalinity in calcium carbonate ($CaCo_3$)	130–280mg per litre
5 Ammonium (NH_4^+)	0.30–1.2mg per litre
6 Nitrate nitrogen	0.10–0.8mg per litre
7 Available phosphate	0.6–0.8mg per litre
8 Biological oxygen demand (BOD)	30.0–116.0mg per litre
9 Combined oxygen demand (COD)	70.0–180mg per litre

Source: Mukherjee et al, 2002a

Table 8.2 *Heavy metal concentrations in East Kolkata wastewater-fed ponds*

Zinc (Zn)	0.04–0.9mg per litre
Copper (Cu)	0.01–0.20mg per litre
Chromium (Cr)	0.008–0.15mg per litre
Cadmium (Cd)	0.001–0.02mg per litre
Lead (Pb)	0.03–0.60mg per litre

Source: Mukherjee et al, 2002a

Table 8.3 *Results of microbial analysis in East Kolkata wastewater-fed ponds*

Test	Inlet water	Settled *bhery* water
Total coliform	> 16 MPN per 100ml	3.6 MPN per 100ml
Colony count	$51.2 \times 10_5$ per millilitre	$12.4 \times 10_5$ per millilitre

Note: MPN = most probable number
Source: Mukherjee et al, 2002a

Existing aquaculture practices in the East Kolkata Wetlands

The practice of fish culture is basically a composite system using different species of fish, which utilize different ecological niches of the pond ecosystem. The poly-culture practices followed in wastewater-fed fish farms are Indian major carp (IMC) – that is, *Labeo rohita, Catla catla* and *Cirrhinus mrigala* – and exotic carps and tilapia poly-culture system. In Rahara (a research sub-station of the Central Institute of Freshwater Aquaculture, Government of India, situated 20km away from peri-urban Kolkata), mourala (*Amblipharyngodon mola*) and freshwater giant prawn (*Macrobrachium rosenbergii*) have been tried. Apart from these, two additional species of Indian carps (*Labeo bata* and *L. calbasu*) and one exotic carp (*Hypophthalnichtys nobilis*) have also been introduced in Kalyani (research station of the Department of Fisheries, Government of West Bengal) sewage-fed fishponds.

In an attempt to utilize wastewater for massive production of tilapia, Ghosh et al (1980) observed that the production of tilapia was not affected even at the highest measured ammoniacal nitrogen level of 5.13mg per litre since the pH (7.2–8.2) and the oxygen level (4.4mg per litre) were favourable to fish. The average production of tilapia has been found to range between 8172–9350kg per hectare per annum in most of the sewage-fed farms of East Kolkata Wetlands. The production of freshwater giant prawn in a wastewater pond of Titagarh at about 499.8kg per hectare per eight months, receiving wastewater of a ratio of 1:3 – that is, one part sewage and three parts water – was observed in another trial (Ghosh et al, 1985).

The approximate annual fish production of carp (tilapia poly-culture system) was estimated to range between 4000–10,000kg per hectare per annum in various ponds using wastewater in the East Kolkata Wetlands (Ghosh et al, 1990). In general, Ghosh et al (1990) showed that fish yields from wastewater-fed ponds are two to four times higher than those from ordinary fish culture practices. It was estimated that the return over investment is 28 per cent, the profit to turnover is 22 per cent, and return over fixed capital cost 7 per cent.

The schematic system shown in Figure 8.1 is the most cost-effective and eco-friendly model suited for the region, and has proved to be an extremely useful model both in terms of fishery and maintenance of ecological balance. It is a hypothetical model of a multidimensional wastewater-fed pond system developed through the experience of the Department of Fisheries, West Bengal.

This type of pond is not seasonal; but seasonal fluctuations in supply of wastewater from wastewater canals are observed. During the dry season, waste-water inflow is very low and does not enter the remote ponds furthest away from the main wastewater canals. In the case of the monsoon season (wet season), supply of water is huge but nutrient load is low. As a result, supple-mentary feeding is necessary for highly stocked fish ponds, which increases the expenses of fish farming. The inflow of water is governed by local authorities and allows a certain amount of wastewater. There is no statutory regulation about this level; it is decided by agreement between local authorities and the pond owners. The wastewater is channelled through the inlet of the ponds. In most ponds, the inlet and outlet canals have well-developed lock gates. The outlet canals flow into wastewater sub-canals. Water hyacinth and duck weed have the ability to absorb a certain amount of pollutants within this system (Culley et al, 1981), and their growth is encouraged (see Figure 8.1).

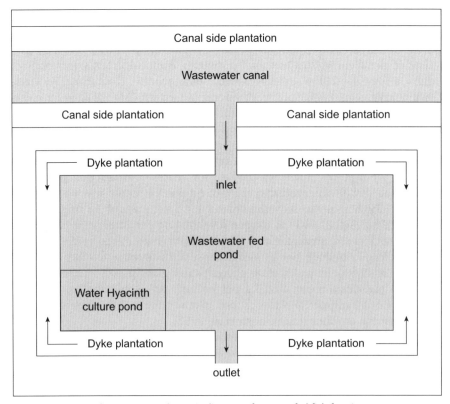

Figure 8.1 A schematic diagram of sewage-fed fish farming

Farmers are encouraged to utilize dyke cultivation, which may enhance their socio-economic status. Dyke farming may control soil erosion, maximize utilization of the farm space and help to maintain the ecological balance of the wetland ecosystem. Drumstick tree (Sagne), different vegetables, mustard and sunflowers are commonly cultured. These are mainly used for human consumption. During the regular de-siltation programme, the excavated mud is gathered on the pond dyke. The cultured plants or vegetables absorb nutrient from the mud, which is nutrient rich. As a result, the farmers gain economic benefit, while the solid waste (mud) is reused by the plants. Therefore, the dyke farming also assists the environmental sustainability of the waste-fed zone.

Fingerlings are stocked in the cultured ponds after being rearing from hatchlings into a nursery pond. Part of a culture pond is used as a nursery pond, separated by a mud-made dyke in order to minimize the threat from predator fishes.

Existing activities under the control of the Department of Fisheries, Government of West Bengal

In March 2001, 13 fishermen societies and 38 fish production groups (FPGs) formed by the Department of Fisheries were working in this area. The sewage-based fish culture with its ancillary activities (such as horticulture and ecotourism) provides employment for about 30,000 full-time people, thus contributing a good share in the local employment scenario. The fishermen's co-operative society has set up a shelter for 10,000 migratory birds at Mudiali Nature Park and has introduced forms of ecotourism (for example, the Nalban Boating Complex). There is a longstanding lotus culture at the Captain Bhery Fishermen Co-operative Society (75 years' old) and a Fisherwomen Co-operative Society has been formed to support the making of fish by-products.

These projects have largely been implemented in various co-operative societies where they are running successfully with the generation of employment and eco-friendly activities.

The Department of Fisheries, Government of West Bengal, also has further activities in the pipeline and is actively trying to obtain money from financial agencies. To date, financial assistance has been received from the National Co-operative Development Corporation (NCDC) for the culture of ornamental fish through BENFISH – the enabling agency of the Fishermen Co-operative Society, Government of West Bengal.

Currently, the sponsored scheme for ornamental fish culture supports 360 units. The principal beneficiaries of the credit and investment scheme of the NCDC are women. There are 360 direct beneficiaries, while other family members are indirect beneficiaries. With an average household size in peri-urban Kolkata of six, the total number of indirect beneficiaries is 2166. In this scheme, loans and subsidies are given simultaneously to the fisherwomen community. Free training is provided by the authority as part of the subsidy.

There are also other funding agencies for various schemes. These funds have been doled out to a number of co-operative societies in the region for dredging, fish culture, development of ecotourism, employment generation and other allied activities for the general improvement of East Kolkata Wetlands. This money will be utilized for:

- increasing the depth of the *bherys* of East Kolkata Wetlands by 1m;
- developing an ecotourist zone in and around the area through the formation of a golf course and picnic spots, extending from Nolban to Sonarpur;
- reconstructing the residential '*kuchcha*' houses (built of bamboo, clay and tiles) into '*pakka*' houses (built of brick and cement);
- arranging the formation of a fish market to enable people to buy and sell fish captured from the *bherys*;
- planting medicinally important plants, and building up plant and animal sanctuaries at a small scale – for example, a deer park – in order to maintain and enhance the eco-tone.

Kolkata is unique in having one of the world's largest peri-urban wetlands where waste can be recycled for resource utilization. The projects have been implemented in phases with the aid of different co-operative societies, and all projects are peculiar to this area.

The East Kolkata Wetlands comprise a natural endowment internationally recognized as the world's single largest integrated low-cost wastewater recycling region by the World Bank-sponsored international symposium held in Kolkata in 1988 (Edwards and Pullin, 1990). This has been acknowledged as a highly productive, remunerative and employment-generating ecosystem that serves as the respiratory system of Kolkata city. This system effectively helps to clean the city's environment and acts as a catalytic agent to change city waste into a protein-rich 'aqua zone', which is also a source of major supplies of vegetable, fruits and horticultural products. This helps to meet the great demand for fish and vegetables of the fast-growing Kolkata city population. Here, the term recycling means the reuses (agriculture, horticulture and floriculture) of wastewater after its discharge from wastewater ponds. Considering the undoubtedly great importance of this wetland, persistent and accomplished care with close vigilance is needed for its conservation and maintenance. It is noted, however, that ever-rising demand for urban land and industries is gradually affecting the socio-economic condition of this sewage-fed fishery area. The East Kolkata Wetlands, which originally extended to an area of approximately 18,100ha, has now being reduced to about 8300ha due to the pressures of urbanization.

A conceptual model for the East Kolkata (waste-fed) Wetlands

Recent advances in information and data processing technologies have dramatically increased the capacity of humans to analyse complex multiple resource-use options and to link up large numbers of people with integrated decision-making structures. New research findings also have greatly broadened the understanding to coordinate common property resource use while maintaining their essential social and cultural attributes (Mukherjee and Maity, 2002). All-round progress has created conditions favourable to the full realization of benefits resulting from the enhanced integration of fisheries, agriculture and livestock, as well as their incorporation within the rest of the economy (Mukherjee, 1998). The integration not only utilizes the waste matters of one sector by the other to mutual benefit, but also acts as a bio-remedy for aquatic problems (for example, by reducing nutrient load and suspended solid particles and by absorbing some amount of pollutants from wastewater) that arise in sewage-fed fish culture, in addition to increased economic return, food security and employment guarantees.

This multidimensional and zero-discharge (no effluent but recycling of the effluent) option (Shome and Banerjee, 2000) includes the following characteristics:

- Dense plantation on the *canal side* maintains the environmental stability through preservation and restoration of ecological balance. It may also control soil erosion, and the plants can absorb excess amounts of nutrients from wastewater and produce sustainable nutrient-rich water for aquaculture. Neem (*Azadirachta indica*), banyan (*Ficus bengalensis*), mango (*Magifera indica*), guava (*Psidiun guajana*) and some mangrove plants decrease the nutrient overload of wastewater, as well as producing fruits that provide an extra source of income for the local people (*Aquaculture Authority News*, 2003). Different types of large and fruit-bearing plants as referred to above are mainly used *upstream* (where the soil is not saline) of Kolkata on both sides of the wastewater canals.
- *Downstream* of the canals, where the soil and water characteristic is saline due to its history of tidal influence, different mangrove plants are used in a plantation programme, with government, non-governmental organization (NGO) and stakeholder participation. The plants are mainly sundari (*Heritiera fomes*), garan (*Ceriops tagal*), jat bain (*Avecennia officenalis*), kankra (*Brugiera gymnorhiza*) and keora (*Sonneratia apetala*). These plants are able to control soil erosion, as well as maintain the ecological stability of this zone.
- Where the canal bed and adjacent area are not suitable for plantation, different types of *fodder* can be grown, because these types of cultivation need less care and the fodder species are very hardy. Cultivation of fodder crops may create new market opportunities for local people. This new dimensional farming system may also encourage livestock farming (for example, dairy animals and goat farming) of the region, while the fodder crops reduce excess nutrient load from wastewater. As a result, the cultivation of fodder crops has both economic and ecological importance.
- Farmers should be further encouraged to establish *dyke plantations* (embankments of the fish ponds/*bherys*). In dyke farming, primarily bushy plants, vegetables and flower trees are introduced which have some economic value, whereas in canal-side plantations, mainly larger trees that

can grow well on the dykes are preferred. This may enhance the socio-economic status of the farmers to provide extra income, apart from the income generated by fish farming and by marketing products (fruits, vegetables and flowers). These are additional agro-products which can be produced alongside the fishery in an integrated system. Not only does dyke farming control soil erosion with maximum utilization of the farm space, but it also maintains the ecological balance of the wetland ecosystem. Drumstick tree (*Sagne*), different vegetables, mustard, sunflowers and other crops can be grown. Excavated mud, which is nutrient rich, is gathered on the pond dyke; from this source, plants or vegetables absorb an additional nutrient supply. Dredging is a general programme that is conducted annually in the dry season, when water level is lower.

- Every FPG (primary co-operative society) and government-controlled co-operative society could start *lotus farming* within the main fish culture pond. Lotus farming has the advantage that it attracts aquatic insects and birds, which helps, respectively, to feed the fish and assist in pollination, while the lotus flower (the national flower of India) has high economic importance.

Integrated aquaculture

In the waste-fed zone of Kolkata, integrated farming should be initiated for the best possible utilization of farm space and the optimum reuse of waste. It is economically advantageous as well as environmentally friendly. Duck, poultry, dairy, pig and goat farming could be successfully established along with fish culture. Dyke culture is also a part of integrated farming.

Local fisherwomen may also participate in integrated farming. Other products, for example, may be made from low-cost fish, especially by fisherwomen. The probable fish by-products, for which there is a ready local market, include fish pickle and fish sandwich. This type of programme may enhance the economic and social status of local fisherwomen.

It is suggested that every co-operative society maintains a freshwater pond, where the harvested fish are stocked for one day, because during this process the odour of sewage and most pathogens are removed from the harvested fish. This is a traditional practice, and it has been observed that there is a reduction of total coliform from 9.2 most probable number (MPN) per 100ml in the inlet water to 1.1 MPN per 100ml in the outlet water of a typical wastewater-fed aquaculture in the region (Mukherjee et al, 2002b).

The question arises as to how this could be implemented. This essentially holistic approach will only be possible if proper land-use planning is carried out from the point of view of social planners, who therefore have an invaluable role to play. This zero-discharge (pollutant-less water) technology for a multi-dimensional (integrated aquaculture) approach in the East Kolkata Wetlands has been designed to involve people's participation, aiming at making the whole process remunerative and eco-friendly.

It is estimated that only 30 per cent of Kolkata's total wastewater is treated and is used for aquaculture or irrigation purposes. The rest of the wastewater is directly discharged into the Bay of Bengal and pollutes the total estuarine region. This discharge also has negative effects on aquatic biodiversity and, in particular, causes huge mortality of estuarine fish seeds (Menasveta, 1997). Therefore, if the total wastewater was able to be used by farmers for aquaculture or agriculture, the problem of uncertain wastewater supply due to the occasional cut-off of supply during the monsoon by the Kolkata Municipal Corporation (for faster discharge of water to the Bay of Bengal in order to prevent inundation in some areas of the city, such as Sonarpur and Bhangor I and II blocks) could be overcome. The estuarine ecosystem would also certainly be improved. A further potential initiative here, therefore, is to consider ways of using the additional 70 per cent of available sewage.

Conclusions

The East Kolkata Wetlands, situated in Kolkata's peri-urban zone, already provide a rich and diverse environment. The use of wastewater in fish culture is well established and contributes an important livelihood opportunity for many of the peri-urban inhabitants. Although not without its problems, the systematic expansion of a holistic approach to land and wastewater use, built around the expansion of aquaculture, would provide both an enhanced environment and augmented livelihood and leisure opportunities, sited in the peri-urban East Kolkata Wetlands, but a resource for Kolkata as a whole.

References

Aquaculture Authority News (2003) vol 1, no 3, March

Cagauan, A. G., Branckaert, R. D. and Van Hove, C. (2000) 'Integrating fish and azolla into rice-duck farming in Asia', *Naga, The ICLARM Quarterly*, vol 23, no 1, January–March, pp4–10

Cagauan, A. G. and Nerona, V. C. (1986) 'Tilapia integrated rice-fish culture with *Azolla* as biofertilizer', *Fisheries Research Journal Philippines*, vol 11, nos 1–2, January–December, pp29–33

Chen, H., Hu, B. and Charles, A. T. (1995) 'Chinese integrated fish farming: A comparative bioeconomic analysis', *Aquaculture Research*, vol 26, pp81–94

Culley, D. D., Raj Pankona, J., Koet, E. and Poye, J. B. (1981) 'Production, chemical quality and use of duck weeds (*Lemnaceae*) in aquaculture, waste management and animal feeds', *Journal of the World Mariculture Society*, vol 12, no 2, pp27–49

Edwards, P. and Pullen, R. S. V. (eds) (1990) *Wastewater-Fed Aquaculture: Proceedings of the International Seminar on Wastewater Reclamation and Reuse for Aquaculture, Calcutta, 6–9 December, 1988*, Environmental Sanitation Information Centre, Asian Institute of Technology, Bangkok

Funge-Smith, S. and Phillips, M. J. (2001) 'Aquaculture systems and species', in Subasinghe, R. P., Bueno, P. B., Phillips, M. J., Hough, C., McGladdery, S. E. and Arthur, J. R. (eds) *Aquaculture in the Third Millennium*, Network of Aquaculture Centres in Asia-Pacific/FAO, Bangkok, pp49–56

Ghosh, A. (1990) 'Wastewater-fed aquaculture in the wetlands of Calcutta – an overview', in Edwards, P. and Pullen, R. S. V. (eds) *Wastewater-Fed Aquaculture:*

Proceedings of the International Seminar on Wastewater Reclamation and Reuse for Aquaculture, Calcutta, 6–9 December, 1988, Environmental Sanitation Information Centre, Asian Institute of Technology, Bangkok, pp49–56

Ghosh, A., Chattopadhyay, G. N. and Mukherjee, A. B. (1990) 'A modular project for recycling sewage effluents through aquaculture and its economic validity', in Edwards, P. and Pullin, R. S. V. (eds) *Wastewater-Fed Aquaculture: Proceedings of the International Seminar on Wastewater Reclamation and Reuse for Aquaculture, Calcutta, 6–9 December, 1988*, Environmental Sanitation Information Centre, Asian Institute of Technology, Bangkok, pp111–118

Ghosh, A., Rao, L. H. and Saha, S. K. (1980) 'Culture prospects of *Sarotherodon mossambicus* in small ponds fertilized with domestic wastewater', *Journal of the Inland Fisheries Society of India*, vol 12, pp74–80

Ghosh, A., Saha, S. K. and Chakraborty, P. K. (1985) *Carp Production Using Domestic Sewage*, Aquaculture Extension Manual, Central Inland Fisheries Research Institute, Barrackpore

Guttman, H. (1999) 'Rice field fisheries – a resource for Cambodia', *Naga, The ICLARM Quarterly*, vol 22, no 2, April–June, pp11–15

Jana, B. B. (1998) 'Sewage fed aquaculture: The Calcutta model', *Ecological Engineering*, vol 11, pp73–85

Jhingran, V. G. (1991) *Fish and Fisheries of India*, 3rd edition, Hindustan Publishing Corporation (India), Delhi

Kongkeo, H. (2001) 'Current status and development trends of aquaculture in Asian region', in Subasinghe, R. P., Bueno, P. B., Phillips, M. J., Hough, C., McGladdery, S. E. and Arthur, J. R. (eds) *Aquaculture in the Third Millennium*, Network of Aquaculture Centres in Asia-Pacific/FAO, Bangkok, pp267–293

Menasveta, P. (1997) 'Mangrove destruction and shrimp culture systems', *World Aquaculture*, vol 28, no 4, pp6–9

Mukherjee, M. (1998) 'Clever manipulation of fishery and recreational activity on any wetland offers an ecofriendly approach towards employment generation', *Meenbarta (Special issue on Wetlands)*, 16 June 1988, pp58–60

Mukherjee, M., Banerjee, R., Datta A. and Sen, S. (2002b) 'Evaluation and comparison of occupation, occupational hazards and socio-economic status of women fishers of three different systems of peri-urban areas of Calcutta', in *Women in Fisheries*, Indian Society of Fisheries Professionals, Mumbai, pp84–88

Mukherjee, M. and Maity, D. K. (2002) 'East Kolkata Wetlands – policy option for the sustainable development – integrated planning has a valuable role to play', in *Department of Fisheries Report*, Department of Fisheries, Government of West Bengal in collaboration with Ministry of Agriculture, Government of India, Kolkata, pp1–26

Mukherjee, M., Nath, U., Kashem, A. and Chattopadhyay, M. (2002a) 'Environmental scenario of sewage-fed fisheries of Kolkata', in *Department of Fisheries Report*, Department of Fisheries, Government of West Bengal in collaboration with Ministry of Agriculture, Government of India, Kolkata, pp27–42

Nair, K. K. (1944) 'Calcutta sewage irrigation fisheries', *Proceedings of the National Institute of Science, India*, vol 10, pp459–462

Raschid-Sally, L., Tuan, D. D. and Abayawardana, S. (2004) 'National assessments on wastewater use in agriculture and an emerging typology: The Vietnam case study', in Scott, C. A., Faruqui, N. I. and Raschid-Sally, L. (eds) *Wastewater Use in Irrigated Agriculture: Confronting the Livelihood and Environmental Realities*, International Water Management Institute and CABI Publishing, Wallingford, pp81–90

Saha, K. C., Sen, D. P., Mukherjee, P. C. and Chakerborty, S. K. (1958) 'Physico-chemical qualities of Calcutta sewage from the view point of pisciculture and the danger of feeding raw sewage to confined fisheries', *Indian Journal of Fisheries*, vol 5, pp144–149

Shome, J. N. and Banerjee, R. D. (2000) 'A conceptual wastewater utilization model: A holistic approach towards zero discharge option', in Jana, B. B., Banerjee, R. D., Guterstam B. and Heeb, J. (eds) *Waste Recycling and Resource Management in the Developing World*, University of Kalyani, Kalyani and International Ecological Engineering Society, Wolhusen, pp515–528

Subasinghe, R. P., Bueno, P. B., Phillips, M. J., Hough, C., McGladdery, S. E. and Arthur, J. R. (eds) (2001) *Aquaculture in the Third Millennium*, Network of Aquaculture Centres in Asia-Pacific/FAO, Bangkok

9

Alternative Strategies in Alternative Spaces: Livelihoods of Pastoralists in the Peri-Urban Interface of Yabello, Southern Ethiopia

Edlam Aberra

Introduction

Pastoralism is one of the main rural livelihood strategies in arid and semi-arid Africa, with more than 20 million people deriving their livelihoods from it in the Horn of Africa alone (IRIN Web Specials, 2002). Broadly, it comprises people living primarily off the products of their domestic animals in environments characterized by resource scarcity (Fratkin, 1997, p235). Pastoralists engage in seasonal migration with their livestock according to the availability of pasture and water, thereby maximizing their access to these resources and facilitating regeneration. There are, however, variations in typologies of pastoralism depending on degrees of mobility, dependence upon non-livestock-based strategies, as well as the purpose of livestock production (Galaty and Johnson, 1990). Furthermore, pastoralism is today undergoing significant transformations, one of which is the increasing permanent settlement of pastoralists in and around urban centres (Fratkin, 1997, p246). Yet, little is known about the nature of pastoralists' livelihoods in these spaces or the impact of such settlement on their well-being. Therefore, this chapter examines the livelihoods of pastoralists permanently settled in the peri-urban interface (PUI) and the extent to which they are able to construct sustainable livelihood options in this space.

Today, the majority of Africa's pastoralists are severely impoverished, lacking the material and political means to sustain their livelihoods (Fratkin, 1997; Lane, 1998; Broche-Due and Anderson, 1999); indeed, many find themselves completely livestock destitute. Without livestock, it is difficult for pastoralists to remain in rural areas where non-livestock-based livelihood opportunities are limited. The overall impoverishment of pastoralists and consequent decline of mutual assistance behaviour among them also means that livestock-destitute households can no longer rely on support from the wealthy to remain in rural areas. They are therefore drawn towards urban centres and the PUI primarily due to perceived non-livestock-based opportunities arising from urban-based wage employment, demand for raw materials and labour. Despite such trends, research on pastoralism has had a strong 'rural' bias with limited emphasis on urban centres and the PUI (but cf Salih, 1985, 1995; El Nagar, 2001; Pantuliano, 2002).

The PUI has been overlooked within existing pastoral research and development programmes for several reasons. First, pastoral research and development agents consider the PUI as being beyond their scope based on a rigid conceptualization of pastoralism as an inherently 'rural' livelihood strategy. Yet, this conceptualization fails to capture ongoing transformations in terms of which pastoralists are moving beyond rural areas to settle in and around urban centres for various reasons (Salih, 1985, 1995; Getachew, 2001; Pantuliano, 2002). Second, researchers and development agents alike assume that pastoralists living in the PUI have access to urban-based livelihood opportunities and are thus better able to support themselves than the poor in rural areas (development non-governmental organization (NGO) personnel, Yabello Borana, pers comm). While there is truth in this perspective, it disregards the need for basic assets such as human and financial capital required to access urban-based opportunities: 'with no skills to secure them jobs in the town's modern sector, pastoralists in town are amongst the most wretched on earth' (Salih, 1991, p52). Third, it ignores recent re-conceptualizations of the simplistic rural–urban dichotomy and ways in which households utilize rural, peri-urban and urban areas flexibly as part of their survival and livelihood strategies, especially in times of stress and vulnerability (Mbiba and Huchzermeyer, 2002; Simon et al, 2004). Finally, there is an assumption that groups with non-pastoral backgrounds dominate the PUI in pastoral areas. Yet, a large number of pastoralists continue to live under squalid conditions in and around urban centres in Ethiopia, as well as several other African countries (Salih, 1991; Grahn, 2001; Pantuliano, 2002).

This chapter thus aims to clarify some of the above misconceptions that result in a 'rural bias' in pastoral research and development programmes. The research on which it is based draws mainly on a household survey conducted with 170 Borana households in 11 settlements located within the PUI of Yabello, southern Ethiopia, between October 2002 and January 2003. Field observations revealed that settlements within an approximately 20km radius are distinct primarily in terms of the inhabitants' livelihood strategies. Subsistence agricultural production dominates, complemented by livestock production where such assets are available (often not). There is also some reliance on urban-based livelihood strategies such as wage labour and trade, the importance of which increases with proximity to town even within this radius – a common phenomenon (Simon et al, 2004) – which therefore can be taken to constitute Yabello's PUI. Beyond 20km, livestock production becomes the dominant activity. Although the PUI may not be identified by local residents and development practitioners using this specific term, they are aware of the distinctive characteristics of these spaces as outlined here.

Purposive sampling was used to select households for the survey based on two main criteria which best fitted the objectives of this study. First, respondents had to have settled in the PUI over the previous 25 years in order to limit the recall period about aspects of their lives prior to settlement. Second, the study targeted only those who were practising pastoralism prior to settlement in the PUI. This was particularly important due to the existence of other groups in the selected communities who had non-pastoral backgrounds. Results from the survey were complemented by results from 34 in-depth interviews and 21 focus group discussions – using some Participatory Rural Appraisal (PRA) tools – undertaken with different men and women between May 2003 and September 2003.

The chapter explores the conceptual framework that informs the analysis here, drawing mainly from the livelihoods approach. It then examines the assets which pastoral households are able to access and the types of livelihood strategies from which they derive a living. Finally, it reviews the key livelihood constraints which limit pastoralists' capacity to achieve sustainable livelihood outcomes.

Conceptual framework: Examining livelihood sustainability

While sustainability is a highly contested concept, it is understood here in terms of the livelihoods approach. This has emerged largely out of changing conceptualizations of poverty that have shifted towards a multidimensional analysis beyond income poverty alone (Rakodi, 2002, pp4–6). Crucially, the approach has adopted Chambers and Conway's (1991, p6) definition of a 'livelihood' as 'the *capabilities*, *assets* (stores, resources, claim and access) and *activities* required for a means of living'. Livelihoods analysis entails an examination of the capital assets (resources) that are available to people and how they are able to transform those capital assets through various livelihood strategies (activities) into positive livelihood outcomes, such as reduced poverty and vulnerability (Carney, 1998; Scoones, 1998). Six types of capital assets are commonly incorporated within livelihoods analysis – namely, natural, human, social, physical, financial and political assets.

In turn, capital assets are central to livelihoods analysis because they affect the ability of individuals or households to pursue particular livelihood strategies (or activities) (Scoones, 1998, p7). Livelihoods analysis also takes into account other contextual factors that influence peoples' choice of livelihood strategies, including institutions and organizations, policies, livelihood opportunities, vulnerability context and socio-cultural factors. In turn, livelihood strategies affect the extent to which individuals or households achieve positive outcomes, such as improved well-being and reduced vulnerability (Chambers and Conway, 1991; Carney, 1998; Moser, 1998; Scoones, 1998; Rakodi, 1999; Rakodi, 2002).

While well-being has been defined in many different ways, there has been a general shift from a focus on income-based indicators to a multidimensional approach that takes into account non-income indicators (Narayan et al, 2000). Crucial to this change has been Sen's influential capability approach, which focuses on people's ability to achieve what they want and the means to achieve it (Sen, 1984, 1985, 1993). Well-being is understood here as a compound concept that refers to people's access to and benefit from a range of tangible and intangible assets, including the freedom to choose and achieve what they desire. When well-being is threatened, households are said to be vulnerable, whereas vulnerability refers to the shock and threats to which they are exposed and their ability to respond to such threats (Moser, 1998). The ways in which households are able to deal with pressures on their livelihoods – and the effectiveness of these strategies – are critical determinants of the sustainability of their livelihoods (Chambers and Conway, 1991, p6). Individuals' and households' capacity to respond to shock and stress is positively correlated with their access to capital assets. As Moser (1998, p3) notes, 'the more assets people have, the less vulnerable they are and the greater the erosion of people's assets, the greater their insecurity'. However, access to assets alone is meaningless if these are not converted into sustainable livelihood outcomes through various strategies (activities).

Livelihoods in the peri-urban interface (PUI)

An increasing proportion of the population in developing countries now lives in the PUI, defined as the transition zone at the edge of cities (Rakodi, 1999; Brook and Dávila, 2000; Mbiba and Huchzermeyer, 2002). A central feature of the PUI is its location between urban centres and rural areas, although the distinctions between these spaces are increasingly becoming blurred (Tacoli, 1998). The PUI is neither urban nor rural, but shares common characteristics with both. For instance, while urban-based employment and trade opportunities provide a source of income for PUI inhabitants, agricultural and livestock production common in rural areas is also practised. Proximity to both urban and rural areas means that the PUI is constantly adapting to new opportunities arising from urban forces of growth and expansion, but also rural processes of development (Rakodi, 1999). The PUI is therefore perceived to be a space that provides multiple opportunities and often attracts impoverished groups from rural areas, but potentially also from urban areas (see Chapter 1 in this volume).

It is argued that inhabitants of the PUI derive a living from multiple livelihood strategies, mostly in the informal economy. However, PUI inhabitants are not a homogeneous group, particularly in terms of capital asset ownership, which, in turn, determines the type of livelihood strategies pursued. Those who own assets such as land engage in more lucrative economic activities, such as agricultural production, whereas poorer groups rely on their labour power and urban-based opportunities largely in the informal sector (Rakodi, 1999). Thus, livelihood opportunities that attract people to the PUI in the first place may be accessible only to those with initial assets, to the exclusion of the poor. Furthermore, livelihood strategies accessible to poorer members often entail physical and health hazards exacerbated by lack of access to clean water, health facilities and housing. Despite the multiple livelihood constraints which characterize livelihoods in the PUI, poor rural migrants such as livestock-destitute pastoralists continue to be drawn to this space, as the Borana case study illustrates.

A changing Borana pastoralism

Pastoralists in Ethiopia number over 8 million, constituting approximately 13 per cent of the country's population (MOFED, 2002, p17). They occupy the arid and semi-arid lowland areas which account for 60 per cent of the country's surface area (Hogg, 1996). Besides numerous smaller groups, the three main pastoral groups in Ethiopia are the Somali, Borana and Afar in the south-east, south and north-east, respectively (Hogg, 1997).

The Borana have occupied the rangelands of southern Ethiopia and northern Kenya probably since the 16th century (Helland, 1997). Like other Ethiopian pastoralists, they have been victimized by the combined impact of drought, conflict, political and economic marginalization (Fekadu, 1990; Hogg, 1997; Beruk Yemane, 2001; CRDA, 2001; Haile-Gebriel, 2003). Since the 1960s, large sums of money have been invested in development interventions among the Borana pastoralists, mainly in the form of livestock development projects focusing on infrastructural development and veterinary service provision (Tamene, 1996). Yet, there have been as many negative consequences as positive changes (Solomon, 1997; Helland, 1997; Aberra, 2001).

The Borana continue to rely on livelihoods that are highly vulnerable to various threats, particularly drought. The probability of drought occurrence remains high, while at the same time several factors are weakening traditional resource management institutions and mechanisms for coping with resource scarcity, such as seasonal migration (Solomon, 2001; Helland, 2001). Privatization and alienation of traditional rights of access to pastoral resources, as well as restrictions on mobility, are key threats to the viability of Borana pastoralism (Baxter, 2001, p245). Declining returns from livestock-based livelihood strategies are causing significant changes in their livelihoods. Already, trends of livelihood diversification have been documented whereby Borana pastoralists are combining livestock production with a variety of other activities, including wage labour and trade (Little et al, 2001). For livestock-destitute pastoralists, an emerging alternative is settlement in and around urban centres such as Yabello in order to access non-traditional and non-livestock-based livelihood strategies.

With a total population of 16,112 at the end of 2002, Yabello (see Figure 9.1) is now the capital of the recently formed Borana zone – the administrative level below a region but above *woredas* and *kebeles* (Ato Sebsibee Gulummaa, deputy head of Yabello City Administrative Office, pers comm). However, Yabello's growing population has not been accompanied by concurrent expansion in social services such as schools, health establishments and water provision. A limited number of educational and health establishments provide services for urban and peri-urban inhabitants (PDOBZ, 2002). The main water supply comes from a tank that was constructed at a time when the town had

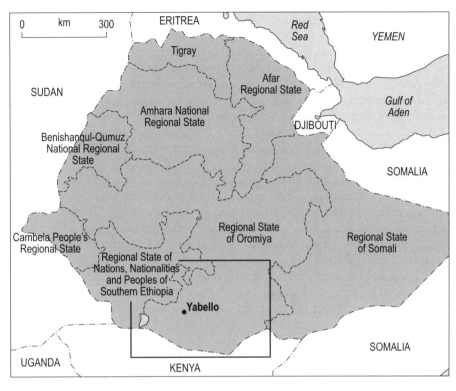

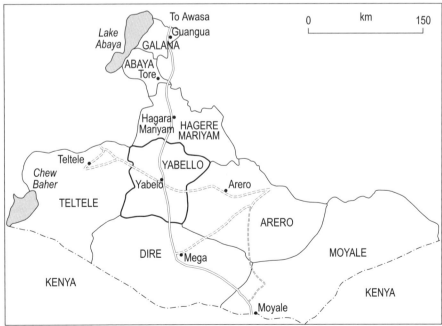

Figure 9.1 Location of Yabello

no more than 6000 inhabitants. The tank now has to cater for the needs of close to 30,000 people, including some peri-urban inhabitants. The lack of infrastructure and services is more acute within the peri-urban zone of Yabello, although this is characteristic of the urban centre itself.

Yabello's administrative office is interested in formally incorporating peri-urban settlements within the urban centre primarily for the purpose of accessing much needed land for the expanding urban administration. Recently, Yabello became a zonal capital, further accentuating this need. Yet, if peri-urban zones are incorporated within the urban centre, its residents are at risk of being displaced.

Yabello's PUI is inhabited by a mixture of long-term residents and recent arrivals from surrounding rural areas, as well as other regions of the country. The predominant production system is agriculture, most of which is for subsistence purposes; but it is also commercial, especially where the land is owned by urban residents. Urban residents who hire labour to cultivate their land and care for their livestock own a large proportion of the land in peri-urban Yabello. Some livestock-rearing activity is also evident in the peri-urban zone, although on a much smaller scale than in rural areas. Peri-urban residents rely greatly on this and other urban-related livelihood opportunities in wage labour and trade, especially where they lack their own land and livestock.

Land in Ethiopia was nationalized under a proclamation by Mengistu in 1975; new peasant associations were entrusted with land allocation and distribution (Bereket, 2003). Despite the change of government, according to the current Ethiopian constitution, the state remains the overall trustee of all land within the national boundaries and has absolute authority over its allocation. This was consolidated in a proclamation in 1991 as follows:

> *The right to ownership of rural and urban land, as well as all natural resources, is exclusively vested in the State and in the peoples of Ethiopia. Land is a common property of the Nations, Nationalities and Peoples of Ethiopia and shall not be subject to sale or to other means of exchange* (Federal Democratic Republic of Ethiopia, 1995, Article 40, No 3).

The constitution also stipulates that every Ethiopian is entitled to obtain land with payment and with protection from eviction regardless of ethnicity or gender. However, tenants are entitled only to usufruct rights, and marketing or permanent land transfers are prohibited.

Peri-urban residents cater for urban labour demands primarily within the informal sector. They also engage in trade of various natural products such as firewood, timber and water, as well as dairy products where these are available to them. The availability of such opportunities is dictated by trends in Yabello's urban economy, which is limited both in scale and specialization.

Yabello's inhabitants derive a living mainly in the service and small-scale industry sectors, while some inhabitants are civil servants (Ato Sebsibee Gulummaa, deputy head of Yabello City Administrative Office, pers comm). Contraband trade used to be a key part of Yabello's economy but has now declined due to tighter government regulations. Despite such limitations, destitute Borana pastoralists continue to be drawn to Yabello's PUI due to perceived livelihood opportunities. But are Borana households really benefiting from such perceived opportunities in the PUI? As a first step in addressing this question, the following section examines the assets and livelihood strategies of Borana households.

Capital assets and livelihood strategies of pastoralists in the PUI

Capital assets are critical determinants of the livelihood choices available to Borana pastoral households. Five main types of livelihood assets were considered here – namely, financial, physical, natural, human and social assets – each of which was operationalized using context-specific indicators (see Table 9.1).

Table 9.1 *Capital assets of Borana households in the peri-urban interface (PUI)*

Assets	Indicators	Findings
Financial	Livestock	Average livestock index declined from 122.5 before settlement to 19 at present[1]
	Banking	98.2% do not have bank accounts
	Savings and credit associations	88.2% of households are not members
Natural	Agricultural land	53.5% of households had no agricultural land
Physical	Housing	81.8% of households owned their own houses
Social	Kinship-based support (KBS)	85.9% of households had not received KBS
	Clan-based support (CBS)	88.2% of households had not received CBS
Human	Medical services	88.2% of households used the Yabello health centre
	Clean water	77.6% of households lack access to clean water

Note: [1] Aggregate livestock assets could not be compared directly due to differences in the value of each type and species. Therefore, a weighted livestock index (LI) was created to allow comparison based on a single figure representing household's livestock assets. Each type of livestock was weighted according to its market price with camels (value 6) being the most expensive, followed by cows (value 5), bulls (value 4), calves (value 3), goats (value 2) and sheep (value 1)
Source: household survey data

As illustrated in Table 9.1, Borana households in peri-urban Yabello had limited access to all five types of assets. Livestock represent a key form of financial capital because they can generate immediate financial income either through the sale of dairy products or using them as draught animals in cultivation, where some of the yield is subsequently sold in market. The livestock ownership status of pastoral households had declined significantly from the period prior to settlement. This is partly explained by the fact that drought-induced livestock loss was the main factor (73.4 per cent of households) that led Borana pastoralists to settle in urban and peri-urban spaces in the first place. In terms of financial services, almost all households did not have bank accounts, primarily due to lack of money to deposit (in 91.1 per cent of cases). The majority of households were not members of informal savings and credit associations, again due to their lack of financial capacity to pay membership fees. In terms of physical assets, housing has been identified as a potential source of income for the urban poor who may run home-based enterprises (Moser, 1998). Although more than 80 per cent of the Borana households owned the houses in which they lived, the poor quality and peripheral location of the houses diminished their value.

Given their limited access to productive physical and financial assets, human capital in the form of labour power was a critical asset for pastoralists in the PUI. Those who owned fewer capital assets or were destitute were particularly heavily dependent upon their labour power to earn a living. As one male interviewee noted, 'Those who have nothing will go and do labour work' (interview on 11 June 2003). Access to health and education services were reviewed as additional aspects of human capital. By virtue of being located in the PUI, pastoral households had physical access to urban-based education and health services. Most pastoralists felt that their access to education and health had improved since settlement. When asked about the advantages of living in the PUI, one woman said, 'If one falls ill here, there is a health centre near by ... for instance, if a woman is in labour, she can be taken to the health centre in Yabello and give birth there.' Yet, physical proximity does not necessarily ensure access in real terms, as elaborated upon later.

Natural capital assets played significant roles in the pastoralists' livelihoods as sources of consumable or marketable goods. Ownership of agricultural land, in particular, was critical for households as it provided them with a means of subsistence, although cultivation required physical and labour inputs that were not always available. Over half of the households did not own any agricultural land, a key asset within the PUI. Among those who did own land, most owned less than 0.5ha (74 per cent of households), which limits production capacities. Water is a further natural capital used by pastoral households not only for domestic consumption, but also as a marketable commodity, given urban demands for water. Pastoralists in peri-urban spaces often lack access to clean water and instead resort to using natural sources such as springs and rivers. The most critical type of natural capital in the livelihoods of pastoralists in the PUI comprises forest resources, which also have a dual purpose as consumable and marketable goods.

Social capital was reviewed in terms of networks of social support and reciprocity, which were found to play a somewhat limited role in pastoralists' livelihoods in the PUI. Traditionally among the Borana pastoralists, several kinship- or clan-based support (KBS and CBS) systems are in place to assist destitute members. For instance, *Busa Gonofa* is a CBS mechanism which allows poor pastoralists to petition the wealthy to redistribute their wealth. Yet, few households had received any such support since settlement in the PUI and were unlikely to do so in the future. Instead, pastoralists in the PUI supported each other at the household level in different productive and reproductive activities. They also shared food and other items in times of need, although such exchange was sporadic and was also restricted by the material poverty of households.

In sum, the evidence suggested that pastoral households' capital asset status was precarious and this was repeatedly identified as a key constraint by pastoralists themselves. This has implications for the types of livelihood strategies which pastoralists are able to pursue in the PUI. Despite the paucity of their assets, Borana households in this study were engaged in 21 different livelihood strategies ranging from trade-related activities to complete reliance on social support (see Table 9.2). Most households were engaged in multiple activities, with over three-quarters (75.1 per cent) of them pursuing at least two or more activities. Yet, a multiplicity of livelihood strategies does not indicate greater benefits – it is more likely to be a matter of necessity and desperation.

Table 9.2 *Livelihood strategies pursued by Borana households in the PUI*

Livelihood strategy	Activity	Percentage of households
Trade	Firewood	59.4
	Sugar and salt	2.4
	Incense (*Kundi*[1])	3.5
	Tobacco	2.9
	Locally brewed alcohol	0.6
	Water	15.9
	Local plant for decoration (*Ergemsa*[2])	2.4
	Shoe-making	7.1
	Construction materials (soil)	0.6
	Khat[3]	0.6
Livestock-based strategies	Livestock herding (own)	27.1
	Livestock brokering	0.6
Agriculture	Agriculture (own)	44.7
Labour work	Hand-pushed cart	1.8
	Paid agricultural work	15.3
	Gold digging	0.6
	Daily labour	10.0
	Paid livestock herding	8.8
Formal-sector employment	Civil employee	1.8
	Driver	0.6
Social support	From neighbours or relatives	7.1

Notes: [1] A local material used as a perfume and incense
[2] A local material used in decorating milk and butter containers
[3] A shrub, the leaves of which are widely used as a stimulant in most parts of Ethiopia
Source: household survey data

The most widely pursued livelihood strategy was selling firewood, followed by agriculture and livestock herding. Other livelihood activities that emerged as significant were selling water and paid agricultural work. Less than one third of the pastoralists continued to engage in livestock rearing, indicating the declining importance of livestock in their livelihoods. Instead, non-livestock-based strategies such as agricultural labour and selling firewood had gained prominence in pastoralists' livelihoods. Trade, mainly in natural resources such as firewood and water, was particularly significant in the livelihoods of pastoralists given their proximity to markets. Market access was an advantage not only for selling goods but also for purchasing basic consumption goods. The ability to purchase grain and other food items in small quantities on a daily basis is critical for most households. Comparing life in rural areas with life in Yabello's PUI, one woman said:

> In the rural area you can only go to the market once a week. In the meantime, your children will be hungry. But here, because it is close to town, I can buy some food for my children when I return from town in the evening.

The range of livelihood strategies in which pastoralists participate in the PUI indicates the existence of diverse urban-based livelihood opportunities, enabling those who have lost their livestock to earn a living. However, the livelihood strategies pursued by pastoral households were not necessarily the most beneficial. Rather, several constraints prevented pastoralists from achieving sustainable livelihood outcomes by means of the livelihood strategies that they pursue.

Livelihood constraints for pastoralists in Yabello's PUI

A key livelihood constraint for Borana pastoralists in the PUI was the paucity of their capital assets. As illustrated earlier, they had limited access to financial, physical, human and social capital assets (see Table 9.1). Furthermore, it emerged that assets interact with one another, with knock-on effects such that access to one asset, especially finance, was linked to – or determined – access to other types of assets. For instance, both formal and informal financial institutions were beyond the reach of most Borana pastoralists given their lack of financial capacity to pay membership fees or contributions. A male interviewee explained his experience in this regard: 'No one will give loans to the poor ... I am poor. In case I go bankrupt, I don't have the capacity to repay; so people do not loan money to us.'

Financial capital also determines access to medical and educational services since the costs of accessing them make these services inaccessible for pastoralists despite their physical proximity. One participant in a group discussion said: 'Due to lack of money, we don't seek medical treatment when we fall ill; we just wait to get better or die.' Although it has been argued that social capital is critical for those who lack tangible financial and physical assets (Narayan and Pritchett, 1997), access to social capital itself may require prior access to tangible assets.

Given the paucity of their assets, pastoral households in the PUI had access to only a limited range of livelihood strategies. Most households were excluded from participating in those which require financial, physical and human capital in the form of skills. In contrast, activities such as selling firewood were pursued widely because they do not require ownership of assets other than labour and a ready supply of wood. Describing the livelihood options available for poor households in the PUI, one interviewee, Bule, said: 'There are plenty of trading opportunities for those who have money ... for the poor, their only means of survival is selling firewood.' Yet, livelihood strategies accessible to pastoralists often entailed multiple constraints as illustrated in the case of selling firewood, which was the most widely pursued livelihood strategy.

As Figure 9.2 indicates, selling firewood entailed a number of physical and health hazards, including risks of falling while climbing trees or carrying firewood to markets, and attacks by wild animals. The process of carrying heavy loads of firewood itself resulted in adverse health complications for women. Such physical burden was exacerbated by the decline in firewood resources, which forced women to walk longer distances to collect it. Despite the physical hardships that women had to withstand when selling firewood, the income generated was barely able to cover basic expenses. Such income insufficiency was characteristic of most of the livelihood strategies accessible to pastoralists in Yabello's PUI (see Table 9.3).

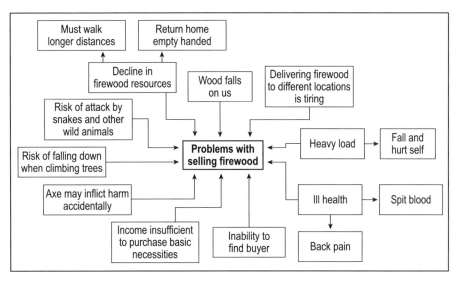

Figure 9.2 Constraints in selling firewood in the Yabello peri-urban environment

Most of the livelihood strategies in which pastoral women and men participated generated less than US$1 per day. Although this is not a comprehensive indicator of poverty, it demonstrates the level of material deprivation among pastoral women and men in urban and peri-urban spaces. The highest daily income was gained from herding other peoples' livestock to markets at US$0.8 per day. Yet this work was rarely available and can be undertaken only by a

Table 9.3 *Daily earnings for some PUI activities*

Activity	Average daily earnings (US$)
Selling firewood	0.12 (men); 0.3 (women)[1]
Selling water	0.18
Selling grass	0.16 (men); 0.3 (women)[1]
Daily labour (house construction)	0.55
Paid livestock herding	0.09
Livestock herding to market	0.80
Agricultural labour	0.55

Note: [1] Women carry larger loads of firewood and grass, thus gaining more income
Source: focus group discussions

limited number of able-bodied men as it may involve walking hundreds of kilo-metres to livestock markets countrywide. By contrast, the activities most accessible to the majority of pastoral women and men, such as the sale of natural products (firewood, water and grass), generated some of the lowest daily incomes.

Fluctuations in market factors and irregularities in urban demand for labour exacerbated income insufficiency. For instance, market prices for fire-wood varied greatly by season and the changing fuel requirements of buyers. As one woman noted: 'There may not be anyone to buy the firewood for up to a week. It all depends on your luck, and some people may not have it.' Other activities in the PUI were also subject to irregularities, creating a sense of liveli-hood insecurity. For example, agricultural production undertaken by pastoralists in the PUI was a largely 'opportunistic' activity dictated by the erratic availability of rainfall. Rudimentary agricultural tools were used, such as an ox-drawn plough or hand hoe, with implications for productivity. As one interviewee noted: 'The harvest is not sufficient for both consumption and sale … there is no other surplus to be sold; the plot is too small.' Although much of the production was subsistence oriented, almost 80 per cent of the house-holds purchased additional grain from the market, implying that production was not sufficient to even meet subsistence requirements.

A third constraint related to the dwindling natural resource base. As noted earlier, firewood and other natural resources are critical for the livelihoods of pastoralists who settle in the PUI. In principle, access to most of these resources is free and open, apart from water purchased from community water points. Yet, access to these vital resources was being threatened by several factors.

A consistent rise in the number of people deriving livelihoods from natural capital assets had led to a dwindling of these resources, and this is likely to continue in future. There is a continual influx of destitute pastoralists from rural areas into the PUI, most of whom resort to selling forest products. In addition, many households sell forest products during crisis periods, such as harvest failure, even if they normally rely on other livelihood strategies. The increasing fuel and construction demands of Yabello's growing population are additional factors that encourage PUI inhabitants to resort to selling forest products as a livelihood strategy. This trend has been accentuated since Yabello became the capital of Borana zone at the end of 2002, which was accompanied by a greater need for fuel and timber as a result of the expansion of government structures and associated personnel, many of whom were transferred from the former capital, Negelle. Demand for timber and firewood therefore increased in order to build new homes, to make furniture for expanded government offices and to meet the growing fuel needs. However, there is a scarcity of timber on the market. While strict government regulations against logging are in place, enforcing these has been problematic. An equally great demand for charcoal exists in Yabello; but this product is in short supply given that charcoal-making is legally prohibited. This combination of factors has precipitated the spread of illegal logging and charcoal-making activities, at times by organized criminal groups. At the same time, forest resources, which are the only sources of livelihood for many poor residents of the PUI, continue to deteriorate. This has had the most direct impact on women and female children who are often the ones responsible for collecting firewood for household consumption and sale.

Water is a further natural resource to which access in the PUI is constrained. Potable water can be purchased from urban community water points; but these are not always physically or financially accessible for pastoral women in the PUI. Instead, most resort to using natural water sources; but the availability of these is seasonal. Women sometimes spend whole days fetching water during the dry season when shortages are particularly acute. This case study's research revealed no evidence of a significant PUI water pollution problem; as in rural and urban areas, it is the shortage of water which poses a serious threat to livelihoods. In terms of quality, water from natural sources such as ponds (which is what most PUI inhabitants use) is often a muddy brown colour, but is purified using branches of a certain local tree.

Access to agricultural land is also becoming increasingly difficult. Pastoralists who settle in the PUI are entitled to apply for a plot of land from the *Kebele* administration or traditional elders may allocate land to them. Yet, it is the actual availability of land that poses a problem. In addition to the competing interests of new entrants to the PUI, such as pastoralists and existing inhabitants, urban residents are also continuously looking to expand their holdings into this space. Consequently, over half of the households who participated in this study did not own any land.

A final livelihood constraint for pastoralists within the PUI is the stigma associated with settlement in this space and the adoption of PUI-specific livelihood strategies. Pastoralist settlers are considered as outcasts and even 'enemies' by rural Borana pastoralists. They are thought to lose their Borana identity by virtue of living among non-pastoral and non-Borana groups, and adopting non-livestock-based strategies in the PUI. Livestock serve not only as symbols of a 'pastoral' identity but also ethnic identity as Borana. Selling firewood is regarded as the most degrading work among Borana pastoralists, indicating complete destitution. In some extreme cases, Borana pastoralists in the PUI may not even be considered as human anymore. As one man said:

> *Those living in the rural area do not consider us as human ... they consider us as monkeys. Monkeys are animals; they live in the forest, eat whatever they can find and then go home, don't they? That is how those living in the rural areas see us.*

Overall, these livelihood constraints have implications for the well-being and vulnerability of Borana pastoralists in the Yabello PUI.

Conclusions

This chapter has demonstrated that pastoralists are, indeed, settling in the PUI as an 'alternative' to rural areas and has highlighted some of the main aspects of these settlers' livelihoods. The existence of non-livestock-based or 'alternative' livelihood opportunities is a major reason why pastoralists are attracted to the PUI. Accordingly, Borana pastoralists are engaged in multiple 'alternative' livelihood strategies in the PUI, although this has not enabled them to achieve sustainable livelihood outcomes in the form of improved well-being and reduced vulnerability. The adoption of multiple strategies by pastoralists in the PUI amidst asset paucity is a matter of necessity and survival rather than a strategy of accumulation. As Rakodi (2002, p6) notes, 'the poorest and most vulnerable households are forced to adopt strategies which enable them to survive but not to improve their welfare'. Due to their lack of initial assets, Borana households engage in livelihood strategies characterized by a number of constraints that will probably preclude long-term improvement in their well-being.

The sustainability of individual and household livelihoods depends on their ability to cope with and recover from shocks, maintain or enhance their capabilities and assets, and preserve the natural resource base. Based on this last criterion, the evidence presented in this chapter suggests that the livelihoods of pastoralists in Yabello's PUI are not sustainable. Survival-oriented strategies do not enable households to accumulate savings or even to access various credit schemes. Without savings, households remain highly vulnerable to potential threats such as harvest failures, market-related declines in urban-based opportunities and declining natural resources. Their ability to recover from such shocks also remains questionable as this requires accumulated assets to buffer the impacts of shocks. Households' ability to maintain and enhance their assets and capabilities is further limited by their lack of initial assets. Paucity of assets also leads households to rely heavily on free or 'open access' natural resources, such as firewood and water, for their sustenance. The natural resource base in Yabello's PUI is therefore dwindling under the pressure of increased numbers of users who are forced to compromise future sustainability of resources in order to meet their pressing current needs.

The influx of livestock-destitute pastoralists is likely to continue in the future given continuing threats of drought, conflict and other factors that cause pastoralists to settle in the PUI. Therefore, there is an urgent need to redress the 'rural' bias of research and interventions in pastoral areas and to adopt a broader approach that takes into account livelihoods in the PUI as well as urban centres. The vulnerability of pastoralists in the PUI and their inability to improve their well-being, underscored by the paucity of their livelihood assets and consequent limited livelihood options, further demonstrates the need to incorporate the PUI within pastoral research and interventions. Finally, urban and peri-urban centres in pastoral areas should be considered in terms of their linkages with rural areas and their potential to contribute to the development of the latter.

Acknowledgements

The following organizations supported fieldwork in Yabello, Borana Zone: SOS-Sahel (UK) International, Action for Development (AFD) and the Southern Rangelands Development Unit (SORDU). Various government offices both in Addis Ababa and in Yabello also facilitated this research. Fieldwork was co-funded by the University of London's Central Research Fund and a studentship from Queen Mary, University of London. Above all, I thank all participants in the research for devoting their valuable time to sharing their knowledge and experiences.

References

Note: Ethiopian names are not inverted in references as they do not use family names

Aberra, E. (2001) *Pastoralists and Development: The Impact of Development Interventions on Borana Pastoralists, Southern Ethiopia*, MPhil thesis, University of Cambridge, Cambridge

Baxter, P. T. W. (2001) 'Immediate problems: A view from a distance', in Salih, M. A., Dietz, T. and Abdel Ghaffar, M. A. (eds) *African Pastoralism, Conflict, Institutions and Government*, Pluto Press, London, pp235–246

Bereket Kebede (2003) 'Administrative allocation, lease markets and inequality in land in rural Ethiopia: 1995-1997', Paper prepared for the DSA Conference on Globalization and Development, University of Strathclyde, Glasgow, UK, 10–12 September 2003

Beruk Yemane (2001) 'The reality of pastoralism in Ethiopia', Paper presented at CRDA Workshop on Non-Governmental Organizations and Sectoral Development, Pastoralism Panel, September 2001, Addis Ababa, Ethiopia

Broche-Due, V. and Anderson, D. (1999) 'Poverty and the pastoralist, deconstructing myths, reconstructing realities' in Anderson, D. and Broche-Due, V. (eds) *The Poor Are Not Us, Poverty and Pastoralism*, James Currey, Oxford, pp3–19

Brook, R. M. and Dávila, J. D. (2000) *The Peri-urban Interface: A Tale of Two Cities*, School of Agriculture and Forest Sciences, University of Wales, Bangor

Carney, D. (1998) 'Implementing the sustainable rural livelihoods approach', *Sustainable Rural Livelihoods, What Contribution Can we Make?*, DFID, London, pp3–23

Chambers, R. and Conway, G. (1991) *Sustainable Rural Livelihoods, Practical Concepts for the 21st Century*, University of Sussex, Institute for Development Studies, IDS Discussion Paper 296, Brighton

CRDA (Christian Relief and Development Association) (2001) *Proceedings of the*

Workshop on Non-Governmental Organizations and Sectoral Development, Pastoralism Panel, September 2001, Addis Ababa, Ethiopia

El Nagar, S. (2001) 'Changing gender roles and pastoral adaptation to market opportunity in Omdurman, Sudan', in Salih, M. A., Dietz, T. and Abdel Ghaffar, M. A. (eds) *African Pastoralism, Conflict, Institutions and Government*, Pluto Press, London, pp247–277

Federal Democratic Republic of Ethiopia (1995) *Proclamation No 1/1995: A Proclamation to Pronounce the Coming into Effect of the Constitution of the Federal Democratic Republic of Ethiopia*, Addis Ababa, Ethiopia

Fekadu Gedamu (1990) 'Pastoral nomadism and rural development', in Pausewang, S., Fantu Cheru, Brune, S. and Eshetu Chole (eds) *Ethiopia, Options for Rural Development*, Zed Books, London, pp205–212

Fratkin, E. (1997) 'Pastoralism, governance and development issues', *Annual Review of Anthropology*, vol 26, pp235–261

Galaty, J. G. and Johnson, D. (1990) 'Introduction, pastoral systems in a global perspective', in Galaty, J. G. and Johnston, D. (eds) *The World of Pastoralism*, Guilford Press, New York, pp1–33

Getachew Kassa (2001) *Among the Pastoral Afar in Ethiopia: Tradition, Continuity and Socio-economic Change*, International Books in Association with OSSREA, Addis Ababa, Ethiopia

Grahn, R. (2001) *Livelihood Diversification in Southern Ethiopia: The Case of Gobicha Settlement*, MPhil thesis, University of Cambridge, Cambridge

Haile-Gebriel Endeshaw (2003) 'Pastoralism in Ethiopia', *The Ethiopian Herald*, 12 April 2003

Helland, J. (1997) 'Development intervention and pastoral dynamics in Southern Ethiopia' in Hogg, R. (ed) *Pastoralists, Ethnicity and the State in Ethiopia*, Haan Publishing, London, pp55–80

Helland, J. (2001) 'Participation and governance in the development of Borana, Southern Ethiopia', in Salih, M. A., Dietz, T. and Abdel Ghaffar, M. A. (eds) *African Pastoralism, Conflict, Institutions and Government*, Pluto Press, London, pp56–79

Hogg, R. (1996) 'Government policy and pastoralism, some critical issues', in Ministry of Agriculture (MOA) (ed) *Full Papers from Conference on Pastoralism in Ethiopia*, MOA, Addis Ababa, Ethiopia, pp29–35

Hogg, R. (ed) (1997) *Pastoralists, Ethnicity and State in Ethiopia*, Haan Publishing, London

IRIN Web Specials (2002) 'Struggling with the legacy of drought', www.irinnews.org/webspecials/drought/default.asp

Lane, C. (1998) 'Introduction' in Lane, C. (ed) *Custodians of the Commons*, Earthscan, London, pp1–25

Little, P., Smith, K., Cellarius, B., Coppock, D. and Barrett, C. (2001) 'Avoiding disaster: Diversification and risk management among East African herders', *Development and Change*, vol 32, no 3, pp401–433

Mbiba, B. and Huchzermeyer, M. (2002) 'Contentious development: Peri-urban studies in Sub-Saharan Africa', *Progress in Development Studies*, vol 2, no 2, pp113–131

MOFED (Ministry of Finance and Economic Development) (2002) *Sustainable Development and Poverty Reduction Programme*, MOFED, Addis Ababa, Ethiopia

Moser, C. (1998) 'The asset vulnerability framework: Reassessing urban poverty reduction strategies', *World Development*, vol 26, no 1, pp1–19

Narayan, D., Patel, R., Schafft, K., Rademacher, A. and Koch-Schulte, S. (2000) *Voices of the Poor: Can Anyone Hear Us?*, World Bank, Washington, DC

Narayan, D. and Pritchett, L. (1997) *Cents and Sociability: Household Income and Social Capital in Rural Tanzania*, World Bank, Washington, DC

Pantuliano, S. (2002) *Sustaining Livelihoods Across the Rural–Urban Divide: Changes and Challenges Facing the Beja Pastoralists of North Eastern Sudan*, IIED, London

PDOBZ (Planning and Development Office of Borena Zone) (2002) *Socio-Economic Physical Planning of Major Towns in Borena Zone*, Unpublished report, Negelle, Borana

Rakodi, C. (1999) 'Poverty in the peri-urban interface', *NRSP Research Advances No 5*, DFID, London

Rakodi, C. (2002) 'A livelihoods approach – conceptual issues and definitions' in Rakodi, C. and Lloyd-Jones, T. (eds) *Urban Livelihoods: A People-Centred Approach to Reducing Poverty*, Earthscan, London, pp3–22

Salih, M. (1985) 'Pastoralists in town: Some recent trends in pastoralism in the north west of Omdurman district', *ODI Pastoral Development Network Paper 20b*, ODI, London, pp1–23

Salih, M. (1991) 'Livestock development or pastoral development?', in Baxter, P. T. W. (ed) *When the Grass Is Gone*, The Scandinavian Institute for African Studies, Uppsala, Sweden, pp37–57

Salih, M. (1995) 'Pastoralist migration to small towns in Africa', in Baker, J. and Aina, T. A. (eds) *The Migration Experience in Africa*, Nordiska Afrikainstitutet, Uppsala, pp181–196

Scoones, I. (1998) 'Sustainable rural livelihoods: A framework for analysis', *IDS Working Paper 72*, IDS, University of Sussex, Sussex, pp3–22

Sen, A. (1984) *Resources, Values and Development*, Harvard University Press, Cambridge, Massachusetts

Sen, A. (1985) *Commodities and Capabilities*, Elsevier Science Publishers, Amsterdam

Sen, A. (1993) 'Capability and well-being', in Nussbaum, M. and Sen, A. (eds) *The Quality of Life*, Clarendon Press, Oxford, pp31–53

Simon, D., McGregor, D. and Nsiah-Gyabaah, K. (2004) 'The changing urban–rural interface of African cities: Definitional issues and an application to Kumasi, Ghana', *Environment and Urbanization*, vol 16, no 2, pp 235–247

Solomon Desta (1997) 'Past and present pastoral development interventions in Ethiopia', in Ministry of Agriculture (MOA) (ed) *Full Papers from Conference on Pastoralism in Ethiopia*, MOA, Addis Ababa, Ethiopia, pp45–49

Solomon Desta (2001) *Cattle Population Dynamics in the Southern Ethiopian Rangelands*, www.glcrsp.ucdavis.edu/project_subpages/PRMPfolder/Research%20Briefs/ PARIMA2_Desta.pdf

Tacoli, C. (1998) 'Rural–urban linkages and sustainable rural livelihoods', in Carney, D. (ed) *Sustainable Rural Livelihoods*, DFID, London, pp67–92

Tamene Yigezu (1996) 'A case study with particular reference to the Boran pastoralist system in Ethiopia', *Full Papers, Conference on Pastoralism in Ethiopia*, Ministry of Agriculture, Addis Ababa, Ethiopia, pp5–8

10

Sustainable Livelihoods in the Peri-Urban Interface: Anse La Raye, St Lucia

Michelle Mycoo

Introduction

Peri-urban settlements reflect persistent neglect, conflict and competition – they are zones in transition that have received less investment, limited land-use planning and no (or ad hoc) attention to environmental management than the more favoured urban centres. However, during the last few decades, the conception of rural and urban areas as discrete physical and social entities has slowly yielded to one based upon intangible and fluid interrelations between the two. There is growing recognition that the sustainability of both cities and rural areas is significantly affected by dynamic and changing flows of commodities, capital, natural resources, people and pollution within the peri-urban interface (PUI) (Allen, 2001). This zone is a place of competing interests, which lacks approaches that strike the balance required to ameliorate poverty, protect the environment, maximize the productivity of human and natural resources, or draw synergy from urban and rural relationships. New solutions are needed to address the conflicts and implement changes in this frontier that will benefit an increasingly excluded population of the PUI.

A definition of the PUI is not straightforward as Brook et al (2003) note. However, there is growing consensus that it goes beyond simply a definition of place. Rather, the PUI is a place that involves many processes that impact on people. Mbiba (2001) sees the PUI as having several elements – spatial, temporal and functional. It is also a zone in which the process of social exclusion is experienced by inhabitants of informal settlements, who are poorly served by infrastructure and services.

Anse La Raye fits the definition of the PUI used by Mbiba (2001) – namely, spatially. The town, which forms part of the quarter of Anse La Raye, is located 9km from Castries, the capital of St Lucia (see Figure 10.1). The Castries PUI comprises a small portion of the island's land area compared to the predominantly rural landscape. Functionally, there is a high degree of interaction between the two places because many residents of Anse La Raye work and conduct business in Castries. The population experiences social exclusion in various forms best illustrated by chronic unemployment, poor-quality infrastructure, inadequate services and substandard housing. Furthermore, it experiences all of the classic symptoms of conflict – namely, competition from built development to convert agricultural land, poor land-use practices and unsustainable livelihoods. Although the Castries PUI, represented here by Anse La Raye is atypical of city PUIs in other parts of the world due to its small size, it represents a micro-case study in absolute terms, important in the Caribbean small island context because of the problems that are manifested and their developmental impacts.

The Anse La Raye peri-urban area is in transition and is characterized by a lack of planning and infrastructure provision that reflects an investment bias towards Castries. The village centre is laid out in a grid pattern, with public buildings along the main streets, and approximately 300 rectangular building lots located on flat land on either side of the Castries–Soufrière main road. However, on leaving its nucleus, housing, which is generally of poor quality, becomes haphazardly laid out. Only 1.8 per cent (see Table 10.1) of households are squatting on land; but settlement generally resembles that of organic, infor-mal development. Family lands have contributed to this unplanned siting of housing; although individuals have security of tenure, the lands cannot be sold on the open market and must be subdivided among each generation of indi-viduals. In many instances two houses have been built on a single parcel of land, increasing housing density. Individual access to property is impossible and access roads cannot be built without the relocation of some properties. The national 2001 census revealed that many residents have septic tanks or no facilities at all and dispose of night soil into existing canals, resulting in the pollution of coastal waters. Spontaneous settlement and haphazard subdivision of family land compromise infrastructure provision and upgrading, reflecting a high level of non-compliance with the existing regulatory controls on land development.

Table 10.1 *Anse La Raye: Tenure of land and dwelling by household, 2001*

Tenure of land			Tenure of dwelling		
Type of tenure	Households		Type of tenure	Households	
	Number	%		Number	%
Freehold	241	55.1	Owned	262	60.0
Rented	116	26.5	Rented	119	27.2
Permission to occupy	5	1.1	Rent free	52	11.9
Squatted	8	1.8	Squatted	1	0.2
Other	6	1.4	Other	1	0.2
Not stated	61	14.0	Not stated	2	0.5
Total	437	100.0	Total	437	100.0

Source: Government of St Lucia Statistics Department, 2001

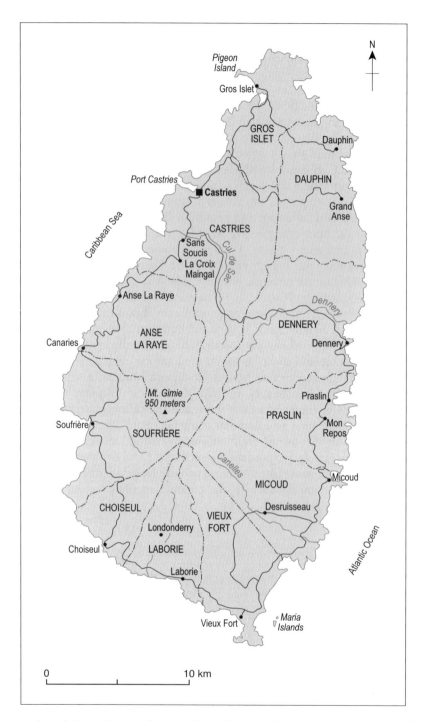

Figure 10.1 Map of St Lucia showing the village and quarter of Anse La Raye as a peri-urban area of the capital and quarter of Castries

Demographically, Anse La Raye is a challenge to policy-makers, not because of its size or density but because of its composition. The 2000 census estimated that the population of Anse La Raye was 1877 persons. Fertility rates are extremely high, as is validated by the fact that 44.45 per cent of the total population are under the age of 20 (see Table 10.2). In low fertility populations, this cohort would be smaller than the others. Furthermore, there is a high dependency ratio of 75 per cent because a high percentage of the population is below 15 years and over 65 years.

Table 10.2 *Anse La Raye: Village population by age group and sex*

Age group	Sex		Total
	Male	Female	
0–4 years	110	108	218
5–9 years	104	102	206
10–14 years	93	103	196
15–19 years	106	94	200
20–24 years	86	75	161
25–29 years	66	68	134
30–34 years	64	55	119
35–39 years	53	63	116
40–44 years	49	42	91
45–49 years	50	32	82
50–54 years	22	35	57
55–59 years	31	23	54
60–64 years	33	25	58
Over 65 years	96	89	185
Total	963	914	1877

Source: Government of St Lucia Statistics Department, 2001

The 2000 census records show that 72 per cent of the labour force had primary education and that 85 per cent of the heads of household had only primary schooling. Additionally, some 21 per cent of the labour force was unemployed. On the basis of the lack of labour market status such as employment status, educational attainment and certified skills, women and youth were found to be the ones suffering the greatest levels of impoverishment.

The poor depended significantly on the coastal environment for livelihoods in fishing and tourism. Gender roles were very distinct. Those who mainly exploited the marine environment in the form of fishing were men, whereas women were involved in agro-processing and certain aspects of tourism.

The profile of Anse La Raye's poor is that of individuals with little education and very poor prospects on the job market. They live in moderate to poor housing areas with inadequate physical infrastructure. Survival of poor households depends on their ability to multi-task, the practice of occupational multiplicity and, in many cases, overseas remittances. Two decades ago

Carnegie (1981) characterized Anse La Raye as having a heavy reliance on non-agricultural income sources such as overseas remittances. Through interviews with persons from the area in 2002, it was established that among young persons there was 'hidden employment' – that is, individuals gained income from the sale of illicit drugs and prostitution.

The demographic characteristics, existing resource utilization, land-use and land tenure patterns, and infrastructural deficiencies pose conflicts in the PUI. Issues of conflict and processes of change, livelihood impacts and sustainable livelihood change strategies are discussed in the following section.

Conflicts and change frontiers in the peri-urban interface (PUI)

Within peri-urban areas there are conflicts over natural resource usage, land-use planning and infrastructure investments that serve to erode sustainable livelihoods. As a consequence, the population of the PUI often seeks opportunities in the more developed urban areas. However, change frontiers exist within the PUI that can curb migration to overburdened urban centres. By using new and improved techniques and approaches, the declining interest of the PUI's younger generation in fishing and agriculture could be revived and new interest stimulated in other livelihood activities, such as agro-processing and tourism. This section discusses conflicts and change frontiers in land-based activity, such as agriculture and tourism, in the Anse La Raye PUI, although fishing is an important livelihood for the older generation. A livelihood is sustainable when it can cope with and recover from stresses and shocks, and maintain or enhance its capabilities and assets both now and in the future, while not undermining the natural resource base (Carney, 1998).

Agriculture

Banana cultivation has been the mainstay of St Lucia's economy since the 1950s following the decline in sugar production (Dujon, 1995). However, the banana industry declined rapidly due to the cash crop's vulnerability to natural catastrophe, disease and, particularly, the change in the General Agreement on Trade Tariffs and Traffic rules in 1993 (Read, 1994), which reduced the preferential conditions under the Lome Convention for the export of bananas to the European Union (EU) market. This resulted in a regime that combined internal liberalization of the EU's banana market with a modified system of external protection. African, Caribbean and Pacific (APC) producers received aid to improve the quality of their bananas, coupled with provisions for marketing and vertical integration, as well as compensation for declining revenues caused by lower prices and falling market share. Read (1994) argues that the introduction of the new rules led to the forced exit from the industry of some higher cost preferential growers like St Lucia in spite of production subsidies. Read (1992) predicted that the growers most severely affected would be labour-intensive smallholders with few alternative sources of income, notably the Windward Islands. Read's predictions have proved accurate as the empirical evidence shows that the contribution of the industry to the gross domestic product (GDP) of St Lucia dropped steadily from 10.3 per cent in 1990 to 3.6 per cent in 2000 (Government of St Lucia, 2001).

Anse La Raye is an interesting case study of a settlement that has depended heavily on banana cultivation and a system of agricultural production that is affected by serious constraints. The population is engaged in agricultural practices on hillsides, given that land in the very narrow coastal zone rises steeply a short distance inland. A symptom of unsustainable agriculture in Anse La Raye is watershed destruction, the root cause being the manner in which key natural resources (land and forest) have been utilized in the past. These practices include forest removal on sloping land, which stripped the natural cover that best protected vulnerable land, the planting of bananas on sloping land exceeding 20 degrees and the introduction of annual crops on sloping land, which exacerbated erosion (Hunting Technical Services and Mott MacDonald, 1998). This is even more problematic given that, like the rest of the Caribbean, a sustainable livelihood in hillside agriculture is constrained by what McGregor (1995) notes as high rates of natural soil erosion arising from the combination of sloping terrain, thin, highly erodible soils and the intense nature of tropical storms that frequently cause flooding, landslides and crop damage.

Despite shifts in hillside farming, land degradation continues because of the system of family lands. An estimated 31.5 per cent of agricultural parcels in Anse La Raye are owned as family lands originating from the use of the Napoleonic Code, in which all family members can lay claim to the land (see Table 10.3). Dujon (1995, 1997, 2000, 2002) argues that family lands have many advantages for the poor; but this is not to say that land degradation does not occur. Since the individual does not have outright landownership, agricultural practices by these farmers are sometimes damaging as there is a tendency to plant short-term seasonal crops that have limited canopies, leaving much of the soil exposed to erosion. This is usually the practice by part-time farmers who are also employed in urban areas, and prefer to cultivate short-term crops because they do not have sufficient time to attend to more demanding long-term crops.

Table 10.3 *Anse La Raye: Number and area of parcels by tenure, 1996*

Form of tenure	Number of parcels	Percentage of parcels	Total area (hectares)	Percentage of area
Owned	113	44.5	516.34	69.6
Family land	80	31.5	150.72	20.3
Rented/private	12	4.6	26.08	3.5
Rented/government	1	0.5	2.02	0.3
Squatting/private	37	14.6	40.98	5.5
Squatting/government	6	2.3	3.23	0.4
Other/no response	5	2.0	2.93	0.4
Total	254	100	742.32	100

Source: 1996 Agricultural Census data, Government of St Lucia, 1996

Agricultural production techniques used in Anse La Raye have had other environmental impacts. The heavy use of pesticides in banana cultivation to control soil-borne pathogens has adversely affected the broad spectrum of soil fauna, including useful species such as earthworms and other organisms involved in the carbon and nitrogen cycles, according to the Windward Islands Bananas Growers Association (WINBAN, 1993). This practice has retarded the recycling of nutrients, requiring increasing use of fertilizers, which has compounded the chemical load of the environment and has caused eutrophication of coastal waters and coral reef damage (Caribbean Environmental Health Institute, 1994, 1995; Government of St Lucia, 1998).

In an effort to shift agriculture from the hillslopes of Anse La Raye, an agricultural project was established by the German government during the early 1990s. The community raised chickens, produced eggs and undertook prawn culture and small-scale tilapia breeding. However, the project did not succeed once the donor agency withdrew (D'Auvergnes, 2002).

Agriculture in the PUI is also under threat arising from a growing demand to convert such lands to housing. Nearly 45 per cent of the land in Anse La Raye, representing around 70 per cent of the overall area classed as agricultural holdings, is individually owned (see Table 10.3). The pressure to convert agricultural lands in Anse La Raye to built development, such as housing, is higher than in St Lucia as a whole because such a high percentage of the land area is under private ownership and can be put on the market for sale (unlike lands that are state owned).

Not all of the population in the Anse La Raye PUI is willing to engage in full-time farming or farming at all. The Anse La Raye focus group meetings revealed that young people are interested in wage labour in urban areas, and many rely on casual work or the less lucrative informal-sector trading and service occupations. Youth unemployment is particularly high as many young persons prefer to remain jobless, rather than farm the land. As noted earlier, fieldwork revealed that the youth are engaged in 'hidden employment', such as illicit drug trafficking, that is more lucrative than farming. The former provides quick money, while the latter necessitates time and patience, as in banana cultivation.

Those farmers who have remained in agriculture are severely constrained by limited access to credit, information on crop cultivation and marketing, as well as inadequate infrastructure, especially irrigation, drains and roads. Figure 10.2 shows small market vendors selling agricultural produce in the centre of Anse La Raye. Farmers are confronted with the threat of forced participation in the global economy that dictates the need for trade liberalization and undermines guaranteed markets for traditional crops such as bananas and, in the future, other commercial crops.

Any transformation of agriculture in the Anse La Raye PUI that brings benefits to the population will require improvement in services, infrastructure and marketing. This involves a transformation of public agricultural institutions. In this context, there is strong justification for a reinvigorated and efficient public agricultural research and extension system. Furthermore, the lethargy of state enterprises in marketing small farmers' produce must be over-

Figure 10.2 Marketing of agricultural produce in Anse La Raye

Source: Mycoo, 2003 field visit

come by more aggressive marketing. Partnerships in research, extension services and marketing between the public and private sectors should be enhanced.

Other sector constraints include exclusion and elitism, still dominant characteristics of the agricultural sector in St Lucia despite land redistribution. The status quo is preserved by the fact that the same elites remain committee and board members for decades. This exclusion makes the voice of the poor farmers mute. Additionally, although grants or loans are made available for farming, the powerful families in the community access and monopolize these grants. Policies formulated to break the monopoly enjoyed by the privileged and the powerful have not yielded results.

The agricultural sector still has the potential to provide a sustainable livelihood, especially since Caribbean agriculturists have noted that yields can be higher; but old paradigms are being used (Pemberton et al, 2002). Technocrats are unwilling or not motivated to try innovative techniques if they are operating in St Lucia's public sector where innovation is stifled, or they are too busy with administrative matters and multi-tasking to spare the time to communicate new ideas to farmers. The status quo must change. The input suppliers are the innovators and they should be challenging old paradigms and linking up with agricultural extension officers to get the new message across. The lack of political will to get the message to the constituencies that need it most – the poor – has stymied the success of sustainable livelihoods in agriculture.

The abandonment of agriculture in the PUI is risky and counter to the practice of multiple livelihoods as a risk reduction strategy of PUI inhabitants. This awareness has influenced agencies and governments to change lending policies in reviving agriculture for the benefit of small farmers. The Caribbean

Development Bank (2002) announced that it will provide financial assistance for a banana production project amounting to US$4.5 million as part of a broader reconstruction programme for St Lucia. The project will provide technical, managerial, agronomic and financial support to improve commercial banana production and productivity, and to capitalize on existing marketing opportunities in traditional and new markets prior to 2008, when preferential treatment will be phased out.

Overcoming constraints and conflicts in peri-urban agriculture, as the Anse La Raye case study demonstrates, is a complex task; but perhaps the most complex of all is changing the political will to introduce reforms that lead to benefits and sustainable livelihoods.

Tourism

The economy of Anse La Raye is in transition in the aftermath of the banana industry collapse and lessening interest of the younger generation in fishing as a livelihood. A growing number of individuals have been forced to seek work in the service sector, including government offices, hotels and restaurants in Castries and Vieux Fort, St Lucia's second largest town. To address the net labour exporter status of Anse La Raye and to induce economic opportunities, heritage tourism has been actively promoted.

On the whole, tourism in St Lucia is characterized by a bifurcation within the sector between high-return activity for large commercial resorts that have access to capital and/or skills, and low-return activities and limited social capital of small-scale operations. The government of St Lucia recognizes that new approaches and strategies for sustainable livelihoods in tourism are essential.

The government has provided incentives for the tourism sector through the 1996 Tourism Incentive Act, which grants tax holidays and waives consumption taxes on materials, furniture and equipment. However, the legislation is skewed in favour of big business and less so for community-based enterprises or small operators. The minimum number of hotel rooms to qualify for incentives is six rooms, which dampens initiatives for small guesthouse operators. Government officials have indicated that small operators below this minimum are considered on a case-by-case basis by the cabinet. Furthermore, the existing act is to be revised to meet the needs of all actors in tourism. This is important in stemming the migration of labour from the PUI to Castries in that small guesthouses and other tourism enterprises, once established, can provide employment for job seekers in Anse La Raye.

Two new initiatives have been embarked upon to improve a sustainable tourism livelihood, given that limited training and access to credit have constrained the entry of small tourism entrepreneurs. The development of a hospitality department is in the pipeline and training is conducted at the Sir Arthur Lewis Hospitality Institute for Training. In addition, the St Lucia Heritage Tourism Programme (SLHTP), which is donor funded, has conducted considerable strategic work, with a specific focus on increasing the poor's basic understanding of tourists and the industry as a whole, training in business skills and institutional capacity-building.

Traditionally, St Lucia has promoted beach tourism as its main product; but with keen competition from the rest of the Caribbean, policy-makers are actively promoting a niche product: heritage tourism. The SLHTP has focused on the development of the heritage tourism sub-sector by placing an emphasis on the use of traditional skills in cooking, farming, artistic expression, craft production or communication – skills that poor people typically possess (Government of St Lucia, 1999). The programme has made inroads into breaking the monopoly of cruise ship tourism by competing for tourists with an interest in cultural tourism through recruiting local operators, developing a new product and attracting tourists to inland initiatives.

In 1998, the Ministry of Tourism determined that the seaward frontage of Anse La Raye had development potential, given its strategic location on the tourist route on the west coast. The goal of the Ministry of Tourism was to generate employment in the fishing, catering, entertainment and crafts sector. The objective was to encourage tourists to spend more in the local communities, rather than only in the resorts. International tourists as well as domestic tourists were targeted. The SLHTP set out to develop a complementary product based on cultural tourism that could be integrated within more conventional tourist packages.

The effort of the SLHTP was successful from all accounts. Every Friday evening St Lucians and visitors travel to Anse La Raye to enjoy a range of seafood on the village beachfront while being entertained by local artists. This event has become known as the 'Fish Fry'. According to Renard (2001), the Anse La Raye seafood night had become the most popular activity of its kind in St Lucia, drawing an estimated 1000 people each Friday. It is an important economic activity, with some 36 vendors, mainly women, involved. The Anse La Raye 'Fish Fry' venture benefits women in particular because it is mainly women vendors who prepare and sell the seafood. With many men displaced by the collapse of the banana industry and declining fishing activity, households are dependent on these women to meet their basic needs. Approximately 95 per cent of the seafood vendors indicated that they earned over East Caribbean $200 per week, which was an increase in their incomes (Government of St Lucia, 2004).

The vendors and bar and nightclub operators make money from the Friday night event. The main bar in the village earned East Caribbean $3000 on Fridays before social problems developed, requiring the bar to be closed earlier. Social impacts have not been always positive. Field visits to Anse La Raye in 2003 revealed that crime, including car thefts (Ashley et al, 2001), violence and drug use, had crept into the 'Fish Fry' event. In an assessment of the Anse La Raye initiative, Renard (2001) noted that a large crowd could destroy the authenticity of the area. The Anse La Raye 'Fish Fry' also impacts on the marine environment because much of the waste left over from the Friday night event does not always get collected and ends up along the watercourses leading to the beach area. Noise and the provision of adequate bathroom facilities have been identified as specific problems. Other constraints include parking space, which stems from the narrowness of the streets and the number of vehicles transporting persons to the event.

While heritage tourism has been successful in generating income for residents, ecotourism in Anse La Raye is affected by infrastructural deficiencies. Unsightly clogged drains and the stench of untreated sewage, coupled with an architecturally unattractive waterfront and haphazard squatter settlement layout, make it difficult to market the town as a tourism attraction with an ecotourism focus – hence the emphasis on heritage tourism. The degraded environment and infrastructure inadequacy have also affected the potential to develop thriving bed-and-breakfast establishments and small hotels. Additionally, despite investments in a rehabilitated jetty, the charter boat community bypasses Anse La Raye.

The neglect of this peri-urban area is also reflected in the lack of land-use planning. The Cinquante pas de la Reine of Anse La Raye, which comprises coastal lands, is allocated for village development by law. Before Hurricane Debbie in 1994, this area was a beautifully landscaped waterfront with almond, coconut and flamboyant trees, and benches and picnic tables. After the destruction caused by the hurricane, the government utilized this coastal land for communal public facilities. However, the outcome has been disorderly development, with buildings haphazardly laid out. Existing land uses have also not been rationalized in terms of priority uses (see Figure 10.3).

The diversity of the tourism product is important in order to reduce vulnerability among the PUI population. Apart from heritage tourism being promoted, ecosystem assets are being used to improve product diversity

Figure 10.3 Anse La Raye's dilapidated waterfront zone

Source: Mycoo, 2003 field visit

marketed to tourists. However, unexplored possibilities remain, such as the fishers using their sea craft to provide water-taxi services in marine parks (Clauzel, 2001) and the marketing of protected areas to satisfy non-consumptive demands such as tourism, recreation, research and education.

Anse La Raye's poor are finding it difficult to develop linkages with the international tourism industry and marketing associations, although these have considerable influence over tourists' itineraries and activities. Partnerships unlock synergies and therefore it is important to create opportunities for the private sector to link up with tourism ventures. One route would be to allow private tour operators and agents to channel their own clients to peri-urban enterprises by including visits on their itinerary, rather than competing in every aspect. There is room for tourism companies to develop complementary products with the villagers to make destinations more attractive, extend the length of stay and provide employment and other income benefits, such as, for example, crafts and entertainment. Tourism companies can also source supplies locally as another means of integrating with the poor of the PUI, especially if their resorts are remote and the only source of agricultural supply is these small villages. After the collapse of the banana industry during the 1990s, Anse La Raye residents explored agro-processing – namely, the manufacture of pepper sauce and seasonings as an income-generating activity. Some producers have begun to link up with the resorts to sell their products.

The Anse La Raye example points to the positive impact of a particular form of tourism in giving hope to a community who faced a devastating decline in the banana industry. However, the negative impact of tourism should not be ignored. Renard (2001) referred to the destruction of the authenticity of an area such as Anse La Raye by large crowds drawn on 'Fish Fry' night. Ashley et al (2001) reported social problems such as crime. Earlier research by Pattullo (1996) also found that tourism is not always a panacea, but a problem. Pattullo cited examples of social alienation of locals from the 'all-inclusive' resorts. There is the very controversial case of the Jalousie Plantation Hilton Resort built near the Pitons as an 'all-inclusive resort' approved by the government with limited public participation, although locals argued that the resort would destroy the ambience of the Pitons and exclude St Lucians. In 2004, the Pitons area was declared a World Heritage Site after years of effort. There are other examples of negative results of tourism, such as reported environmental impacts that include coastal water pollution, stemming from poor wastewater disposal from the tourism establishments that do damage to coral reefs.

Conclusions

Natural physical characteristics of land in the PUI in the Caribbean are not easily modified, so that interventions are needed to modify human activity that triggers soil erosion, landslides and pollution. Furthermore, relaxation of agricultural constraints is necessary to make agriculture a sustainable livelihood.

New cultivation techniques should also be introduced to small farmers to alleviate environmental impacts and improve productivity levels. This requires agricultural research and information dissemination by agricultural extension officers.

Few governments in the South, argue Hardoy et al (1999), appreciate the extent to which productive intensive agriculture can support development goals of the urban and peri-urban areas. Ironically, many governments want to slow migration to cities; yet they do little to support peri-urban livelihoods, protect agricultural lands and prevent resource degradation. The role of the state is paramount in supporting sustainable agriculture, for without this the population of the PUI will be unable to improve their living standards. State activity is needed in ensuring that the population can access reasonably performing, stable markets for finance, as well as agricultural inputs and output, improved access to good farming land, infrastructure and credit.

Tourism also presents a viable alternative income-generating activity provided that constraints to achieving a sustainable livelihood in this sector are addressed. Currently, most job opportunities in tourism require the population to work in resorts located outside the peri-urban area. Tourism remains a source of income for economic elites, but less so for the poor because policy incentives have not had a pro-poor focus. The Anse La Raye case study shows that poor communities can earn a living from heritage tourism.

A major constraint to tourism in Anse La Raye is the significant infrastructure deficiencies, which have caused negative environmental externalities that deter visitors from staying overnight. Infrastructure upgrading and architectural interventions are crucial to retrofitting and redesigning peri-urban areas, though state investment is critical. These measures will also mitigate negative environmental impacts that result from debilitated or non-existent infrastructure.

Physical changes will be insufficient to promote tourism. Other measures include reducing entry barriers in tourism through human resource development in the form of training and better utilization of existing skills, access to credit, and the creation of an enabling environment for forging commercial and political partnerships involving poor people.

The proposed alternative income-generating sustainable livelihoods for the PUI's poor population require the state to play a pivotal role in unlocking possibilities for these communities. The complexity of the constraints demand state intervention, otherwise the poor, in particular, cannot independently remove the barriers to achieving sustainable livelihoods. While economic liberalization and privatization are being advanced by the World Trade Organization (WTO) as measures to improve global trade, disadvantaged members of society, such as the poor, will remain trapped in poverty. Increasing poverty and crime, witnessed in the Caribbean during the era of post-structural adjustment, are lessons that should not be ignored in the context of globalization and trade liberalization. Poverty and crime, if exacerbated by these processes, may make these societies ungovernable.

Acknowledgements

This publication is an output from a project funded by the UK Department for International Development (DFID) for the benefit of developing countries (Project R8135 Alternative Coastal Resource Livelihoods Strategies). The views expressed are not necessarily those of DFID.

References

Allen, A. (2001) 'Environmental planning and management of the peri-urban interface: A changing conceptual landscape', Keynote paper for the conference on Rural–Urban Encounters: Managing the Environment of the Periurban Interface, London, 9–10 November
Ashley, C., Roe, D. and Goodwin, H. (2001) *Pro-poor Tourism Strategies: Making Tourism Work for the Poor – A Review of Experience*, ODI, London
Brook, R., Purushothaman, S. and Hunshal, C. (2003) *Changing Frontiers: The Peri-Urban Interface Hubli-Dharwad, India*, Books for Change, Bangalore
Carnegie, C. (1981) *The Rural Population of Saint Lucia: A Preliminary Analysis*, Mimeo, Organization of American States Technical Report, Castries, St Lucia
Carney, D. (1998) *Sustainable Rural Livelihoods*, Russell Press Ltd, Nottingham
Caribbean Development Bank (2002) Press Release No 07/02, Bridgetown, Barbados
Caribbean Environmental Health Institute (1994, 1995) *Environmental and Coastal Resources Project Report. Environmental Monitoring Component: Water Quality Monitoring at the St Lucia Local Site*, Castries, St Lucia
Clauzel, S. (2001) *Developing a Complementary Tourism Product to Benefit Local Communities: The Case of Vieux-Fort, St Lucia*, MSc thesis, University of Greenwich, London
D'Auvergnes, C. (2002) Interview with Chris D'Auvergnes of Sustainable Development and the Environment Department, Ministry of Planning
Dujon, V. (1995) *National Actors against World Market Pressures: Communal Land, Privatisation and Agricultural Development in the Caribbean*, PhD thesis, University of Wisconsin, Madison
Dujon, V. (1997) 'Communal property and land markets: Agricultural development policy in St Lucia', *World Development*, vol 25, no 9, pp1529–1540
Dujon, V. (2000) 'Caribbean peasants in the global economy: Popular resistance to the privatization of communal land in the twentieth century and beyond', *Global Development Studies*, vol 2, pp199–221
Dujon, V. (2002) 'Local actors, nation-states and their global environment: Conceptualizing successful resistance to the anti-social impacts of globalization', *Critical Sociology*, vol 28, pp372–388
Government of St Lucia (1996) *1996 St Lucia Census of Agriculture Final Report*, Planning and Statistical Unit, Ministry of Agriculture, Lands, Fisheries and Forestry, Castries, St Lucia
Government of St Lucia (1998) *Biodiversity Country Report*, Castries, St Lucia
Government of St Lucia (1999) *St Lucia Heritage Tourism: Anse La Raye Consultation Report on Nature Heritage Tourism*, Castries, St Lucia
Government of St Lucia (2001) *St Lucia National Report to the World Summit on Sustainable Development*, Castries, St Lucia
Government of St Lucia (2004) *St Lucia Heritage Tourism Programme Draft Socio-Economic Impact Assessment of the Weekly Anse La Raye Seafood Festival*, Castries, St Lucia

Government of St Lucia Statistics Department (2001) *2001 Population and Housing Census Report*, Castries, St Lucia

Hardoy, J. E., Mitlin, D. and Satterthwaite, D. (1999) 'The rural, regional and global impacts of cities in Africa, Asia and Latin America', in Satterthwaite, D. (ed) *Sustainable Cities*, Earthscan, London, pp426–462

Hunting Technical Services and Mott MacDonald (1998) *Report on Protecting St Lucia's Watersheds*, Hunting Technical Services, Hemel Hempstead

Mbiba, B. (2001) 'Peri-NET origins, obstacles and options', in Mbiba, B. (ed) *Review of Urban and Peri-Urban Transformation and Livelihoods in East and Southern Africa*, Urban and Peri-Urban Research Network, South Bank University, London

McGregor, D. F. M. (1995) 'Soil erosion, environmental change and development in the Caribbean: A deepening crisis?', in Barker, D. and McGregor, D. F. M. (eds) *Environment and Development in the Caribbean*, The Press, University of the West Indies, Kingston, Jamaica, pp189–208

Pattullo, P. (1996) *Last Resort*, Ian Randle Publishers, Kingston, Jamaica

Pemberton, C., Wilson, L., Garcia, C. and Khan, A. (2002) 'Sustainable development of agriculture', in Goodbody, I. and Thomas-Hope, E. (eds) *Natural Resources Management for Sustainable Development in the Caribbean*, Canoe Press, University of the West Indies, Kingston, Jamaica, pp277-306

Read, R. (1992) 'Small-scale banana growers in the Windward Islands: External implication of the single European market', University of Lancaster Management School Discussion Paper EC 13/92, Lancaster

Read, R. (1994) 'The EC internal banana market: The issues and the dilemma', *World Economy*, vol 17, no 2, pp119–235

Renard, Y. (2001) 'Practical strategies for pro-poor tourism: A case study of the St Lucia Heritage Tourism Programme', *PPT Working Paper No 7*, Centre for Responsible Tourism, International Institute for Environment Development and ODI, London, pp1–23

WINBAN (Windward Islands Bananas Growers Association) (1993) *Report of the Productivity Constraints Phase I*, Winward Islands Banana Growers Association, Research and Development Division, Castries, St Lucia

Part 3

Planning and Development of the Peri-Urban Zone

11

The Inevitable Illusiveness of 'Sustainability' in the Peri-Urban Interface: The Case of Harare

Tanya A. S. Bowyer-Bower

What constitutes the peri-urban interface (PUI)?

Assumptions and questions

The peri-urban interface (PUI) is one zone of cities that has commanded a mounting volume of attention among geographers during recent times (Allen, 2003). The designation PUI suggests that it refers to where urban areas interface around their periphery with non-urban areas, usually assumed to be rural. It thus suggests three categories of land: urban, rural and peri-urban (the latter presumably could equally be accurately called peri-rural interface).

Several questions arise from this interpretation:

- Does the PUI exist as a physically locatable zone for any given urban area, and if so, what criteria best identify its physical location?
- Are there types of activities that are distinctive to the PUI that help to distinguish peri-urban from urban and rural?
- Are there activities that are, in fact, found in all three areas, but – if located in the peri-urban – which take on a particular distinctiveness from the same activity undertaken in either urban or rural areas?
- If the PUI does not exist as a physically locatable zone, how instead is it identifiable, and what is the benefit to geographical research of the widespread use of the term PUI?
- Does the PUI have value as a theoretical concept that proves useful to types of geographical enquiry; if so, what is this distinctive value that would apparently be lacking if the concept of the PUI did not exist?

Attempts to identify criteria for locating the PUI as a peripheral zone of an urban area

It is unlikely that there are land uses, whether in the developed or developing world, that are universally distinctive to the PUI. Instead, such factors as the distinctive topography, hydrology, politics, economics, society or culture of an area are likely to be more dominant in determining the location of land-use types (Potter and Lloyd-Evans, 1998). For example, industry or housing may be located in satellite towns some way distant from the main urban area (for example, Kafue, an industrial satellite town for Lusaka, and Chintungwiza, a residential satellite town for Harare) or adjacent to a node of transport that could be in the urban centre (such as an estuary or highway), rather than on the urban periphery. Waste processing may occur in urban centres since this is closer to the supply of wastes, or because of the growth of the city beyond its original urban periphery (as, for example, modelled in Asia by McGee and Greenberg, 1992), or instead outside the urban area on rural land where such locations often prove more economical, or where the task may be environmentally less challenging. Equally it is not uncommon to find agricultural practices within the urban core of cities, frequently despite being against regulations and by-laws (see UNDP, 1996, for examples). Occurrences of this nature suggest there is not, in fact, any distinctive type or set of land uses that identifies an urban periphery.

It has been suggested that a spatial definition of what constitutes peri-urban can, instead, be based on the livelihoods present – specifically, where livelihoods undertaken involve the natural resources present, such as land for food, water and fuel, and space for living (see, for example, Brook and Dávila, 2000). No criteria have been set, however, that define the extent to which livelihoods need be dependent upon natural resources, either in terms of what proportion of the population present should be engaged in these natural resource-based livelihoods or what proportion of the livelihoods undertaken should be based on natural resources. Furthermore, some studies interpreting the PUI in this way have a poverty focus such that they exclude from their analysis natural resource use by the non-poor and therefore may not be representative of what actually constitutes the peri-urban area. Others exclude practices of the livelihood in the urban core or rural areas, or exclude non-resource livelihoods that might also coexist. While such studies are valid in their own right, they tend to end up being livelihood-based studies focused on, for example, market gardening (Manshard, 1992), livestock rearing (Orskov, 1994; Schiere, 2000), waste processing (Furedy, 1992; Hasan, 1999) and brick-making (Ngweyama and Nyasulu-Ng'ombe, 2000), rather than being PUI-focused studies. The livelihoods in question are probably also present in the urban core or in rural areas; thus, the peri-urban distinctiveness of such studies is unclear.

It could be considered that some threshold in the population density or land use could, instead, be a deciding factor in what is urban, rural or peri-urban. This, however, would undoubtedly be site specific and so again, even relatively quantifiable universal rules are unlikely. Ribbons of urban development (urban) and lack of urban development (rural) also frequently exist within any one 'urban' area, often depending upon such factors as landscape, politics, land-use history, and/or demography (Potter and Lloyd-Evans, 1998).

A municipal boundary generally delimits the land area that is managed and controlled by municipal bodies based on municipal laws and other rules of governance. The area of land included in such boundaries often changes through time as cities evolve. Some are generous in their size, ready to accommodate urban growth, and thus incorporating significant proportions of 'rural' land (for example, Lilongwe in Malawi). Others are already well overtaken by urban growth, with urban land uses having long since spilled over their boundaries (McGee and Greenberg, 1992), often with no shift in administrative boundaries to reflect this spread. Some cities accommodate both of these features simultaneously (for example, Lusaka in Zambia). It follows that if the PUI zone is taken as the land in the proximity of the municipal boundary of an urban area, depending upon the urban area in question, this could be predominantly urban or predominantly rural, rather than any peri-urban distinctiveness having validity.

It thus becomes apparent that identifying the physical location of a PUI zone in terms of land-use type, density or location of administrative boundaries is problematic. More conceptual understandings of what constitutes the PUI thus also need exploration and provide a better key to achieving peri-urban sustainability.

Identifying the PUI conceptually

Conceptually, the PUI could instead be interpreted as being where rural and urban land uses co-exist. Such coexistence can be in the core of urban areas (urban based), within what otherwise are rural areas (rural based), or in a clear interface or mixed area between the two (mixed location). Some areas of the 'interface' for any one region may be contiguous, and others may be fragmented. Critical issues, which may be the focus of research, would then be those that arise from this coexistence of rural and urban land uses wherever that may be (that is, not confined to the urban periphery); for example, rural land areas being taken over by urban sprawl, agriculture being undertaken within the urban core, or industry and housing development taking over the agricultural land of rural areas. The drivers behind such dynamics can be both forces of wealth (for example, urban industry or high-income housing development taking over the agricultural land of rural areas) and forces of poverty (for example, agriculture being undertaken in the urban core as a self-help strategy of the urban poor).

In determining the PUI as where rural and urban land uses coexist, it is the impacts of the interaction of these rural and urban land uses that may well be unique. The impacts of interaction typical of these areas may include competition for land where essential but low-value uses may become priced out of the area; issues of pollution; contamination; loss of amenity; and so on. A range of forces (probably interrelated and including, for example, social, political, economic, market, demographic and environmental factors) are likely to be involved; as such, in studies of, for example, their sustainability, the peri-urban areas would benefit from multidisciplinary study.

Are governance issues part of what makes the PUI distinct?

A main argument in this chapter with regard to the view that the PUI exists where rural and urban land uses merge is that, particularly in the developing world, governance issues add important distinctiveness to these peri-urban areas.

Although governance issues for urban and rural land uses are generally incorporated within urban and rural governance structures, respectively, where the PUI involves rural land uses in urban areas or urban land uses in rural areas, sometimes these end up being outside the jurisdiction of the governance structures that prevail in the area. Second, where they occur in proximity to the urban periphery, there are instances where such peripheral areas of competing land uses may not be recognized by either the urban or rural governance structures due to a lack of clarity of where officially defined urban land ends and where rural land officially begins (Bowyer-Bower, 1996a). A third factor is simply weak, ineffective or corrupt governance (Bowyer-Bower, 1996b), which is not distinctive to the PUI but may have particularly severe impacts there, such as the effects being more irreversible.

A fourth factor is that where there is a void of clear and/or effective formal governance, informal governance in the form of community negotiated and administered rules of management and control may develop (Santos, 1979; Castells, 1996). Such means of informal governance are by no means confined to the peri-urban, but may dominate due to the prevalence of these circumstances that weaken the effectiveness of formal governance. Informal means of governance may well coexist with the formal, and this may be in harmony or in conflict.

The extent to which these governance attributes characterize the PUI of developing countries and the implications for achieving sustainability in the PUI are now explored in more detail by analysing the practices of cultivating urban public land in the urban core and periphery of Harare, Zimbabwe.

Investigating constraints to achieving sustainability in the PUI

Empirical case study: Cultivating urban public land in Harare, Zimbabwe

The need for the urban poor to cultivate urban public land
From the late 1980s, economic structural adjustment programmes (ESAPs) were being implemented in Zimbabwe, with their effects increasingly felt from the early 1990s. Main features of such adjustments include trade liberalization, streamlining the public sector, privatization and cost-recovery measures on public services (Seralgeldin, 1989; Government of Zimbabwe,

1991). The implications for worsening hardship among the urban populations in particular are recognized (Seralgeldin, 1989; Jesperson, 1992). Public-sector jobs were not compensated by private employment and local industries collapsed on becoming undermined by trade liberalization. At the same time, price controls were removed, resulting in dramatic increases in the prices of some goods (for example, of fuel, with implications for the costs of transport, and some staple foods) such that average and minimum wages rapidly declined in real terms (Balleis, 1993) and government expenditure on public services was cut (health by 20 per cent and education by 14 per cent between 1991 and 1992 alone; Balleis, 1993), resulting in consumer charges for these services being introduced.

Of all the needs of the urban poor, food is among the most fundamental. In 1990, low-income families in Harare were typically spending more than 70 per cent of their income on food, compared with 10–40 per cent for higher income families (Drakakis-Smith and Kivell, 1990). This meant that when, for example, in August 1992 the effects of ESAP measures (in this instance, the removal of price subsidies) resulted in a 50 per cent increase in the cost of maize meal (the staple food) and 65 per cent increase in the cost of bread in one day alone (*The Herald*, 6 August 1992), the ability of urban poor families to meet their food needs became particularly challenged.

Unsurprisingly, therefore, the urban population's dwindling formal livelihood options have been accompanied by a rise in informal livelihood options as a survival strategy. These include opportunistically planting crops in otherwise unused tracts of urban public land (for example, roundabouts, roadside verges, vacant building plots, parkland and railway embankments) at the onset of the rainy season in the hope of obtaining a harvest of subsistence food crops (mostly maize) using rain-fed cultivation techniques to supplement the family food supply and, possibly, also income (Bowyer-Bower and Drakakis-Smith, 1996).

The prevalence of the cultivation of urban public land in Harare during the 39-year period of 1955–1994 is presented in Table 11.1.

Studies investigating the prevalence of such urban agriculture in developing world cities include Bowyer-Bower and Drakakis-Smith (1996) and Mbiba (1995) for Zimbabwe; Freeman (1991) for Kenya; Maxwell and Ziwa (1992) for Uganda; Mlozi et al (1992) for Tanzania; Rakodi (1985) for Zambia; Ganapathy (1983) for India; Thaman (1978) for Fiji; Losada et al (1998) for Mexico; Dasso and Pinzas (2000) for Peru; Yi-Zhang (1999) for China; and Yue-man (1985) for Asia.

The suitability of open space areas in Harare for rain-fed cultivation

Another reason why the cultivation of urban public land in Harare became widespread is the fact that Harare is built on the headwaters of five drainage basins where the city and its suburbs are dissected by vlei land (seasonally waterlogged drainage ways). Such land in urban areas is not favoured for construction (Tomlinson and Wurzel, 1977), and in rural areas is a prized location for agriculture because of its favourable hydrology, being the first to receive water from the surrounding area at the onset of the rains and the last

Table 11.1 *Extent of area of cultivated public land in Harare, 1955–1994*

Year of aerial photograph coverage	Area of public land cultivated (hectares)	% of total land area of Harare[3] that is cultivated	% of open space area of Harare[4] that is cultivated
1955	267[1]	0.5	1.0
1965	1066[1]	1.9	4.0
1972	1399[1]	2.5	5.5
1978	3696[1]	6.6	14.0
1980	4762[1]	8.5	18.5
1990	4822[2]	8.6	26.9
1994	9288[2]	16.6	33.50[5]

Notes: [1] Information obtained from Mazambani (1982)
[2] Information derived from ENDA (1994)
[3] 55,900ha (land area of the Harare Municipality determined from *1989 Surveyor General 1:33,333 Map of Harare*, Government Printer, Harare)
[4] 41% of the total area of the Harare Municipality (determined from *1989 Surveyor General 1:33,333 Map of Harare*, Government Printer, Harare)
[5] Estimated 57% of this cultivated area is vlei land
Source: adapted from Bowyer-Bower and Drakakis-Smith, 1996

to retain water as the dry season progresses (Rattray et al, 1953, Theisen, 1975; Whitlow, 1983). These 'wetlands in drylands' (Scoones and Cousins, 1991) are therefore also favoured for rain-fed cultivation in the urban environment.

The prohibition of city cultivation

Cultivation in vlei areas and, indeed, elsewhere in the city is, however, illegal. First, the cultivation of vlei land is prohibited by the Streambank Protection Regulations of the Natural Resources Act (Government of Zimbabwe, 1952), forbidding cultivation in any wetland or within 30m of the banks of any body of water or stream (including ephemeral water courses). Chapter 125 of the Protection of Lands By-Laws of the Municipal Act (Government of Zimbabwe, 1973) also forbids cultivation of any sort on municipal land without the prior written approval of the authorities, and gives the authorities permission to destroy, without prior notice, any cultivation in contravention of this by-law. Similar legislation in other African countries is widespread; but the extent, severity and effectiveness of implementation vary.

The minutes of Harare City Council document well that there has been a confusing hierarchy of city organizations and officials involved in implementing the legislation since the 1970s. It includes the Department of Health, Housing and Community Services (DHHCS) through its mandate to determine and manage the provision of the community's needs; the Department of Town Planning and Works (DTPW) through its role in land-use planning; the Finance and Development Committee (FDC) through obtaining rents for activities carried out on municipal land; the municipal police, providing agronomic supervision; the Natural Resources Board (NRB), providing information on the regulations of the Natural Resources Act; AGRITEX (Agricultural Extension Services) for their research informing the guidelines used in land conservation and management; the Ministry of Education for undertaking awareness programmes educating school children of the illegality of cultivating public land; the director of works and the director of community services for overseeing the control of the cultivation activities in low-density and high-density suburbs, respectively; and the town clerk, whose role includes communicating the actions, findings, recommendations and requests between the above mentioned bodies and people (Bowyer-Bower, 1996c).

During the 1980s and 1990s, in particular, actions by the Harare authorities to prohibit the cultivation of public land were considerable. They included air drops of leaflets stating the Natural Resources (Protection) Regulations and warning of the authorities' entitlement to destroy cultivation undertaken in defiance of the regulation. Similar leaflets were delivered to households and placed as advertisements in newspapers. In 1985, the city council physically demarcated Harare's stream banks with wooden stakes, and notices were attached warning that cultivation between the notice and the riverbank was illegal. Many such stakes were uprooted for homestead fencing, and iron supports firmed with concrete were recommended for future use (*The Herald*, 6 September 1985). The municipal police patrolled the wetlands and watercourses to report activities undertaken illegally, and to warn those involved of the illegality of their actions (*The Herald*, 23 October 1982). The destruction of crops grown in contravention of the relevant legislation has been undertaken by council 'slasher squads' (*The Herald*, 7 November 1985). Crucially, given how widespread the cultivation has been, since it is illegal, it falls outside the remit of the agricultural extension services responsible for advising and helping to facilitate environmentally sustainable practices.

Despite all of the actions implemented to curb the cultivation of urban public land, not only has the practice continued, but it has also become more and more widespread (see Table 11.1; see also *The Herald*, 16 December 1984, 28 November 1990, 1 March 1992).

Factors controlling unsustainable practice

Bowyer-Bower and Tengbeh (1997) demonstrated how very simple indigenous soil conservation measures and guidelines could significantly reduce the more negative environmental impacts (where present) of cultivation activities in Harare. The implementation of such measures, however, made cultivation more visible (and thus more risky) and required greater investment (so that cultivators had more to lose if they had their crop destroyed). However, agricultural extension services to advise on the greater environmental sustainability of these measures could not be provided as this cultivation was illegal. Thus, it was the illegality of the practice that resulted in it being undertaken in ways that caused environmental damage (Bowyer-Bower and Tengbeh, 1997). If legalizing urban agriculture meant agricultural extension services would become available to urban cultivators, not only could city cultivation become a secure livelihood option where suitable land was available, but also an environmentally sustainable one. Moreover, the further benefits to improved urban food security, reduced urban poverty, reduced rural dependency of urban populations, improved urban health, and released income for the purchase of other goods and service could also be enjoyed.

Conflict between formal and informal governance: Inevitable illusiveness of sustainability in the PUI

Because of the evident need for the urban poor to be able to undertake this opportunistic activity, an ongoing pattern of conflict has been in existence from at least a decade prior to independence in 1980. This is a conflict between the episodic prevalence of formal and informal governance, which has manifested itself in a conflict between those who want to cultivate and those who want to prohibit cultivation (Bowyer-Bower, 1997a). The annual pattern to this conflict is summarized in Figure 11.1.

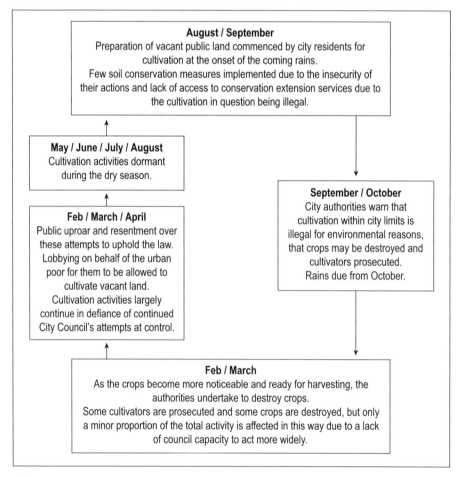

Figure 11.1 Typical annual pattern of conflict surrounding illegal cultivation activities in Harare

Source: collated from minutes of meetings of the Harare City Council, 1974–1992

A conceptual analysis to identify governance controls on achieving sustainable PUI: Case study of cultivating urban public land in Harare

Analysis of this pattern reveals six distinct groups of 'actors' (see column 1 of Table 11.2), each of distinct motive (column 2 of Table 11.2), which condense into three sets of actors when viewed in terms of their desired result (column 3 of Table 11.2). Four conflicting required governance scenarios then become apparent if each of the three sets of actors is to achieve its desired result (column 4 of Table 11.2), with each having different implications for the sustainability of the environment and for meeting the needs of the poor (columns 5 and 6 of Table 11.2).

Deconstruction of the situation presented in Table 11.2 shows that those who are 'pro-all cultivation' (groups e and f) are, in fact, the more powerful players in the existing conflict. The dominance of their actions is being helped by inadequate formal governance and is environmentally unsustainable since it is undertaken outside formal controls. An alternative governance scenario for this group of actors would be a change in the law to allow the occurrence of urban cultivation to be controlled by market forces (whereby a main controlling factor would be, for example, the price of land). However, this would undoubtedly result in the urban poor being denied access to the livelihood (by being priced out by market forces) that has long since been a relatively available coping strategy. In the absence of the availability of other livelihood options to replace what the practice of cultivating urban land can offer the poor, a change to a situation of urban cultivation being controlled by market forces will not be popular. If unsustainable in human terms, then the status quo is likely to resume and environmental sustainability will again be threatened.

The 'pro-poor cultivators' and 'pro-environment; anti-cultivators' are the other two sets of actors depicted in Table 11.2. The 'pro-poor cultivators' (groups a and b) want cultivation by the urban poor to be allowed. Their activities again are controlled by informal governance structures and processes. They require the implementation of formal governance to be inadequate, and they use moral argument to justify their actions.

The 'pro-environment; anti-cultivators' (groups c and d) believe cultivation should be prohibited on environmental grounds and base their argument on the existing law, the need for environmental protection, and/or the need for urban areas to exist for urban functions. They require adequate effective implementation of the existing formal governance structures and processes to achieve this. If effective, this would be a means of achieving a sustainable environment. Effectiveness, however, is unlikely in the prevailing economic climate as this option would not address the needs of the poor.

With regard to this case study in Harare, much lip service has been paid to the need for policy changes to resolve the ongoing conflict, which is typical of a number of developing world cities, but without progress (Bowyer-Bower, 1997a, 1997b; Mbiba, 1999, 2000). This chapter has revealed that this is, perhaps, not surprising – the existing scenario is one of a three-way power play between moral argument, the law and governance. The effectiveness of

Table 11.2 *Analysis of components controlling the sustainability of cultivating urban public land in Harare*

Groups of actors involved	Motive of group	Desired result	Required governance scenario to achieve desired result	Whether this would be environmentally sustainable	Whether this addresses the needs of the poor
Pro-poor cultivation					
(a) Urban poor cultivators	A self-help strategy for withstanding economic hardship	Cultivation should be allowed to be undertaken by the urban poor	A change in the law to allow and support pro-poor cultivation	Yes	Yes
(b) City authority bodies and employees who fail to uphold the law	Support for the moral right of low-income residents				
Pro-environment; anti-cultivation					
(c) Residents who wish the law to be upheld	Concern for the urban environment/ proper urban activities	Cultivation should be prohibited on the grounds of environmental protection	Existing law to be upheld and implemented effectively	Yes	No
(d) City authority bodies and employees who uphold the law	Law abidance/the needs of the urban environment				
Pro-all cultivation					
(e) Non-poor urban-resident cultivators	Opportunistic gain	Cultivation should be allowed to be undertaken and governed by market forces	Continued failure to implement existing law or	No	To some extent
			change in the law to allow urban cultivation based on market forces	Yes	Unlikely
(f) City authorities and employees whose actions to prohibit the cultivation of urban public land are ineffective and/or incomplete	Political favour/ corruption/ management actions constrained by capacity				

governance here is controlled by the interplay between coexisting formal and informal governance structures and processes, with a play of power between the two. The environmental sustainability of the PUI is at the mercy of this. This issue is thus one of vested interest and power played out in a perpetual conflict between formal and informal governance structures and processes where, as reported by Bowyer-Bower (1997a, 1997b) and Mbiba (1999, 2000), little progress has been made in decades to either identify or resolve the nature of the conflict within and between the many factions involved.

Conclusions

This chapter has thus argued that a conceptual understanding of what constitutes the peri-urban – in particular, that it is where rural and urban land uses coexist, which may be in contiguous or fragmented units in any one area – has greater validity as a basis for peri-urban studies than identifying the PUI as an urban periphery (suggesting an outer edge). It is then easier for the distinctiveness of such areas to lie in the dynamics of the juxtaposition of rural and urban, wherever these may occur in otherwise urban or otherwise rural locations, or a mixed location on an urban periphery.

Focusing on the idea of distinctive governance issues being important in determining the sustainability of these coexisting land uses, the illegal cultivation of public land in Harare has been explored as a case study. This chapter has shown that a power play exists between coexisting formal and informal means of governance that perpetuate conflict. A consistent pattern of contrasting motives of differing groups of actors, requiring four possible but divergent governance scenarios if their desired outcomes are to be achieved, has been revealed. It is argued here that circumstances of coexisting formal and informal governance, often typical of the PUI, can be manipulated too readily to perpetuate this conflict.

The importance of effective governance in determining whether land-use practices are undertaken sustainably is clear; but in peri-urban Harare, this has not been achieved. It is argued here that a means of bringing together formal and informal processes of governance will be required in order to change the current illusiveness of sustainability in the PUI. It is suggested that approaches of this nature to analysing the sustainability of land-use activities where rural and urban land uses coexist are vital if the sustainability of the PUI is to be more readily understood and, ultimately, secured.

References

Allen, A. (2003) 'Environmental planning and management of the PUI: Perspectives on an emerging field', *Environment and Urbanization*, vol 15, no 1, pp135–147
Balleis, P. (1993) *A Critical Guide to ESAP*, Mambo Press, Gweru
Bowyer-Bower, T. A. S. (1996a) *A Review of the Environmental Implications of the Urban and Peri-Urban Farming Activities of Kano City, Northern Nigeria*, Report of the NRI-BUK City Cultivation Project, Natural Resources Institute, Chatham

Bowyer-Bower, T. A. S. (1996b) 'Criticism of environmental policy for land management in Zimbabwe', *Global Ecology and Biogeography Letters*, vol 5, pp7–17

Bowyer-Bower, T. A. S. (1996c) 'Environmental protection and the control of urban agriculture in Harare, Zimbabwe', in Eden, M. J. and Parry, J. T. (eds) *Land Degradation in the Tropics: Environmental and Policy Issues*, Pinter Press, London, pp222–233

Bowyer-Bower, T. A. S. (1997a) 'The potential for urban agriculture to contribute to urban development in Africa – dilemmas of current practice and policy', *Geographical Journal of Zimbabwe*, vol 28, pp1–6

Bowyer-Bower, T. A. S. (1997b) 'Conflicts for resolution and suggestions for consensus: Legalising urban agriculture in Harare', *Geographical Journal of Zimbabwe*, vol 28, pp53–59

Bowyer-Bower, T. A. S. and Drakakis-Smith, D. (1996) *The Needs of the Urban Poor versus Environmental Conservation: Conflict in Urban Agriculture*, Final Report of ODA-ESCOR Project R5946, Overseas Development Administration, London

Bowyer-Bower, T. A. S. and Tengbeh, G. (1997) 'Environmental implications of (illegal) urban agriculture in Harare', *Geographical Journal of Zimbabwe*, vol 28, pp7–24

Brook, R. M. and Dávila, J. D. (eds) (2000) *The Peri-Urban Interface: A Tale of Two Cities*, School of Agricultural and Forest Sciences, University of Wales and Development Planning Unit, University College London, Bangor and London

Castells, M. (1996) *The Rise of the Network Society*, Blackwell, Oxford

Dasso, A. and Pinzas, T. (2000) 'NGO experiences in Lima targeting the urban poor through urban agriculture', in Bakker, N., Dubbeling, M., Gundel, S., Sabel-Koschella, U. and de Zeeuw, H. (eds) *Growing Cities, Growing Food, Urban Agriculture and the Policy Agenda*, DSE, Feldafing, pp349–361

Drakakis-Smith, D. and Kivell, P. (1990) 'Urban food distribution and household consumption: A study of Harare', in Findlay, M. A., Paddison, R. and Dawson, J. A. (eds) *Retailing Environments in Developing Countries*, Routledge, London, pp235–247

Freeman, D. B. (1991) *A City of Farmers: Informal Urban Agriculture in the Open Spaces of Nairobi, Kenya*, McGill-Queen's University Press, Montreal

Furedy, C. (1992) 'Garbage: Exploring non-conventional options in Asian cities', *Environment and Urbanization*, vol 4, no 2, pp213–218

Ganapathy, R. S. (1983) *Development of Urban Agriculture in India: Public Policy Options*, Ahmedabad

Government of Zimbabwe (1952) *The Natural Resources Act*, Government Printers, Harare

Government of Zimbabwe (1973) *The Municipal Act*, Government Printers, Harare

Government of Zimbabwe (1991) *Zimbabwe: A Framework for Economic Reform (1991–1995)*, Government Printers, Harare

Hasan, A. (1999) *Understanding Karachi: Planning and Reform for the Future*, City Press, Karachi

The Herald (23 October 1982) 'City cops to watch for river bank crops', *The Herald*, Harare

The Herald (16 December 1984) 'Streambank cultivation on the increase in Harare', *The Herald*, Harare

The Herald (6 September 1985) 'Streambank cultivation tour ends in fiasco', *The Herald*, Harare

The Herald (7 November 1985) 'Streambank slasher squads strike', *The Herald*, Harare

The Herald (28 November 1990) 'Streambank cultivation rife', *The Herald*, Harare

The Herald (1 March 1992) 'City plans strategy on illegal cultivation', *The Herald*, Harare

The Herald (6 August 1992) 'Shock rise in price of meal and bread', *The Herald*, Harare

Jesperson, E. (1992) 'External shocks, adjustment policies and economic and social performance' in Cornia, G. A., van der Hooven, R. and Mkandawire T. (eds) *African Recovery in the 1990s: From Stagnation and Adjustment to Human Development*, St Martin's Press, New York, pp9–52

Losada, H., Martinez, H., Vieyra, J., Pealing, R. and Cortes J. (1998) 'Urban agriculture in the metropolitan zone of Mexico: Changes over time in urban, sub-urban and peri-urban areas', *Environment and Urbanization*, vol 10, no 2, pp37–54

Manshard, W. (1992) 'Agricultural change: Market gardens in West African urban communities – the case of Ouagadougou, Burkino Faso', in Raza, M. (ed) *Development and Ecology: Essays in Honour of Professor Mohammad Shafi*, Rawt Publications, Jaipur and New Delhi

Maxwell, D. and Ziwa, S. (1992) *Urban Farming in Africa: The Case of Kampala Uganda*, ACTS Press, Acts studies, Nairobi

Mbiba, B. (1995) *Urban Agriculture in Zimbabwe: Implications for Urban Management and Poverty*,Ashgate Publishing, Avebury

Mbiba, B. (1999) 'Urban agriculture in Southern and Eastern Africa: Policy questions and challenges', in Grossman, D., van den Berg, L. M. and Ajaegbu, H. I. (eds) *Urban and Peri-Urban Agriculture in Africa*, Ashgate Publishing, Avebury, pp36–48

Mbiba, B. (2000) 'Urban agriculture in Harare: Between suspicion and repression' in Bakker, N., Dubbeling, M., Gundel, S., Sabel-Koschella, U. and de Zeeuw H. (eds) *Growing Cities, Growing Food: Urban Agriculture on the Policy Agendas – A Reader on Urban Agriculture*, DSE, Feldafing, pp285–302

McGee, T. G. and Greenberg, C. (1992) 'The emergence of extended metropolitan regions in ASEAN', *ASEAN Economic Bulletin*, vol 1, no 6, pp5–12

Mlozi, M. R. S., Lupanga, I. J. and Mvena, Z. S. K. (1992) 'Urban agriculture as a survival strategy in Tanzania', in Baker, J. and Pedersen, P. O. (eds) *The Rural–Urban Interface in Africa: Expansion and Adaptation*, Scandinavian Institute of African Studies, Uppsala, Sweden, pp284–294

Ngweyama, D. C. and Nyasulu-Ng'ombe, M. V. (2000) *An Economic Analysis of Environmental Impact of Small Scale Quarrying in Zambia: The Case of Lusaka Province*, Publication ESF/005, Pilot Environmental Fund, Environmental Support Programme, Ministry of Environment and Natural Resources, Lusaka, Zambia

Orskov, R. (1994) 'Landless livestock keepers', *ILEIA Newslette*, vol 10, no 4, p24, Centre for Information on Low External Input Sustainable Agriculture, The Netherlands

Potter, R. B. and Lloyd-Evans, S. (1998) *The City in the Developing World*, Addison Wiley Longman, Singapore

Rakodi, C. (1985) 'Self reliance or survival? Food production in African cities with particular reference to Zambia', *African Urban Studies*, vol 21, pp53–63

Rattray, J. M., Cormack, R. M. M. and Staples, R. R. (1953) 'The vlei areas of Southern Rhodesia and their uses', *Rhodesia Agricultural Journal*, vol 50, pp456–483

Santos, M. (1979) *The Shared Space: The Two Circuits of the Urban Economy in Underdeveloped Countries*, Methuen, London

Schiere, J. B. (2000) *Peri-Urban Livestock Systems: Problems, Approaches and Opportunities*, FAO, Rome, and IAC, Wageningen

Scoones, I. and Cousins, B. (1991) *Wetlands in Drylands – The Agroecology of Savannah Systems in Africa, Part 3f, Key Resources for Agriculture and Grazing: The Struggle for Control over Dambo Resources in Zimbabwe*, IIED, London

Seralgeldin, I. (1989) *Poverty, Adjustment and Growth in Africa*, World Bank, Washington, DC

Thaman, R. (1978) 'Urban agriculture and home gardening in Fiji: A direct road to development and independence', *Transactions of the Proceedings of the Fiji Society*, vol 14, pp1–28

Theisen, R. J. (1975) 'Development in rural communities', *Zambezia*, vol 4, pp93–98

Tomlinson, R. W. and Wurzel, P. (1977) 'Aspects of site and situation', in Kay, G. and Smout, M. (eds) *Salisbury, Rhodesia*, Hodder and Stoughton, London

UNDP (United Nations Development Programme) (1996) *Urban Agriculture – Food, Jobs and Sustainable Cities*, UNDP Publication series for Habitat II, vol 1, UNDP Press, New York, and University Press, Oxford

Whitlow, R. (1983) 'Vlei cultivation in Zimbabwe', *Zimbabwe Agricultural Journal*, vol 80, pp123–135

Yi-Zhang, C. (1999) 'Case study: Urban agriculture in Shganghai', *GATE Technology and Development*, no 22 (April–June), pp18–19

Yue-man, Y. (1985) *Urban Agriculture in Asia*, United Nations University, Food-Energy Nexus Programme, Paris

12

Peri-Urban Development in Gampaha District, Sri Lanka

Nimal Dangalle and Anders Närman

Introduction

The urban–rural interface, variously known as the urban fringe, the rurban zone, the urban field, the peri-urban area or the urban periphery, performs an important role in the urbanization process of a country. Since peri-urban areas are involved in a process of transition, they cannot be precisely defined spatially. However, it is not difficult to identify a set of common characteristics specific to these areas. They are situated within the metropolitan areas of a country but often outside the formal urban boundaries (of municipalities and urban councils) and urban jurisdictions. Describing the peri-urban area of Metropolitan Bangkok, Webster (2004) identifies it as an area beyond suburbia where industrialization is occurring rapidly, yet agriculture and other rural activities coexist with the modern economy. Being a zone in transition, both agricultural and non-agricultural activities can be found in these areas. However, the agricultural and rural characteristics are gradually being replaced by urban landscapes with attendant changes in people's lifestyles. Demographically, this is a fast-growing area. The continuous inflow of people from both the urban core and the rural hinterland has resulted in a complex social fabric.

The rapid transformation that has been taking place in the demography, society, economic structure, land-use and infrastructure network in peri-urban areas has both advantages and disadvantages. From the perspective of a development planner, the peri-urban zone offers a number of solutions to the industrial, commercial, residential and urban problems faced by the economy. The locational advantages possessed by these areas have, in many instances, made them the focus of modern economic activity such as export promotion zones. In the case of Sri Lanka, both the Katunayake-Katana and Biyagama export promotion zones have been located in the urban periphery. In Thailand, the Eastern Seaboard Industrial Estate and Ayutthaya, new industrial estates producing automobiles and electronics, respectively, have been located outside Bangkok's daily commuter radius (Webster, 2004).

Furthermore, in accordance with the new economic policies that promote the private sector as the 'engine of growth', the urban periphery is being considered an ideal location for a number of modern high-tech and high-value industrial ventures. In Sri Lanka, for instance, computer software manufacturing companies and educational institutes specializing in information technology are increasingly being located in the peri-urban area of the capital, Colombo. The high return from the enterprises compared to the costs of land and other amenities, room for future expansion, location away from the established industrial areas, ability to attract skilled and semi-skilled labour from both the urban core and rural periphery, and favourable response from the local government administration have been some of the factors that have encouraged the location of high-tech enterprises in the peri-urban areas. Furthermore, property developers are locating upper middle-class housing complexes in these areas. The increasing demand for land has pushed land values upward, thereby tempting rural residents to sell their land and migrate into the rural periphery.

Viewed from a micro-local perspective, on the other hand, these changes, accompanied by an increase in population, have created a number of problems in peri-urban areas. It may be said that the social, economic and infrastructural capacities of peri-urban areas, in most cases, were not prepared for the changes to take place in a short period of time. For instance, the rapid rate of industrialization in these areas has resulted in a number of environmental problems due to the inadequacies in drainage and waste disposal facilities. The problem has further been aggravated by the conversion of agricultural land into residential blocks by the real estate industry. Industrialization and expansion of settlements have increased the demand for services; but the service infrastructure, in many instances, is inadequate to meet even basic needs. As van den Berg et al (2003) reveal, farmers in the southern outskirts of Hanoi, Vietnam, face a number of problems, such as the loss of agricultural land-use rights, increased seasonal flooding and water contamination by city wastes. As in many other cities, the relationship between urban planners, consumers, rural communities and horticultural producers is uneasy and generally not constructive.

Although not apparent at first glance, the economic, social, cultural and political implications of urban development cannot be underestimated. The declining agricultural economy, caused mainly by the loss of agricultural land and displaced labour, has been replaced by a dependent economy controlled by the urban core. Rural youth who seek employment in the new industrial and service sectors find it increasingly difficult to adapt themselves to the norms and standards stipulated by the companies controlling the employment market in these urbanizing areas. At the same time, the high rate of migration has changed the social mix of the residential population. The disappearance of agriculture and rural lifestyles has not only changed the rural economy, but also the rural normative value systems. A more or less closely knit rural society has now become a heterogeneous and loosely knit collection of individuals with different religious, ethnic, social and political identities.

Objective

The main objective of this chapter is to examine the social, economic and environmental costs of peri-urban development in one metropolitan district in Sri Lanka – Gampaha. It is one of the three districts that constitute the Colombo Metropolitan Region (CMR). Although Gampaha became a separate administrative district in 1979 after being part of Colombo district for a long time, the significant role it has been playing as an urban field to the urban core of Colombo has not diminished. Figure 12.1 shows the spatial distribution of the peri-urban area of Colombo that spreads over a vast area of Gampaha and Kalutara districts (see also Wanasinghe, 1984; UDA, 1998). This peri-urban area has been described as having mixed urban/rural uses by the Urban Development Authority of Sri Lanka (UDA, 1998). The spatial extent of this area, however, has been marked in terms of administrative divisions: in the Colombo district, for example, it covers the district secretariat divisions (DSDs) of Kaduwela, Maharagama and Kesbewa; in Kalutara district, the divisions of Matugama, Dodanduwa, Bandaragama and Milleniya; and in Gampaha district, the divisions of Gampaha, Biyagama and Mahara have been identified as a zone with mixed urban and rural uses. Understandably, the total area covered by these DSDs cannot be designated as peri-urban: in some instances, the area adjacent to the urban core is predominantly urban, as in the case of Maharagama in the Colombo district. At the other extreme, some divisions identified as rural are fast becoming peri-urban – for example, Gampaha division in Gampaha district. The peri-urban zone around the urban core is in transition, being constantly pushed outwards towards the rural periphery.

It is interesting to note that almost all of the area identified as peri-urban in this study has been designated as rural in the 2001 Census of Population and Housing. An urban population has been enumerated only in the Gampaha DSD; but it comprised only a very small percentage of the total population (5.9 per cent) (DCS, 2001). The underestimation of the urban characteristics in the peri-urban zone reflects the administrative criteria applied by the government in the demarcation of urban areas: all local government areas administered by municipalities and councils are considered to be urban areas. A major characteristic of the peri-urban zone, therefore, is the underestimation of its urban population. However, the use of land for urban purposes in this zone has been increasing at a very rapid rate during recent times (UDA, 1998).

Gampaha district: An overview

The district of Gampaha, located in the north of Colombo district, covers an area of 1387 square kilometres. For administrative purposes, the district has been divided into 13 DSDs (see Figure 12.2). These 13 DSDs comprise 1177 *Grama Niladhari* divisions (GNDs), the lowest spatial unit of the administrative hierarchy. According to the 2001 Census of Population and Housing, Gampaha was the second-most populated district in the country with 2 million people. However, the increase in population between the census years of 1981

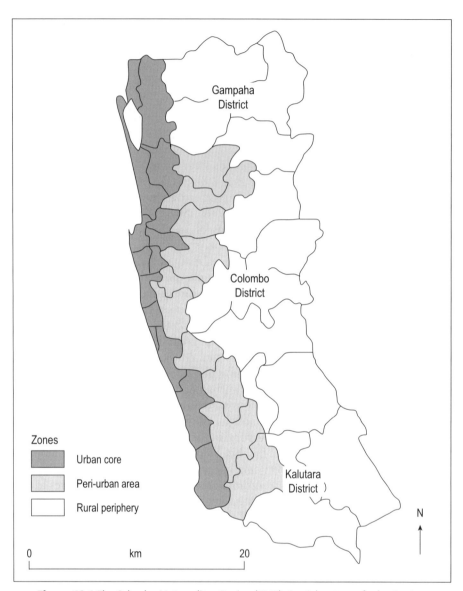

Figure 12.1 The Colombo Metropolitan Region (CMR): Spatial pattern of urbanization

Source: Redrawn by Jenny Kynaston from author's original

and 2001 was much higher in Gampaha (48.5 per cent) compared to that in Colombo district (31.5 per cent). The net addition of population in Gampaha district over this period was 675,000, the highest experienced by any district in Sri Lanka (DCS, 2001). In some of the DSDs, however, the growth rate has been much higher, such as in Katana DSD. In terms of population density, with 1541 persons per square kilometre, Gampaha is second only to Colombo district in the country. A main contributory factor to the increase in population and population density has been net migration. In some DSDs, nearly 30 per

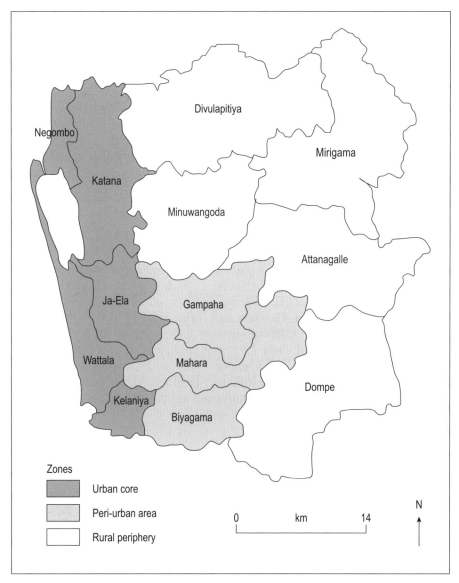

Figure 12.2 Gampaha district: Spatial pattern of urbanization

Source: Redrawn by Jenny Kynaston from author's original

cent of the population have been born outside the district (DCS, 1997).

In comparison to most other Sri Lankan districts, Gampaha is relatively developed from a modernization and economic point of view. It has been identified as belonging to the developed core of the country, where economic and social development standards are above the national average. Moore's (1984) study of spatial patterns of development in Sri Lanka identified Colombo district together with Kalutara, Galle and Matara as constituting the core of the country; and Gampaha was part of Colombo district at that time. According to O'Hare and Barrett (1996), development in Sri Lanka has occurred along an axis/corridor extending from the south-west to north-east, and Gampaha was in the south-west corner of the development corridor:

> *... there is evidence of a swathe of districts with high development running from the south-west of the island (Colombo, Gampaha, Kalutara, Galle and Matara) through the central highlands (Kegalle, Nuwara Eliya and Kandy) to the north and east (Polonnaruwa and Trincomalee) ... [and] on either side of the development axis there are districts with significantly lower development levels (Badulla, Anuradhapura, Kurunegala, Batticaloa)* (O'Hare and Barrett, 1996, p121).

The United Nations Development Programme's (UNDP's) national human development report identified Gampaha as a wealthy industrial district (UNDP, 1998, p14). Nearly 20 per cent of the total industrial enterprises in Sri Lanka (the second largest concentration of industries in any district) are located in Gampaha district. The district also enjoyed a higher level of human development, with a Human Development Index of 0.851 in 1994, well above the national average of 0.753. Disaggregation of the components of the Human Development Index would show how well Gampaha district fared in some areas of social development. For instance, access to knowledge and information, on average, was high: the adult literacy level was 95 per cent, the highest in the island, and the combined primary-, secondary- and tertiary-level enrolment rate was around 40 per cent.

Peri-urban development in Gampaha district

However, Gampaha is still a largely rural district, with only 14.6 per cent of the total population classified as urban (DCS, 2001). It is evident from the district land-use maps that only 1.6 per cent of the total area can be classified as urban land. Nearly 91 per cent of the land, including homesteads, has been classified as agricultural. However, the land classified as homesteads is being used mainly for residential purposes. On the other hand, the percentage of urban land area in some of the DSDs is much higher than the district average – for example, Kelaniya (7.6 per cent), Negombo (6.2 per cent), Ja Ela (4.8 per cent) and Wattala (3.7 per cent). Furthermore, the built-up urban area has grown rapidly in the recent past. Although Gampaha, as a whole, has been classified as a rural/agricultural district, its urban characteristics are increasing. Some of the DSDs of Gampaha district – for example, Kelaniya, Wattala, Ja Ela, Negombo and part of Katana – already lie within the urban core (see Figure 12.2). Since the 1980s, with the spatial diffusion of the effects of economic reforms, the adjacent divisions such as Biyagama, Mahara, Gampaha and some parts of Katana have become the peri-urban area of the district. The remaining divisions – namely, Divulapitiya, Mirigama, Minuwangoda, Attanagalle and Dompe – are considered as the rural periphery (UDA, 1998).

In the process of peri-urban expansion, the residential or dormitory utility of the district has played a pioneering role. In 1996, nearly 53 per cent of the land area of the district was being utilized as homesteads – that is, for residential purposes (see Table 12.1; see also DCS, 1996). The pioneering dormitory areas of the 1970s have changed their functions and have now become part of the urban core (for example, Kelaniya, Ja-Ela and Peliyagoda). However, the fact that the residential utility of land has been increasing implies that the residential frontier would move further into the fringe. As some studies have shown, people from other districts find residence in Gampaha district mainly due to its proximity to Colombo. A study carried out on a housing scheme located in Nittambuwa township in Gampaha district, a few kilometres from the city of Colombo, revealed that out of a total of 161 families surveyed, 77 (48 per cent of the total) have migrated from Colombo district. Another 29 families, 18 per cent of the total, had migrated from districts further away, such as Kurunegala, Kegalle and Kandy. A considerable number of these migrants are employed in Colombo (Hettiarachchi, 2000).

Table 12.1 *Gampaha district, Sri Lanka: Changes in land-use pattern, 1981–1996*

Land-use category	1981		1996		
	Extent (hectares)	% of total	Extent (hectares)	% of total	Change (hectares)
Urban built-up area[1]	2220	1.6	3217	2.3	997
Homestead [2]	69,670	49.8	73,991	52.9	4,321
Trees and other					
Tea	10	0.0	10	0.0	–
Rubber	5190	3.7	4336	3.1	–854
Coconut	25,000	17.9	20,981	15.0	–4019
Other	1920	1.4	1920	1.4	–
Cropland					
Paddy	22,550	16.1	18,743	13.4	–3807
Abandoned	120	0.1	3776	2.7	3656
Other	2140	1.5	2238	1.6	98
Forest	1390	1.0	1259	0.9	–131
Scrub and grass	940	0.7	940	0.7	–
Wetland	3490	2.5	3077	2.2	413
Water	4620	3.3	4620	3.3	–
Barren land	610	0.4	699	0.5	89
Total	139,870	100.0	139,870	100.0	–

Notes: [1] Urban built-up area: residential (including hotels), industrial, commercial, institutional, administrative, transportation, power plants and urban open spaces
[2] Homesteads: family residential units surrounded by home gardens and open space; cultivation includes fruit trees, spices, vegetables and small holdings of coconut, rubber, tea and plantation crops
Source: UDA,1998

The centrality index value (29.0) of the Colombo municipality area, which contains the heart of Colombo district, is more than twice the value of Gampaha district's highest-order urban locality, the Negombo municipality area (13.1) (UDA, 1998). Compared to Colombo's index value, all urban centres in Gampaha district score relatively low. The fact that the Colombo urban core offers a wide variety of services and Gampaha lies in close proximity to the core has enabled the residents of Gampaha district to utilize those services while remaining in the urban periphery. A study on commuting from Gampaha to Colombo conducted during the mid 1990s revealed the number of people who utilize these services: more than 125,000 people commute daily from Kirillawela (a locality situated on the Colombo–Kandy Road) to the Colombo municipality area (Department of Geography, 1996).

The increase in the utility value of Gampaha district as an urban field of the Colombo core region could also be attributed to the district's extensive transport network. The Colombo–Kandy Road crossing the district has created a few nodes, from which extensive road networks extend into the interior. These networks, accompanied by major railroads passing the district, have not only facilitated people to commute to Colombo, but have also acted as arteries along which the urbanization process has reached the peripheral boundaries of the capital metropolis.

Another contributory factor to the urban transformation of the district has been the expansion of industrial activities. Gampaha was a preferred district for the location of industrial estates by the government even at the beginning of the process. In 1963, as a counter-magnet to the private sector-dominated Ratmalana industrial complex in the southern outskirts of Colombo district, an industrial estate was located by the government at Ekala in the Ja Ela division. Subsequently, during the late 1970s and early 1980s when the government decided to establish export processing zones, Gampaha district again became a preferred location. Compared to the area south of Colombo, which was already congested with industrial establishments, the relatively less densely populated Gampaha district in close proximity to Colombo was ideal for the location of new industries.

The industrial expansion in Gampaha district exerted a multiplier effect that resulted in an increase in population, service industries and other related enterprises. Between 1985 and 1993, the number of industrial units increased by 96.4 per cent (see Table 12.2). However, in the DSDs of Biyagama (757 per cent), Katana (728 per cent), Gampaha (620 per cent), Kelaniya (447 per cent), Wattala (404 per cent), Ja Ela (300 per cent) and Negombo (288 per cent), the growth was very much higher than average. The rapid growth in the number of industrial units in the DSDs of Biyagama and Gampaha indicates the increasing significance of the peri-urban region in locating the new industries. Although the increase was somewhat slower in the DSDs of Mirigama (187.5 per cent) and Attanagalle (184.6 per cent), it does show that urban activities are also expanding into the rural periphery.

Table 12.2 *Gampaha district: Industries and industrial employment*

District secretariat division (DSD)	1998 status[1]	Number of industrial units (1985)	Number of industrial units (1993)	Number of persons employed (1985)	Number of persons employed (1993)
Gampaha	PU	10	72	802	3488
Minuwangoda	R	12	9	2025	1054
Ja Ela	C	34	136	3776	22672
Wattala	C	24	121	1646	13531
Weke	R	10	8	270	2108
Mahara	PU	122	31	2250	3534
Kelaniya	C	19	104	1763	13997
Divulapitiya	R	25	12	2140	250
Katana	C	18	149	1450	71289
Mirigama	R	8	23	589	379
Attanagalle	R	13	37	818	4735
Negombo	C	16	62	2501	6839
Biyagama	PU	7	60	522	34059
Total		425	835	60549	386984

Notes: [1] C = core; PU = peri-urban; R = rural
Source: UDA, 1998

The increase in the number of industrial units has also resulted in an increase in the number of industrial workers. In Gampaha district, as a whole, the number of persons employed in industries increased by 539 per cent between 1985 and 1993. The most remarkable growth took place in peri-urban Biyagama DSD, where the number of persons employed in industries increased by 6424 per cent; by comparison, Gampaha DSD's 335 per cent increase appears almost modest. The rate of growth in Mahara DSD is somewhat lower, being only 57 per cent. In fact, the growth has occurred in spite of a decline in the number of industrial units, suggesting that there has been an increase in their size. The DSDs of Wattala (722 per cent), Kelaniya (694 per cent), Ja Ela (500 per cent) and Katana (482 per cent) in the urban core also registered high growth rates. The DSD of Attanagalle, identified as rural but located next to peri-urban Gampaha and crossed by the Colombo–Kandy highway, also recorded a high growth rate (479 per cent). Meanwhile, some other rural DSDs – for example, Minuwangoda and Divulapitiya (see Figure 12.2) – experienced a decrease in the number of industrial units and industrial workers between 1985 and 1993 at the expense of the increase in peri-urban areas.

The cost of peri-urban development

The process of peri-urban development involves, among other things, a rapid increase in population coupled with a change in the demographic and social structure, transformation in land use from agriculture to urban, and expansion

in economic activities in favour of industries and services. As long as prepara-
tory measures have been adopted to take care of the changes taking place,
hardly any major problems should arise. However, in the absence of such
preparations, unplanned peri-urban development will result in a number of
problems. In this section, an attempt is made to show that although Gampaha
district has achieved a comparatively high level of economic and social development, the process has not been cost free.

In Gampaha district, as elsewhere, peri-urban development has been associated with two main transformations: first, a rapid increase in the size and
density and a change in the composition of population and, second, a spatial
expansion of urbanization-related economic activities in the form of industries
and services into the urban fringe. Although the effects of these transformations on the economic, social, cultural and political landscape have been
substantial, the authorities' attention has been focused more on the changes
that have taken place in the environmental profile of the region.

The situation in Gampaha district is no exception. For example, in the
Colombo Metropolitan Regional Structure Plan's volume on Gampaha district,
attention has been focused particularly on the environmental problems associated with the increase in the district's urban population. According to the
report, the rapid conversion of agricultural land into residential uses has
created a number of problems. These include extensive and often uncontrolled
filling of low-lying land, resulting in blocked drains and canals and frequent
floods during rainy seasons, indiscriminate dumping of domestic wastes on
vacant land, increasing use of marshy areas as waste dumping sites, and health
problems due to foul odours and toxic gases emanating from the dumps,
resulting in diseases related to flies and mosquitoes (UDA, 1998).

The resource profiles prepared by the respective divisions of the district
provide ample evidence for these environmental problems. For instance, the
resource profile of the Ja Ela DSD has pointed out that due to the unavailabil-
ity of proper drainage systems, waterlogged areas polluting the environment
could be seen within the city limits of Ragama, Kandana and Ja Ela (Ja Ela
District Secretariat, 1990). According to the data profile of the Gampaha
district, environmental problems associated with sewage due to the small size
of landholdings could be seen even in peripheral divisions such as Divulapitiya
(Gampaha District Secretariat, 2002). Problems associated with the disposal of
solid waste can be attributed to the increase in residential area, as well as to
industrialization.

According to the Ministry of Forest Resources and Environment (1999)
report on the disposal of solid waste by local governments in Sri Lanka,
Gampaha district ranks third most problematic after Colombo and Jaffna
districts. In some of the divisions in the district, however, there were no suitable methods for the disposal of solid waste. For instance, in the Mahara
Pradeshiya Sabha (PS) area (located in the peri-urban region), waste is collected
once a week; but there is no method to dispose of it. At present, marshy areas
are being used as dumping sites by the authorities. In fact, in some of the local
government areas such as Negombo Municipal Council (core), Kelaniya PS
(core), Peliyagoda Urban Council (core), Gampaha PS (peri-urban) and

Katana PS (core), no land is available for dumping purposes (Ministry of Forest Resources and Environment, 1999). As officially demarcated sites are not available, refuse is dumped into the vacant lands and marshes.

Perhaps the most visible ill effects of urban expansion on the environment are associated with increasing industrialization. As mentioned earlier, Gampaha district has been a popular site for industrial location due mainly to its proximity to Colombo. However, the unplanned location of industries without adequate attention to their environmental implications has resulted in a number of problems. UDA (1998) has identified a large number of enterprises in the divisions of Wattala, Ja Ela, Negombo and Katana as high-polluting industries.

The Ekala Industrial Estate in Ja Ela DSD provides an example of a severe environmental problem: contamination of drinking water. Established in 1963 with 17 industries, the Ekala Industrial Estate now has 105 industrial enterprises. This increase, accompanied by rapid growth of population due to migration, has adversely affected the carrying capacity of the industrial estate. A recent study of the Ekala area found that 60 per cent of the industrial enterprises, whose products are chemicals, asbestos, textiles, plastics and dry batteries, are responsible for severe water contamination. The absence of waste-water treatment methods and release of polluted water into canals and natural water bodies have polluted the wells from which nearly 70 per cent of the residents of the area obtain drinking water (Department of Geography, 1999).

The resource profile of Ja Ela division mentioned above has commented specially on the water pollution and environmental damage caused by one factory, Union Carbide, located just outside the Ekala Industrial Complex (Ja Ela District Secretariat, 1990, p65). A similar problem has been detected in the Japalawatte Industrial Estate located in the Minuwangoda DSD. Due to the absence of a proper drainage system, the wastewater discharged from the industries flows through private landholdings, resulting in contamination of local wells, the principal drinking water sources (Gampaha District Secretariat, 2002, p44).

Economic and social problems

The peri-urbanization of Gampaha district through industrialization and expansion of residential areas has affected the economic base of the district in many ways, most importantly the declining significance of agriculture. For example, in 1984, according to the district land-use maps published by the Sri Lankan Department of Survey, 51.4 per cent of the total area of Gampaha district was occupied by residential uses (49.8 per cent) and urban built-up area (1.6 per cent). This had risen to 55.2 per cent (residential area, 52.9 per cent, and built-up area, 2.3 per cent) by 1996, registering an increase of 3.8 per cent – that is, 5318ha (UDA, 1998). Almost all of this increase had been at the expense of agricultural land, mainly coconuts, paddy and rubber. As pointed out by UDA: 'The changing pattern of the land-use characteristics during the last 15 years indicates that the concentration of urban growth and urban activities in lands formerly under agricultural use remains very high' (UDA, 1998, p31). Table 12.1 shows that the district's coconut and paddy area declined by some 4000ha and 3800ha, respectively between 1981 and 1996.

The loss of agricultural land has been acute in the peri-urban divisions. For example, a study of the conversion of coconut lands into residential lands, using data provided by auctioneers and advertisements appearing in the news-papers, revealed that during the decade of 1980 to 1990 a vast number of coconut lands were transformed into housing plots in the peri-urban DSDs of Mahara, Gampaha and rural Attanagalle (Department of Geography, 1992). In Mahara DSD, for instance, where the total area was only 98.8 square kilo-metres, the number of coconut lands that were converted into housing plots increased from 4 in 1980 to 55 by 1990 (see Table 12.3). It is also evident that conversion of coconut lands into housing plots has been relatively less in both the urban and rural divisions, an indication of the pressure exerted on agricul-tural land in the peri-urban area.

The loss and forced abandonment of paddy land has been another prob-lem faced by local people, especially in low-income groups. The filling-in of paddy lands and other low-lying areas for residential and commercial purposes is a common sight along the Colombo–Kandy road. As official sources reveal, the abandonment of paddy land is greater in the DSDs of Gampaha, Katana and Mahara, where the rate of urbanization is at a high level. In the divisions of Dompe, Attanagalle, Biyagama and Minuwangoda, too, the pace of paddy land being put to other uses has been on the increase. It must also be noted that the unplanned and uncontrolled way of land filling and building construc-tion have resulted in poor drainage and loss of wetlands; in some instances, the storm-water floods during the rainy season have become a severe problem (Chandrasena, 2001).

Table 12.3 *Gampaha district: Number of coconut lands converted into housing plots, 1980–1990*

District secretariat division (DSD)	1980	1990	Increase
Gampaha	3	31	28
Minuwangoda	1	11	10
Ja Ela	2	17	15
Wattala	1	3	2
Dompe	0	15	15
Mahara	4	55	51
Kelaniya	0	9	9
Divulapitiya	0	6	6
Katana	0	3	3
Mirigama	0	9	9
Attanagalle	3	24	21
Negombo	0	10	10
Biyagama	0	6	6
Gampaha District	14	199	185

Note: The study did not report the area of each landholding
Source: Department of Geography, 1992

The change in land use has not only reduced the area under food crops but has also, through increased demand, resulted in an escalation of land values. During the last two decades, paralleling the introduction of the liberalized economy, Gampaha district has witnessed a sharp increase in land values. The residential and commercial utility value of land in the district, especially in the DSDs served by main roads and feeder roads, could be seen in the proliferation of real estate agents participating in the land market and increased fragmentation of agricultural land. The availability of land for residential purposes at relatively cheap rates compared to that in Colombo and Kalutara, the other two districts of the Colombo Metropolitan Region, has attracted a large number of migrants into the district.

As the demographic survey of Sri Lanka showed, in some of the divisions located in the peri-urban area of Gampaha district, migrants constitute a sizeable proportion of the total population. For example, in Mahara DSD, only 59.6 per cent of the total resident population had been born in the same division; 27.7 per cent had migrated from other districts; and another 12.6 per cent had come from the other divisions in the Gampaha district (see Table 12.4). As revealed by studies, land values in some of the peri-urban locations have been increasing at an alarming rate. In Yakkala, between 1980 and 1990, land values rose by 600 per cent; in Gampaha, by 150 per cent; and in Ganemulla, by 100 per cent (Chandrasena, 2001). Land values have risen not only in peri-urban localities, but also in rural areas with accessibility. As Abeygunawardana (1995) has shown, the value of land increased at an annual rate of 19.3 per cent in Mahara PS area between 1978 and 1994; during the same period, Biyagama PS area recorded an annual rate of increase of 27.7 per cent.

Table 12.4 *Gampaha district: Population by place of birth and usual residence by district secretariat divisions (DSDs)*

DSD of usual residence	Status[1]	Place of birth				Total %
		Same as DSD of usual residence	Outside DSD but within district	Other district	Outside Sri Lanka	
Gampaha District		68.2	10.9	20.8	0.1	100
Attanagalle	R	73.4	10.7	16.0	0.0	100
Biyagama	PU	63.9	11.1	25.0	0.1	100
Divulapitiya	R	78.5	11.2	10.3	0.0	100
Dompe	R	79.8	9.1	11.0	0.1	100
Gampaha	PU	67.2	11.7	21.0	0.1	100
Ja Ela	C	71.5	10.7	17.6	0.2	100
Katana	C	57.8	15.0	27.0	0.1	100
Kelaniya	C	53.8	7.9	38.2	0.1	100
Mahara	PU	59.6	12.6	27.7	0.1	100
Mirigama	R	74.4	11.7	13.9	0.0	100
Minuwangoda	R	73.9	11.4	14.6	0.0	100
Negombo	C	77.6	7.5	14.8	0.1	100
Wattala	C	60.5	9.4	29.7	0.4	100

Notes: [1] C = core; PU = peri-urban; R = rural
Source: DCS, 1997, 1996

It must also be noted that real estate has become a lucrative business and many investors have entered the land market during recent years. According to Abeygunawardana (1995), an investment made in land would yield a much higher return compared to that from a fixed deposit in the National Savings Bank. For example, an investment of 100 rupees with the National Savings Bank made in 1978 would have increased to 1158 rupees by 1994; but the same investment in land in Biyagama area would have yielded 4678 rupees during the same period. The entry of migrants and speculators to the land market has affected the poor adversely and they have been pushed further into the periphery and environmentally sensitive areas in their search for land.

As stated in the Colombo Metropolitan Regional Structure Plan, the urbanization process in Gampaha district will be intensified with the sponsored development of three growth centres – namely, Katunayake-Negombo, Gampaha and Biyagama. The UDA of Sri Lanka has projected a high rate of population growth (3 to 5 per cent per annum) in these growth centres for the next 20 years in terms of population and land use (UDA, 1998, p14). In the Katunayake-Negombo Growth Centre, according to the plan, population will grow at a rate of 3.3 per cent per annum, and by the year 2010 there will be a population of 430,000. It is expected that the industrial, residential and commercial share of land use will be 71 per cent of the total land area. In the Gampaha Growth Centre, on the other hand, the population will increase at 4 per cent per annum to reach 262,000 by 2010. A major portion of the total land (40 per cent) will be devoted to residential purposes; but the land used for industrial purposes will also be substantial. In the third growth centre, Biyagama, population growth was forecast at 2.5 per cent annually, and in the year 2010 it is expected to have a population of 285,000. Industries will occupy 40 per cent of the land area and residential use 15 per cent.

Conclusions

Since the liberalization of economic policies during the late 1970s, urbanization in Sri Lanka has been increasing at a rapid rate. This is especially true of the urban expansion that has taken place in the CMR that encompasses the Western Province. The urban core of the CMR has been invading the existing peri-urban zone; in turn, the peri-urban zone is expanding into the rural periphery. During the recent past, the peri-urban zone has been an area of attraction in locating modern enterprises associated with a large number of migrants from the periphery.

Even if there have been plans to expand industrial activities in certain parts of the larger metropolitan region into the peri-urban areas, this is also the reason for pollution and an uncontrolled informal-sector industrialization. This will lead to a demand for land which will create a competition with other uses such as agriculture. The same is the case for demand required for new residential areas, both for high-class buildings for the elite, as well as squatter settlements. In a way, the demand for land is making it increasingly more difficult to provide for the daily demands of food in a growing urban environment.

References

Abeygunawardana, G. W. G. (1995) 'Land values in the Colombo urban areas', *Economic Review*, June/July, pp34–36

Chandrasena, U. A. (2001) 'Land use changes and related issues in the suburban environment in Colombo Metropolitan Region of Sri Lanka', in Singh, R. B., Fox, J. and Himiyama, Y. (eds), *Land Use and Cover Change*, Science Publishers, Inc, Enfield (NH), US

DCS (Department of Census and Statistics) (1996) *Demographic Survey, 1994, Sri Lanka: Report on Housing and Basic Amenities, Release 2*, DCS, Ministry of Finance and Planning, Colombo, Sri Lanka

DCS (1997) *Demographic Survey, 1994, Sri Lanka: Report on Demographic Characteristics of the Population, Release 3*, DCS, Ministry of Finance and Planning, Colombo, Sri Lanka

DCS (2001) *Census of Population and Housing 2001*, Preliminary Release Department of Census and Statistics, Ministry of Finance and Planning, Colombo, Sri Lanka

Department of Geography (1992) *Utilization of Coconut Lands for Housing Development in Gampaha District*, BA thesis, University of Kelaniya, Kelaniya, Sri Lanka, SL 2131

Department of Geography (1996) *An Analysis of Daily Commuting between the City of Colombo and Suburbs*, BA thesis, University of Kelaniya, Kelaniya, Sri Lanka, SL 2867

Department of Geography (1999) *Water Pollution due to Industries in the Ekala Area*, BA thesis, University of Kelaniya, Kelaniya, Sri Lanka, SL 3750

Gampaha District Secretariat (2002) *Compendium of Data: Gampaha District*, District Planning Secretariat, Gampaha, Sri Lanka

Hettiarachchi, K. G. P. (2000) *Social Mobility and Urban Housing Schemes*, MSc thesis, University of Kelaniya, Kelaniya, Sri Lanka

Ja Ela District Secretariat (1990) *Resource Profile*, Planning Division, Divisional Secretariat, Ja Ela

Ministry of Forest Resources and Environment (1999) *Data Compendium on Solid Waste Disposed by the Local Government Institution Areas in Sri Lanka*, Colombo

Moore, M. (1984) 'Categorising space: Urban–rural or core-periphery in Sri Lanka', in Harriss, J. and Moore, M. (eds) *Development and the Rural–Urban Divide*, Frank Cass, London, pp102–122

O'Hare, G. P. and Barrett, H. R. (1996) 'Spatial socio-economic inequalities in Sri Lanka: Core-periphery frameworks', *Tijdschrift voor Economische en Sociale Geographie*, vol 87, no 2, pp113–123

UDA (Urban Development Authority of Sri Lanka) (1998) *Colombo Metropolitan Regional Structure Plan, vol 2*, UDA, Ministry of Housing and Urban Development, Colombo

UNDP (United Nations Development Programme) (1998) *Sri Lanka: National Human Development Report*, UNDP, Colombo

van den Berg, L. M., van Wijk, L. S. and Van Hoi, P. (2003) 'The transformation of agriculture and rural life downstream of Hanoi', *Environment and Urbanization*, vol 15, no 1, pp35–52

Wanasinghe, Y. A. D. S. (1984) 'Rural–urban fringe of Colombo: A zone in transition', *Vidyodaya Journal of Arts, Science and Letters, Special Jubilee Issue*, vol 12, pp152–170

Webster, D. (2004) 'Bangkok: Evolution and adaptation under stress', in Gugler, J. (ed) *World Cities beyond the West: Globalization, Development and Inequality*, Cambridge

University Press, Cambridge, pp82–118

Zelinsky, W. (1977) 'Coping with the migration turnaround: the theoretical challenge', *International Regional Science Review*, vol 2, pp175–178

13

The National Highway Bypass around Hubli-Dharwad and Its Impact on Peri-Urban Livelihoods

Kiran C. Shindhe

Introduction

Future population growth will be particularly rapid in the urban areas of less developed regions, averaging 2.4 per cent per year during 2000 to 2030, consistent with a doubling time of 29 years (United Nations Population Division, 2001). The projections of this study mean that the need for urban infrastructure development is bound to increase. The development of roads is one of the prime necessities. This is validated by the current Golden Quadrangle project to develop a four-lane highway connecting India's four metropoles: New Delhi, Mumbai, Bangalore and Kolkata.

Urban infrastructure development almost always occurs at the cost of rural livelihoods and the main resource affected is almost invariably peri-urban and rural land, which in India, a predominantly agricultural economy, provides the major source of livelihood for the poor. There is a very definite relation between development of roads, land-use changes and livelihoods.

However, there have been relatively few studies in India of the development of roads and the effects on land-use changes and livelihoods. Studies using geographical information systems (GISs) have charted urban growth along the roads (for example, Jothimani, 1992; Fazal, 2000, 2001a, 2001b). Fazal (2001a, 2001b) notes that Indian cities tend towards linear development along the roads, leading to speculative purchases of agricultural lands, which are left vacant for considerable time. Thangvel's (2000) study of Chennai concludes that linear development of cities along transport corridors will occur unless there is planning intervention to facilitate development of other areas.

The comparable study conducted by Salau and Baba (1984) of a Nigerian highway examined the effect of development of a road on its immediate locality. This study stressed the need for both macro- and micro-analysis in order to understand the complex forces engendered by the road development. Salau and Baba note that most development projects at that time only conducted a narrow cost-benefit analysis on the basis of road usage only.

The Hubli-Dharwad peri-urban interface (PUI)

There are broadly two approaches to defining the peri-urban interface (PUI): spatially, as a transitional zone around a city and, second, as a zone of intense interactions, flows and linkages between urban and rural areas.

With reference specifically to land transactions in relation to urban–rural interactions, Tacoli (1998) suggests that land markets and land uses in many rural areas around cities 'become increasingly influenced by real-estate developments. Intensive land development, sub-division and sale may take place although with little building construction as many urban residents make speculative purchases in anticipation of increases in land value linked to urban expansion.' Speculative land purchasing is understood to be characteristic of peri-urban areas, where competition for land, particularly between agricultural uses and more 'urban' activities is prevalent (Brook and Dávila, 2000).

The baseline study for UK Department for International Development (DFID)-funded research in the Hubli-Dharwad PUI (University of Birmingham et al, 1998) states that the Hubli-Dharwad PUI may loosely be defined as the area included within the Hubli-Dharwad city region, but outside the core urban area and encompassing the villages connected to Hubli and Dharwad by city bus services. Brook and Dávila (2000, p16) further proposed that the Hubli-Dharwad PUI can be defined as the area undergoing changes due to growth of the twin cities and the increased connectivity with them, and that such areas can be represented by the villages outside the twin cities which have experienced such changes.

For the purposes of this chapter, the PUI is regarded as an area (or, more correctly, areas) of intense urban–rural interaction, which includes more intense purchase of agricultural land, particularly for urban and speculative purposes, than that seen in other areas within and around a city. Such intense land transactions have implications for governance and policy, as well as for agricultural practice, for both rural and urban authorities.

As Nunan (2001, p390) notes, there are 'challenges concerning coordination and cooperation between institutions that arise within the peri-urban interface', requiring planning and management approaches that integrate the aspirations of urban and rural areas and better reflect the dynamic nature of the interface. There is, therefore, a need to investigate the opportunities and threats posed by urban development such as a major road to the livelihoods of the people in the PUI, and to study how women and children are affected, particularly the poor, and what are the coping strategies adopted. This study is needed to inform policies to make the whole process of inevitable urbanization more acceptable and the ensuing transition smoother.

This study has been conducted to identify the effects of urban infrastructure development in the form of a national highway bypass, the associated land-use changes and the effects on the livelihoods of the people. Of the 12 villages through which the bypass road passes, two villages with peri-urban features were selected for detailed analysis.

The study area

Hubli-Dharwad, located in Karnataka State, south-west India (see Figure 13.1), is a conurbation comprising the urban areas of Hubli and Dharwad, which are some 20km apart. It is about 400km north-west of the state capital, Bangalore, and approximately 600km south-east of Mumbai (formerly Bombay). The two were brought together under the Hubli-Dharwad Municipal Corporation (HDMC) in 1962, thus making it the third largest urban agglomeration in Karnataka State after Bangalore and Mysore. In 1991, Hubli-Dharwad had a population of 648,298, which grew to 786,018 by the 2001 census (a 21.2 per cent increase).

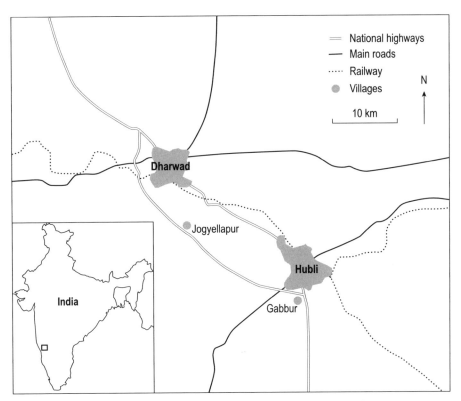

Figure 13.1 Location of the Hubli-Dharwad bypass and study villages

A national highway bypass was proposed during 1981, as the traffic on the then National Highway NH-4 connecting Bangalore and Poona, passing through Hubli and Dharwad cities, had become dense, leading to congestion and frequent accidents. The cities also grew along this major transport corridor, resulting in increased traffic-related problems. The bypass spans a distance of 31 km, passing through 12 villages (see Figure 13.1).

The planning of the bypass originated with a survey; but little information was given about the purpose to the local residents. The advent of the bypass was heralded through land acquisition notices served to the landowners in 1982, and land acquisitions started in 1986. A system of compensations was agreed, and some compensation was paid at this time. Initially, it was proposed that the government, specifically the National Highway Department, would construct and maintain the bypass. The work started at different spots; but the project ran into problems regarding acquisition. There were also insufficient funds and the project was not prioritized by the state government. During 1997–1998, the project resumed when the government awarded the contract to a private company, Nandi Highway Developers (NHDL), as per the build–own–operate–transfer (BOOT) scheme. Accordingly, the NHDL had to fund the construction, pay the remaining compensations and contract to maintain the road for a period of 26 years. The company would be allowed to collect a toll. However, the villagers contend that the terms of contract between the government and NHDL have not been disclosed to them.

According to the contract, the road was to be constructed as per the regulations of the Ministry of Surface Transport (MOST), which stipulate that for major roads such as this, fences must be constructed along both sides of the road to prevent people and livestock crossing the road, to ensure smooth flow of traffic, prevent accidents and avoid structures leading to congestion. The road has to be patrolled by security guards to prevent any traffic flow problems. Underpasses, culverts and pipelines have to be constructed to facilitate the movement of traffic, people, livestock and water. On either side of the bypass a service road is to be constructed for local traffic.

Construction eventually began in 1998 and the bypass was opened in 2000. However, service roads were not constructed at all appropriate places along the bypass.

Gabbur and Jogyellapur were the villages selected for this study (see Figure 13.1). The selection criteria were as follows:

- villages affected by construction of the bypass;
- villages exhibiting peri-urban characteristics such as rural–urban flows and linkages (Adell, 1999);
- speculative land purchases were occurring (Brook and Dávila, 2000).

Gabbur is located at the junction of the old national highway and the new bypass (see Figure 13.1). It is closer to the urban centre than Jogyellapur. Gabbur was absorbed within the HDMC three decades ago. Lands in Gabbur are irrigated using the sewage from Hubli city since the stream carrying sewage from Hubli courses through the village. Gabbur has a population of 600.

Jogyellapur (population 800) is located at about the mid-point of the bypass (see Figure 13.1) and is further from urban centres than Gabbur. The bypass cuts through the village, dividing the village lands. Jogyellapur was absorbed within the municipal corporation only in 1998. Almost the entire village has been severely affected by the lack of service road along the bypass and the people have organized protests. There are number of litigations regarding compensation issues. The main occupation of the villagers is agriculture and horticulture, growing rice and mangoes. There are a number of mango and sapodilla (*sapota*) seedling nurseries.

Survey methodology

The information for the study was collected from different sources. Village maps and survey data were obtained from the Revenue Office and the Roads Department of the Public Engineering Office. The bypass map was obtained from the National Highway Authority of India. The names of the landowners whose lands have been acquired were obtained from the village accountants, and the information regarding livelihoods before and after the bypass, compensation, involvement in litigation and problems faced was obtained from individual interviews with the landowners who have lost their lands.

Both villages were first reconnoitred to understand their general status. In order to investigate the effects of the bypass on the entire village, focus group interviews were conducted with villagers who have lost lands; villagers who have not lost their lands; landless labourers; and people commuting from the village to cities for jobs and trading. The landowners were both male and female. The size of the focus groups varied from 15 to 25 members, with women representing at least 25 per cent of each group. In order to ensure that their voice was properly heard, the women were also interviewed separately to obtain their opinions about the bypass.

To study the effect of the new bypass on the service providers and traders (grouped here under the term 'vendors') along the old national highway, a varying number of vendors from each village on the old highway were selected, based on their businesses such as tea shops, petty shops and shops for minor vehicle repairs. However, in one particular village where the majority of the women do all the fruit vending, all vendors were interviewed.

There have been two categories of landownership changes due to the advent of the bypass. Initially, land was acquired through government acquisition notices along the line of the road in order that road building could take place. Subsequently, speculative land purchases have taken place.

However, the limitations of the study are due to non-availability of all the private individuals who have acquired land near the bypass since most are city dwellers who purchased the lands for speculative purposes and, hence, do not live locally. It also became clear that the correct land sale price could often not be obtained because neither seller nor buyer would disclose it. Hence, the price recorded here is the price fixed by the government, where compensation for the land is based on the land value as decided by the Land Revenue Department. This varies from village to village and over time, and depends on factors such as type of soil, crops grown, proximity to village or city, and access to national or state highway.

The objective of the present study is not to explore the Land Revenue Department's methodology for calculation of compensation, but to identify problems caused by the land acquisitions and sales that should be considered for compensation. This is critical for villages on the bypass since these problems affect the livelihoods of people who do not (or no longer) own the land, but who have been directly or indirectly affected by the redistribution of land during and since the bypass construction.

Results and discussion

The data show that during the year 1997–1998, when it was decided that a bypass would be constructed, land prices of the villages increased (see Figure 13.2). The amount of land sold also increased in both villages. This peaked during the period of 1998 to 2000 in Jogyellapur, but was sustained through to 2001 in Gabbur. However, neither the landowners nor the buyers were aware that the bypass would be fenced and that direct access would be officially denied. When this became known, the price of land did not appreciate and the number of sales also decreased since the lands had lost the potential for commercial venture. The lands were mostly purchased by city dwellers hoping to start commercial ventures that needed access and, hence, were left fallow. This speculative land purchase is a typical peri-urban feature.

Gabbur

From the focus group interviews, it could be inferred that children are exposed to accident risk while (illegally) crossing the bypass (national highway) to go to school, located on the other side of the bypass. The women of the village who work as manual labourers in the fields have to spend more time reaching fields separated from the village by the bypass; there is no nearby service road and the bypass has to be crossed only at places where under-passes are located, some distance from the village. There is a shortage of grazing lands as the bypass has taken away some of the land and traversing the bypass is not feasible because of fencing on either side of the road.

Looking specifically at landowners whose land had been acquired by government, the information in Tables 13.1 to 13.4 was obtained through in-depth interviews with six such landowners. There were a further five landowners whose lands had been acquired. They were not available for interviewing as they could not be contacted.

It was observed that 45 per cent of the people in the village as a whole are not from Gabbur and are recent immigrants, and that many former residents have settled in Hubli City, abandoning cultivation. Some lands had been purchased for commercial activities, such as garages and hotels. These have been left fallow, the owners hoping to utilize them for commercial purposes. Most of the acquired lands in Gabbur were irrigated, prior to acquisition,

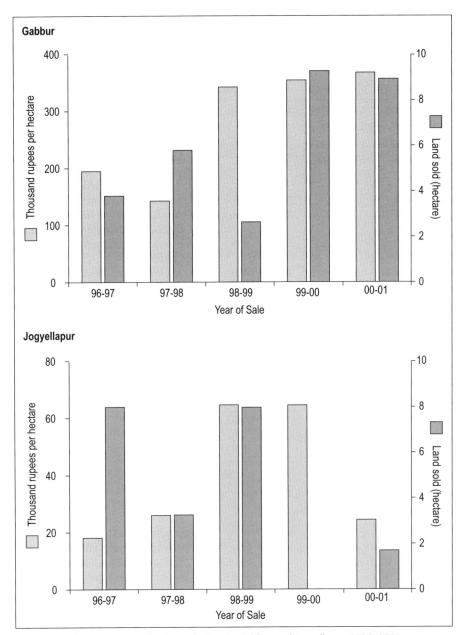

Figure 13.2 Land sales and prices in Gabbur and Jogyellapur, 1996–2001

Source: various Land Revenue Department records

using sewage flowing in a stream from the city. Crops such as sorghum, cotton, groundnut and vegetables were grown. Vegetable growing is lucrative because of the ready and continuous availability of nutrients from sewage, proximity of urban market and access to the national highway.

Table 13.1 *Details of land acquired: Gabbur survey*

Code for landowner	Land (hectares)		Loss %	Road passes through the land	Effect
	Total	Acquired			
SRM[1]	2.4	0.4	16.7	Yes	0.2ha fallow because of water logging in monsoon season. Problem of access to land. Deprived of sewage water.
SM	2	0.2	10	Yes	1.8ha fallow because of water logging in monsoon season. Problem of access to land. Deprived of sewage water.
ARM[1]	2.4	0.04	1.7	No	Unable to cultivate; sold the land.
SFS	5.6	1.4	25	Yes	Sold 1.8ha of land to Nandi Highway Developers (NHDL) and leased remaining land. Changed traditional occupation.
VRM[1]	3.2	1.1	34.4	Yes	0.2ha fallow because of difficulty to access land. Deprived of sewage water.
BRM	0.6	0.272	45.3	Yes	Water logging in monsoon season. Problem of access to land. Deprived of sewage water. Changed occupation.

Note: [1] Landowner residing in Hubli City

Table 13.2 *Income from land before and after the bypass: Gabbur survey*

Code for landowner	% of land lost	Income (thousand rupees)		Decrease %	Remarks
		Before	After		
SRM[1]	16.7	100–120	50	50–58	Sewage water not available; cannot grow vegetables and cash crops.
SM	10	150–180	Nil	100	Stopped cultivating in the land adjacent to road. Cultivating in other land away from bypass.
ARM[1]	1.7	50	Nil	100	Unable to cultivate; sold the land.
SFS	25	150–200	36	82–76	Leasing amount for 2ha land.
VRM[1]	34.4	80–90	50–60	37.5–33.3	Sewage water not available; cannot grow vegetables and cash crops.
BRM	45.3	40–50	10–15	70–75	Sewage water not available; cannot grow vegetables and cash crops. Size of land very small.

Note: [1] Landowner residing in Hubli City

In 1996, NHDL acquired more land from two additional farmers to set up a truck terminus, but later returned their land saying that they did not need it any more. Over this period, these farmers were neither allowed to enter their land to cultivate, nor were they compensated for this land.

Table 13.3 *Occupation before and after the bypass: Gabbur survey*

Code for landowner	Before	After
SRM[1]	Agriculture	Agriculture
SM	Agriculture	Agriculture
ARM[1]	Agriculture	Migrated to city; grocery shop
SFS	Agriculture	Transport business
VRM[1]	Agriculture	Shifted to growing mulberry
BRM	Agriculture	Hotel business, milk vending, agriculture labour

Note: [1] Landowner residing in Hubli City

Table 13.4 *Compensation and litigations: Gabbur survey*

Code for landowner	Land acquired (hectares)	Compensation details in 1986 (rupees)	Remarks
SRM[1]	0.4	15,000	No litigation
SM	0.2	10,000	No litigation
ARM[1]	0.04	5000	No litigation
SFS	1.4	36,000	No litigation
	1.8	430,000	Acquired for truck terminus in 1999; no litigation
VRM[1]	1.1	38,000	No litigation
BRM	0.272	13,500	No litigation

Note: [1] Landowner residing in Hubli City

Jogyellapur

The bypass has cut through the village lands. On one side lies the entire village, along with agricultural lands, and on the other side lie the other cultivated lands, school and cemetery. During construction of the bypass, in addition to the agricultural lands, lands with full-grown fruit-bearing mango trees were also acquired. One of the lands acquired contained a dam, which used to irrigate about 2ha of rice fields downstream. The bypass road has destroyed this dam and farmers downstream are deprived of the irrigation facility. In this case, a compensation payment was made for land as well as the check dam. The bypass passes over a local road leading to the village cemetery, also connecting other village lands. A service road on either side of the bypass has not been provided. The bypass itself is supposed to be inaccessible to the villagers and they cannot legitimately make use of it.

The bypass acts as a physical barrier causing water logging of lands, thus making the land unfit for growing crops. This effect is compounded by the wrong placement of drainage pipes at the higher levels despite people's advice.

Due to the lack of service roads, farmers cannot easily access their lands and the only way is to use the bypass illegally. Vehicles ply at high speed and the drivers of the vehicles, according to the regulations pertaining to national highway status, do not expect the road to be used by carts and pedestrians. Therefore, it is dangerous to travel in the carts (the main means of transportation in villages), especially at night. Furthermore, once the crop is standing, the farmers cannot access their land through other farmers' fields.

Due to a wrong classification of the planned local service road, this was designated in the construction phase as a cattle pass. Accordingly, the height and width of the passage has been constructed as 2.75m × 2.75m, respectively; but for a local service road it should be 3.75m in height × 3.75m in width. Due to this discrepancy, it is not possible to use laden tractors; thus, the villagers are forced to use carts, which can transport only one third of the quantity. Therefore, more labour, money and time are needed to transport the same quantity of materials. This was pointed out at the planning stage by local people; but their protests were ignored.

Another problem with this wrong classification is the source of embarrassment to the entire village. The major community of the village is of Hindu Lingayat caste. At funerals, the dead body is borne by four people on their shoulders. The body itself is placed on a coffin in a sitting posture. The coffin is in the form of a dome structure. The total height, inclusive of the coffin and its bearers, will exceed the height of the present cattle pass. As a result, the body has to be lowered to go across the cattle pass. According to the traditional customs, the body should be lowered only at the cemetery, which is on the other side of the village across the bypass. This causes a lot of embarrassment to the villagers, more so because people from other villages attend the funerals.

In addition, as the school is on the other side of the bypass from the village, parents have to accompany their children, resulting in loss of productive work time. People have engaged in protests and demonstrations because of the lack of service roads and have also gone to court seeking proper compensation. All of this has resulted in a loss of productive work time as well as money. The bypass has destroyed the dam and deprived the people downstream of the crop that they would have grown. The truck drivers plying on the bypass harass the village women when they use the bypass to cross over to the fields on the other side.

The outcome of eight in-depth interviews, considering the effects individually on those who have lost lands, are tabulated in Tables 13.5 to 13.8.

When the overall impacts on the two villages are considered, it is evident that the negative effects on Gabbur are less than those on Jogyellapur. For example, a wider range of alternative livelihood options appear to be present in Gabbur compared with Jogyellapur (see Tables 13.3 and 13.8). Social conflicts are also fewer in Gabbur compared to Jogyellapur, indicating a smoother acceptance of the inevitable change. A factor in this may be that Gabbur has already had the impact of urbanization well before Jogyellapur; as a result, its adaptability is much faster and smoother.

Taken as a whole, from the findings reported here and in the wider survey, it could be inferred that the division of lands into smaller fragments renders them uneconomical to cultivate and also makes them more difficult to sell. This usually more strongly affects the poor, whose land holdings are small.

Table 13.5 *Details of land acquired: Jogyellapur survey*

Code for landowner	Land (hectares)		Loss %	Road passes through the land	Effect
	Total	*Acquired*			
MBP	6.4	0.932	14.5	Yes	Loss of access to tank; 0.4ha land uncultivated since 1998 due to water logging
GCP	16	1.72	10.8	Yes	Settled in city; land leased for cultivation; loss of 35 mango trees
HDP	3.2	0.72	22.5	Yes	Intervention of road. Increase in expenses due to access problem
SDP	8.4	0.92	10.8	Yes	Loss of tank as the road passes through; 120 trees lost
SAM	3.0	1	33.3	Yes	Intervention of road. Increase in expenses due to access problem
VNV	4	2.4	60	Yes	Land is divided into three parts; difficult to cultivate; 0.2ha is fallow
CSH	10	1.26	12.6	Yes	Intervention of road. Increase in expenses due to access problem
VBA	6	1.4	23.3	Yes	Intervention of road. Increase in expenses due to access problem

Table 13.6 *Income from land before and after the bypass: Jogyellapur survey*

Code for landowner	% of land lost	Income (thousand rupees)		Decrease %	Remarks
		Before	*After*		
MBP	14.5	100–120	80–90	20–25	
GCP	10.8	500	300	40	Loss of 35 trees
HDP	22.5	40–50	20–25	50	
SDP	10.8	250–300	100–150	40–50	Loss of 120 trees
SAM	33.3	30–40	20–25	33.5–37.5	
VNV	60.0	80–90	45–50	43.2–44.4	Fallow land
CSH	12.6	150–180	120–130	20–38.4	
VBA	23.3	100–150	70–100	37.2–41.3	

Compensation is not paid pending judicial decision wherever there is a conflict for ownership, and the normal judicial procedures take quite some time as these cases are treated on a par with other (numerous) litigations.

People have less land as result of the construction of the bypass; in order to minimize this loss, they have resorted to less land-intensive practices, such as developing plant nurseries for mango and sapodilla. People who have lands on either side of the bypass have resorted to share cropping, where farmers who have lands on either side of the road will cooperate and will cultivate the

Table 13.7 *Compensation and litigations: Jogyellapur survey*

Code for landowner	Land acquired (hectares)	Compensation details (rupees) Before litigation in 1986	After litigation	Remarks
MBP	0.92	57,058	645,000	For land
			80,000	For 20 mango trees
GCP	1.72	30,000	1,016,000	For land
			140,000	For 35 mango trees
HDP	0.72	9000	300,000	
SDP	0.92	16,000	320,000	For land
			480,000	For 120 mango trees
SAM	1	Not received	Not received	Ownership to be decided
VNV	1.4	40,000		
	1 (in 1999)		440,000	
CSH	0.46	9000		
	0.8 (in 1999)	–	Not received	Ownership to be decided
VBA	0.8	60,000	–	
	0.6 (in 1999)		400,000	Including 35 mango trees

Table 13.8 *Occupation before and after the bypass: Jogyellapur survey*

Code for landowner	Before	After	Remarks
MBP	Agriculture	Agriculture; grafting and nursery	Shift
GCP	Agriculture; advocate	Leased land; practising in city	Change
HDP	Agriculture	Nursery of mango and sapodilla	Shift
SDP	Service in city; agriculture	Service in city; agriculture	No change
SAM	Agriculture	Grocery shop; grafting and nursery	Change
VNV	Agriculture and horticulture	Grafting and nursery	Shift
CSH	Agriculture	Agriculture	No change
VBA	Agriculture	Agriculture	No change

lands of both on only one side. By doing so, a person can work on one side of the road only. Poor farmers have either sold their fragmented lands or have kept them fallow, resorting to manual labour under farmers with larger land holdings since they do not have any other skills.

Effects on vendors along the old national highway

Before construction of the bypass, the national highway was catering for all the traffic, such as trucks and tourists who had to compulsorily pass through Dharwad, several intervening villages and Hubli. Vendors were dependent for their livelihoods on this road. They ran small businesses such as tea shops, petty shops and shops for minor repair of vehicles. The villagers, mainly women, were selling fruits such as guava, mango and sapodilla. The road was very convenient because of its proximity to their houses and fields.

A random survey revealed that their business had reduced from between half to zero. They wanted to begin similar business on the bypass; but regulations do not permit this. As a result, vendors are forced to rely on local customers. The women fruit vendors from villages are the most affected because they cannot leave their houses and start the same business.

Conclusions and policy recommendations

The bypass, like any other urban infrastructure, will affect rural livelihoods. The impact is more on people who lose lands and natural resources associated with the land. The poor, who have fewer lands, are affected the most as it is they who are forced to change their traditional livelihoods. They do not possess appropriate skills and have to compete with skilled urban people. This introduces a lot of uncertainty and insecurity within their lives. In contrast, people who have larger land holdings or other assets have the opportunity to change their livelihoods by adopting less land-intensive practices such as sericulture and plant nurseries, or by sinking bore wells and irrigating the remaining lands with the compensation received.

When impact on the village as a unit is considered, it is suggested that the negative effect on Gabbur is less than that of Jogyellapur. Although survey numbers are small, respondents in Gabbur showed a more diverse range of 'post-bypass' livelihood options compared to Jogyellapur. Social conflicts are also less in Gabbur compared to Jogyellapur, indicating a smoother acceptance of the inevitable change. This can most simply be explained by the fact that Gabbur is closer to the city and has better access to it, resulting in more alternate livelihood options. Another factor is that Gabbur has already experienced the impact of urbanization well before Jogyellapur; as a result, its adaptability is much faster and smoother.

The following policies are suggested so that the inevitable process of urban expansion at the cost of rural livelihoods and environment can be made more acceptable and in order to mitigate the impacts on rural lives, especially the poor in the peri-urban zone:

- The process of planning and execution should be made more participatory. This will help to identify local features and customs that will be affected.
- The current compensation procedures account for the loss of existing natural resources. Some natural resources such as dams and sewage

streams will benefit people other than those who have lost lands. Policies are needed to compensate for the loss of benefits from such resources. Such policies will address people who have not lost land but were dependent on affected resources, resulting in loss of livelihoods.

- The poor are the most affected and they are most likely to change occupations; but they lack skills for changing occupation successfully. Credit policies to help such people are needed. Policies for capacity-building are required in order to provide the necessary skills for changing occupations.
- Special judicial mechanisms to deal with ownership issues of the acquired lands only should be instituted so that quicker compensation payments can be made.
- It is necessary that areas which are affected by urbanization for the first time are given priority over previously affected areas. Policies should reflect this aspect.
- Preference should be given to rehabilitate the vendors on the previous road.

Only by learning the lessons of the mistakes made while implementing the Hubli-Dharwad bypass, and by careful and systematic planning, will the negative effects of such road schemes on those whose lands are affected be avoided. This requires a degree of political will to plan with local villagers, rather than plan without taking account of their voices.

Acknowledgements

The author wishes to acknowledge the UK Department for International Development (DFID); Dr R. M. Brook, project manager, School of Agricultural and Forest Sciences, University of Wales; Dr C. S. Hunshal, Department of Agronomy, University of Agricultural Sciences, Dharwad, India; research assistants Dr S. M. Patil and Dr Suresh; and the management of SDM College of Engineering and Technology, Dharwad, India, for continuous support and encouragement.

References

Adell G. (1999) *Theories and Models of the Peri-Urban Interface: A Changing Conceptual Landscape*, Literature review for the Strategic Environmental Planning and Management for Peri-Urban Interface Research Project, Development Planning Unit, University College, London

Brook, R. M. and Dávila, J. D. (eds) (2000) *The Peri-Urban Interface: A Tale of Two Cities*, School of Agricultural and Forest Sciences, University of Wales and Development Planning Unit, University College London

Fazal, S. (2000) 'Urban expansion and loss of agricultural land – a GIS based study of Sharanpur City, India', *Environment and Urbanization*, vol 12, pp133–149

Fazal, S. (2001a) 'The need for preserving farmland: A case study from a predominantly agrarian economy (India)', *Landscape and Urban Planning*, vol 55, no 1, pp1–13

Fazal, S. (2001b) 'Land re-organization in relation to roads in an Indian city', *Land Use Policy*, vol 18, pp191–199

Jothimani, P (1992) 'Operational urban sprawl monitoring using satellite remote sensing: Excerpts from the studies of Ahmedabad, Vadodara and Surat, India', Paper presented at annual meeting of National Association of Geographers, Bangalore

Nunan, F. (2001) 'Rural–urban interactions: The purchase of urban waste by farmers in Hubli-Dharwad, India', *Third World Planning Review*, vol 23, no 4, pp387–403

Salau, A. T. and Baba, J. M. (1984) 'The spatial impact of the relocation of a section of the Zaria-Kano road: A study of change and development in rural Zaria', *Applied Geography*, vol 4, pp283–292

Tacoli, C. (1998) 'Rural–urban interactions: A guide to the literature', *Environment and Urbanization*, vol 10, no 1, pp147–166

Thangvel, C. (2000) 'An empirical estimation of the effect of some variables on land subdivision in Madras', *Urban Studies*, vol 37, no 7, pp1145–1146

United Nations Population Division (2001) *World Urbanization Prospects: The 2001 Revision*, Population Division, Department of Economic and Social Affairs, United Nations Secretariat, Washington, DC

Universities of Birmingham, Nottingham and Wales, Birmingham, Nottingham and Bangor (1998) *Baseline Study and Introductory Workshop for Hubli-Dharwad City-Region, Karnataka, India*, Final Technical Report, vol 2, 'Appendices', University of Birmingham, Birmingham, pp129–216

14

Conflict and Cooperation in Environmental Management in Peri-Urban Accra, Ghana

Katherine Gough and Paul Yankson

Introduction

Peri-urban areas in the developing world have received much attention in recent years (see, for example, Tacoli, 1998, 2003; Mbiba and Huchzermeyer, 2002; Simon et al, 2003). Despite the lack of consensus on the definition of the peri-urban interface (PUI), there is widespread recognition that rural and urban features are increasingly present both within cities and beyond their limits (Allen, 2003). The changes taking place are often contentious, with widespread conflicts between those competing for entitlements to land corresponding with inequalities in the respective contenders' powers and resources (Mbiba and Huchzermeyer, 2002). Accra, the capital of Ghana, is no exception and studies have shown how the rapid changes in land use and livelihoods have resulted in conflicts within communities, between different communities, and between communities and governmental authorities (Kasanga et al, 1996; Kufogbe, 1996; Gough and Yankson, 1997, 2000; Maxwell et al, 1999). This chapter illustrates that it is important to recognize that the transactions taking place in peri-urban Accra also reflect a wide degree of consensus and cooperation among a range of actors.

The chapter draws on fieldwork conducted in five villages within the peri-urban area of Accra: La Bawaleshie, the closest to the centre of Accra and which has been totally surrounded by urban development; Pantang, which lies beyond the physical limit of the city; and Ashale Botwe, Agbogba and Gbawe, which are located between these in the area experiencing the most rapid land-use change (see Figure 14.1). These villages were first studied during 1995/1996, when focus group discussions were held with the chief and elders, youth groups and women's groups, and a census survey, questionnaires and in-depth interviews were conducted in each village. Our interest in these settlements has been ongoing informally since 1995; but in February 2003 we again conducted formal focus group discussions with the same three groups, enabling us to trace the changes that have taken place.

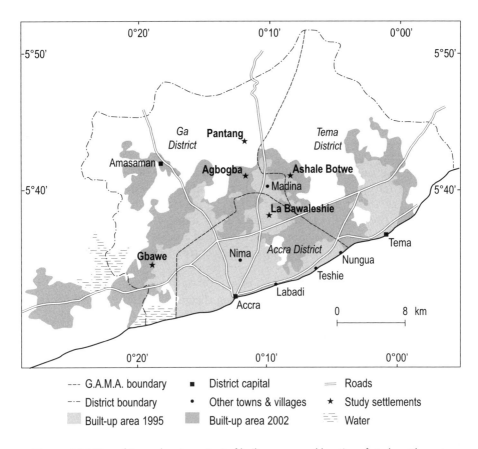

Figure 14.1 Map of Accra showing extent of built-up area and location of study settlements

Source: limits of built-up area developed from figures in Yankson et al (forthcoming) based on texture-based classification of Landsat (E)TM satellite images

Whereas our previous papers have explored topics across the five settlements, such as land, environment, governance and management (Gough, 1999; Gough and Yankson, 1997, 2000, 2001, 2003; Yankson and Gough, 1999), this chapter takes a different approach. For each village, the most striking theme is presented. In La Bawaleshie, it is resisting the construction of a new road through the old settlement; in Gbawe, it is the actions of the astute chief; in Ashale Botwe, changing livelihoods; in Agbogba, the changing provision of a range of services; and in Pantang, it is the disputes between the youth and the chief and elders. By telling a 'story' from each village, diverse aspects of the changes taking place in peri-urban Accra are highlighted. The extent to which the settlements are characterized by both cooperation and conflict is clear, with many issues linking back to the land question, which is paramount to the development of the whole PUI.

Peri-urban Accra

As already indicated, definitions of the PUI can vary widely. Like Simon et al (2004), we consider the peri-urban zone to be an extension of the city rather than an entirely separate area, and as being characterized by strong urban influences such as easy access to markets and services and the possibility of commuting to urban-based employment. Parts of the peri-urban zone also experience the direct impact of the urban centre, including changes in land use due to urban growth.

Accra's peri-urban area comprises a broad zone beyond the legal boundary of Accra Metropolitan Area (AMA), especially in westerly, northerly and north-easterly directions. Rapid land-use change from rural land use to urban uses is widespread in Ga District, particularly along the major transport arteries as a result of greater accessibility to central Accra. The areas between the major transport arteries radiating from the centre of Accra are now also developing as a result of increased pressure for residential development (see Figure 14.1). As could be expected (Simon et al, 2004), the intensity of land conversion to urban uses declines with increasing distance from the centre of Accra and from the main transport arteries and feeder roads.

The *umland*, the area of continuous sphere of influence of AMA, includes industrial centres, dormitory towns and market centres such as Nsawam (an industrial town to the north), Kasoa (a market and dormitory town to the west) and Buduburam (a refugee settlement also to the west of Accra). These are functionally linked with Accra but are not contiguous with the AMA because of the intervening rural spaces. There is also a belt of dormitory towns on the Akwapim ridge to the north of Accra, which is attracting real estate developers. Despite recognizing that determining the spatial limits of peri-urban areas has little value due to the rapid changes taking place (Simon et al, 2004), the peri-urban zone of Accra can be considered to comprise areas located between 10km and 40km from the centre of Accra, including the whole of Ga District, parts of Tema Metropolitan Area, Akwapim South District in the Eastern Region, and Gomoa and Effutu-Awutu-Senya districts in the Central Region.

Whereas only a decade ago, peri-urban Accra still consisted of dispersed rural settlements where subsistence agriculture was widely practised, today these settlements are surrounded by new housing at various stages of construction and little farming land remains. Richer households are moving into the newly completed houses, whereas poorer households seek rooms to rent, often within the indigenous settlements. These newcomers are referred to as strangers. Accra Metropolis experienced a rapid population increase between 1984 and 2000, from just under 1 million to almost 1.7 million (see Table 14.1). The most marked increases occurred in the peri-urban areas. For example, the population on Gbawe land increased dramatically from a mere 837 in 1984 to almost 29,000 16 years later. The population of Ashale Botwe exhibited a similar growth rate (data for the other settlements studied are not available).

Table 14.1 *Population increase in Accra, 1970–2000*

	1970	1984	2000
Accra Metropolis	624,091	969,195	1,658,937
Gbawe	608	837	28,989
Ashale Botwe	383	410	11,974

Source: Republic of Ghana Statistical Service, 2002

A basic understanding of the land market in Accra is imperative in under-standing the nature of the changes taking place (see Gough and Yankson, 2000, for further details). Most peri-urban land falls under customary land tenure and is thus controlled by chiefs and elders (or family heads). The customary owners hold the allodial title, but have only usufruct rights and should use the land so that the interests of the future generations are not jeop-ardized (Amankwaah, 1989). This stems from the belief underpinning the whole customary land tenure system – namely that 'Land belongs to a vast family of which many are dead, few are living and countless numbers are still unborn' (Ollenu, 1962, p4).

As demand for residential land in Accra has risen, peri-urban land has increased in value. Although the land cannot be sold outright, leaseholds may be sold. The new land acquirers must present the chief or family head with drink money (a monetized version of the traditional chiefly tribute); but this amount has come to reflect its economic value rather than being merely a token sufficient to buy a few drinks as in the past. The new land acquirers tend to be middle- and higher-income people who gradually build large villas ('self-contained houses'), often in areas where there are no or few services. Some of the proceeds from the land sales are fed back into villages in the form of improved services; but in some cases no benefits from the land sales are appar-ent. Although all peri-urban development plans should be drawn up by the Town and County Planning Department offices and all land transactions should be registered with the Lands Commission, development is taking place at a faster pace than these government offices can cope with. Hence, it is largely uncontrolled.

La Bawaleshie: Resisting the new road

La Bawaleshie lies east of the Accra–Aburi road and approximately 13km north-east of central Accra (see Figure 14.1). The village is about 200 years old and was founded by Abraham Djanie from Labadi. The chief of La Bawaleshie is only a caretaker and the Labadi chief has ultimate control over village affairs. By 1995, the old village had already been completely surrounded by new homes and the new area, East Legon, has become one of the most prestigious in Accra. In 1995, La Bawaleshie was served by piped water and electricity and there was an asphalt road leading into and out of the village, but not through it, so all traffic had to traverse the village on a dirt track, which had an increas-ing number of potholes (see Figure 14.2).

Figure 14.2 The road in La Bawaleshie while under dispute, 1995

This situation arose because the original plan drawn up for the development of the area by the Town and Country Planning Department had totally ignored the existence of the old settlement. As a town planning officer informed us, they had assumed that the old settlements with their mud compound houses would be demolished. Therefore, on the plans the plot layout for the new housing development was just superimposed over the existing indigenous settlements. As it became apparent that the indigenous villages were not going to disappear, the planners started to 'cut' around the old villages in their plans and just plan for the new areas. They subsequently realized the need to include the old settlements in their planning for the area as a whole, and this became the policy by the mid 1990s.

The plan for East Legon was drawn up in the first phase outlined above; this included a new, very straight access road which would cut through several houses on the south side of La Bawaleshie. The contractors subsequently constructed it up to the edge of the settlement and continued on the other side; however, due to resistance from the inhabitants, they were not able to enforce the demolition of the existing houses. Thus, the main access road to some very expensive houses in East Legon included a stretch around the edge of the village which was unpaved and deteriorated progressively with the ever increasing traffic. This stalemate persisted for years until finally, in 2002, the authorities gave in and paved the old road in its original position, curving around the southern edge of the village. This was seen as a success for the indigenous inhabitants.

This case illustrates the power of the indigenous landowners and how it is almost impossible to demolish parts of existing settlements without their consent. It also shows how there have been improvements in the planning for the peri-urban area of Accra and a realization that the new and old settlements need to be planned in harmony.

Gbawe: The astute chief

Gbawe is an old farming settlement approximately 10km west and slightly inland from the centre of Accra (see Figure 14.1). The people belong to the Ga Asne clan of central Accra but possess the allodial rights to their land. Already in 1995, many newcomers had built houses on Gbawe land; but there were considerably more eight years later. The old settlement was adequately served by water and electricity, and the access road to the village was paved in 1996.

The chief spends much time at court contesting land cases. However, he is both very able and wealthy (see Figure 14.3), in sharp contrast to many of the other chiefs in peri-urban Accra, some of whom lack formal education and live modestly. The ways in which the chief manages the affairs of Gbawe are clearly innovative, and he has both the will and the ability to improve overall living conditions.

Figure 14.3 The chief's palace in Gbawe contrasts sharply with nearby compound houses, 1995

His most innovative policies relate to land, with which the Gbawe stool (chief-dom) is well endowed. It is managed by the chief and elders, together with a land committee that they have established. Trained surveyors have been employed to demarcate plots and many leaseholds have been sold. Despite the costly land disputes with neighbouring stools, which are being contested in the courts, the chief and elders have invested money from the sale of stool land in the old settlement. For instance, they paid for the access road to be paved, for electricity and for the provision of toilets and other facilities. In 1995, Gbawe was the only stool we were aware of in peri-urban Accra that had set aside land for the indigenous inhabitants to enable them to continue farming.

As Accra continues to expand, Gbawe's chief and elders are no longer able to keep the land that they had demarcated as farmland since the Lands Commission instructed that the area should be allocated for residential use. Since farming was barely profitable, partly due to poor rains, this was not considered to be problematic by Gbawe's inhabitants. Members from each old compound house were subsequently invited to a meeting where they were allocated two plots of land each for future residential construction. This land should enable the youth who cannot be accommodated within the old compound houses to build on the new plots. With the aid of the chief, some family heads are opting to sell one plot of land and use the proceeds to rehabilitate the old houses, many of which are in poor condition due to lack of maintenance. Consequently, many of the old houses in Gbawe have now been rebuilt with cement blocks. A few families are still farming on the two plots that they have been allocated.

The chief also has a good relationship with the residents' associations set up by the new land acquirers. They hold frequent meetings to discuss development and security issues, including plans to build a police station. The Gbawe chief has provided free land for the police station and every adult is being asked to contribute to the project. Likewise, land has been allocated for a fire station and for schools. In the case of the latter, the chief has made an agreement with a private senior secondary school that, in exchange for providing land, the school will establish two scholarships for Gbawe children, to be allocated on the basis of achievement in the junior secondary school (JSS).

The importance of good relations between the chief and the inhabitants of Gbawe was stressed by a woman participant in a 2003 focus group discussion:

> *Because there is peace in the town ... improvements have come. There is peace through the efforts of the chief and there is no question of litigation between the families. Here a lot of people have come to hire rooms and rent and strangers have built new houses. We live in common with the new people and do everything with them.*

The case of Gbawe clearly illustrates how, under the leadership of a highly capable chief, the customary land tenure system can operate in a very sustainable way and to the benefit of all peri-urban residents. This success is now widely recognized in Accra and efforts are being made to spread the knowledge gained to other chiefs.

Ashale Botwe: Changing livelihoods

Ashale Botwe is about 17km north-east of central Accra (see Figure 14.1). The indigenous people originated mainly from Teshie and Labadi. The current chief still resides in Teshie, but usually visits Ashale Botwe on Saturdays. A whole new township, Ashale Botwe New Town, has developed on land previously owned by the indigenous people. In 1995, the village was served by electricity but not by piped water and the road was paved during 1996.

By 2003, not very much appeared to have changed in the indigenous settlement, although many new houses had been erected nearby. There is still no piped water in the village, so residents still have to buy from people who own containers, which are filled by tankers. Our discussions, though, revealed that there have been major changes in people's livelihoods. During the mid 1990s, many of the inhabitants of Ashale Botwe were farmers and appeared to be engaged in the most lucrative farming out of the five villages studied. This was due to the existence of a dam on their land, about 0.5km from the village, which had originally been built by Fulani herders coming from northern Ghana with their cattle. The dam continually held water and many farmers had set up nurseries close to the water's edge. This facilitated frequent watering of the crops, principally tomatoes and peppers, but also watermelons and other fruits. When the plants had grown to a certain size, the farmers would move them out to their farms. After harvesting, the crops were sold mainly in Accra. Several farmers told how there was good money in farming and one had even quit his job as a tractor operator for a German firm because he could make more money farming.

By 2003, this lucrative vegetable gardening had ended as some of the land surrounding the dam had been built upon and some had been acquired by a company. Several farmers were still growing maize and cassava on farms about 3km from the village; but much of this was for home consumption. The elders confirmed this trend:

> *We are losing our lands to housing projects. The farming is dying gradually. Now only a few people are farming. Before almost everyone was a farmer. The rain pattern has changed, too, so if you get into farming you'd better be careful. Only the old people are farming now. Farming does not interest the young. It does not pay anymore.*

However, the story is not entirely negative. The women, who are mainly traders, said that they were selling their goods faster now than before and that although there were many doing the same trade, more people could afford to buy from them. The arrival of numerous strangers, both renting rooms within the community and living in the newly constructed villas, was seen in a positive light as the newcomers had increased demand for their goods: 'It has improved our living conditions that the strangers have come.' There was also increased employment in construction, with the men working as artisans or labourers and the women carrying water. Trucks also pass by on the paved road to pick up labourers to work in sand and stone quarrying (known locally as 'winning').

The case of Ashale Botwe clearly illustrates the common peri-urban phenomenon that land-use changes result in livelihood changes, including the enforced abandonment of previously lucrative farming. However, it cannot be assumed that those affected are necessarily worse off as new livelihood opportunities also arise from the changes in land use. As the elders of Ashale Botwe said: 'The new development has drawn Accra closer', which they saw as resulting in new opportunities.

Agbogba: Changing level of services

Agbogba lies about 15km north of Accra off the Accra–Aburi road (see Figure 14.1) and comprises two sections. One is occupied by the indigenous Ga people, who came primarily from Labadi and settled in Agbogba over 200 years ago. The other section of the village was originally settled by a non-indigenous group who came from the north over 150 years ago. Today, the two settlements appear as one village and the northerners have adopted the Ga language and traditions. In 1995, most of the land surrounding the village had been sold; but there was no piped water or electricity, and there was only a gravel road through the village, along which the *tro-tros* (minibus taxis) weaved to avoid the worst potholes, throwing up much dust.

In 2003, we were immediately struck by the main village road, which had been tarred and lined with storm drains (see Figure 14.4). This had been carried out by the government, some say in readiness for when they will need it as a bypass while they upgrade the main Accra–Aburi road. The volume of traffic had increased, with many *tro-tros*, trucks and buses passing by. The greater danger from the high vehicle speed does not seem to worry the inhabitants. It is more important to them that it is now easy to catch a vehicle to and from Agbogba at almost any time. This has greatly facilitated market access for the women, who have consequently experienced improved sales. The increase in the number of trucks passing by has also improved the chances of the young men obtaining work in construction or sand and stone quarrying. They form themselves into small groups and wait daily under the tree outside the chief's house (see Figure 14.4) in anticipation.

The new road was not all good news, though. During construction, the mains water pipe was accidentally ruptured and had not been repaired. Agbogba was thus without running water for a year. The chief and elders, with the help of the local district assemblyman, were still chasing the construction company to solve the problem. Meanwhile, the inhabitants of Agbogba needed to find alternative water sources. There is a nearby pond from where people collect water; but according to the women, it is not safe to drink due to the cattle that also use it, so it is used only for washing. The initial water pipe had been installed by the community in collaboration with the new land acquirers, the former paying just one quarter of the cost. Some of the newcomers living south of where the pipe was damaged still have running water and some of them sell water by the bucket. Others have large containers, which they pay to have filled from tankers and then sell water to other residents. Even when the water was flowing, most houses in Agbogba lacked their own taps, partly due to the cost but also due to the disputes that can arise in compound houses over how much water each household has used. However, there was a communal tap from which people could buy water by the bucket. A man appointed by the

Figure 14.4 The improved road in Agbogba, 2003

chief and elders was in charge of selling the water and was able to take a salary from the profits. This system was both more convenient and cheaper than having to buy from the newcomers.

Another major change in Agbogba was the arrival of electricity. The inhabitants were fortunate in that a nearby horticultural export company had brought electricity close to the village. Using stool money, the chief and elders were thus able to buy poles and wire. They used communal labour to erect the poles and paid the electricity company to do the wiring. Consequently, the majority of the houses now have light that is metered, although there are a number of illegal connections. The women were especially eloquent about the ways in which the arrival of electricity had improved their lives:

> *Now we have electricity in our homes. It has brought a big change. We can watch TV. We can put water in the fridge and sell ice water. Instead of selling small we have changed to selling ice water, ice kenkey [boiled fermented maize meal and raw maize dough wrapped in leaves] and ice cream. It has improved the work of hairdressers and seamstresses. Some welders were not working before, but have now started. Some have changed to block-making; they use the electricity to cut the blocks. If we drop something we can see it and it helps the school children to learn in the night. We don't go to bed so early so it has helped family planning.*

The increasing number of residents has resulted in greater pressure on the schools as there is still only one primary school and one JSS. Many children do not gain admission, so their parents have to try to pay the fees of the nearby private schools. For those who make it into the state school, class sizes often exceed the official maximum of 60. The residents hope that their assemblyman will pressurize the district assembly to build more schools. One service that has improved is the provision of toilets. The chief and elders have built a Kumasi ventilated improved pit latrine (KVIP) for five men and five women, so sanitation is much better.

The example of Agbogba has shown how the provision of, and access to, different services in peri-urban villages can change both positively and negatively over time. Some of these changes are attributable to the land issue since the money gained from the sale of stool land has been used by the chief and elders to bring in electricity and toilets; but there have also been elements of both good and bad luck.

Pantang: Conflict between the youth and elders

Pantang is about 20km to the north of Accra (see Figure 14.1), west of the Accra–Aburi road at Oyarifa. The landowners are four families who still reside in Teshie. In 1995, Pantang was still principally a farming community and although many of the surrounding plots of land had been sold, very few purchasers had started to build. By 2003, many new houses were complete and the level of farming had declined. The road to Pantang, though, was still a mud track with fairly infrequent vehicles and the village was served by neither piped water nor electricity.

In February 2003, some young men began spontaneously to voice their grievances. It turned out that there had been an incident of disappearing electricity poles, which had split the village, especially between the generations. Although the youth, elders and women's group and local assemblyman related different accounts, in essence the problem revolved around villagers' efforts to electrify the village under the Ghanaian government's Self-Help Electricity Programme (SHEP), whereby the community provides some of the necessary electricity poles, following which the district assembly provides the remainder provided that the project has the support of the Electricity Corporation.

Attempts to levy all households for the necessary contribution had failed due to widespread poverty. Some of the new land acquirers who had built large houses close to the indigenous village, however, donated money towards this end to the assemblyman. Together with the youth, he then approached the elders in Teshie (who hold the allodial land rights) and requested that they sell a portion of land which had previously been allocated for the youth to use. Part of this land was sold and the combined money was used to buy 15 electricity poles. The assemblyman then convinced the district assembly to donate the remainder. However, before this could happen, the secretary of the electricity project (a village resident) and an employee of the Electricity Corporation removed and presumably sold the poles. The youth were very angry as they had played an important role in obtaining the poles; the assemblyman had to intervene and the elders maintained that the project was the government's responsibility and therefore refused to help. The youth demonstrated and threatened, in effect, to strike until the elders solved the problem.

The youth were also very angry that the elders had sold a plot of land located at the top of the slope by the pond, which is one of their main water sources. The youth destroyed the building work which had started there, claiming that the new residents would pollute their water. The assemblyman had to intervene again. Eventually, the elders agreed to relocate the new land acquirers away from the pond. They also realized by then that if the area had electricity, they could sell the plots for more money; as a result, they promised to help retrieve the poles. However, by late 2003, no progress had been made. The offender had soon left the village for Teshie and the police seemed unable to locate him despite being given an incentive by the assemblyman. The youth, though, blame the elders of Pantang for not doing more to solve these problems: 'The fault comes from the elders not realizing the problems.'

Importantly, this is not an isolated incident. Ever since we started working in peri-urban Accra in 1995, Pantang has been the village where conflict among indigenous members has been the most prevalent, especially between the youth and the chief and elders. During a focus group discussion in February 1996, the youth stated that: 'The elders are not treating the youth well. We are being cheated by the elders. We are not informed and are not involved in matters concerning the village.' Further discussions revealed that the youth were particularly discontented with the way in which the land was being disposed of, stating: 'We are suffering; there is no land for the youth.' This statement really identifies the crux of the problem, which is the land issue. In Pantang, the chief and elders are only caretakers of the land, which belongs to landowning families living in Teshie. When land is sold, the money stays in Teshie. This creates a situation quite different from that in the villages where the chief and elders have ploughed some of the land sale profits back into the village. The youth were venting their anger on the chief and elders of Pantang; but, in reality, the source of the problem appeared to lie elsewhere – with the landowning families. The issue, however, ran very deep in the community as one of the tenets of Ga culture is showing respect for elders. Already in 1996, the chief and elders were complaining: 'In the past, we had respect for our parents and elders; but this is not seen today. The young do not listen to what we say; they are not respectful. They ignore our advice.'

Although the deterioration of the relationship between the youth and elders was markedly more pronounced in Pantang, it simmers below the surface in many other settlements. The youth often feel that the elders have disposed of their inheritance without giving adequate regard to how they will earn a living in the future or where they will find the space to construct dwellings.

Conclusions

As Accra continues to grow, more indigenous peri-urban settlements are being incorporated within the urban fabric. This longitudinal study of five villages in peri-urban Accra has explored some of the changes taking place by means of a story from each village. These stories have illustrated the complexity and diversity of change; at the same time, they have also highlighted certain similarities.

Although the case of Ashale Botwe was emphasized, in all of the settlements studied many of the inhabitants' livelihoods have changed. These changes were not necessarily for the worse as peri-urban studies sometimes assume. Increased accessibility to the city, better transport and higher population densities are resulting in new livelihood possibilities. However, not only have the possibilities for farming decreased; but farming as an occupation has also become increasingly difficult and few of the youth are interested in becoming farmers. All the settlements are experiencing changing fortunes in service provision. Where the stool is wealthy and the chief astute, as in Gbawe, service levels have improved. In other areas, increasing population densities are resulting in services being overstretched and, thus, declining, though the higher population densities can also result in greater collective wealth and hence greater possibilities of improving services.

Although the conflict between the youth and the elders was most pronounced in Pantang, there was also evidence of dissatisfaction with leaders elsewhere. Not only the youth but, in some cases, also the women expressed their dissatisfaction with the chief and elders, especially regarding the sale of land and subsequent disposal of the proceeds. Although Pantang was the only settlement where direct conflict was found, Simon et al (2004) relate a similar tale from a peri-urban settlement near Kumasi where the disappearance of copper wire has prevented the planned installation of electricity, to the great frustration of the inhabitants. This suggests that the Pantang tale of internal conflict within a peri-urban settlement, linked to the wider peri-urban changes taking place, is not just an isolated case.

Many actors are involved in the transformations taking place in peri-urban Accra, and in all cases there are instances of cooperation and conflict between them. In all of the 'stories', however, the land issue emerges as being fundamental though often highly problematic. The indigenous settlements are here to stay and planners are now more aware of the need to plan for these, as well as the newly developing residential areas. The case of Gbawe has illustrated how customary land tenure managed by a competent chief can result in sustainable development practices. Partly based on that experience, attempts are under way to offer more support to chiefs and elders to better enable them to tackle the new challenges facing them. In 2002, Kasim Kasanga, the then minister of lands and forestry, claimed that:

> *In spite of their weaknesses, the customary tenurial systems and institutions are better placed to ensure accountability to the local communities and villagers than the public land administration machinery. Community land secretariats backed by their own hired professionals would promote positive land management and community participation. Any income accruing from stool lands should be retained by stools, community land secretariats and families, and only taxable by government in accordance with the income*

tax law. The contention here is that there are better checks and balances at the community level, ensuring that the right thing is done, than is currently the case with public land administration. (Kasanga, 2002a, p16).

The Ghanaian government has already taken some initiatives to address the land constraints and integrate land issues within the broader development agenda by adopting a *National Land Policy* (Ministry of Lands and Forestry, 1999). A Land Administration Project (LAP) has become the main tool for implementing the *National Land Policy*. LAP is a medium- to long-term (5- to 15-year) project, supported by the World Bank and other donors. It aims to reduce poverty and enhance social growth through improving security of tenure, accelerating access to land by the populace and fostering efficient land management by developing efficient systems of land titling and administration, based on clear, coherent and consistent policies and laws supported by appropriate institutional structures (Kasanga, 2002b). The impact of these policies remains to be seen.

The PUI is very complex, with a wide range of changes occurring rapidly and at differing rates in different areas. These changes, in turn, have differential impacts upon service provision and residents' livelihoods. It is important, therefore, that environmental management and planning systems take account of these differences and that governance systems evolve to facilitate collaboration across the different jurisdictions into which the peri-urban zone typically falls.

References

Allen, A. (2003) 'Environmental planning and management of the peri-urban interface: perspectives on an emerging field', *Environment and Urbanization*, vol 15, no 1, pp135–148

Amankwaah, H. A. (1989) *The Legal Regime of Land Use in West Africa: Ghana and Nigeria*, PLP, Tasmania

Gough, K. V. (1999) 'The changing nature of urban governance in peri-urban Accra, Ghana', *Third World Planning Review*, vol 21, no 4, pp397–414

Gough, K. V. and Yankson, P. W. K. (1997) *Continuity and Change in Peri-Urban Accra: Socio-Economic and Environmental Consequences of Urbanisation*, Final report to Danish Council for Development Research, Copenhagen

Gough, K. V. and Yankson, P. W. K. (2000) 'Land markets in African cities: The case of peri-urban Accra, Ghana', *Urban Studies*, vol 37, no 13, pp2485–2500

Gough, K. V. and Yankson, P. W. K. (2001) 'The role of civil society in urban management in Accra', in Tostensen, A., Tvedten, I. and Vaa, M. (eds) *Associational Life in African Cities: Popular Responses to the Urban Crisis*, Nordic Africa Institute, Uppsala

Gough, K. V. and Yankson, P. W. K. (2003) 'Associational life in urban Ghana', SEREIN Occasional Paper No 15, Proceedings of the 15th Danish Sahel Workshop, Copenhagen

Kasanga, R. K., Cochrane, J., King, R. and Roth, M. (1996) *Land Market and Legal Contradictions in the Peri-Urban Areas of Accra, Ghana: Informant Interviews and Secondary Data Investigations*, Land Tenure Centre, University of Wisconsin, Madison, US, and LARC, UST, Ghana

Kasanga, K. (2002a) 'Ideology and land policy in Ghana – the third way', Paper presented at USAID- and World Bank-sponsored side event to the World Summit on Sustainable Development, Property Rights: Reflection on Governance, Assets and Stewardship, Johannesburg, South Africa, The Export House, 30 August 2002

Kasanga, K. (2002b) 'Integrating land issues in poverty reduction strategies and the broader development agenda: The case of Ghana', Paper presented at Regional Workshop on Land Issues in Africa and the Middle East. Kampala, Uganda, 29 April–2 May 2002

Kufogbe, S. K. (1996) 'Urbanization and changing patterns of land use in the peri-urban zone along the Airport–Ayimensah Transect of Accra, Ghana', *Our Common Estate*, Royal Institution of Chartered Surveyors, London

Maxwell, D., Larbi, O., Lamptey G. M., Zakariah, S. and Armar-Klemesu, M. (1999) 'Farming in the shadow of the city: changes in land rights and livelihoods in peri-urban Accra', *Third World Planning Review*, vol 21, no 4, pp373–391

Mbiba, B. and Huchzermeyer, M. (2002) 'Contentious development: Peri-urban studies in sub-Saharan Africa', *Progress in Development Studies*, vol 2, no 2, pp113–131

Ministry of Lands and Forestry (1999) *National Land Policy*, Ministry of Lands and Forestry, Accra

Ollenu, N. A. (1962) *Principles of Customary Land law in Ghana*, Sweet and Maxwell, London

Republic of Ghana Statistical Service (2002) *2000 Population and Housing Census Report*, Republic of Ghana Statistical Service, Accra

Simon, D., McGregor, D. and Nsiah-Gyabaah, K. (2004) 'The changing urban–rural interface of African cities: Definitional issues and an application to Kumasi, Ghana', *Environment and Urbanization*, vol 16, no 2, pp 235–247

Simon, D., McGregor, D. F. M., Nsiah-Gyabaah, K. and Thompson, D. A. (2003) 'Poverty elimination, North–South research collaboration, and the politics of participatory development', *Development in Practice*, vol 13, no1, pp40–56

Tacoli, C. (1998) 'Rural–urban interactions: A guide to the literature', *Environment and Urbanization*, vol 10, no 1, pp147–166

Tacoli, C. (2003) 'The links between urban and rural development', *Environment and Urbanization*, vol 15, no 1, pp3–12

Yankson, P. W. K. and Gough, K. V. (1999) 'The environmental impact of rapid urbanization in the peri-urban area of Accra, Ghana', *Danish Journal of Geography*, vol 99, pp89–100

Yankson, P. W. K., Kofie, R. and Møller-Jensen, L. (forthcoming) 'Monitoring urban growth: urbanisation of the fringe areas of Accra', *Danish Journal of Geography*

15

Re-evaluating People–Environment Relationships at the Rural–Urban Interface: How Sustainable Is the Peri-Urban Zone in Kano, Northern Nigeria?

Tony Binns and Roy Maconachie

Introduction

The high rural population densities and intensive agricultural systems surrounding the city of Kano, northern Nigeria's largest city, have long been a topic of great interest to observers. As early as the mid-19th century, the explorer Heinrich Barth (1857) noted the unusually high concentration of people supported by the landscape around Kano. This region later became known as the Kano Close-Settled Zone (CSZ) and was originally defined by Mortimore in 1967 as the essentially rural area surrounding Kano's urban core, sustaining population densities above 350 people per square mile (circa 135 people per square kilometre) (see Figure 15.1). Today, this densely settled area stretches some 100km from metropolitan Kano and is one of the most intensively cultivated areas in sub-Saharan Africa (SSA). The so-called 'inner CSZ' has a radius of about 30km and is effectively the range of a donkey's day journey (Mortimore, 1993).

Kano and its region currently support over 5 million people, with densities between 250 and 500 people per square kilometre (Mortimore, 1993). As population densities have steadily increased, Kano's CSZ has become a focus of debate on whether agriculture can support an increasing population without causing land degradation (Harris, 1996). Despite being one of the most densely populated rural areas in semi-arid Africa, observers have been impressed by the apparent sustainability of farming systems, and studies suggest that the CSZ could support sustainable intensification for many years to come (Harris, 1996; Mortimore, 1998).

It seems likely that Kano's CSZ, and its less distant peri-urban interface (PUI), have long been arenas of competition. For many years, the landscape has been shaped by a variety of anthropogenic forces, and an early paper by

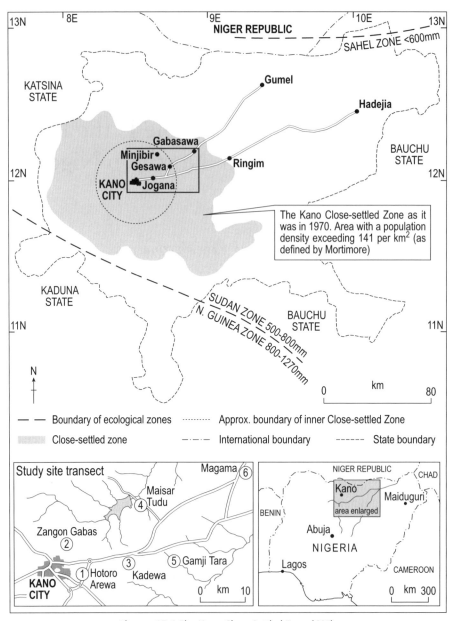

Figure 15.1 The Kano Close-Settled Zone (CSZ)

Source: Redrawn by Jenny Kynaston from author's original

Mortimore (circa 1960s) suggested that the zone has been continually subjected to pressures associated with competition for land, markets and off-farm employment. As the region of spatial transition between the urban tract and rural environs has grown substantially, consuming greater expanses of Kano's hinterland, levels of competition have intensified. More recently, Mortimore (1993) noted that the peri-urban area extended to the limits of the inner CSZ, and the entire region has become a zone of mixed land use.

As the distinction between 'rural' and 'urban' has become progressively less pronounced, and rural–urban networks have become the focus of renewed interest among policy-makers and researchers, there is an urgent need to explore the wider implications of these linkages. This chapter will consider how Kano's peri-urban areas are becoming contested zones and can be constructed as arenas of conflict and struggle. It is argued that a fuller appreciation of the forces currently shaping livelihoods in and around Kano is necessary if changing patterns of resource use and availability are to be understood. As a number of researchers have highlighted, many urban households operate across the urban–rural divide, maintaining close ties with their rural-based kin (Potts, 1997). In such situations, it is therefore neither useful nor relevant to draw the traditional distinction between 'urban' and 'rural', since rural and urban areas have become blurred and livelihoods in the two areas have become progressively intertwined. Tacoli (1998) observes that urban livelihoods frequently depend on a geographic area which is substantially larger than the built-up city area in order to supply basic resources and ecological functions. A number of studies have acknowledged the increasing importance of peri-urban zones as arenas for rural–urban exchanges in household livelihood strategies and family networks (Swindell, 1988).

For present purposes, the peri-urban region is perhaps best regarded as a transitional environment of mixed land use between a city's continuously built-up area and its rural hinterland, where 'economic and social activities are directly affected (beneficially, as well as to their detriment) by the presence and expansion of the city' (Mwamfupe, 1994, p12). Although urban and peri-urban agriculture is now widely considered as an important survival strategy for urban residents (Lynch et al, 2001), there has been little attention given to the future sustainability of peri-urban livelihoods. Past experience suggests that the political stability and economic sustainability of 'exploding' sub-Saharan cities will be vitally dependent on the accessibility of reasonably priced food supplies (Walton and Seddon, 1994). There is a pressing need for field-based research into the sustainability of environment and development in peri-urban zones.

Exploring the sustainability of Kano's peri-urban zone

Most research into land–society issues in Kano's CSZ, and more widely in dryland Africa, has focused on the impact of population growth on resource use, and has often been framed by an overarching theoretical perspective, or 'meta-narrative'. As Roe (1991, p228) explains, these narratives or development 'stories' tell us not so much about what *should* happen, as they do about what *will* happen, and they have had tremendous power in 'standardizing' and 'stabilizing' environmental problems into a 'one size fits all' scenario (Leach and Mearns, 1996). Relationships between population and environment are understandably complex and are the focus of an ongoing debate between proponents of neo-Malthusian and neo-Hardinian views concerned with environmental limits to population growth, and neo-Boserupians, who see increasing population densities as stimuli to innovation and conservation.

Where many anthropogenic-focused studies in Africa have seen human activity as being essentially destructive, Mortimore's (1967, 1970, 1993, 1998) detailed work on the Kano CSZ suggests that in high-population density areas, small-scale farmers often invest considerably more in land improvement than in low-density areas in order to meet increasing demand for food. Mortimore (1998) reminds us that the 'diversity, flexibility and adaptability' of dryland households are perhaps their greatest resource. Identifying the role of indigenous knowledge in risk management will undoubtedly play a key role in ensuring the sustainability of livelihoods and natural resources in the Kano CSZ. Mortimore's work is particularly important because it challenges the legitimacy of neo-Malthusian environmental orthodoxies which distort and misrepresent the issues. However, it might be argued that Mortimore presents an overly optimistic picture of the Kano CSZ at a time when life has become progressively more challenging due to Nigeria's deteriorating economic situation.

While it is true that in the past many actors have relied on strong social networks to cope in difficult times, Watts (1983) convincingly suggests that such adaptation is often no longer possible as the penetration of capitalist production and exchange relations in Nigeria has undermined the so-called 'moral economy', which once played a central role in the survival of rural communities. Although Watts's initial statement on 'how farmers perceive their (hazardous) environment' (1983, pxxvii) was formulated over 20 years ago, it can, perhaps, still be argued that as traditional safety nets have continued to erode, peasant households have become even more paralysed by a crisis of reproduction. Over the last three decades, as the economy in Nigeria has continued to decline, indigenous land management systems have been challenged and the consequences for rural, urban and peri-urban environments have often been devastating. Although it remains imperative to consider grassroots voices when formulating meaningful environmental policies in Kano's CSZ, it may be equally dangerous to over-romanticize the role that indigenous knowledge can play in conservation, in light of the many constraints faced by local actors. While research approaching the causality of land degradation and the articulation of alternatives must be rooted in the outlook and aspirations of local people, so, too, must it consider how such local solutions are embedded in regional, national and global systems.

Urban growth and Kano's Close-Settled Zone (CSZ): Sustainability under threat?

Linkages between cities and their hinterlands through food supply networks are complex, and it is necessary to understand the dynamic relationships between the two. In the Kano PUI, mounting pressures on resources, which have been intensified by increasing population densities, have not only made it more difficult to access farmland and agricultural inputs, but have forced many farmers to diversify income strategies and engage in non-farm activities to ensure subsistence. As Bryceson and Jamal (1997) note, although the majority of SSA's population remains rural, each year the population is actually becoming less agrarian as farmers respond to decreasing agricultural productivity and can no longer rely solely on farming for survival.

Against a backdrop of apparent sustainability in the Kano CSZ, the large and growing influence of metropolitan Kano on land use and ownership, economic activities and labour markets is having a significant impact on agricultural production and rural livelihoods. Kano has enjoyed a long historical relationship with its hinterland through employment and food trading, and rural–urban interaction has always played a role in defining the contours of transformation and development in both city and countryside. The long-established local and regional trading systems in Hausaland have been well documented (Hill, 1972), and dry season circular migration from villages to towns or cities, known as *cin rani* in Hausa, has been an enduring livelihood strategy. These relationships between city and countryside have intensified over recent years, and diverse flows and linkages of people, food, goods, capital, information and wastes serve as 'bridges' spanning the rural–urban divide, and have become key forces in shaping the process of regional change.

Households operating at the rural–urban interface have had to become much more reliant on the resilience of Sahelian resource management systems, as detailed by Mortimore (1998). While a variety of livelihood survival strategies in the peri-urban area have become increasingly significant, remarkably little attention has been given to their sustainability. It is essential to understand patterns and processes at the local level within the broader context of change at regional, national and global levels.

A comparative study along a distance–decay transect

Six study sites were sampled on a distance–decay transect along a major tarmac road extending north-east from Kano in order to test for the attenuation of peri-urban influences with increased distance from the city (see Figure 15.2). A detailed field-based investigation was undertaken over ten months during 2001/2002 to explore local knowledge and perceptions of rural–urban linkages and peri-urban land use. Quantitative and qualitative methods were used to provide evidence of the real and perceived severity of land and resource degradation. Household and farmer surveys were undertaken, along with extensive focus group discussions, in-depth interviews and on-site transect walks with local actors. It soon became apparent that 'land degradation' is a socially constructed concept that is interpreted differently by different individuals. In the light of these considerations, the methodology employed an interdisciplinary 'actor-oriented' approach within a spatial sampling frame.

Chambers (1983) has written extensively on the notion of 'rural development tourism' and associated research biases that impede an 'outsider's' appreciation of the community being studied. Chambers (1983, pp13–16) is particularly critical of spatial biases that often occur in research practice, notably 'urban', 'tarmac' and 'roadside' biases. If, as Chambers (1983) suggests, land is used differently and more intensively near the roadside, the

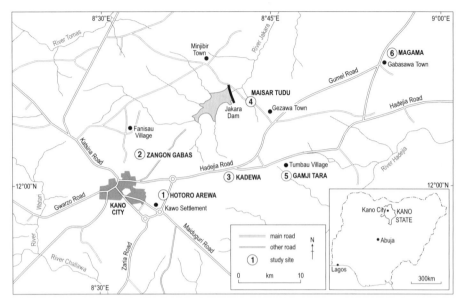

Figure 15.2 Study sites in the Kano CSZ

Source: Redrawn by Jenny Kynaston from author's original

question of how this is having an impact on the incidence of land degradation becomes relevant. A number of questions emerge concerning the relationship between urban areas, their rural hinterlands and the transportation networks which provide the 'connectivity' between the two. The presence of a tarmac road is therefore crucial to the sampling frame for this research and played a key role in determining the selection of research sites.

Focus group sessions were undertaken with key informants selected for their particular knowledge or position on issues relevant to the investigation. Five different groups of actors were identified to take part in these discussions – namely, young farmers, those who had received Western education, elders, Fulani herders and women. Local modesty considerations preclude a male researcher from interviewing women directly; they could therefore not partic- ipate in any mixed groups. A women-only group was thus established and interviewed by a female research assistant. After extensive discussions with the five actor groups at each site, a clear picture of land degradation began to emerge and an appreciation gained of how perceptions of the environment vary, both spatially and between actors.

Discussions with actors at the two transect sites closest to Kano, where the most 'peri-urban' characteristics were exhibited, revealed recurring concern about three degradation themes: soil fertility, the quality of irrigation water and a perceived reduction in the number of trees. Many peri-urban land users recognized the inter-linkage between various types and manifestations of degradation identified, and these issues are considered in the following section.

Competition for land

Many stakeholders suggested that heightened levels of resource competition, particularly increases in the incidence of 'land hunger', were exacerbating land degradation in Kano's hinterland, with potentially disastrous consequences for livelihoods. While most households interviewed in this study confirmed that individual plots were now smaller, 36.7 per cent of households reported that the total size of family land holdings had decreased during recent years. Such competition for land is by no means a new development in the region. For many years, the traditional subdivision of farm plots through inheritance has led to land fragmentation, and local actors acknowledged that cultivated areas are now much smaller than in the past. Mortimore (1970) suggests there has long been a steady decline in the size of average family landholdings; referring to records between 1932 and 1964, he notes:

> *The number of separately occupied plots on the 448 acres [181ha] which were surveyed increased by 42% to 185 ... During the same period, the cultivated area increased by 26 acres [10.5ha] [of] mostly marginal land ... Of all plots registered in 1932, 41% had been subdivided by 1964, while only 16% had been consolidated ... Fragmentation is also increasing. The average plot decreased in size by 22% between 1932 and 1964, [and] the average holding by 11%* (Mortimore, 1970, p385; cited in Watts, 1983, p353).

As farm plots have been required to feed increasing numbers of people, smaller parcels of land have been forced to 'work harder' to ensure household survival. This increased stress on available land has both constrained and transformed management practices. Further exacerbating the incidence of land hunger, a number of pressures associated with an expanding rural–urban interface have reduced land availability, leading to greater competition for resources and markets. For example, as urban development has increased the value and demand for land in peri-urban Kano, many residents have abandoned farming altogether and have sold their plots to urban developers. Poor farmers have frequently been driven to sell their land out of desperation. In other situations, high peri-urban real estate prices have enticed farmers to liquidate their land assets and purchase farmland in less expensive, more peripheral, areas. As a growing percentage of peri-urban land has come under the control of developers, farming has become increasingly difficult for those who continue cultivating.

After a plot has been sold, urban developers typically have the land surveyed, and lay the cornerstones of a building to indicate their formal ownership and eventual intention to develop the property (see Figure 15.3). However, in most cases, the plot is bought for speculative reasons, with the land remaining idle for many years in the hope that property values will increase. Land hunger has sometimes become so acute that peri-urban cultivators may continue farming inside the walls of unfinished buildings. Legality of land use and security of land tenure are vital considerations in ensuring the sustainability of peri-urban livelihoods, and almost 25 per cent of surveyed households admitted insecurity of land tenure. One farmer, who was cultivating a plot that was on loan to him, suggested that because he did not own his land and was only farming there temporarily, there was little point in him using soil conservation practices to improve the quality of the land. Other respondents without security of tenure agreed that they had possibly exacerbated land degradation because they had been forced to cultivate marginal and/or unproductive land through sheer desperation.

Figure 15.3 Cornerstones laid on plots by developers indicate an 'intention' to build

Adding further complexity to the land security issue, the 1978 Land Use Decree gave the federal government control of all urban land, with powers allocated to the state governor to grant customary rights of occupancy. The right of government to appropriate privately held land instantly has, quite understandably, increased feelings of insecurity, even among those who legally own their plots. Farmers experiencing insurmountable pressures are sometimes forced into adopting practices that are not sustainable. For example, one farmer admitted that the only reason he had sold his plot to an urban developer was because he feared that the government would confiscate it. He also confessed that immediately before selling his plot, he completely deforested the property so that he could earn some additional income from selling firewood. Such feelings of land insecurity, perpetuated by suspicions of government motives, are shared by many peri-urban residents.

Soil infertility

Field-based research revealed widespread concern about declining soil fertility in peri-urban areas. Many actors believe that 'nutrient mining' (van der Pol, 1992) is a common cause of soil infertility in peri-urban Kano. Although intensive cultivation has placed great pressure on the land, in the past most farmers integrated crop production with livestock raising, and soil fertility was maintained by the constant application of manure, compost or urban refuse (Yusuf, 1996). Micro-level studies conducted by Harris (1996, 2000) into soil nutrient management by smallholders in the village of Gamji Tara, 35km north-east of Kano, appear to reinforce the evidence concerning the sustainability of the region, and her work celebrates the role of indigenous management strategies in low-output farming systems.

Like the extensive studies undertaken by Mortimore, Harris's research has contributed usefully to understanding how Kano's rural production systems operate. However, recent discussions with land managers in the region, including those in Gamji Tara, reveal that the present-day situation has made access to traditional farm inputs increasingly challenging, and many people believe that declining yields are now commonplace. In fact, the questionnaire survey revealed that 62.2 per cent of households believed that fertility rates were declining each year and that soil nutrients were not being replenished in the farming system. Such sentiments are summarized in the words of one elderly farmer from Gamji Tara:

> *Before, a person would just use one piece of land to plant his crops and the land would produce as many as 100 bundles. But last year, that old man over there farmed 18 different pieces of land, and before the rainy season he had to sell some cattle because he had run out of food. The land has to work harder, and we don't have enough* taki *[animal manure] for our plots. If we use* taki *this year, there is a need to reapply it again next year. Sometimes, we have to cultivate without applying any* taki *at all* (Ahamed, pers comm, 2002).

Conventional wisdom concerning herder–farmer relations holds that a harmonious and symbiotic relationship once prevailed between pastoralists and sedentary farmers in the Kano CSZ, whereby Fulani cattle herders were permitted to graze their animals on field stubble during the dry season in exchange for animal manure to fertilize land (Binns, 1994). However, land hunger and mounting resource pressures have radically changed the way that land is managed, and Harris and Yusuf (2001, p321) note that due to exceedingly high population densities, the region now has relatively few cattle in comparison with other parts of West Africa. In peri-urban localities, virtually all traditional rangeland (*makiyaya*) and cattle paths (*burtali*) have disappeared due to pressure on the land, and Fulani cattle herders have sought to diversify their livelihoods. One Fulani respondent confirmed the transformation in traditional lifestyles:

Here, the land use is mixed: some of us want to farm, some keep animals, some build houses and some are doing business. Some people are taking sand from holes to make building blocks. This is causing erosion and decreasing the productivity of the land. Now, we Fulani are farming as well as rearing animals. We are lucky because at least we can use some of the taki *[manure] from our animals. This increases the productivity of the land* (Ali, pers comm, 2002).

Although Fulani still traverse the Kano CSZ during the dry season when migrating to greener pastures further south, in reality, most manure used on farms now comes from draught animals, donkeys and small ruminants that are actually kept by farmers themselves. The significance of animal manure in the nutrient management strategies of farmers is well documented (Harris, 1996; Harris and Yusuf, 2001); but it is unclear whether supplies of manure in the Kano region will be able to keep pace with the growing future demand. As Stocking and Murnaghan (2001) point out, by increasing manure inputs, the effects of land degradation can be 'hidden'; but production will continue at a cost. Unfortunately, as Harris and Yusuf (2001) reveal, although farmers appreciate the role that manure plays in maintaining soil fertility, resource pressures may not permit them to use manure optimally, and the high cost and erratic availability of chemical fertilizer often exclude it as a viable option.

Soil erosion

Although soil erosion in the Kano CSZ is not as serious as in more humid parts of southern Nigeria, local perceptions indicate that human-induced erosion in peri-urban Kano is increasing. In particular, it was widely recognized that poor land stewardship practices, such as ridge-making across land contours or ill-advised channelization of storm runoff into gullies, could accelerate soil erosion. Respondents also acknowledged the detrimental consequences of poorly planned road and housing construction projects, where inadequate side drainage and plant cover could lead to soil erosion. Such observations were shared by a number of peri-urban residents, who believed that as competition for scarce resources increases, financially strained municipal, state and federal governments will be unable to manage the environment effectively. This scenario is of concern since it is likely that the resolution of environment and development issues in peri-urban areas could, to varying degrees, be determined by the quality of different levels of governance.

Field research revealed a common view that the dramatic acceleration of urban growth in Kano, and the subsequent expansion of the PUI, had certainly contributed to the erosion hazard. A significant number of respondents were specifically concerned about erosion caused by indiscriminate removal of building materials, such as sand and gravel from gullies, which has now become a widespread practice in peri-urban Kano (see Figure 15.4). Sand extraction has become a very profitable income-generating strategy since the demand for construction materials in the city has increased spectacularly over recent years. According to one sand excavator, a lorry load of good-quality sand could be sold for as much as 9000 Nigerian naira (circa UK£47 in April 2002). Such high-profit margins have led to a proliferation of sand collectors and, in the absence of any proper regulation, a number of violent conflicts have developed between land users.

Figure 15.4 Sand collectors at Hotoro Arewa

According to one peri-urban farmer, 'sand carriers' began extracting building materials from his plot without permission. When local farmers observed these activities and realized that they could not prevent them, many thought that it would be better to sell their land to the sand collectors in an effort to gain some compensation. This is said to have resulted in increased gullying and a reduction in the area of cultivable land.

Changes in tree cover

Challenging deforestation orthodoxies, the widely cited studies by Cline-Cole et al (1990a, 1990b) suggest that the maturity and density of trees in the Kano CSZ actually increase in localities that are closer to urban centres and where population densities are greater. These findings appear to be amplified in forest research carried out elsewhere in West Africa, most notably by Fairhead and Leach (1996) who conclude that in certain situations people's activities can enrich the forest, as in the creation of anthropogenic peri-village forest islands in Kissidougou, Guinea. However, discussions with a diverse range of actors in the Kano CSZ revealed that there is currently widespread concern about changes in tree cover. In particular, peri-urban residents lamented the perceived decline in valuable indigenous species, such as *Dorawa* (*Parkia biglobosa*), *Rimi* (*Ceiba pentandra*) and *Kuka* (*Adansonia digitata*). It is worth noting that the studies carried out by Cline-Cole et al (1990a, 1990b) were based on field research undertaken during the late 1980s, and local voices now suggest that there is a pressing need to reconsider issues concerning trees in the CSZ.

When asked about changes in tree cover, most respondents perceived that there were now fewer trees than previously, even though they acknowledged that there were conservation laws in place to regulate the felling of trees on farmland. Over 82 per cent of households sampled reported fewer trees on their land than 20 years ago. Moreover, as indicated in Table 15.1, although the perception that tree cover is diminishing was high at all six sites, households sampled at the three communities in closest proximity to Kano – Hotoro Arewa, Zangon Gabas and Kadewa – demonstrated a strong belief that tree numbers were declining.

Table 15.1 *Are there fewer trees on your land today than 20 years ago?*

Site	Yes		No	
	n = 15	%	n = 15	%
Hotoro Arewa	13	86.7	2	13.3
Zangon Gabas	13	86.7	2	13.3
Kadewa	13	86.7	2	13.3
Gamji Tara	12	80.0	3	20.0
Maisar Tudu	11	73.3	4	26.7
Magama	12	80.0	3	20.0
Total sample (N = 90)	74	82.2	16	17.8

Source: authors' fieldwork

The perceived recent decline in tree numbers was thought to be the result of a number of factors. Specifically, in addition to an increase in the domestic use of trees for house building, it was believed that more wood was needed for cooking and heating water. This belief was not just based on the perception that a growing population was consuming more resources, but also that the rising cost and unreliability of kerosene supplies had increased the demand for wood as the main source of fuel. Many respondents who had previously used kerosene as a primary fuel source reported that they had been forced to switch to wood. Table 15.2 summarizes the main types of household fuel being used in peri-urban areas, according to 100 households surveyed randomly in Hotoro Arewa and Zangon Gabas. Table 15.3 summarizes the main factors determining household choice of fuel selection.

Table 15.2 *Primary fuel sources in Hotoro Arewa and Zangon Gabas*

Main type of household fuel used	% of households (N = 100)
Wood	38
Kerosene	31
Wood and kerosene	26
Millet/sorghum stalks and wood	2
Millet/sorghum stalks	1
Ayafa (refuse from plastics factories)	1
Charcoal	1

Source: authors' fieldwork

Table 15.3 *Reasons for household fuel choice*

Fuel type	Reason for choice of household fuel	% of households (N = 100)
Wood	Wood is the cheapest	25
Wood	Family is large, so wood is more economical	18
Wood	Food tastes better cooked on wood	4
Wood	Cannot cook some foods with kerosene, so wood must be used	2
Wood	Wood is more available	3
Wood	Cannot afford to buy a kerosene stove	1
Kerosene	Family is small, so kerosene is easier and more cost effective	19
Kerosene	Kerosene is easier to use than wood	9
Kerosene	Kerosene is cheaper than wood	8
Kerosene	Do not like the smoke from wood	6
Kerosene	Kerosene is more easily available than wood	4
Kerosene	Kerosene is better for the environment	1

Source: authors' fieldwork

Some individuals also admitted that economic desperation had driven them to harvest trees on their property and sell them for fuelwood. Even in Gamji Tara, a community that Harris described in her 1995 study as being 'away from the bias of the city ... [where] farmers were not in frequent contact with Kano businesses and trade' (1995, p49), residents now report that fuelwood lorries from Kano visit the village regularly to buy supplies from anyone who wishes to sell. Fuelwood sales were often associated with the need for cash during the so-called 'hungry season', immediately preceding the crop harvest, or in fulfilling cultural obligations, such as weddings or naming ceremonies.

Apart from the perceived increase in domestic wood use, the reasons given for the decline in tree cover generally concerned conflicting peri-urban land-use patterns. To increase the cultivable area and allow more sunlight to reach crops, many farmers cleared all the trees on their property. Several respondents also admitted that in the past trees had been the cause of land-use conflicts between Fulani pastoralists and local cultivators. To discourage pastoralists from bringing cattle on to agricultural land, some farmers chopped down all *Gawo* (*Faidherbia albida*) trees, an indigenous species the branches of which are traditionally used by Fulani for fodder. The problem is illustrated in the response of one young farmer:

> *Some trees are good for the land, but some are bad. The Gawo tree causes problems for us because of the Udawa [Fulani from the Republic of Niger] who come and cut the branches. Sometimes, the Udawa bring their animals onto my plot after the crops have already germinated, and they damage the plants. So for this reason, to keep the Udawa off my land, I have cut down my* Gawo *trees* (Yakubu, pers comm, 2002).

Reports of conflict between cultivators and pastoralists in the Kano CSZ are common, and increasing competition for key resources has often led to violent clashes. Respondents suggest that as the number of *Gawo* trees has been significantly reduced in Kano's hinterland, and the landscape has become progressively more 'urban' in character, pastoralists now rarely use peri-urban areas for grazing. Several local farmers believed that the reduction in tree cover has played a role in progressive soil deterioration.

Water quality and peri-urban pollution

Increasing water pollution is also recognized as a key problem in peri-urban Kano. Of particular threat to *fadama* (lowland) irrigation crops in dryland peri-urban areas are industrial effluents from manufacturing plants, which contaminate irrigation channels. Laboratory analysis of peri-urban water samples confirms this problem, with a particular threat from the large number of tanneries that discharge substantial quantities of chromium salts and other toxins into water courses (Binns et al, 2003; Maconachie, 2004). In addition to health hazards associated with contaminated peri-urban water sources, other studies indicate a concern that stagnant water may favour mosquito breeding sites, leading to a greater risk of malaria and other vector-borne diseases (Trape et al, 1992).

At Kano's three peri-urban industrial estates – Bompai, Challawa and Sharada – untreated liquid waste is routinely deposited in open drains, sewer systems and water courses. These water sources are vital to peri-urban livelihoods, with over 60 per cent of local people depending on rivers and groundwater aquifers (Osae-Addo, 1992). Many residents also rely on this water to irrigate small vegetable plots, and in recent years, peri-urban livelihoods have become dependent on this food production, both in terms of household consumption and income generation (Lynch et al, 2001). Cultivators generally possess a good level of environmental knowledge and are keenly aware of the conditions that constrain their production. Farmers can usually distinguish water toxicity levels by colour and can provide detailed descriptions of temporal variations in water quality. One respondent commented:

> *There are three bad colours [of water] that come at different times. The oily red one and the green one will kill the crops, and when we see these colours in the channel, we turn off our pumps immediately. The bluish water is corrosive and causes a red rash when it comes in contact with the skin. We always wash our hands after we have come in contact with the blue water* (Sadanu, pers comm, 2002).

Waste treatment facilities that do exist in peri-urban Kano are either inadequate or non-functioning and little, if any, enforcement of pollution control takes place. Poor zoning and enforcement by-laws in the industrial estate areas exacerbate problems, as landowners continue to sell their property to housing developers, since new manufacturing facilities are now rarely being established in Kano. As long as such practices continue, housing encroachment and urban agriculture will occur alongside industry, pollution rates will increase at an alarming rate and the health of the local population will be threatened.

Conclusions

In contrast with the rhetoric of Malthusian apocalypse, researchers such as Mortimore, Harris and Cline-Cole have usefully challenged received wisdom on dryland livelihood systems. These more optimistic models of sustainable land use reframe the issues and suggest that many of the standard prescriptions for environmental problems have often been highly inappropriate and draconian in nature. However, at the same time, it would be erroneous to suggest that serious environmental problems do not exist in Kano's CSZ. As has been suggested here, it has become apparent that so-called 'closed systems', which once formed the basis of many early seminal studies in the Kano area, are becoming increasingly difficult to find and new external forces are taking their toll on the landscape. Indeed, Mortimore (2002, p137) himself concedes:

> *It should be noted ... that the drylands are not and, in general, never have been closed economic systems. Trading networks and diasporas were a feature of their pre-colonial histories [and] political linkages between arid and sub-humid regions gave expression to fundamental complementarities. Mining and urbanization have intensified these linkages through offering new employment opportunities to migrants.*

This being the case, in undertaking present-day explorations of the 'sustainability' of the Kano CSZ, it is vital to move beyond the dichotomous Malthusian versus Boserupian debate which has dominated the focus of so many previous studies. In particular, there is a need to consider environmental and social implications of recent developments in and around the burgeoning city of Kano, where urban and rural livelihoods have become blurred and competition for resources has become extreme. Reflecting Watts's (1983) contentions, the combined effects of social, political and economic factors, in conjunction with population-driven resource pressures in Kano's growing PUI, have certainly intensified contests among various actors at the micro-level, and have rendered traditional smallholder mechanisms of adaptation and resilience increasingly difficult. Although it is acknowledged that some rural–urban linkages have positive implications for local actors, at the same time, physical evidence of land degradation, together with 'insider' perceptions of key environmental issues, provide significant warning signs that new stresses are breaking down the sustainability of the system.

As economic conditions in Nigeria have deteriorated, so life has become increasingly challenging for those living in peri-urban Kano. In cities and hinterlands, survival has become more difficult as coping mechanisms have been eroded and competition for scarce resources has continued apace. Indicators suggest that actors at all levels will find it increasingly difficult to manage their environments, and more research into indigenous institutions is critically sought. Specifically, more studies are needed that explore how the effectiveness of community-based institutions has become challenged during recent years, as well as how they might operate more effectively in the future. As Leach and Mearns (1996) point out, although more research will not necessarily translate into the formulation of more appropriate and effective policy, there is a need for better understanding of how mutual support between institutions at different levels can be fostered, particularly in times when fewer resources are available and environmental management has become increasingly difficult.

In short, substantial investment and community action are urgently sought in the management of Kano's PUI if future livelihood and environmental sustainability are to be ensured. Coordination among communities, environmental agencies and government bodies currently remains weak, and a new concerted programme of action is vital to stimulate effective strategies for sustainable management. Future research must identify the positive roles that the state can play in supporting local resource management initiatives in the Kano CSZ, taking into account the interests of grassroots actors. At the same time, although local actors may be both powerless and marginalized, they frequently possess a detailed understanding of the environment–society interactions and are generally in the best position to evaluate and safeguard their resource base. Acknowledging the perceptions and knowledge of a wide range of peri-urban actors, and determining how they fit into the macro-level forces that currently shape Nigeria's development trajectory, will undoubtedly be a key component in ensuring the future sustainability of livelihood systems in the Kano CSZ. There must surely be lessons here for peri-urban areas under pressure elsewhere in SSA and beyond.

References

Ayodele Ariyo, J., Voh, J. P. and Ahmed, B. (2001) *Long-Term Change in Food Provisioning and Marketing in the Kano Region, 1960–2000*, Working Paper 34, Kano-Maradi Study of Long-Term Change: Niger-Nigeria series, Drylands Research, Crewkerne

Barth, H. (1857) *Travels and Discoveries in North and Central Africa*, vol 3, Longman, London

Binns, T. (1994) *Tropical Africa*, Routledge, London and New York

Binns, T., Maconachie, R. A. and Tanko, A. I. (2003) 'Water, land and health in urban and peri-urban food production: The case of Kano, Nigeria', *Land Degradation and Development*, vol 14, pp431–444

Bryceson, D. F. and Jamal, V. (eds) (1997) *Farewell to Farms: De-Agrarianisation and Employment in Africa*, Africa Studies Centre, Leiden, Research Series 1997/10, Ashgate, Aldershot

Chambers, R. (1983) *Rural Development: Putting the Last First*, Longman, Harlow

Cline-Cole, R., Falola, J., Main, H., Mortimore, M., Nichol, J. and O'Reilly, F. (1990a) *Wood fuel in Kano*, United Nations University Press, Tokyo

Cline-Cole, R., Main, H. and Nichol, J. (1990b) 'On fuelwood consumption, population dynamics and deforestation in Africa', *World Development*, vol 18, no 4, pp513–527

Fairhead, J. and Leach, M. (1996) *Misreading the African Landscape: Society and Ecology in a Forest-Savanna Mosaic*, Cambridge University Press, Cambridge

Harris, F. (1995) *Nutrient Dynamics of the Farming System of the Kano Close-Settled Zone Nigeria*, PhD thesis, Department of Geography, Cambridge University, Cambridge

Harris, F. (1996) *Intensification of Agriculture in Semi-Arid Areas: Lessons from the Kano Close-Settled Zone, Nigeria*, Gatekeeper Series 59, IIED, London

Harris, F. (2000) *Changes in Soil Fertility under Indigenous Agricultural Intensification in the Kano Region*, Working Paper 36, Kano-Maradi Study of Long-Term Change: Niger-Nigeria Series, Drylands Research, Crewkerne

Harris, F. and Yusuf, M. A. (2001) 'Manure management by smallholder farmers in the Kano Close-Settled Zone, Nigeria', *Experimental Agriculture*, vol 37, pp319–332

Hill, P. (1972) *Rural Hausa: A Village and a Setting*, Cambridge University Press, Cambridge

Leach, M. and Mearns, R. (eds) (1996) *The Lie of the Land: Challenging Received Wisdom on the African Environment*, IAI and James Currey, Oxford

Lynch, K., Binns, T. and Olofin, E. (2001) 'Urban agriculture under threat: The land security question in Kano, Nigeria', *Cities*, vol 18, no 3, pp159–171

Maconachie, R. A. (2004) *Sustainability Under Threat?: Urban Pressure and Land Degradation in the Kano Close-Settled Zone, Nigeria*, DPhil thesis, Department of Geography, University of Sussex, Brighton

Mortimore, M. (circa 1960s) 'Peri-urban pressures', Unpublished paper, Mimeo, Department of Geography, Ahmadu Bello University, Zaria

Mortimore, M. (1967) 'Land and population pressure in the Kano close-settled zone, northern Nigeria', *The Advancement of Science*, vol 23, pp677–688

Mortimore, M. (1970) 'Population densities and rural economies in the Kano Close Settled Zone, Nigeria', in Zelinsky, W., Kosinski, L. and Prothero, R. M. (eds) *Geography and a Crowding World*, Oxford University Press, London, pp380–388

Mortimore, M. (1993) 'The intensification of peri-urban agriculture: The Kano close-settled zone, 1964–1986', in Turner, R., Kates, R. and Hyden, G. (eds) *Population Growth and Agricultural Change in Africa*, University Press of Florida, Gainesville, Florida, pp358–400

Mortimore, M. (1998) *Roots in the African Dust: Sustaining the Sub-Saharan Drylands*, Cambridge University Press, Cambridge

Mortimore, M. (2002) 'Development and change in Sahelian dryland agriculture', in Belshaw, D. and Livingstone, I. (eds) *Renewing Development in Sub-Saharan Africa: Policy, Performance and Prospects*, Routledge, London and New York, pp135–152

Mwamfupe, D. G. (1994) *Changes in Agricultural Land-Use in the Peri-Urban Zone of Dar es Salaam, Tanzania*, PhD thesis, Department of Geography and Topographic Science, University of Glasgow, Glasgow

Osae-Addo, A. (1992) *Nigeria: Industrial Pollution Control*, Sector report draft, cited in World Bank (1995) *Nigeria: Strategic Options for Redressing Industrial Pollution*, vol 1, no 3, February 1995, Enterprise Development and Public Sector Management Division, West Central Africa Department, Washington, DC

Potts, D. (1997) 'Urban lives: Adopting new strategies and adapting rural links', in Rakodi, C. (ed) *The Urban Challenge in Africa: Growth and Management of Its Large Cities*, United Nations University, Tokyo, pp447–494

Roe, E. (1991) 'Development narratives or making the best of blueprint development', *World Development*, vol 19, no 4, pp287–300

Stocking, M. A. and Murnaghan, N. (2001) *Handbook for the Field Assessment of Land Degradation*, Earthscan, London

Swindell, K. (1988) 'Agrarian change and peri-urban fringes in tropical Africa', in Rimmer, D. (ed) *Rural Transformation in Tropical Africa*, Belhaven, London, pp98–115

Tacoli, C. (1998) *Bridging the Divide: Rural–Urban Interactions and Livelihood Strategies*, Gatekeeper Series 77, International Institute for Environment and Development, London

Trape, J.-F., Lefebvre-Zante, E., Legros, F., Ndiaye, G., Bouganali, H., Druilhe, P. and Salem, G. (1992) 'Vector density gradients and the epidemiology of urban malaria in Dakar, Senegal', *American Journal of Tropical Medicine and Hygiene*, vol 47, no 2, pp181–189

Van der Pol, F. (1992) *Soil Mining: An Unseen Contributor to Farm Income in Southern Mali*, Royal Tropical Institute Bulletin 325, Royal Tropical Institute, Amsterdam

Walton, J. and Seddon, D. (1994) *Free Markets and Food Riots*, Blackwell, Oxford

Watts, M. (1983) *Silent Violence: Food, Famine and Peasantry in Northern Nigeria*, University of California Press, London

Yusuf, M. A. (1996) 'The farming system of Tumbau, Kano State, Nigeria', *Soils, Cultivars and Livelihoods in North-East Nigeria*, *Working Paper No 1*, Department of Geography, Bayero University, Kano

Part 4

Strategies for Sustainable Development

16

Community-Based Waste Management Strategies: Peri-Urban Interface, Kumasi, Ghana

Abdullah Adam-Bradford, Duncan McGregor and David Simon

Introduction

The increasing pollution and waste disposal problems found in many sub-Saharan cities have become distinctive features of Kumasi and its immediate peri-urban areas (Onibokun, 1999; Adam, 2001; Simon et al, 2001, 2003), where rapid growth, widespread poverty, inadequate and weak local governance and limited financial resources all contribute to the waste problem (Onibokun, 1999; Adarkwa and Post, 2001; Simon et al, 2001, 2003). Rapid urbanization in Kumasi is resulting in major challenges to environmental protection, waste management, food security and urban and peri-urban agriculture (Brook and Dávila, 2000; Mensah et al, 2001). The pollution and waste disposal problems are most acute in peri-urban areas, where waste management services are seldom provided despite rapidly increasing settlement densities (Adam, 2001). Although this poses problems, there are substantial opportunities for community-based waste management strategies that promote nutrient recycling. These strategies turn organic waste into compost at community and household levels for use as an agricultural fertilizer in urban and peri-urban agriculture. Such approaches have the potential for creating a classic win–win situation by increasing urban and peri-urban agricultural production through appropriate soil fertility management; protecting the environment through the recycling of organic waste; and income and livelihood generation, which enhance urban and peri-urban food security (Drechsel and Kunze, 2001; Leitzinger, 2001).

This chapter reports on an experimental implementation of such approaches in selected peri-urban interface (PUI) communities around Kumasi.

Kumasi, Ghana

Currently, about 36 per cent of Ghana's population are classified as urban, although due to rapid migration this proportion is estimated to reach 50 per cent by the year 2015 (Naylor, 2000). Kumasi is Ghana's second largest city and the regional capital of Ashanti. In 1948, the city's population stood at 71,436; by the 2000 population census the figure was reported at 1,170,270 and the population growth rate was 5.2 per cent per annum (GOG, 2002).

Urban and peri-urban agriculture in the Kumasi PUI

There is no universally accepted definition of 'peri-urban' (Birley and Lock, 1999), although, in simple terms, it can be defined as the areas around cities and towns characterized by rapid demographic, economic, environmental, social and cultural interactions and changes. General commonalities in peri-urban discourse emphasize the importance of these transitional processes rather than the geographical location (Binns, 1994; Rakodi, 1999; Brook and Dávila, 2000; Nunan, 2001; Tacoli, 2003; Simon et al, 2004). As Simon et al (2004, p239) highlight: 'This is more appropriate for examining the continuum between the poles of urban and rural and understanding the dynamics of change as they affect particular parts of the peri-urban zone, as well as shifts in the position of the zone as a whole.'

Arable land within the city totals 15,920ha, of which 11,930ha are currently under cultivation (Anon, 2003). The dominant farming system is sedentary agriculture with monocropping and mixed cropping of cassava, exotic vegetables, maize, plantain and sugarcane. In peri-urban areas, cassava, maize and plantain are the main crops and in both urban and peri-urban areas backyard gardening features extensively. Despite the important role that urban agriculture plays in contributing to food security and income generation, the sector faces many constraints. Lack of water for dry season farming, low-income levels, the high cost of farm inputs and a lack of storage and processing facilities all hinder agricultural production. However, the loss of agricultural land for constructional activities is one of the main constraints within and around the metropolis, not only destroying livelihoods but also resulting in the intensification of agriculture on remaining lands. Consequently, nutrient depletion of soils and inappropriate use of chemical fertilizers occur. In peri-urban areas, in general, this poses particular problems as female-headed households are still dependent upon agriculture as their main livelihood activity.

Research methodology

The research project was implemented using a participatory action research (PAR) approach. In essence, PAR is a problem-solving, iterative and systematic approach to research where a range of 'intellectual resources' are drawn upon to find a solution to a problem or to improve current practices (Hoggart et al, 2002). The research tools used during the fieldwork – Participatory Rural Appraisal (PRA) techniques, semi-structured interviews, micro-projects and workshops – were predominantly qualitative methods and, hence, bestowed several important advantages, which are crucial if a PAR approach is to be successful and truly participatory. These included flexibility of research design and methods; increased holistic understanding of the issues; more natural settings; and inclusion of local perceptions and viewpoints (Curry, 1996).

The first phase of fieldwork consisted of an orientation and familiarization survey of six selected peri-urban villages (see Figure 16.1). This provided an opportunity to make initial contact with the respective village chiefs (traditional village head), unit committee representatives (elected village body) and, where established, the community level facilitators (CLFs) – community-chosen representatives working with a Ghanaian non-governmental organization (NGO) on a UK Department for International Development (DFID)-funded livelihoods project – thereby introducing the research and identifying some of their main issues and concerns. The second phase consisted of a household survey in which semi-structured interviews were used to collate household, waste, sanitation, health and agricultural details, as well as to determine micro-project participation willingness in each of the villages (Adagya, n = 52; Apeadu, n = 50; Asago, n = 58; Domeabra, n = 54; Esereso, n = 56; and Kyerekrom, n = 53).

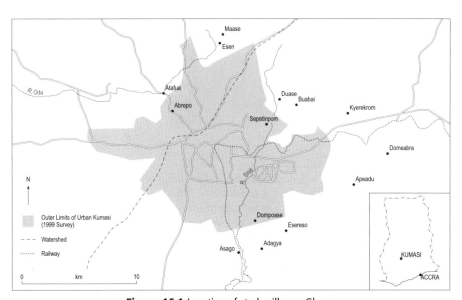

Figure 16.1 Location of study villages, Ghana

Results from preliminary and household surveys indicated high potential for a household-level waste separation and composting programme. This was reinforced by the communities' willingness to participate and by their eagerness to improve village sanitation, while also contributing to their agricultural livelihoods since the composting and reuse of organic waste is a means of recycling nutrients and restoring soil fertility (Drechsel and Kunze, 2001). Once appropriate interventions were identified, they were implemented using micro-projects and training workshops. These were conducted through the CLFs of each village, thereby also contributing to the enhancement of the CLFs' capacity to produce and analyse knowledge (Douglass, 1992).

Implementation sites

Village selection criteria were based on environmental, geographical, social, economical and political factors, each selected to ensure that villages with a range of different peri-urban characteristics were represented (see Table 16.1). The single universal characteristic that applied to all the six villages was that open refuse dumps were used – that is, that no waste collection service existed. The remaining seven criteria can be clustered into geographical (village size, location and access), economical (agricultural based or alternative livelihood strategies; level of small-scale enterprises) and, finally, social (level of community mobilization) categories.

Table 16.1 *Village selection criteria*

Criteria	Adagya	Apeadu	Asago	Domeabra	Esereso	Kyerekrom
1	✓	✓	✓	✓	✓	✓
2	2000	> 1000	2000	> 1000	> 4000	2000
3	✓	✗	✓	✗	✓	✓
4	✓	✗	✓	✓	✗	✗
5	✓	✓	✗	✗	✓	✗
6	BAKDA[1]	KMA[2]	BAKDA[1]	EJDA[3]	BAKDA[1]	EJDA[3]
7	3km	5.3km	4km	4.2km	0km	1.5km
8	✗	✓	✗	✗	✓	✓

Criteria	Description
1	No waste collection provision (i.e. open refuse dumps are a characteristic feature)
2	Range of village sizes (from approximately < 1000 to > 4000)
3	With/without community level facilitator (CLF) mobilization
4	Agriculture main livelihood/alternative livelihood strategies
5	With/without small-scale enterprises (light industries)
6	Located in different political boundaries (districts/KMA[2])
7	Distance from arterial road
8	With/without good-quality feeder routes

Notes: [1]   BAKDA: Bosomtwe-Atwima-Kwanwoma District Assembly
[2]   KMA: Kumasi Metropolitan Assembly
[3]   EJDA: Ejisu-Juabeng District Assembly

Waste management in peri-urban Kumasi

In peri-urban areas without waste collection services, community members use an allocated site, often within the village boundary, where solid waste is simply dumped and allowed to accumulate, to be burned occasionally. Progressive urbanization has led to higher waste flows and, coupled with the increasing accumulation of non-biodegradable plastic waste on open dumps, the effectiveness of any natural decomposition is reduced, resulting in the growth of unsightly and unsanitary conditions.

In the past, dumping of organic waste posed a low public health and environmental risk because it consisted mainly of organic matter, which was either eaten by livestock or decomposed naturally and thus never accumulated to the scales that can be observed today.

Despite differing social and economic circumstances and geographical locations among the six villages, several characteristics were common, including unmanaged open waste dumps; indiscriminate dumping of waste on village peripheries; open defecation by children on waste dumps; and disposal of human excrement in plastic bags on waste dumps. The last phenomenon is now so common in many cities that terms such as 'precious package', 'wrap and throw' or 'flying toilets' are used to describe the practice (Hardoy et al, 2001). The public health hazards of such practices are high as open refuse dumps encourage fly breeding, which may result in an increase in faecal-oral infections (for example, diarrhoea, dysentery, hepatitis A, cholera and typhoid). When dumps are located near traditional pit latrines, the infection risk is higher. Mosquitoes that spread viral and parasitic infections (dengue, malaria and yellow fever) may breed in the refuse itself (for example, water in tin cans, tyres and plastic), while diseases associated with rats (*salmonellosis*, plague, endemic typhus rat-bite fever and *leptospirosis*) may also be promoted. Parasitic worms (for example, hookworm) can be transmitted through the soils (Caincross and Feachem, 1993), particularly at sites where human waste is dumped and open defecation occurs. During rainy periods, leachates that contain high levels of pathogens may contaminate drinking water sources.

These conditions have resulted in the growth of unsanitary conditions in many peri-urban villages, and the current in-migration trends are likely to lead to further deterioration. Within the Kumasi Metropolitan Assembly (KMA) boundary, the poor quality of feeder roads linking peri-urban areas is the often-cited excuse for the limited services (M. O. Danso, head of waste management, KMA, pers comm, 2002). However, the Kumasi Waste Management Department has limited financial resources and, considering the highly political implications of urban sanitation, clearly prioritizes the more affluent areas. Peri-urban locations become marginalized regardless of which side of the municipal/district boundary they are located on, and likewise the priorities of the district assemblies lie within the district interior and not on the district periphery that borders the KMA.

Backyard container composting

Daily domestic waste consists mainly of food scraps (cassava, yam and cocoyam peels and plantain skins) and wood ash, with only small quantities of sand and plastic bags. In the light of these high proportions of organic matter in domestic waste, the high engagement (90 per cent) in local (≥ 4km) agricultural activities and the need for soil ameliorates in these same areas (Nsiah-Gyabaah and Adam, 2001), domestic waste composting is one strategy that can be adopted by households to reduce waste and to provide much needed soil inputs for agriculture. In addition to producing natural fertilizer, backyard composting reduces the amount of domestic organic waste destined for open refuse dumps or municipal landfill sites, thus contributing to a cleaner environment and, where waste collection services are provided, a reduction in collection and transport costs (GFA-Umwelt, 1999).

Backyard composting requires suitable composting containers to stop disease vectors, such as flies, mosquitoes, cockroaches and vermin, from being attracted to the compost pile, thereby ensuring that the composting process remains safe, hygienic and acceptable to local residents and conforms to district and municipal sanitation by-laws. Compost containers can be made from recycled materials such as tyres, blocks, bricks, wood, plastic barrels or 250-litre drums, making the technology accessible for low-income groups. When the technology is implemented appropriately, it can not only improve environmental sanitation, but can also enhance local livelihoods.

Decomposition process

When left long enough, all organic matter decomposes due to the breakdown of the matter by bacteria and other living organisms. Composting is a method of controlling this process by accelerating the decomposition rate while also minimizing the nutrient loss (Mason, 1997). This is best achieved by providing optimal conditions for the bacteria and other living organisms through the best combination of air, moisture, temperature and type of organic material (Agromisa, 1999). Compost containers can be used to obtain the optimal decomposition conditions by regulating the air, humidity and temperature during the composting process. With appropriate handling, the decomposition rate can be greatly accelerated; good practices include the cutting up and shredding of the organic matter, sprinkling water on the pile if it becomes too dry, mixing the pile to increase aeration and keeping the container closed during heavy rains to prevent waterlogging.

For effective decomposition, it is equally important to supply the micro-organisms within the compost pile with the optimal carbon/nitrogen ratio of 25–30:1 (C/N ratio). To obtain a suitable C/N ratio, materials with a high ratio such as sawdust (up to 400) must be mixed with materials with a low ratio such as chicken manure (about 7). If the C/N ratio is incorrect and there is too little nitrogen, decomposition will be slow and the compost of low quality. Conversely, if there is too much nitrogen, the compost will become putrid, acidic and compact and the quality will deteriorate (Agromisa, 1999). Turning the pile and adding dry porous materials, such as leaves, sawdust or straw, can easily rectify this problem. Likewise, if the compost releases an ammonia odour (indicating nitrogen richness), carbon-rich materials such as leaves, sawdust or straw should be added.

Micro-projects

Simple and easily replicable demonstration micro-projects were distributed at prominent points in each of the six villages. By conducting composting workshops using the demonstration sites, the dissemination capacity was increased and a wider community audience reached. However, due to the time required to produce compost there could be a prolonged period before outputs are available for use or sale – hence, the intervention must be well planned and sustainable, with local people participating actively in all stages of the planning and implementation process.

The main container-composting method demonstrated was block-built compost bins, chosen because of the wide availability of building blocks, standard bricks or the traditional sun-baked blocks, all of which can be used to construct a compost container. The block-built compost bins consist of a double chamber with covering lids (see Figure 16.2). Cement can be used when a permanent structure is required, otherwise the blocks can be left un-mortared for temporary use or portability. Gaps are left between the bricks in the bottom course to facilitate airflow; making holes in and mixing the compost pile provides additional aeration. The chambers are filled sequentially. When the second chamber is full, the compost in the first chamber can be emptied and the mature compost stored until ready for use. Each compost bin is sufficient for a household with an extended family. Larger versions consisting of three high-capacity chambers were also demonstrated (see Figure 16.3). The larger version is suitable for up to five households, which reduces the cost of materials per household. The back wall, sidewalls and dividing walls are mortared, while the blocks on the front of the bins are left un-mortared to facilitate emptying.

Figure 16.2 Double-chamber block-built compost bin

Source: Abdullah Adam-Bradford

Figure 16.3 High-capacity block-built compost bin

Source: Abdullah Adam-Bradford

The 'Suame compost tumbler' (see Figure 16.4) has a smaller capacity and is therefore only suitable for smaller households since rapidly filling the drum may result in waste putrefaction. The tumbler was an outcome of collaborative work with the Intermediate Technology Transfer Unit, Kumasi, and is designed to accelerate organic decomposition while ensuring hygienic conditions. Design features were included to ensure suitability for tropical conditions and ease of use by children. The tumbler comprises a 250-litre drum mounted horizontally on to a steel axis that is supported by a frame made from 50mm angle iron. The opening is made by cutting out a section in the side of the barrel, which is then reattached with hinges to form a door. Holes are added underneath the barrel to allow drainage while also standing at each end of the drum to allow additional aeration.

Other container composting methods that were demonstrated included barrel composting, which was constructed from locally sourced recycled materials. Disused 250-litre drums were used simply by making aeration holes around the drum and providing a cover. If the base of the barrel was still intact, then drainage holes were made in the base, which allows any seepage to be collected. This can then be added to the decomposing organic matter in the barrel, thereby minimizing nutrient loss (Agromisa, 1999).

Similarly, old 250-litre or plastic drums can be used to build simple vermi-composting units. The drum, with aeration and drainage holes, is located in a

Figure 16.4 Compost tumbler

Source: Abdullah Adam-Bradford

shaded area, stones are placed in the bottom for drainage and are covered with a perforated wooden board or nylon sacking with slits to stop the worms from escaping, mature compost is added to a depth of 10cm for the worm bed, and then local varieties of red worms (for example, *Lumbricus rubellus*) and brandling worms (for instance, *Eisenia foetida*) are added. A few handfuls of organic waste are added to start the process. Once the container is full, the top 10cm of compost containing most of the worms is retained to start the next cycle and the remainder of the compost is emptied.

After construction of a compost bin or allocation of a tumbler, the respective household members received training in waste separation and composting techniques. In addition, information leaflets in both English and the local Twi language were distributed. The leaflets provided clear instructions in environmental sanitation, household waste separation and container composting, and included sketches. The demonstrations were then monitored over several weeks during which further training and technical assistance was provided, as necessary.

Anaerobic composting

The final method implemented and demonstrated at community level was anaerobic composting, where compost is produced in sealed plastic bags or in small piles covered with plastic sheeting (see Martin and Gershuny, 1992). Rather than using small piles, a windrow measuring approximately 1.5m wide and 1m high was formed, with organic waste added daily to the end of the windrow. The windrow was covered with two (recycled) tarpaulins (waterproof canvas covers), which served to protect the pile from waterlogging during heavy rains, to prevent access to livestock, rodents, flies and mosquitoes, and to prevent the pile from drying out.

This technique was implemented in the village of Kyerekrom, where specific conditions provided an opportunity to trial the method. The village chief had financed the construction of a pit (measuring approximately 8m by 4m by 2m deep) at the site of the refuse dump to be used for the incineration of domestic waste produced within the community. Rather than burning all waste types, a suggestion was made to employ a community member to oversee the separation of organic and non-organic waste at the site of the pit, to compost the organic element in covered heaps and to use the pit to incinerate non-organic material. The village unit committee adopted this idea and a suitable candidate was selected. The commitment of both the village chief and the unit committee was instrumental in successfully implementing this composting method. In addition, the relatively small community size (approximately 2000 people) ensured that the waste flow was manageable for one person. The anaerobic composting process has worked very well, with good temperatures being reached (> 60° Celsius) and without the windrow drying out during the process.

School composting programme

In Ghana, recent environmental initiatives have been targeted at schoolchildren through the medium of school environment clubs in an attempt to raise environmental awareness among younger community members. The Ghana Environmental Protection Agency (EPA) is now tasked with forming the clubs at all junior secondary schools (JSSs) (age group of 12- to 15-year olds) throughout Ghana. The Ashanti Regional Office has commenced the programme in and around Kumasi, with several environmental clubs inaugurated by late 2003. Selected topics that are addressed include water quality, conservation and harvesting; tree planting; soil erosion; waste pollution; and community clean-up programmes. While the EPA has supplied some materials, such as leaflets, posters and tree seedlings, the agency generally faces financial constraints. Therefore, in collaboration with the EPA, funding was provided to construct triple-chamber block compost containers (see Figure 16.3) at each of the JSSs in the six peri-urban locations.

The first aim of the school composting programme was educational, enabling school pupils to gain practical hands-on experience of composting techniques, rather than just learning theory. The educational aspect was enhanced through the provision of compost thermometers to enable students to monitor the compost temperature during the decomposition, conversion and synthesis phases, thereby increasing the scientific understanding of the compost process. The second aim of the programme was actual compost production for use on school projects, especially vegetable growing, horticulture and lawn improvement. All of the participating schools have small school farms with a high potential for compost use.

Training was given to the teachers on how to manage and use the compost bins. Teachers then organized the collection of domestic organic waste from their community; where pupils bring domestic organic waste from home to compost in the school compost container. This has not only raised awareness among the wider community, but has also reduced the amount of organic waste that is deposited on the open waste dumps.

A further strategy to raise 'waste' awareness has incorporated school excursions to the KMA's co-composting plant at Buobai and to the new World Bank-funded landfill site at Dompoase (see Figure 16.1). The excursions were strongly supported by the waste management and education departments of the KMA and by the EPA Ashanti Regional Office. Following the visit, all participating pupils entered a writing competition on a local waste management theme. The best essay from each school was chosen, with each winner being awarded an EPA certificate and a copy of *Nature Kicks Back* (Adarkwa-Dadzie, 2001). The school excursions have provided an additional means to raise awareness of environmental issues among the pupils. Through this medium, the message is taken home and is also spread widely throughout the community, contributing to greater environmental awareness. The school environmental clubs and the compost programme received national media coverage in the main Ghanaian daily newspaper, the *Daily Graphic* (2003).

Performance and problems

All containers proved effective for decomposing organic waste, particularly when good composting practices were followed, specifically where organic materials were shredded and the compost pile frequently aerated. Problems encountered included rapid filling of containers, which resulted in the waste inside compacting and putrefying. During the implementation phase, the enthusiasm of some project participants to fill their containers extended to inviting their neighbours and friends to use them. As the double-chamber block-built containers were designed for individual household use, over-rapid filling, compaction and putrefaction resulted. Removing the top layers and increasing aeration of the remaining compost pile remedied this. Where the larger capacity triple-chamber containers have been used, this problem has not materialized. Teething problems were also encountered with the compost tumbler due to insufficient aeration holes, which was rectified by making additional holes at each end of the drum.

In economic terms, the most cost-effective containers have been those constructed from recycled materials, requiring no financial inputs. These included barrel composting and un-mortared block-built compost bins constructed from recycled blocks. Whereas the average construction cost of each double-chamber block-built compost bin was approximately 13 Euros, the construction cost of each compost tumbler was approximately 58 Euros.

Despite the compost tumbler being highly effective in decomposing small quantities of organic waste, the construction cost exceeds the purchasing power of most peri-urban farmers and, therefore, is not the most appropriate solution. Conversely, the wide availability of building blocks (both modern and traditional sun baked) increases the viability of block-built compost bins, particularly the larger triple-chamber container, as the cost can be shared by several households. However, if wider uptake of such techniques is to be promoted, assistance (either with finance or with materials) would be required, particularly for poorer households.

Early spontaneous uptake of the technology was encouraging, with the number of installations almost doubling within three months of project initiation (see Table 16.2).

Table 16.2 *Implemented composting micro-projects and take-up after a three-month period*

	Demonstrations	Take-up (after three months)	Total (after three months)
Adagya	3	2	5
Apeadu	3	1	4
Asago	4	4	8
Domeabra	3	1	4
Esereso	3	4	7
Kyerekrom	4	5	9
Total	20	17	37

Policy implications

Separating and composting domestic waste at the household level can lead to substantial decreases in waste outputs and, thus, contribute to a cleaner environment, particularly in peri-urban areas that are plagued by open waste dumps. Furthermore, composting and reusing domestic organic waste is a means of recycling nutrients and restoring soil fertility, contributing to soil structure and humus, increasing organic matter and improving the water-holding capacity of soils. However, the successful implementation of backyard composting programmes requires substantial educational and training inputs across a range of topics, including establishing compost sites, constructing compost containers, appropriate compost handling and compost use. Successful implementation can be enhanced through the provision of demonstrations and information leaflets and the running of composting workshops. Financial assistance may also be required to purchase any required materials to build compost containers. However, the success of backyard composting is not dependent upon the composting method or container, but principally on 'intensive care and know-how of the individual' (GFA-Umwelt, 1999), which can only be fostered through well-planned educational and training programmes with the beneficiaries participating in all stages of the planning and implementation process.

Conclusions

A demonstration and participatory approach has been shown in peri-urban Kumasi to be highly appropriate in implementing a household waste separation and composting programme. The establishment of micro-projects within a community can be a catalyst for change, particularly when the strategy is affordable, has obvious benefits and contributes directly to the enhancement of local livelihoods. Micro-projects were used to provide simple demonstration sites that can be easily replicated, particularly after other villagers have observed the direct benefits. However, there will be a time lag, so the intervention must be well planned and sustainable, with villagers actively participating in all stages of the planning and implementation process. Failure to adopt such an approach may result in the implementation of inappropriate technologies (Hamdi, 2004).

Interest in the introduced low-cost technologies has been high within the selected communities; but while several households have spontaneously adopted the techniques (see Table 16.2), supplying their own materials to construct compost containers, if such programmes are to be implemented on a wider and systematic scale, then financial assistance will be required. In the context of household waste management strategies, a variety of interventions that meet low-cost requirements and that are appropriate in the peri-urban areas of Kumasi are feasible.

Acknowledgements

Project participation by the villagers of Adagya, Apeadu, Asago, Domeabra, Esereso and Kyerekrom was crucial. Abdullah Adam-Bradford acknowledges receipt of UK Economic and Social Research Council Research Studentship No R42200134386. The research was conducted in collaboration with the Ghana office of the International Water Management Institute (IWMI), which provided funding for the micro-projects. The Suame compost tumbler was built by the Intermediate Technology Transfer Unit (ITTU), Kumasi.

References

Adam, M. (2001) 'Definition and boundaries of the peri-urban interface: Patterns in the patchwork', in Drechsel, P. and Kunze, D. (eds) *Waste Composting for Urban and Peri-Urban Agriculture: Closing the Rural–Urban Nutrient Cycle in Sub-Saharan Africa*, IWMI, FAO, CABI Publishing, Wallingford, pp193–208

Adarkwa-Dadzie, A. (2001) *Nature Kicks Back: Poems on the Degradation of the Natural Environment*, Advent Press, Accra

Adarkwa, K. K. and Post, J. (eds) (2001) *The Fate of the Tree: Planning and Managing the Development of Kumasi, Ghana*, Thela Thesis, Amsterdam, pp41–58

Agromisa (1999) *Preparation and Use of Compost: Agrodok-Series No 8*, Agromisa Foundation and the Technical Centre for Agricultural and Rural Cooperation (CTA), Wageningen

Anon (2003*) Agricultural Profile: Kumasi Metropolis*, Leaflet issued by the Metropolitan Director of Agriculture, Kumasi, 6 June

Binns, J. A. (1994) *Tropical Africa*, Routledge, London

Birley, M. H. and Lock, K. (1999) *The Health Impacts of Peri-Urban Natural Resource Development*, Liverpool School of Tropical Medicine, Cromwell Press, Trowbridge

Brook, R. M. and Dávila, J. D. (eds) (2000) *The Peri-Urban Interface: A Tale of Two Cities*, School of Agricultural and Forest Sciences, University of Wales, Bangor and Development Planning Unit, University College London

Caincross, S. and Feachem, R. (1993) *Environmental Health Engineering in the Tropics: An Introductory Text*, second edition, John Wiley and Sons, Chichester

Curry, J. (1996) *An Introduction to Qualitative Research*, University of Wales, Bangor

Daily Graphic (2003) 'EPA initiates moves', *Daily Graphic*, 31 March, p23

Douglass, M. (1992) 'The political economy of urban poverty and environmental management in Asia: Access, empowerment and community based alternatives', *Environment and Urbanization*, vol 4, pp9–32

Drechsel, P. and Kunze, D. (eds) (2001) *Waste Composting for Urban and Peri-Urban Agriculture: Closing the Rural–Urban Nutrient Cycle in Sub-Saharan Africa*, IWMI, FAO and CABI Publishing, Wallingford

GFA-Umwelt (1999) *Utilisation of Organic Waste in (Peri-) Urban Centres*, GFA Infrastruktur und Umweltschutz GmbH, Bonn (GFA Umwelt), Deutsche Gesellschaft für Technische Zusammenarbeit GmbH (GTZ), Eschborn and Ingenieurgemeinschaft Witzenhausen Fricke & Turk GmbH (IGW), Witzenhausen

GOG (Government of Ghana) (2002) *Development Plan for Kumasi Metropolitan Area (2002–2004)*, Kumasi Metropolitan Assembly, Ministry of Local Government and Rural Development, Government of Ghana, Kumasi

Hamdi, N. (2004) *Small Change: About the Art of Practice and the Limits of Planning in Cities*, Earthscan, London

Hardoy, J. E., Mitlin, D. and Satterthwaite, D. (2001) *Environmental Problems in an Urbanizing World*, Earthscan, London

Hoggart, K., Lees, L. and Davies, A. (2002) *Researching Human Geography*, Arnold, London

Leitzinger, C. (2001) 'The potential of co-composting in Kumasi – quantification of the urban and peri-urban nutrient balance', in Drechsel, P. and Kunze, D. (eds) *Waste Composting for Urban and Peri-Urban Agriculture: Closing the Rural–Urban Nutrient Cycle in Sub-Saharan Africa*, IWMI, FAO and CABI Publishing, Wallingford, pp150–162

Martin, D. L. and Gershuny, G. (eds) (1992) *The Rodale Book of Composting*, Rodale Press, Emmaus, Pennsylvania

Mason, J. (1997) *Sustainable Agriculture*, Kangaroo Press, East Roseville

Mensah, E., Amoah, P., Drechsel, P. and Abaidoo, R. C. (2001) 'Environmental concerns of urban and peri-urban agriculture: Case studies from Accra and Kumasi', in Drechsel, P. and Kunze, D. (eds) *Waste Composting for Urban and Peri-Urban Agriculture: Closing the Rural–Urban Nutrient Cycle in Sub-Saharan Africa*, IWMI, FAO and CABI Publishing, Wallingford, pp55–68

Naylor, R. (2000) *Ghana: An Oxfam Country Profile*, Oxfam Publishing, Oxford

Nsiah-Gyabaah, K. and Adam, M. (2001) 'Kumasi: Farming systems and farming inputs in and around Kumasi', in Drechsel, P. and Kunze, D. (eds) *Waste Composting for Urban and Peri-Urban Agriculture: Closing the Rural–Urban Nutrient Cycle in Sub-Saharan Africa*, IWMI, FAO and CABI Publishing,

Wallingford, pp96–111

Nunan, F. (2001) 'Rural–urban interactions: The purchase of urban waste by farmers in Hubli-Dharwad, India', *Third World Planning Review*, vol 23, no 4, pp387–403

Onibokun, A. G. (ed) (1999) *Managing the Monster: Urban Waste and Governance in Africa*, International Development Research Centre, Ottawa

Rakodi, C. (1999) *Poverty in the Peri-Urban Interface: NRSP Research Advances No 5*, DFID, London

Simon, D., McGregor, D. F. M., Nsiah-Gyabaah, K. and Thompson, D. A. (2003) 'Poverty elimination, North–South research collaboration and the politics of participatory development', *Development in Practice*, vol 13, no 1, pp40–56

Simon, D., McGregor, D. F. M. and Nsiah-Gyabaah, K. (2004) 'The changing urban–rural interface of African cities: Conceptual issues and an application to Kumasi, Ghana', *Environment and Urbanization*, vol 16, no 2, pp235–247

Simon, D., Poku, O. and Nsiah-Gyabaah, K. (2001) *Survey of Large Industries in Kumasi: Water Use and Environmental Impacts*, CEDAR/IRNR Kumasi Paper 6, Centre for Developing Areas Research, Royal Holloway, University of London and Institute for Renewable Natural Resources, Kwame Nkrumah University of Science and Technology, Kumasi

Tacoli, C. (2003) 'Editor's introduction: The links between urban and rural development', *Environment and Urbanization*, vol 15, no 1, pp3–12

17

Measuring Sustainability in Peri-Urban Areas: Case Study of Mexico City

Rocio A. Diaz-Chavez

Introduction

Since the 1992 Earth Summit in Rio, there have been many initiatives to promote and measure sustainable development (UN, 1992). Indicators of the degree of sustainability are widely regarded as useful tools for gaining insight about the progress made towards achieving sustainable development. They are a flexible means of producing quantified or quantifiable information that can be readily understood and used by a range of specialists. They are not, in themselves, statistics, standards or criteria; rather, they are a way of ordering information in order to give a synoptic view of a situation or a process. Among the main functions of indicators proposed by the Organisation for Economic Co-operation and Development (OECD) are simplification, showing changes over time; quantification, based on theory and science; reliability and information; and ability to update. However, ease of understanding by general users is also important (OECD, 1978, 1997a).

Numerous indicators have been proposed and can be grouped in different ways. A first grouping called 'individual indicator sets' represents the least amount of data aggregation and features lists of indicators, such as the OECD's framework of 'pressure–state–response' (OECD, 1998, 2000), the United Nations Commission for Sustainable Development (CSD) indicators programme (UNDP, 1999) and the preliminary set of indicators developed for the UK (DETR, 1999). A second grouping classifies indicators according to the main dimensions of sustainability, called thematic indicators (economic, social, environmental and integrated) (Eurostat, 1997; Seattle, 1998; Hart, 1999). A third grouping refers to the spatial scale (local, national and global) (Pender et al, 2000). A fourth grouping classifies them according to the environmental medium (air, water, biota and land) (Mckenzie et al, 1992), and a final grouping follows a hierarchical order (headline or core, local or basic, detailed or area specific) (World Bank, 1997; Briassoulis, 2001).

An indicator framework comprises the structuring of sets of indicators in a manner that facilitates their interpretation in measuring progress towards sustainable development (OECD, 2000). The major tendency in the development of indicator frameworks has been to consider first, organization into a specific theme (mainly economic or environmental); second, focus primarily at a national level; third, promotion of international comparisons. Nevertheless, there is still a need to develop frameworks which consider more the social dimension of sustainable development and properly link social aspects with economic and environmental dimensions. Frameworks should also enable valid comparison at the same geographical scale (for example, countries, cities and regions) with broadly similar characteristics (Siniscalo, 2000; Diaz-Chavez, 2003). Another consideration relates to the tendency to aggregate information into a single value or index, such as the Human Development Index, the Poverty Index and gross domestic product (GDP). According to Jenkins and Midmore (1999), aggregation can mask the effects of some indicators in the index, while obscuring relations between them. Instead of an aggregated index, some authors have relied on presenting an array of indicators, limited in number with an appropriate suite of linked measures to promote integrated decision-making (Jenkins and Midmore, 1999; Pender et al, 2000).

One of the frameworks extensively used is the OECD's 'pressure–state–response' framework (OECD, 1978). In this, 'pressure' indicators represent sectoral trends of environmental significance and related driving forces; 'state' indicators represent interactions with the environment and natural resources; and 'response' indicators represent related economic and policy considerations (Avérous, 1997). This model is based on a causal logic – namely, action-response relationships between the economy and the environment (INE, 1997).

This approach was adopted at the national level for Mexico under a United Nations (UN) programme for developing sustainability indicators (UN, 1996; INE, 1999; INEGI/INE, 2000). As with environmental indicators, the *UN Habitat Agenda* has provided another set of indicators following the Istanbul 1996 summit on human settlements (UNCHS, 2000). It is recommended that for each country, indicators should be collected and analysed for at least one major city in order to establish the dimensions of national urban conditions, trends and issues. Nevertheless, indicators for peri-urban areas or for assessing relationships between rural–urban environments have yet to be developed (Potter, 1989; Segre, 1997; UNCHS, 1998).

This chapter introduces an indicator framework developed specifically to assess sustainability in peri-urban areas. The framework is based on a thematic structure, considers linkages within and between themes, and uses a geographical information system (GIS) to visualize the indicators through a case study in the south of Mexico City.

Peri-urban areas

According to the United Nations Human Settlements Programme (UN-Habitat), more than 3 billion people will live and work in urban areas during the 21st century (UNCHS, 2000). Among the main problems that will have to be faced are lack of employment, increased poverty, insecurity, improper land use, inadequate water supply, rising traffic congestion, increasing pollution, lack of green spaces, uncoordinated urban development and an increasing vulnerability to disaster (Burgess et al, 1997). Furthermore, the impacts of economic growth and physical expansion of the urban area are not confined within urban boundaries; they reach into much wider areas surrounding urban centres, creating so-called 'rurban areas', 'urban fringe areas' or 'peri-urban areas' (OECD, 1979).

In this particular research, peri-urban areas were defined under the sustainable development concept as 'the areas with urban and rural characteristics within urban limits, where primary sector activities are performed in order to sustain the natural resources without compromising their existence for future generations but providing the basic needs to their local populations' (Diaz-Chavez, 2003). This definition assumes that local socio-economic and environmental characteristics impact in a positive or negative way upon the lives of local people.

This peri-urban interface (PUI) constitutes the habitat for different kinds of populations, including lower income groups who are vulnerable to the impacts and negative externalities of both rural and urban systems. This includes risk to health, lack of access to basic services, risk of hazards (natural and human made). Environmental changes also affect these areas and their inhabitants by decreasing access to resources such as land, water and energy (OECD, 1979; Brook and Dávila, 2000). Furthermore, there is a noticeable absence of tools to assess sustainability in peri-urban areas; as a result, there are no indicators developed to provide information for decision-makers and the general public (Diaz-Chavez, 2003).

Mexico City

The Basin of Mexico is a closed and now artificially drained hydrological watershed of approximately 7000 square kilometres. The Valley of Mexico is surrounded by volcanic mountains and much of the area was formerly a saline inland lake. Today, most of the original lake is gone and the area is now covered by low-income settlements (Ward, 1998). Mexico City, also known as the Federal District (DF), a political unit created in 1928, enjoys a unique administrative status. It is probably one of the most cited cities in the world because of its environmental problems and many examples of rapid urban sprawl. Internally, it is divided into 16 political-administrative units known as *delegaciones* (delegations). As a result of the metropolitan growth, the built-up area of Mexico City extends into 34 municipalities of the surrounding State of Mexico, making one of the biggest metropolitan areas in the world (Ward, 1998; Ezcurra et al, 1999; INEGI, 2000). In 2000, Mexico City had a population of 8.6 million inhabitants, with a total of 17.8 million in the metropolitan area (INEGI, 2000, 2001).

Of the 16 delegations or political divisions, seven of them in the south-west of the city were classed as peri-urban in this research. This area is classified, mainly in the rural areas, as conservation land, including the delegations Alvaro Obregon, Cuajimalpa, Magdalena Contreras, Milpa Alta, Tlahuac, Tlalpan and Xochimilco (see Figure 17.1) (INEGI, 2000). They are referred to by the government as rural delegations (GDF, 1996). This zone is characterized as an area where some natural ecological communities remain, but where overexploitation of natural resources is present (SEMARNAP, 1996; Ezcurra et al, 1999). It comprises 85,986ha of conservation land with different land uses (INEGI, 2000). This PUI shows a mixture of rural and urban activities, forming a mosaic of social, economic and environmental characteristics and problems. It is an area mainly of urban infrastructure and influence while retaining a dominant rural ambience (Losada et al, 1998).

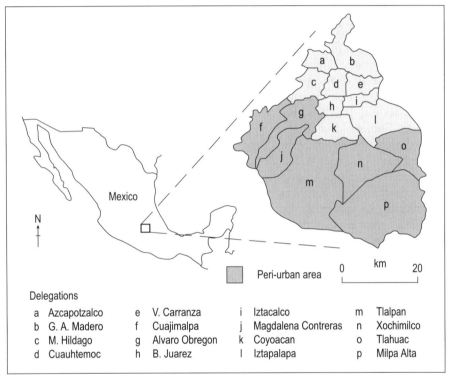

Figure17.1 Mexico City: The Federal District (DF) and peri-urban area

Source: Diaz-Chavez, 2003; INEGI, 2000

In Mexico there are three types of land tenure: private, *ejidal* and communal. After the Revolution of 1910, *ejidos* were created. *Ejido* is a collective of the rural population, which owns a group of lands, forests or water sources for the population's own benefit, independently of the type of land property, the type of activities and the municipality in which they are located (INEGI, 2000). Article 27 from the Mexican Constitution of 1917 was reformed in 1992 and gives *ejidos* and communal lands recognition and protection over their lands for either human settlements and/or productive activities. It also allows them to divide and sell the property, which was not originally permitted (México, 1992; SRA, 2002). The later privatization (legal and illegal) of *ejidal* lands also helped to expand the city. The result is a fragmented mosaic of social, spatial, political and administrative aspects. As a consequence, the south of the city is not homogeneous in terms of density, land use and land value (Negrete et al, 1995; Ward, 1998). This sprawl had an effect on changes in land use, demands on services (water and sewage), housing and transport, among others.

Some of the other factors which influenced land use and the shape of Mexico City are the economic crisis leading to illegal selling of protected land, the more recent concern over conservation of natural resources and local government planning projects. Regarding legal instruments, the new Land Use Plan for Mexico City (GDF, 2002a) defines eight zones: agro-ecological; special agro-ecological (including the swamps and canals of Xochimilco and Tlahuac); agroforestry; special agroforestry; protected forestry; special protected forestry; conservation forestry; special conservation forestry.

Livelihoods of the peri-urban population depend on income from both rural land and urban employment. Thus, family incomes are likely to be the sum of several activities, including, perhaps, permanent employment within the city. Some of the PUI communities comprise indigenous groups who, according to the government's Programme of Attention to Indigenous Towns in the Federal District (GDF, 2002b), have been recognized as groups deserving special attention. An additional factor, which influences the urban link in the peri-urban area, is the transport system. This may either reinforce the link beneficially or adversely by inhibiting the movement of products to the markets. Other environmental problems in the PUI are the loss of biodiversity, reduced forest area, water resources and land-use change. Air and water pollution as well as problems of domestic waste affect the whole city.

The main rural activity across all peri-urban delegations is still small-scale arable farming, followed by forestry and livestock rearing for market (UAM-I, 1997; Losada et al, 1998). Even though the area for rural activities is considerable (18,548ha), the working population engaged in primary production in the PUI is comparatively small. It is important to note that self-consumption of rural production is an essential component of local livelihoods, even though it cannot be measured in terms of income. This indicates that local rural production makes almost no contribution to GDP. Nevertheless, the preservation of these activities contributes to the maintenance of the conservation area.

Some initiatives to develop environmental and sustainability indicators have already been undertaken in Mexico. In 1997, a pilot programme was implemented with the aim of applying a core set of sustainability indicators at a national level. A second report on indicators was submitted to the United Nations Development Programme (UNDP) in 1999. In this second report, most of the environmental indicators were applied; but it was noted that some gaps in the methodology and data availability still existed (INE, 1997, 1999; OCDE, 1998).

At a local level with the government of Mexico City, some initiatives have also been undertaken (Saldívar, 1998; Torres and Rodriguez, 1998). Nevertheless, these initiatives have not shown a complete picture of the links between the different issues of sustainability, mainly due to the application of a general index which masks the relations and links between and within themes. Saldívar (1998) calculated an Index of Sustainable Development (IDS) for the south of Mexico City (considering economic, environmental and social indicators), which indicated a lack of progress towards sustainability, especially in the environmental system. Torres and Rodriguez (1998) focused on regional agriculture development and sustainability indicators for Mexico City. Their conclusion was that a lack of resources exists to promote sustainable agriculture in the PUI, including lack of infrastructure, low economical support and poor organization, as well as inadequate programmes and policy.

Developing the sustainability indicators of the peri-urban indicators framework

To develop the present framework, five sets of indicators from established international organizations were compared. Table 17.1 shows the characteristics of these sets. The UN (1996) sustainable development set included the social, economical, environmental and institutional classes or themes. This set was later modified in 2001 and the number of indicators was reduced (UN, 2001). The OECD (1998) environmental set included climate change; water; forest and fish resources; biodiversity; socio-economic factors; transport; agriculture; and expenditure classes. The OECD urban set included housing, services and employment; ambient quality (environment and nuisances); and social and cultural classes (OECD, 1997b). The UN-Habitat programme has two sets of indicators which include shelter; social development and eradication of poverty; environmental management; economic development; and governance and international cooperation classes (UNCHS, 1998, 1999). Finally, the World Bank considered forestry; biodiversity; land use; water pollution; air pollution; global environmental problems; and institutional capacity as the main classes at project level (Segnestam, 1999). It is important to note that the five sets of indicators are not exhaustive and may be adapted to each project, or to city- or country-specific conditions.

After comparing the sets of indicators, a checklist (Glasson et al, 1995) was used to select a list of indicators. The checklist was primarily based on existing national and local statistical information from Mexican government sources, such as the National Institute of Statistics, Geography and Informatics of Mexico (INEGI). A preliminary list of 108 indicators was derived, and to allow comparison with other approaches, the categories of the OECD process–state–response framework were assigned to each indicator. They were divided broadly into urban and rural according to the influence they may have in the PUI.

A thematic, rather than an aggregated framework, was adopted for the peri-urban indicators. Four themes were selected (societal, productivity, environment and quality of life). In this framework, the economic dimension was replaced with 'productivity' in order to reflect the importance of rural

Table 17.1 *Synopsis of the five sets of indicators reviewed*

Organization	Year	Type	Level	Number of classes	Number of indicators
United Nations (UN)	1996 2001	Sustainability	National	4	134
Organisation for Economic Co-operation and Development (OECD)	1998	Environmental	National	9	50
OECD	1978 1997	Urban	Local (city)	4	23
United Nations Centre for Human Settlements (UNCHS) (*now* UN-Habitat)	1996 1998	Urban	Local (city)	6	40 (maximum) 23 (minimum)
World Bank	1999	Environmental	Project	7	34 approximately

Source: Diaz-Chavez, 2000

activities. The type of settlement was designated as urban (U), rural (R) or peri-urban (PUI).

The definition of the themes followed the criteria:

- *Societal:* the characteristics that belong to society (individuals, populations and communities) and all the components derived from it (political orga-nizations and political activities).
- *Productivity:* not just economic measures linked to other themes, but production itself as part of the 'rural' PUI activities.
- *Environment:* the total global environmental system and the conditions (human activities or natural causes) affecting its components (physical and biological).
- *Quality of life:* the minimal issues necessary to promote a better life for people living in a peri-urban area as part of sustainable development, including alleviation of poverty.

From the preliminary list of 108 indicators, 30 were chosen and balanced to give approximately equal numbers in the four themes selected (see Table 17.2). This chapter considers that the way in which communities live in the PUI is different from the way in which communities live in contiguous urban and rural areas. Since the PUI is, in fact, a mixture of rural and urban activities, people's livelihoods are different and their income sources are mixed. Lifestyles are also differentiated. In this framework, 'quality of life' is consid-ered instead of 'well-being' due to the economic and social conditions of communities in peri-urban areas, especially in developing countries. 'Well-being' implies some ethical concepts; but here the emphasis is on providing better living conditions for people without endangering the environment.

Table 17.2 *Set of indicators selected for the peri-urban area*

Number	Societal	Productivity	Environment	Life quality
1	Population change	Total area for rural activities	Land use (total area in significant categories)	Housing density
2	Population growth rate	Working population per sector	Environmental disturbances	Households and services
3	Population density	Employment and unemployment rate	Changes in urban land use	Literacy level
4	Urban/rural population	Income (wages)	Pollution (waste, air and water)	Access to health services
5	Habitable area per person	Agriculture production	Water resources	Access to transport services
6	Policy instruments	Livestock production	Relation between conservation and urban areas	Marginality and human development indexes
7	Public participation	Forestry production and collection of forest products	Environmental response measures	
8		Production destination	Amount invested in environmental protection measures	
9		Gross domestic product (GDP)		

Source: Diaz-Chavez, 2003

Rural–urban links in the PUI are more complicated than in rural and urban systems themselves. In this case study, however, a simplified approach was used to build the framework for peri-urban areas. In the PUI, urban and rural links are interrelated and intra-related. Furthermore, the indicators are interrelated within and between themes. The resilience or 'elasticity' of linkages in the PUI has been discussed by a number of authors (Ezcurra and Mazari-Hiriart, 1996; Holland et al, 1996; Losada et al, 1998; Meadows, 1998; Pezzoli, 1998; Ward, 1998; Ezcurra et al, 1999; Brook and Dávila, 2000), although particular links may also be easy to break under specific conditions. An example of how these links were analysed is given in the following section.

A database was created from the secondary information and integrated in a geographical information system (GIS) to show the indicators data on a base map of Mexico City (ESRI, 1992–1999). The main emphasis was on the seven peri-urban delegations. The original selection of indicators was tested using a computer model called Sequential Interactive Model for Urban Sustainability (SIMUS). SIMUS is a decision tool that helps to select indicators according to the importance values assigned to the attributes. The model uses relationships between these attributes and their numerical values through the signs < (less than), > (greater than) or = (equal) (Munier, 2002).

Finally, a format was created to standardize the presentation of the indicators, which were categorized following the thematic framework. Table 17.3 shows its characteristics.

Table 17.3 *Characteristics for selected indicators*

Characteristic	Interpretation
Settlement characteristics	Whether it belongs to the urban area only (U), the rural area (R) or the peri-urban area (PUI)
Presence in other frameworks	United Nations (UN); Organisation for Economic Co-operation and Development (OECD); United States Environmental Protection Agency; United Nations Human Settlements Programme (UN-Habitat); other
Process–state–response scheme	According to the OECD framework, to allow comparison
Goal	Specific aim of the indicator
Theme	According to each of the four presented in the framework
Definition	Explanation of the characteristics or proper definition for the indicator
Methodology	Form to measure or establish the indicator
Collection level	City or delegation level
Source of data	Local government, census, other
Linkages	Link with another indicator, other theme or other settlement
Timing	Time series (if available); future trends or projections (if available)
Other characteristics	Particular characteristic per indicator
GIS file	According to the database created

Source: Diaz-Chavez, 2003

Subcategories of some indicators were set up in order to facilitate their utility – for example, the environmental indicator 'pollution', which considers waste, air and water pollution. Table 17.4 shows some examples of the available data used to measure the indicators.

Some indicators are well-known statistics used in the census, such as population density or housing density. In this framework, they were adapted and applied to the PUI. Thus, instead of simply using housing density, what was used was housing density in the urban land-use type within the conservation area. An important outcome of using these alternative criteria is that it was possible to establish the relationships between some indicators within certain themes. As an example, linkages were established between indicators such as housing density within the quality of life theme with the change in urban land-use indicator within the environment theme.

Applying indicators to the case study

The objective of these key indicators is to present instant, easily understandable and accurate information. The data were obtained from a variety of secondary sources, both public and academic (Diaz-Chavez, 2003). The results are intended to be used by a spectrum of audiences, from the general public to policy-makers and specialists. Of the 30 chosen indicators, 4 correspond exclusively to the city level, 6 to the city/delegation (C/D) level and 20 to the delegation level.

Table 17.4 *Examples of the data used for indicators*

Productivity theme

Agriculture production	Cultivated surface and production (tonnes and value in Mexican pesos) of main crops per delegation
Livestock production	Livestock categories, production levels in tonnes and production value in Mexican pesos per delegation
Forestry production	Forestry production in cubic metres per species and number of rural units with forest products (resin, firewood or others)
Production destination	Percentage of the destination of the rural production in the rural delegations (self-consumption, local, national and export)

Environmental theme

Pollution (waste, air and water)	Air: time series of maximum values of the Metropolitan Index of Air Quality (IMECA), specifically of ozone
	Water: time series of wastewater discharge into deep sewage system
	Waste: average production or recovery of domestic waste
Water resources	Sources of water supply (in cubic metres) and water consumption amount in cubic metres per inhabitant per day

Quality of life theme

Households and services	Number of dwellings with access to infrastructure services (piped water, electricity and access to sewage system per delegation)
Literacy level (population over 15 years of age who can read and write)	Size of the total literate population per delegation in a time series of at least 20 years; show gender differences
Access to health services	Size of the population per delegation with access to health services per delegation and per health institution; show the ratio to the total size of population per delegation

Some of the indicators have sufficient data to produce a time series over a period of years, as in the case of the societal indicator 'urban–rural population', which shows the population in localities of ≤ 2500 (rural population) over a period of ten years (see Figure 17.2). These data can be used to create a GIS database.

Some indicators, however, lack the data for time series presentation, but they may be displayed as a ratio or percentage chart in the GIS. Nevertheless, the graphic representation in the form of a map is easier to visualize and interpret. In the case of indexes that had already been produced, such as GDP, human development and marginality indices, the information may be presented graphically.

As the framework does not use aggregation, the relationships between indicators over time helped to provide an overview of the progress towards sustainability under the four different themes. For example, Figure 17.3 shows the relationships of the indicators within the productivity theme.

It can be observed that relationships exist not just between the indicators within a particular theme, but also between indicators of different themes. The productivity theme contains the largest number of indicators and includes those indicators traditionally described as economic, such as, GDP, working population and income, along with indicators specifically selected for the PUI,

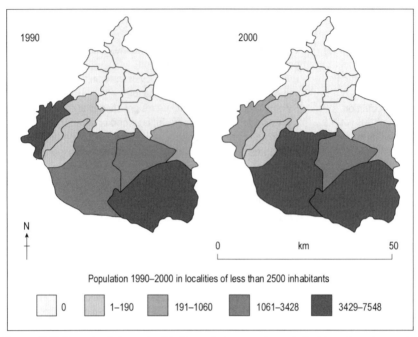

Figure 17.2 Example of the societal indicator 'urban–rural population' in a short time series

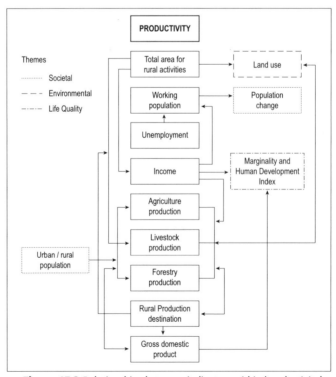

Figure 17.3 Relationships between indicators within 'productivity'

Source: Diaz-Chavez, 2003

including primary-sector activities such as agriculture (crop production), livestock and forestry production (see Figure 17.3). The land-use indicator is related to the total area for rural activities and to the various types of production in the PUI.

In terms of between-theme linkages, the production-type indictors of the productivity theme, for example, are linked to the urban–rural population indicator from the societal theme, as this is the population engaged in primary-sector activities. The urban–rural population indicator is, in turn, directly related to the working population indicator of the productivity theme.

A further example relates to one of the main problems of the PUI: the loss of conservation land to urban development. Table 17.5 shows how the environmental theme indicator 'change in urban land use' has been derived, and how it is logged within the GIS database.

Table 17.5 *Example of the database setup of the environmental theme indicator 'change in urban land use'*

Characteristic	Change in urban land use
Settlement characteristics	Urban/peri-urban
Presence in other frameworks	United Nations (UN)
Pressure–state–response (P-S-R) scheme	Pressure (P)
Goal	To establish changes in urban land use through time
Theme	Environmental
Definition	Urban areas are defined as localities with more than 2500 inhabitants (National Institute of Statistics, Geography and Informatics of Mexico, or INEGI); it also considers the areas where no rural activities are performed
Methodology	Define the surface area in hectares of urban land use per delegation on the basis of a time series
Data collection level	Delegation level
Data collection sources	INEGI/Gobierno del Distrito Federal (GDF); Federal District of Mexico City (Distrito Federal, or DF); Secretaria de Medio Ambiente (SMA); Instituto Nacional de Estadisticas (INE)
Linkages	Land use Relation between conservation and urban areas Housing density Population density
Timing	Available data for at least the last 20 years
Other characteristics	Human settlements in conservation area
GIS file	Urban land.apr

Figure 17.4 shows the corresponding GIS time series of change in urban land use between 1970 and 2000. Each year, up to 600ha of forest are lost to the urbanization process. It has been estimated recently that of the 8842ha of

conservation land, 3457ha hold 800 illegal settlements and 179 legalized settlements (Sosa, 2002).

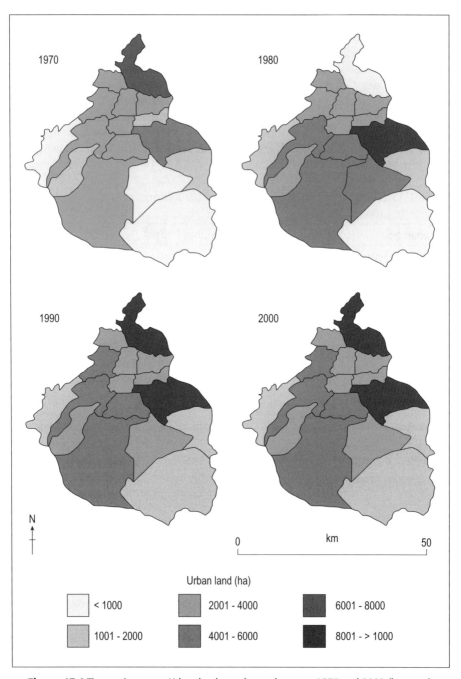

Figure 17.4 Time series maps: Urban land-use change between 1970 and 2000 (hectares)

Source: Diaz-Chavez, 2003

As can be seen from the 'linkages' characteristics, the change in urban land use (from the environment theme) is linked to the housing density and population density indicators from the societal theme. Also linked in a practical way, the 'habitable area per person' indicator (of the societal theme), defined as the density of urban land use, has shown an increment from 1970 to 2000. This reflects a rise in the urban area and a reduction of the conservation area within the peri-urban delegations. However, there is still the need to increase housing in the DF. Given the lack of housing in Mexico City, the south of the city has been the target of irregular settlements, reflected in this framework in the environmental indicator 'environmental disturbances' (J. Hernández, 2002; M. Hernández, 2002; Sosa and Botello, 2002). Therefore, the linkages between different indicators, such as population change, population density and habitable area per person within the societal theme also show a direct linkage with and impact upon the land-use indicator within the environmental theme.

The same process was applied to each indicator in the four themes and the results were analysed and compared to existing previous frameworks, such as Saldívar (1998) and Torres and Rodriguez (1998). The outcome of this analysis provided the information to determine the progress or lack of sustainability in the PUI.

Assessing sustainability

One of the main concerns with respect to the peri-urban area in Mexico City is urban growth and contraction of the conservation area (including rural land used for agriculture and grassland). Since land use is a major link between the existing local population and their rural activities, it was important to review these changes over time. For instance, INEGI (2000) reports that the area of conservation land has decreased during the last 25 years.

The results of the four themes of indicators showed progress towards sustainability in some issues, such as those from the societal theme, while others are still lagging behind in terms of sustainability, such as the environment theme. These differences, along with the features that characterize peri-urban areas, are important outcomes of the applicability of the framework in the case study. With respect to the environment theme, there has been some progress related to protection of the conservation area and environmental response measures to improve environmental quality in the whole city.

Table 17.6 depicts some of the outcomes of the research. It shows those indicators which demonstrated progress towards sustainability, or at least did not reveal a great difference over time, and those which are still lagging behind. Some indicators show a dual achievement because they depict progress in one aspect and a lack of progress in another. For example, 'total area for rural activities' from the productivity theme may be considered as a progress due to the legal changes in land tenure. Nevertheless, it lacks progress towards sustainability regarding the reduction of land surface useful for rural activities.

Table 17.6 *Indicators assessment towards sustainability*

Progress towards sustainability	Lack of progress towards sustainability
Societal	*Societal*
Population change	Urban–rural population
Population growth rate	Habitable area per person
Population density	
Policy instruments	
Public participation	
Productivity	*Productivity*
Total area for rural activities	Total area for rural activities
Employment and unemployment rate	Working population per sector (primary, such as
Agriculture production	rural activities)
Livestock production	Employment and unemployment rate
Forestry production	GDP (except primary sector)
Production destination	
Gross domestic product (GDP)	
Environment	*Environment*
Land use (conservation)	Land use (total area in significant categories)
Environmental response measures	Environmental disturbances
Amount invested in environmental protection	Changes in urban land use
measures	Pollution (wastes, air and water)
	Water resources
	Relation between conservation and urban area
Quality of life	*Quality of life*
Households and services	Housing density
Literacy level	Marginality and human development indices
Access to health services	(Milpa Alta and Xochimilco)
Access to transport services	
Marginality and human development indices	

Source: Diaz-Chavez, 2003

It is important to indicate how these linkages were analysed. Assessing links in this case study was based on several criteria – namely, knowledge of the site and its historic antecedents; logical assessment using a network methodology; and cause–effect relationships. The most influential indicators are those that affect other factors, both within and between themes. The characteristics of peri-urban areas mean that the land-use indicator showed links in three of the four themes, while the population change indicator was defined as a basic indicator for each of the four themes. This was based upon a causality methodology, which was applied to a local scale for easier assessment of previous and actual conditions in the four themes. However, as suggested by Ramos et al (2004), linear relationships do not obstruct the view of more complex relationships within and between the themes. The present conditions may depend on the total effects of multiple factors. They suggest an integrated approach that relates different indicators with multiple aspects that interact with each other. In this study, this was followed through the different linkages between and within themes and was related to a well-known area: the south of Mexico City.

Comparing the results of this research with the work of Saldívar (1998), it is possible to track progress towards sustainability through the use of a non-aggregated indicator framework. In addition, the analysis can rely upon the secondary data and the links between indicators. In both frameworks, it was the environmental theme which showed less progress towards sustainability.

Conclusions and final recommendations

In this case study, the assessment of progress towards sustainability in the peri-urban area was facilitated by the use of specific indicators. The value of rural activities in the peri-urban area was also highlighted, as well as the need to consider local livelihoods. Presenting the characteristics of the area also provides a useful tool for public comment and future public participation regarding the policy and planning of the south of Mexico City.

The main outcomes of this chapter are, first, the use of indicators as a tool to assess progress towards sustainability; second, the use of a thematic framework for indicators that provides rapid, easy and understandable information for various stakeholders such as decision-makers and the general public; and, third, the conceptualization of peri-urban areas and the need to measure sustainability in such areas in order to provide decision-makers with better policy instruments and management tools to improve the quality of life of local populations.

In addition, the use of various tools in the framework may help to facilitate the task of decision-making, as the maps created through GIS helped to track progress towards sustainability without using a single index of sustainability. The use of a predefined format for presenting indicators integrates the information, which is necessary for measuring sustainability. The 13 features that make up the format allow for comparisons with other frameworks and with other geographic areas. Three visual aids (graphs, tables and time series maps) fulfil the objective of indicators by providing information that is easily understood.

Another important feature observable from links between indicators is that the peri-urban area is not just the sum of its various components. The links between indicators clearly show interaction between components, such as land use, population, working population and sector of activities. These constitute a set of different and unique dynamics beyond individual issues. Thus, many issues (measured by indicators) act to reinforce or counteract one another. This dynamic is the result of the relations between natural and anthropological elements, called 'sub-systems' by other authors (Peri-Urban Research Project Team, 2001). To measure progress towards sustainability and to present information in a comprehensive form, the use of links among indicators both within and between themes reduces the subjectivity involved in creating a single index of sustainability. Such aggregate indices may mask important information and conceal relationships within the framework. Even though the debate over a single sustainability index will continue, using links between indicators will provide additional information and reinforce the results of the analysis using disaggregated indicators.

Although the current framework was not constructed as a set of community indicators, community participation in studies in the area was witnessed in previous research by the author (UAM-I, 1997). Nevertheless, sustainability is a concept which relies upon social participation. Therefore, the adoption of the framework in another area would necessarily require public participation in testing the applicability of the indicators. The framework allows for modifications, while preserving the same conceptual structure.

Finally, the use of indicators can be extended to different areas of environmental management such as auditing, environmental assessments and the creation of standards. A universally applicable and unique framework does not exist. Similarly, the perfect sustainable city or peri-urban area does not exist. Nevertheless, the applicability of the general framework to different cases suggests that it provides an easy means of analysing and measuring progress towards sustainability.

References

Avérous, C. (1997) 'Evaluación del desempeño ambiental', in OCDE (ed) *Desarrollo Sustentable: Estrategias de la OCDE para el Siglo XXI*, OCDE, Paris, pp41–58

Briassoulis, H. (2001) 'Sustainable development and its indicators: Through a (planners) glass darkly', *Journal of Environmental Planning and Management*, vol 44, no 3, pp409–427

Brook, R. M. and Dávila, J. D. (eds) (2000) *The Peri-Urban Interface: A Tale of Two Cities*, School of Agricultural and Forest Sciences, University of Wales and Development Planning Unit, University College London

Burgess, R., Carmona, M. and Kolstee, T. (1997) 'Contemporary spatial strategies and urban policies in developing countries: A critical review', in Burgess, R., Carmona, M. and Kolstee, T. (eds) *The Challenge of Sustainable Cities: Neoliberalism and Urban Strategies in Developing Countries*, Zed Books, London, pp111–124

DETR (Department for Transport, Local Government and the Regions) (1999) *Quality of Life Counts: Indicators for a Strategy for Sustainable Development for the United Kingdom – A Baseline Assessment*, DETR, London

Diaz-Chavez, R. (2000) *PhD Internship Report at the Mexican Representation before the OECD*, OECD, Paris, July–August, p19

Diaz-Chavez, R. (2003) *Sustainable Development Indicators for Peri-Urban Areas: A Case Study of Mexico City*, PhD thesis, EIA Unit, IBS, University of Wales Aberystwyth, Aberystwyth

ESRI (Environmental Systems Research Instsitute) (1992–1999) *ArcView GIS 3.2*, Geographic Information System software, ESRI, Aylesbury

Eurostat (1997) *Indicators of Sustainable Development*, Eurostat, Luxembourg

Ezcurra, E. and Mazari-Hiriart, M. (1996) 'Are megacities viable? A cautionary tale from Mexico City', *Environment*, vol 38, no 1, pp6–15, 26–35

Ezcurra, E., Mazari-Hiriart, M., Pisanty, I. and Aguilar, A. (1999) *The Basin of Mexico. Critical Environmental Issues and Sustainability*, United Nations University Press, New York

GDF (Gobierno del Distrito Federal) (1996) *Programa General de Desarrollo Urbano del Distrito Federal*, Gaceta Oficial del Distrito Federal, Mexico DF
GDF (2002a) *Programa General de Desarrollo Urbano del Distrito Federal 2000–2006 (Propuesta)*, GDF, Mexico
GDF (2002b) *Programas del DF*, GDF, www.df.gob.mx/secretarias/programas/index.html, accessed 2003
Glasson, J., Therivel, R. and Chadwick, A. (1995) *Introduction to Environmental Impact Assessment*, UCL Press, London
Hart, M. (1999) *Guide to Sustainable Community Indicators*, 2nd edition, Sustainable Measures, North Andover, Massachusetts
Hernández, J. (2002) 'Sorprenden a invasores de terrenos', *Reforma*, 24 June, Mexico
Hernández, M. (2002) 'Prevé Xochimilco regular asentamientos', *Reforma*, 3 September, Mexico
Holland, M., Kasanga, R., Lewcock, C. and Warburton, H. (1996) *Peri-Urban Baseline Studies: Kumasi, Ashanti Region, Ghana*, Report for DFID, Natural Resources Institute, London
INE (Instituto Nacional de Estadisticas) (1997) *Preliminary Report on the Development of Environmental Performance Indicators in Mexico*, SEMARNAP, INE, Mexico
INE (1999) *Mexico: Sustainable Development Indicators. Final Report (Draft)*, SERMANAP, Mexico
INEGI (National Institute of Statistics, Geography and Informatics of Mexico) (2000) *Estadísticas del Medio Ambiente del Distrito Federal y Zona Metropolitana 2000*, INEGI/SMA/GDF, Aguascalientes, Mexico
INEGI (2001) *XII Censo General de Población y Vivienda 2000*, INEGI, Aguascalientes, Mexico
INEGI/INE (2000) *Indicadores de Desarrollo Sustentable en México*, INEGI, Mexico
Jenkins, T. and Midmore, P. (1999) 'Towards an integrated understanding of environmental quality', in O'Connor, M. and Spash, C. L. (eds) *Valuation and the Environment: Theory, Method and Practice*, Edward Elgar, Cheltenham, pp263–285
Losada, H., Martinez, H., Vieyra, J., Pealing, R., Zavala, R. and Cortés, J. (1998) 'Urban agriculture in the metropolitan zone of Mexico City: Changes over time in urban, suburban and periurban areas', *Environment and Urbanization*, vol 10, no 2, pp37–54
Mckenzie, D., Hyatt, D. and Macdonald, V. (eds) (1992) *Ecological Indicators: Proceedings of an International Symposium, Fort Lauderdale, Florida, 1990*, Elsevier Applied Sciences, London
Meadows, D. (1998) *Indicators and Information Systems for Sustainable Development: A Report to the Balaton Group*, The Sustainability Institute, Vermont
México (1992) *Constitución Política de los Estado Unidos Mexicanos*, Government of Mexico, Mexico City
Munier, N. (2002) 'Impact assessment with urban sustainable indicators', Paper presented at 22nd Annual Conference: Assessing the Impact of Impact Assessment. for Informed Decision Making, IAIA, The Hague, 15–21 June
Negrete, M., Graizbord, B. and Ruiz, C. (1995) *Población, Espacio y medio Ambiente en la Zona Metropolitana de la Ciudad de México*, El Colegio de México, Mexico City
OCDE (Organización para la Cooperación y el Desarrollo Económicos) (1998) *Análisis del Desempeño Ambiental: México*, OCDE, Mexico City
OECD (Organisation for Economic Co-operation and Development) (1978) *Urban Environmental Indicators*, OECD, Paris
OECD (1979) *Agriculture in the Planning and Management of Peri-urban Areas*, OECD, Paris
OECD (1997a) *OECD Environmental Performance Reviews: A Practical Introduction*, OECD, Paris

OECD (1997b) *Better Understanding Our Cities: The role of Urban Indicators*, OECD, Paris

OECD (1998) *Towards Sustainable Development: Environmental Indicators*, OECD, Paris.

OECD (2000) 'Accounting frameworks', in *Proceedings of OEDC Rome Conference on Towards Sustainable Development: Indicators to Measure Progress*, OECD, Rome, pp66–74

Pender, A., Dunne, L., Convenry, F., Dilworth, C., Doddy, M., Fennelly, R., Kealy, L., Keane, P., Ryan, C. and Scully, F. (2000) *Environmental Indicators for the Urban Environment*, Environmental Institute, National University of Ireland, Dublin

Peri-Urban Research Project Team (2001) *Guidelines for Strategic Environmental Planning and Management of the Peri-Urban Interface*, Development Planning Unit, University College London

Pezzoli, K. (1998) *Human Settlements and Planning for Ecological Sustainability*, MIT Press, Massachusetts

Potter, R. B. (1989) 'Urban–rural interaction, spatial polarisation and development planning', in Potter, R. B. and Unwin, P. T. H. (eds) *The Geography of Urban–Rural Interaction in Developing Countries*, Routledge, London, pp323–333

Ramos, T. B., Caeiro, S. and de Melo, J. J. (2004) 'Environmental indicator frameworks to design and assess environmental monitoring programs', *Impact Assessment and Project Appraisal*, vol 22, no 1, pp47–62

Saldívar, A. (1998) *Diseño y Metodología para una base de datos para crear un Sistema de Información para evaluar Sustentabilidad y Ordenamiento Ambiental de la Ciudad de México*, Desarrollo Sustentable y Recursos Naturales, Gobierno del DF CONSERVA, Mexico City

Seattle (1998) *Indicators of Sustainable Community*, Seattle, Seattle/King County

Segnestam, L. (1999) *Environmental Performance Indicators: A Second Edition Note*, Environmental Economic Series, Paper No 71, World Bank, Washington, DC

Segre, R. (1997). 'The inner periphery of the city: Symbol and cultural expression in the urban scenery of Latin America', in Burgess, R., Carmona, M. and Kolstee, T. (eds) *The Challenge of Sustainable Cities: Neoliberalism and Urban Strategies in Developing Countries*, Zed Books, London, pp125–135

SEMARNAP (Secretaría de Medio Ambiente, Recursos Naturales y Pesca) (1996) *Programas de Desarrollo Sustentable (PRODERS)*, México, SEMARNAP, Mexico City

Siniscalo, D. (2000) 'Chair's conclusions', in *Proceedings of OEDC Rome Conference Towards Sustainable Development: Indicators to Measure Progress*, OECD, Rome, pp13–15

Sosa, I. (2002) 'Urgen a contener expansión urbana', *Reforma*, 11 December, México

Sosa, I. and Botello, B. (2002) 'Reconocen 419 asentamientos irregulares', *Reforma*, 9 October, México

SRA (Secretaría de la Reforma Agraria) (2002) *La Reforma Constitucional de 1992 Secretaría de la Reforma Agraria*, SRA, www.sra.gob.mx/sraweb/srahistoria/reforma_01iniciativa.htm, accessed 2002

Torres, P. A. and Rodriguez, L. M. (1998) *Desarrollo Agrícola Regional e Indicadores de Sustentabilidad en la Ciudad de México*, Desarrollo Sustentable y Recursos Naturales, Secretaría del medio Ambiente del DF CONSERVA, Mexico City

UAM-I (Universidad Autonoma Metropolitana – Iztapalapa) (1997) *PRODERS de la Región Sur Poniente del Distrito Federal: Diagnóstico*, SEMARNAP, Mexico City

UN (United Nations) (1992) *Report of the United Nations Conference on Environment and Development*, UN, Rio de Janeiro, p5

UN (1996) *Indicators of Sustainable Development: Framework and Methodologies*, UN, New York

UN (2001) *Indicators of Sustainable Development: Guidelines and Methodologies*, UN/ESA, New York

UNCHS (United Nations Centre for Human Settlements) (1998) *Global Urban Indicators Urban Indicators Programme*, UNCHS, www.urbanobservatory.org/indicators/guidelines/abridged/dataset.html, accessed 14 April 2000

UNCHS (1999) *Comprehensive Guidelines for Urban Indicators Urban Observatory*, UNCHS, www.urbanobservatory.org/indicators/guidelines/comprehensive/collecting.html, accessed 14 April 2000

UNCHS (2000) *The Habitat Agenda*, UNCHS, www.unchs.org/unchs/english/hagenda/ch-1a.htm, accessed 2000

UNDP (United Nations Development Programme) (1999) *Indicators of Sustainable Development: From Theory to Practice*, UNDP, www.un.org/esa/sustdev/isd.htm, accessed 2000

Ward, P. (1998) *Mexico City*, Wiley, New York

World Bank (1997) *Expanding the Measure of Wealth: Indicators of Environmentally Sustainable Development*, World Bank, Washington, DC

18

Promoting the Interests of the Poor in the Peri-Urban Interface: The Experience of the Intermediate Technology Development Group in Kenya

Lucy Stevens, Rachel Berger and Michael K. Kinyanjui

Introduction

The Intermediate Technology Development Group's (ITDG's) work focuses on promoting the interests of the poor in ways that are environmentally, economically, socially and institutionally sustainable, with the aim of delivering practical answers to poverty by supporting communities in harnessing technologies that meet their needs. At the same time, ITDG aims to increase the programme's impact on poverty and sustainable development by sharing knowledge and influencing policy and practice.

There is, as yet, no consensus on the definition of the peri-urban interface (PUI) apart from recognition that it is a zone where urban and rural features coexist (see Chapter 1 in this volume). The management of natural resources in the 'peri-urban' regions surrounding an urban centre is of great importance to the livelihoods of many groups (see Chapters 2 and 3 in this volume). Equally, the rapid changes in socio-economic conditions and the environment that occur in the peri-urban area have a major impact on the opportunities and constraints facing people living in that area (Tacoli, 1999). The encroachment of the expanding urban area into the surrounding rural land threatens the productivity of natural resources and the livelihoods of small farmers. The PUI is frequently characterized by the degradation of natural landscapes, soil and quality of natural water sources, together with growing population and urbanization in a generally unregulated manner. ITDG sees the PUI as a zone where much of the land remains undeveloped and available for exploitation, although subject to many competing interests and an inadequate institutional framework for mediating the conflicts which arise. These conflicts can be between poor resource users and larger commercial interests, and between economic interests, of both commercial and poor users, and environmental requirements to protect the natural resource base from degradation. ITDG's interventions in the PUI have focused on developing the institutional framework (regulating the use and tenure of land) and building the capacity of poor resource users to negotiate access to resources.

Much of the recent research on the PUI is the output of UK Department for International Development (DFID)-funded research programmes under the Natural Resources Systems Programme (NRSP), examining the effects of growth on natural resource management on two cities, Kumasi in Ghana and Hubli-Dharwad in India. One project under the programme focused on waste management and the extent to which this was a source of livelihoods for peri-urban dwellers and a source of nutrients for agriculture in or near the urban areas (Universities of Birmingham and Bangor, 1998–1999). An issue identified was the affordability and availability of this material to poorer farmers. The programme, while assessing the poverty impact of natural resource management or lack of it, was primarily examining management systems. One issue addressed is the valuation of natural resources in urban and peri-urban areas in a way that reflects not merely short-term economic value, but longer-term issues related to the environmental services that they provide. Both of the case studies in this chapter are concerned with issues of maintaining the natural resource base while improving livelihoods for local users.

Another major research project under this programme, Strategic Environmental Planning and Management for the Peri-Urban Interface, was carried out within the Development Planning Unit (DPU) at University College London (UCL). Draft reports from this programme (Allen et al, 1999; Budds and Minaya, 1999; Tacoli, 1999) also cover the issues illustrated by the case studies: the competition for land in which the wealthier stakeholders win, resulting in the concentration of resource-poor households on environmentally unsuitable sites with little or no security of tenure.

A research project under DFID's Knowledge and Research Programme (R7132: Improved Irrigation in Peri-Urban Areas) looked at the situation in Kumasi and Nairobi. The findings of the first phase of this research for Mavoko, a municipal district just outside Nairobi, were similar to those of the ITDG survey (ITDG-EA, 2003a): squatting and insecurity of tenure are widespread among those engaged in agriculture in the PUI (Hide and Kimani, 2000).

Much of this research focuses on city-level ways of tackling natural resource management problems relating to waste and water. While community involvement is increasing (Budds and Minaya, 1999), capacity-building and social mobilization, key aspects of ITDG's approach, are not yet widespread.

ITDG's interventions focus on the physical characteristics of the PUI in terms of how these affect the poor. In the case studies below, the issues covered include the increase in land values and insecurity of tenure for many of the people living in the PUI, and the issues surrounding poor management of natural resources. Kenya is a rapidly urbanizing country, with urban populations growing at a rate of 4.9 per cent per annum between 1995 and 2000 (UN, 2000).

This creates growing demands for natural resources such as fuelwood, agricultural produce and building materials. Peri-urban areas have a comparative advantage in supplying these resources, and their supply can be key to the livelihoods of peri-urban populations. Natural resources are also used in peri-urban areas for meeting subsistence needs to a greater extent than in urban areas.

However, for a variety of reasons, natural resources are often exploited unsustainably in peri-urban areas. Environmental regulations and legislation are often weak and governments lack the capacity to enforce those that exist. Where poor people make a living that relies on natural resource use, the lack of effective regulation and the intense competition of the informal sector mean that the lowest-cost methods are chosen. Land tenure is often insecure. In Kenya, many people are tenants or squatters, and are at risk of eviction should the land be developed for housing or industry. As a result, there is little incentive for investing in sustainable methods. Even where sustainable methods would benefit the poor, they rarely have the power or voice to influence business or the government to adopt them. Finally, the environmental problems which are of most concern to many of the people living in urban and peri-urban areas are not linked to natural resource use, but to a lack of services, especially water, sanitation, refuse removal and shelter. Others are simply linked to their location on marginal land that is prone to flooding, landslides and pollution from industry.

ITDG's approach to promoting the interests of the poor in this context is through:

- technology that can improve their productivity and reduce environmental impacts; ITDG defines 'technology' to include physical infrastructure, machinery and equipment, and the associated knowledge and skills, as well as the capacity to organize and use all of these;
- building the capacity of poor people to organize and engage with more powerful stakeholders;
- working with a wide range of stakeholders to seek win–win solutions that take the needs of the poor fully into account.

To help conceptualize the situation of the peri-urban poor, and ITDG's approach to working with them, the sustainable livelihoods framework is used (DFID, 2000). This considers the causes of vulnerability of the poor, their assets and the policies, processes and institutions that affect their use of those assets. These combine to produce the wide variety of ways in which urban and peri-urban people construct their livelihoods (see Figure 18.1).

The distorted shape of the assets pentagon in Figure 18.1 indicates the relative reliance on natural resources of peri-urban residents, and their limited access to financial or physical assets. The three points of ITDG's approach are mapped on to the diagram (numbered). These actions help to improve the asset base of the poor and change the policy environment to be more pro-poor, which improves livelihoods (shown in the bottom-left box).

The aim of this chapter is to illustrate ITDG's approach in two different Kenyan 'case study' contexts. The first looks at sand extraction on the outskirts

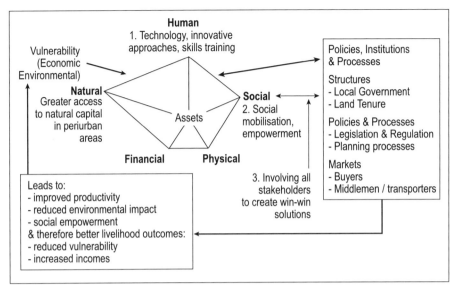

Figure 18.1 Sustainable livelihoods framework: Working with the poor in peri-urban areas

of the town of Nakuru. This has caused significant environmental damage to the ecology of nearby Lake Nakuru and its large population of flamingos. The second looks at urban agriculture in the municipal district of Mavoko near Nairobi. Here the issue is not so much environmental damage, but the unproductive use of the land and other available natural resources for nutrient inputs and irrigation. In both cases, there are problems of land tenure, inappropriate and ineffective regulations, a lack of finance, weak social organization, and a lack of power in decision-making or the market. We outline the approaches that are being taken to address these problems, incorporating the lessons from previous work in Kenya.

Sand extraction in Nakuru, Kenya

Background

Nakuru is Kenya's fourth largest town, located 160km north-west of Nairobi on the main highway between Nairobi and Kisumu. It has a population of just under 290,000, growing at 5.7 per cent per year (Central Bureau of Statistics, 2001). The population of the whole metropolitan area within and immediately outside the municipal boundary of the town is estimated at 350,000 (Majale and Albu, 2001). It is the headquarters of the surrounding district and of the Rift Valley Province. Seventy per cent of the population live in informal settlements, and 41 per cent live below the poverty line (Government of Kenya, 2000). The economy of the town is largely based on agro-processing from the surrounding agricultural hinterland (for example, dairies, oil-seed mills and cereal processing). Other industries have also developed and there are numerous informal commercial activities.

There are seven low-income settlements in Nakuru (see Figure 18.2), on the fringes of two of which (Kaptembwo and Kwa Rhonda) sand extraction takes place. Most of the people who work as labourers or whose business depends upon the labourers (for example, food sellers) come from these two settlements. The majority of residents rely on running small businesses (60 per cent of households in three of the low-income areas, including Kaptembwo) or providing casual labour in the town's industries (20 per cent) (Mwangi, 2003). Incomes in these settlements are very low, and the neighbourhoods suffer from very poor access to services. The main environmental issues which concern the residents of these settlements are the immediate ones of a lack of sanitation and clean drinking water, and inadequate wastewater drains and refuse collection (see Figure 18.3).

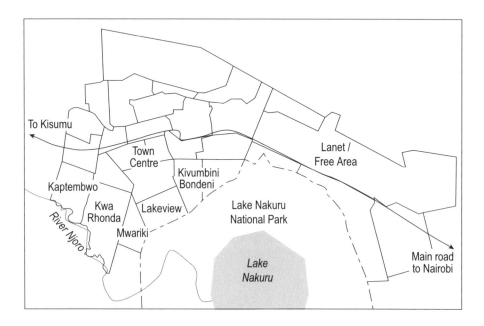

Figure 18.2 Nakuru Municipality (the names of the seven low-income settlements are shown)

Source: base map of block boundaries from Mbuguah and Ehrensperger, 2003

The land in the settlements of Kaptembwo and Kwa Rhonda slopes gently towards the Njoro River. Between the settlements and the riverbed, deposits of sand are found covered with a layer of loose volcanic soils. Quarrying of this sand takes place along a 1.5km stretch of the riverbank. There are about 15 of such quarries, varying in size between 0.3ha and 0.5ha.

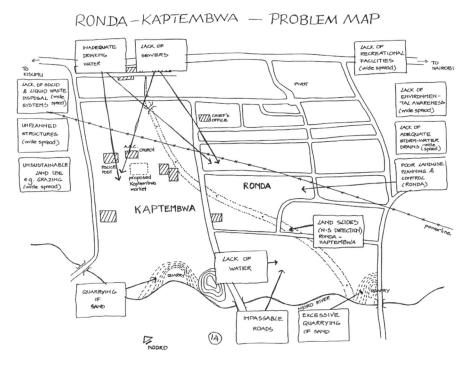

Figure 18.3 Map created at participatory workshop, 1997

Impact of sand extraction

Figure 18.4 indicates the main impacts of sand extraction. The positive impacts (the upper half) are largely related to the town's economy and the livelihoods of the poor. The negative impacts are largely linked to the environment (the lower half).

Contribution to the economy and livelihoods of the poor

One of the positive impacts of sand extraction is that it provides a source of cheap sand for the town's construction industry (see box 1 in Figure 18.4). The nearest alternative source is Naivasha, some 95km away. Sourcing sand from here would greatly increase the costs of construction because of the high cost of transport. The construction sector is estimated to employ around 2600 people in Nakuru (Central Bureau of Statistics, 2000), although this is probably an underestimate as official data do not accurately capture informal and casual employment (see boxes 1.2 and 1.3 in Figure 18.4). The private sector plays the dominant role in housing construction. Recently, formal-sector construction has been affected by the poor national and local economic performance. However, the informal sector for housing is still growing at a rapid rate to cater for the town's growing population and because there is still land available for development (Majale and Albu, 2001). Cheap sand, therefore, makes

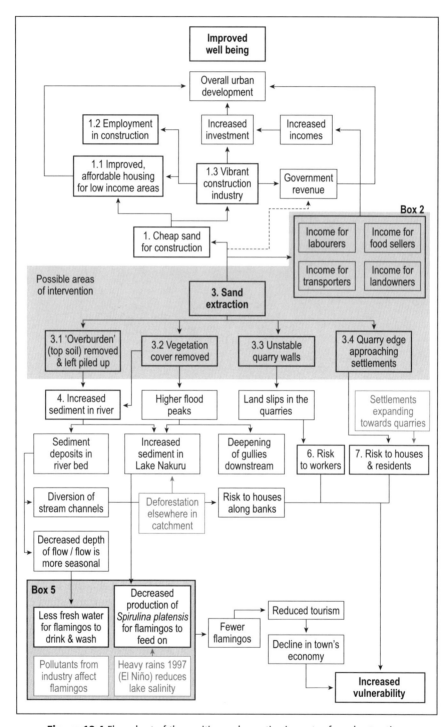

Figure 18.4 Flow chart of the positive and negative impacts of sand extraction

Note: Grey lettering indicates factors beyond those linked to sand extraction. Dotted line shows a potential link

it possible to develop relatively low-cost housing in the low-income settlements (see box 1.1 in Figure 18.4).

Sand extraction also provides a source of employment for about 200 labourers (mostly men) and around 20 others (mostly women) who sell food at the sites (see box 2 in Figure 18.4). However, the labourers tend to be exploited, receiving very little of the final price for the sand. Those who profit most are the landowners and those who transport the sand into the town. A labourer is generally paid about 400 Kenyan shillings (approximately UK£3.60) per lorry load. They can generally sell three to four loads per week. This is divided, with a cut (about half) being paid to the landowner and 60 Kenyan shillings paid to others to assist with loading the lorry. The labourer is left with 140 Kenyan shillings (approximately UK£1.30). The load is sold in town for 2100 Kenyan shillings (approximately UK£19.10), with most of the profit going to the lorry owners. Incomes fluctuate by season. There is less demand for sand during the rainy season because at this time of year it is more difficult for the construction industry to operate. In addition, some of the tracks leading to the sand extraction sites become impassable (marked on Figure 18.3).

Negative impacts of sand extraction

Sand extraction has a range of serious environmental consequences, illustrated in the lower half of Figure 18.4. In the process of extracting the sand, the overburden (top layers of soil) are removed and piled up (see box 3.1 of Figure 18.4). Vegetation cover is removed (box 3.2). These extraction activities (see Figures 18.5 and 18.6) lead to greater soil erosion and a greater volume of sediments in the river. Monitoring of the river undertaken by the World Wide Fund for Nature (WWF) between March 2001 and November 2002 found that the average concentrations of dissolved solids in the Njoro River were nearly twice as high as in any of the other rivers or springs which feed the lake (see Table 18.1).

Figure 18.5 Soil erosion and sedimentation in the Njoro River caused by sand extraction

Source: ITDG/Lucy Stevens, May 2003

Figure 18.6 Sand being dug

Source: ITDG/Lucy Stevens, May 2003

Table 18.1 *River flows and sediment loads to Lake Nakuru: March 2001 to November 2002*

River/spring	Days of flow per year	Average flow (millimetres per day)	% contribution of flow to lake per year	Average total dissolved solids (milligrams per litre)
Njoro River	240	52,116	58.3	1986
Makalia River	240	26,065	29.2	735
Nderit River	90	13,703	5.8	625
S/drain	360	2194	3.7	1086
B/springs	360	1831	3.1	1052

Source: Lake Nakuru Conservation Project, Kenya Wildlife Service; data originally collected by WWF

The lake is at the lowest point of its catchment, which means that it maintains a high level of alkalinity. This provides the habitat for the blue-green alga *Spirulina platensis* upon which large numbers of lesser flamingos (*Phoeniconaias minor*) feed. The numbers of flamingo at the lake vary during the year as they travel to Tanzania's Lake Natron to breed, and from year to year as they move between a string of soda lakes in the Rift Valley area. However, Nakuru has tended to be their favourite location, and in 1993, 1.5 million birds were counted on the lake. They provide the major draw for visitors to the Lake Nakuru National Park, bringing with them an income of around US$3 million per year.

The high levels of sediment in the river affect the flamingo population in two ways (see box 5 of Figure 18.4). First, they reduce the depth and increase the turbidity of water in the lake. The algae require clear water to thrive, so the sedimentation reduces the production of algae. Second, sediment is deposited on the riverbed, reducing its flow and making it more seasonal. The flamingos rely on this source of clean water for drinking and washing their feathers.

Sand extraction is not the only cause of increased levels of sediment, nor is it the only threat to the flamingos. In 1993 and again in 1997, for example, large numbers of flamingos died at Lake Bogoria. The majority had come from Lake Nakuru and had been killed or severely weakened by high levels of agricultural and industrial pollution. They were also affected by dilution of the lake's salinity by heavy rains in 1997, which reduced the production of algae. Since then, however, efforts have been made with industries to reduce levels of pollution. A spokesman for the Kenya Wildlife Service now describes sand extraction as the major threat to the lake's ecosystem.

There are also risks to the labourers and local residents from the current methods of sand extraction. Steep cliffs are exposed, which often collapse during the rainy season and risk burying labourers (see Figure 18.6 and box 6 of Figure 18.4). The dug areas are expanding steadily towards the nearby settlements, and in some places houses are dangerously close to the edge. Similarly, further downstream, gullies have been deepened and widened, and nearby houses are at risk (see box 7 of Figure 18.4).

Regulations controlling sand extraction

Sand extraction has been largely unregulated in Kenya. The 1940 Kenya Mining Act, last revised in 1987, did not cover sand, aggregates or rock. In relation to stone quarrying, Uglow (1999) noted that the practice 'can commence on private land without reference to any authority – unrecorded, unregulated and with no environmental obligations'. In general, the enforcement of environmental regulations in Kenya has been very weak. They have been affected by:

- poor or weak administrative structures;
- an absence of provisions to specify standards of performance;
- inadequate deterrents and incentives;
- gaps and overlaps in the institutional framework, making enforcement difficult;
- low levels of active or participatory awareness among the population;
- a preference for short-term gains rather than sustainable alternatives;
- poverty promoting the unsustainable use of resources (Uglow, 1999).

In Nakuru, attempts have been made to deal with the problems caused by sand extraction through the district environment committee. The committee, with membership from a range of organizations including WWF and the Kenya Wildlife Service, favoured banning the practice altogether. However, there is no available legislation to effect or enforce such a ban. There is general support for environmental control from the Municipal Council of Nakuru, especially given its adoption of a Local Agenda 21 programme (with support from UN-Habitat). At the same time, however, it is in the council's interest to support the economy of the town – balancing the interests of the environment, the tourism industry, the construction industry and the residents (the majority of whom are poor). More recently, ITDG has been successful in lobbying the committee to support the adoption of sustainable extraction practices. The difficulty is making this happen in practice. By September 2004, there was still a standoff between the various parties, and unrestricted sand extraction was still continuing.

Lessons of ITDG's work on stone quarrying

Lessons for addressing the problem can be learned from an earlier ITDG project working with stone quarrying in Nairobi's peri-urban areas (Shadmon, 1999). A similar set of stakeholders was involved, and environmental damage was being caused in terms of deforestation, soil erosion and flooding. The project worked on three issues (as suggested in the model in Figure 18.1):

- *Improvement of technologies and quarrying practices.* The labourers were trained by ITDG in improved mining methods, which reduced wastage and improved site safety. A training manual was produced to disseminate the training practices to other areas.

- *Social mobilization and empowerment of the poor.* Quarry-workers' associations were established and registered. Training in technical skills, marketing of the stone, saving and credit schemes, and simply being involved in regular meetings helped to build their confidence. They developed a shared agenda of concerns which they were able to present to landowners and policy-makers.
- *Involvement of all stakeholders to find a win–win solution.* A number of quarries had been closed due to environmental and safety concerns. In an attempt to avoid this drastic measure, workshops were held with all stakeholders. An environmental impact assessment was carried out which helped to define clear rules and policy to guide quarry managers and owners in the rehabilitation of the quarried land. A tree nursery was established on some of the reclaimed land. This provided an incentive for the owners to reclaim the land, in addition to the increased incomes they gained from better practices. Workers benefited from higher productivity, higher incomes and a safer environment, as well as work in rehabilitating the land. A centre was opened as a focal point for all stakeholders: quarry owners, workers, brokers and customers.

A similar approach could be taken in addressing the question of sand extraction. Figure 18.7 shows some suggested actions, including rehabilitating the quarries and planting woodlots. Some of these are detailed in Nakuru's strategic structure plan, developed through the Local Agenda 21 initiative. This will be supported by recent changes in legislation. A new Environmental Management and Coordination Act came into force which covers rock, aggregates and sand under the provisions for quarrying and mineral exploitation, and requires environmental impact assessments to be carried out. An environment department has recently been created at the council, which plans to include conservation measures in its environmental by-laws. Despite this legislation, action will only be effective with the support of the stakeholders involved, especially the landowners and labourers. A lesson from the stone-quarrying work is the need for continual dialogue between all partners to maintain awareness and support for whatever legislation or regulations are put in place. This may only be feasible if funding can be found for a non-governmental organization (NGO) such as ITDG to facilitate the process.

Peri-urban agriculture in Mavoko, near Nairobi

Background

Mavoko is an expanding urban area around 30km south east of Nairobi, in Machakos district, and is adjacent to Nairobi National Park on the River Athi at the junction of the Nairobi–Mombasa railway line and the highways from Arusha (Tanzania) and Mombasa (see Figure 18.8). Mavoko is a rapidly growing secondary town, where land values are rising as opportunities for investment in industry open up, while an influx of people seek work and

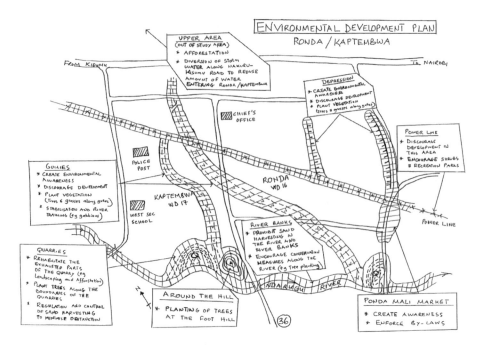

Figure 18.7 Environmental development plan created during participatory workshop

Note: The River Njoro is sometimes know as the Ndarugu, as shown here
Source: Environmental Development Plan and Action Plans – Kwa Rhonda and Kaptembwo, Workshop under the Environmental and Urban Development Training Project, supported by Green Town, Municipal Council of Nakuru and UN-Habitat, January 1997

housing. Its population was estimated at between 50,000 to 60,000 in 1998, up from 40,000 in 1989 (Koti, 2000). Its economy and environment are dominated by two cement factories and newer industries in the export processing zone within its boundaries. The municipal boundary has been enlarged to include a large area of agricultural land, while at the same time 65 per cent of its population live in informal settlements.

ITDG is managing a programme entitled Improving Urban Livelihoods (funded by the UK National Lottery), and Mavoko is one of the programme sites. The programme builds on an earlier project that has been working with communities and partnerships in Mavoko to change regulations to regularize land tenure and enable the construction of affordable housing.

Contribution of peri-urban agriculture to the livelihoods of the poor

ITDG commissioned a study (ITDG-EA, 2003a) of the stakeholders and their activities in peri-urban agriculture in Mavoko in order to determine appropriate interventions to develop its commercial viability for the urban poor.

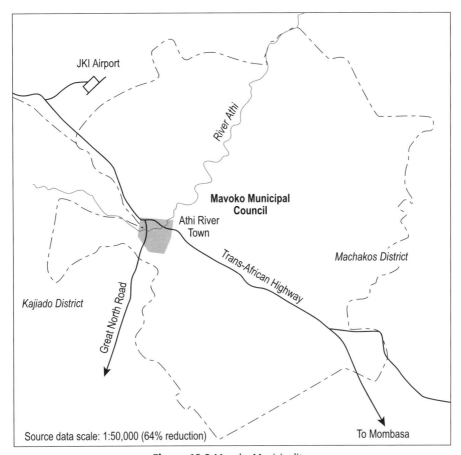

Figure 18.8 Mavoko Municipality

Source: Koti, 2000

The findings are based on focus group discussions and key informant interviews with farmers engaged in crop production, officials of the Ministry of
Agriculture, retailers of farm produce and municipal officials in the three
settlements within the municipality.

Besides a poor environment and lack of infrastructure services, a key issue
in Mavoko is the lack of livelihood options. Despite the presence of industry,
many residents do not find work in the formal sector, which is poorly established, and live a hand-to-mouth existence (ITDG-EA, 2003b). Peri-urban
agriculture is widespread in Mavoko despite low financial returns because it is
one way of gaining a livelihood without formal skills and because of the lack of
alternatives for ensuring food security at the household level. Peri-urban agriculture contributes to the urban economy in a number of ways by providing:

- a subsistence livelihood, improving food security and some income from
  selling crops (see Figure 18.9);

- seasonal employment in the commercial horticulture sector for poorer residents;
- a valuable source of nutrition (particularly for the under-fives);
- rents for absentee landlords and tax revenue for the local authority;
- an outlet for composted organic waste, thereby relieving the local authority of the duty and cost of waste disposal and providing an environmental service to the poor, as well as employment in the collection and processing of the waste (Gordon et al, 2000).

Figure 18.9 Maize cultivation outside squatter housing (cement factory in the background)

Source: ITDG/Theo Schilderman, July 2001

While the situation varies between different parts of Mavoko's large area, there are certain common issues. Commercial agriculture is a key source of wage employment for many residents of the informal settlements who work on horticultural and flower farms located within the municipal area (although outside the currently developed area), where emphasis is on export crops, mainly grown under irrigation.

Most peri-urban agriculture is not of this commercial high-input nature. Instead, most cultivation is conducted on the flat land below the settlement and adjacent to the River Athi. The main crops grown by poorer farmers are cabbages, tomatoes, *sukumawiki* (a local variety of kale), onions and spinach sold in the local market. Maize, sold as green maize because of its lower demand on cooking fuel, is the food of the poor.

This land belongs to individuals who had acquired it for residential development; however, since the land floods during the rainy season, it is unusable for building and therefore people can engage in 'squatter' cultivation (see Figure 18.10). Even here, there is a spectrum in the scale of operation. Longer-established residents, who have obtained access to larger areas of land (often on a first-come, first-served basis) may be paying rent and are able to produce enough for sale in local markets or even for transport to Nairobi. For produce sold in Athi River and Nairobi, middlemen and retailers purchase directly from the farms. However, farmers perceive that power relations favour the middlemen due to the large number of producers. In the absence of a unified markets structure among farmers, middlemen are able to manipulate prices in their favour.

Figure 18.10 Squatter housing on wasteland close to high-income housing; this area is likely to be developed and, therefore, agriculture offers a limited and insecure livelihood

Source: ITDG/Lucy Stevens, May 2003

Factors limiting the productivity of peri-urban agriculture in Mavoko

Annual precipitation in the range of 500mm–1000mm means commercial agriculture is heavily dependent on irrigation. Rain-fed production of maize and beans is carried out on plots further away from the river mainly for subsistence production. Crop production in this manner is limited to two growing seasons per year, making it unattractive for commercial production. Soil is poorer and lack of water limits the range of crops, which can only be grown during the rainy season. Parcels further inland are as yet cultivated only to a very limited extent; most of the land is used for grazing.

Large areas are in private ownership, primarily owned by corporations no longer operating in the area. Private ownership of available land makes residents engaging in squatting cultivation vulnerable. Up to 60 per cent of the municipality's land area is uncultivated and belongs to the government; the risk of eviction is an ever present threat for those who cultivate there. Secure access to land for the poor is therefore a key issue. Interviews conducted with residents of the settlements reveal that the land they can cultivate rarely supplies all of their households' food requirements, let alone provides them with a cash income.

There is apparently low usage of appropriate technologies in the locality for resource management. Those engaged in agriculture for subsistence or local markets lack any training and appear to have little technical knowledge. They rarely practise composting, instead buying cheap fertilizers. Residents involved in farming expressed disappointment over the quality and nature of extension services available to them, and discussions with extension officers confirmed that Mavoko has been neglected in this respect by the Ministry of Agriculture.

Opportunities for increasing positive impacts of peri-urban agriculture

Several key issues have emerged from the study. There has been very little social organization in the town. Farmers operate as individual enterprises and prior to ITDG's intervention, no community-based groups existed. Where land parcels are of a minimum size or where there is a shortage of idle land and high rents, this precludes access to the poorest, who currently squat. Land access is therefore the prime issue.

Based on the study of peri-urban agriculture, technology areas where capacity of urban farmers can be improved include:

- biological pest control methods to reduce expenditure on pesticides and the associated chemical pollution;
- composting and other soil-improving practices to raise productivity of poorer land;
- post-harvest technology to reduce wastage;
- water-saving approaches to cultivation, such as drip irrigation, to increase the area of land capable of growing higher value vegetable crops;
- identification of new crops to widen opportunities for income generation.

The ITDG programme is investigating the viability of alternative access to markets in order to provide a greater return to poor producers.

Prior to engaging the farmers in technology development, ITDG encouraged group formation through social mobilization. This enabled capacity-building for group-based enterprises and the piloting of financial assistance (savings and credit schemes). This last was the most requested intervention. Most of the respondents to the study are low-income earners and therefore are unable to afford capital and input items necessary for commercial production. As a result, providing access to credit is critical to expanding peri-urban agriculture. Through social mobilization, credit and savings groups have developed and, as a result, one group of 25 people (the Kimongo farming group) was able to borrow money and obtain a lease of 5ha of land some distance from the town for five years. The land is close to the river; the group bought an irrigation pump and began cultivating the land for horticulture in 2004. The costs of renting the land and installing irrigation pipes and a pump have been shared between ITDG and the group. Skills are available among the community members to access the ready market for horticultural products.

ITDG's parallel project in Mavoko on Regulatory Guidelines for Urban Upgrading ended in March 2004. The project involved working closely with the municipal council, which has, as a result, made a number of changes that now facilitate landownership by poor residents:

- agreeing reductions to the minimum plot size;
- simplifying land allocation procedures;
- improving access to information on land.

The council now maintains a land allocation register that will help to prioritize areas for regularization or resettlement. Undoubtedly, the outcome of this project has facilitated the success of the Kimongo farming group in obtaining a lease.

Enabling urban farmers to join together will facilitate the provision of appropriate training, enterprise and marketing services, and will give them a voice in dealing with other stakeholders, whether official or market based. ITDG will seek to involve the Ministry of Agriculture in discussions with farmers on rain-fed production and low-cost pest control to develop extension services that meet their needs. ITDG's own training on farm and crop management has led to successful development of urban agriculture enterprises in Mavoko.

In another programme on Integrated Approach to Housing with the Urban Poor in Marginal Settlements in Kenya and Zimbabwe, ITDG is currently working in Nairobi and Nakuru to link community-based waste management to income generation. A later stage of the programme hopes to develop sales of compost, which would lead to improved food production in small-scale urban and peri-urban agriculture. In parallel, ITDG has worked jointly with the University of Nairobi and the city councils in developing ecological sanitation systems jointly with community groups; pilot blocks were completed in 2004. If successful, there is the opportunity for replication and development of these activities with the communities in Mavoko.

The flow diagram in Figure 18.11 illustrates some of the linkages between peri-urban agriculture, livelihoods and the environment.

Conclusions

Livelihoods in peri-urban areas are complex. Many of the residents have moved either from the urban area, or from the rural hinterland, in search of improved livelihoods. A key opportunity is the greater availability of natural

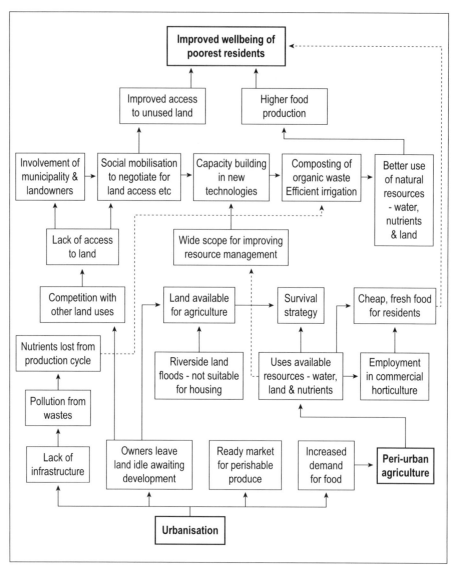

Figure 18.11 Linkages between peri-urban agriculture, livelihoods and the environment

Source: Rachel Berger, 2003

resources than in town (such as land and water), on the one hand, and opportunities for waged labour, on the other. In the absence of formal employment opportunities, natural resources are important to the livelihoods of the poor in peri-urban areas to the extent that they have access – which is often very limited and insecure. The dependence on natural resources with insecure tenure leads to increased vulnerability of the poor. Since they lack voice and are often not mobilized to act as groups, more powerful stakeholders will readily take over exploitation of resources in the absence of an institutional framework that balances the interests of all stakeholders. The lack or weakness of regulatory frameworks protecting the environment also means that these resources are often exploited unsustainably.

Improving livelihoods through better resource management in peri-urban areas is possible, but requires a detailed understanding of the interests and asset base of the poor. In order to improve livelihoods while, at the same time, improving environmental management and using available resources more productively, a range of barriers needs to be overcome that is associated with land allocation and tenure, as well as the weakness of organization among the poor. Finding workable, sustainable solutions depends not on legislation and enforcement alone, but on a process of negotiation between all stakeholders. These interests are often deeply entrenched (as in Nakuru), and initiating this process can require funding and facilitation from an NGO. ITDG has found that a process that places the interests of the poor at the centre can be effective. The process begins with social mobilization to empower the poor, which enables them to improve their assets. A process of participatory technology development – that is, the introduction of appropriate technology, developed with the communities and relevant to their situation – enables improvement to livelihoods through increasing incomes both from the natural resources in the PUI, as well as from other opportunities. The result of this process is that financial and social capital for these groups is increased, thereby reducing the distortions shown in Figure 18.1.

References

Allen, A., da Silva, N. and Corubolo, E. (1999) *Environmental Problems and Opportunities of the Peri-Urban Interface and their Impact upon the Poor*, Draft paper, Development Planning Unit, University College London, www.ucl.ac.uk/DPU/pui/research/previous/epm/allen.htm

Budds, J. and Minaya, A. (1999) *Overview of Initiatives Regarding the Management of the Peri-Urban Interface*, Draft paper, Development Planning Unit, University College London, www.ucl.ac.uk/DPU/pui/research/previous/epm/budds_minaya.htm

Central Bureau of Statistics (2000) *Economic Survey 2000*, Government of Kenya, Nairobi

Central Bureau of Statistics (2001) *1999 Population and Housing Census*, Government of Kenya, Nairobi

DFID (Department for International Development) (2000) *Sustainable Livelihoods Guidance Sheets*, DFID, London, www.livelihoods.org/info/ info_guidanceSheets.html

Gordon, A., Davis, J., Long, A. and Meadows, K. (2000) 'The role of natural resources in the livelihoods of the urban poor', *Policy Series 9*, Natural Resources Institute, University of Greenwich, London, www.nri.org/publications/policyseries/PolicySeriesNo09.pdf

Government of Kenya (2000) *Welfare Monitoring Survey WMS III of 1997*, Government of Kenya, Nairobi

Hide, J. M. and Kimani, J. (2000), *Informal Irrigation in the Peri-Urban Zone of Nairobi Kenya: Findings from an Initial Questionnaire Survey*, Unpublished report, Hydraulics Research Wallingford

ITDG-EA (Intermediate Technology Development Group, East Africa) (2003a) *Commercial Agriculture – A Case Study of Kimongo, Kaswitu and Kijiji 39, Mavoko Municipality*, Unpublished report, ITDG, East Africa, Nairobi

ITDG-EA (2003b) *Mavoko – People Stories*, Unpublished report, ITDG, East Africa, Nairobi

ITDG-EA (2003c) *Regulatory Guidelines for Urban Upgrading – Project Report*, Unpublished report, ITDG, East Africa, Nairobi

Koti, F. T. (2000) *Production of Urban Space in Kenya: Central–Local Government Power Relations in Mediating Space in Athi River Town*, MA thesis, University of West Virginia, US, www.etd.wvu.edu//ETDS/E1319/koti_f_etd.pdf

Majale, M. and Albu, M. (2001) *Tools for Understanding Sustainable Livelihoods Based on Enterprise: Livelihoods around the Roofing Construction Subsector in Nakuru, Kenya*, Unpublished report, ITDG, East Africa, Nairobi

Mbuguah, S. and Ehrensperger, A. (2003) *Analysis of Field Survey on Urban Development Priorities and Needs for Information on Urban Development Issues*, Unpublished report, Nakuru Local Urban Observatory, Nakuru

Mwangi, S. W. (2003) *Needs Assessment Report of Three Low-Income Neighbourhoods in Nakuru Municipality*, Unpublished report, ITDG, East Africa, Nairobi

Shadmon, A. (1999) *Kenya Improved Stone-Workers Project: Evaluation of Research Project – Training and Policy Guidelines for Artisanal Quarrying*, Unpublished report, ITDG, East Africa, Nairobi

Tacoli, C. (1999) 'Understanding the opportunities and constraints for low-income groups in the peri-urban interface: The contribution of livelihood frameworks', Draft paper, Development Planning Unit, University College London, www.ucl.ac.uk/DPU/pui/research/previous/epm/tacoli.htm

Uglow, D. (1999) *Mitigating the Environmental Impact of Artisanal Quarrying: Consideration of Awareness and Incentives*, Report for DFID/ITDG, Mining and Environment Research Network, University of Bath, Bath

UN (United Nations) (2000) *World Population Prospects: The 1999 Revision*, UN Population Division, New York

Universities of Birmingham and Bangor (1998–1999) *Improved Utilisation of Urban Waste by Near-Urban Farmers in the Hubli-Dharwad City Region*, Inception Report and Phase 1 Report, DFID Natural Resources Systems Programme, London

19

A Co-Management Approach to Sustainable Watershed Utilization: Peri-Urban Kumasi, Ghana

Duncan McGregor, David Simon, Donald Thompson, James Quashie-Sam, Sampson Edusah and Kwasi Nsiah-Gyabaah

Introduction: The Kumasi peri-urban interface (PUI)

A three-year project (R7330: Peri-Urban Natural Resources Management at the Watershed Level – Kumasi, Ghana, February 1999–March 2002) was designed as an important element in the progressive research programme under the UK Department for International Development (DFID) Natural Resources Systems Programme (NRSP) peri-urban interface (PUI) production system in Kumasi, Ghana. Kumasi has grown rapidly in recent years from a population of 71,000 in 1948 to the 2000 census estimate of 1.17 million (Government of Ghana, 2002), with commensurate physical expansion (see Figure 19.1). Pressures on land for building and for extraction of building aggregates has increased within the boundary shown in Figure 19.1 and up to about 30km–40km beyond. Most of the land annexed for these activities was traditionally under agricultural land use.

Whereas earlier NRSP projects in Kumasi had been concerned essentially with baseline studies and characterization of Kumasi's peri-urban environment (see Brook and Dávila, 2000), this project moved the emphasis to environmental management at the watershed scale. Questions regarding levels of community awareness of water and environmental issues, and the development of participatory local environmental co-management structures and tools appropriate for poor and under-resourced peri-urban villages were a major focus. To that end, the project has formulated and piloted a framework for sustainable natural resource co-management, which forms the subject of this chapter.

Following reconnaissance, the PUI was characterized (Simon et al, 2004) and a contribution was made to refining the concept as constituting more or less a continuum from essentially rural to urban, but without a necessarily

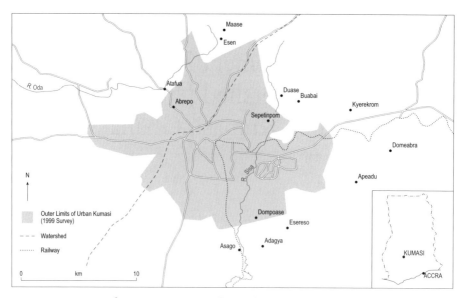

Figure 19.1 Kumasi and peri-urban research locations

linear relationship between physical distance and the degree of 'urbanness' or 'rurality', as represented in Table 19.1. Key features of the PUI include the rapidity of change as urban pressures increase, the changing locations that are 'peri-urban' and, hence, the changing identity and diversity of people within the PUI. Our more flexible approach than others that focus on concentric rings or cardinal distances is well suited to the rapid change in such parameters and even the particular areas identifiable as 'peri-urban'. Mbiba and Huchzermeyer (2002) provide a detailed and complementary critical review of the DFID and other approaches to defining the PUI.

The project emphasized the watershed or catchment principle in which temporal and spatial linkages in nutrient and pollutant flows are determined by the location of activities within the hydrological pathways that link slopes and sub-catchments to the main drainage systems. The effects of peri-urbanization on environmental quality thus depend upon the location of changing activity patterns with respect to the hydrological system. Our purposive sample of villages reflected these considerations, enabling us to assess a transect of two key (sub-) catchments, the north-western part of the Oda (the Owabi and the eastern and southern Sisa, from Maase to Atafua) (see Figure 19.1).

This chapter focuses on the final phase of the project – namely, development of a set of principles for managing the local environment – the Watershed Management Framework (WMF) – which stakeholders at local and district/metropolitan level can utilize to improve long-term environmental quality within the catchments. A key environmental issue in peri-urban Kumasi is the (mis)use of water; this chapter explores the development and dissemination of (as well as reactions to) the WMF, principally at the community level.

Table 19.1 *Major differences among the eight selected Kumasi peri-urban villages, ordered from most rural to most urban*

Village	Similarities and major differences
Adagya	Slow growth
	Moderate influence of Kumasi Metropolis
	Farming is the major occupation
	Loss of some farmlands to housing and sand winning
	Strong communal spirit
	Easy access to Kumasi
	Poor level of infrastructure
	Poor sanitation and drainage system
Asago	Slow growth
	Moderate influence of Kumasi Metropolis
	Farming is the major occupation
	Loss of some farmlands to housing and sand winning
	Strong communal spirit
	Poor access to Kumasi
	Poor level of infrastructure
	Poor sanitation and drainage system
Maase	Moderate growth
	Moderate influence from Kumasi Metropolis
	Farming is the major occupation
	Loss of some farmlands to housing
	Strong communal spirit
	Moderate access to Kumasi
	Appreciable level of infrastructure
	Poor sanitation and drainage system
Duase	Moderate growth
	Moderate influence of Kumasi Metropolis
	Major occupation is still farming
	Nevertheless, farming is on the decline
	Increasing loss of some farmlands to housing
	Easy access to Kumasi
	Strong communal spirit
	Appreciable level of infrastructure
	Poor sanitation and drainage system
Esereso	Moderate growth
	Strong influence of Kumasi Metropolis
	Farming on the decline
	Most people still engaged in farming
	Loss of some farmlands to housing
	Strong communal spirit
	Easy access to Kumasi
	Appreciable level of infrastructure
	Poor sanitation and drainage system

Table 19.1 *Continued*

Village	Similarities and major differences
Atafua	Increasingly rapid growth Easy access to Kumasi Strong influence from Kumasi Metropolis Farming on the decline Farming is still important Increasing loss of farmlands to housing Strong communal spirit Appreciable level of infrastructure Poor sanitation and drainage system
Sepetinpom	Strong influence of Kumasi Metropolis Easy access to Kumasi Growing rapidly Loss of almost all farmlands to housing Most people now engaged in non-agricultural occupations Large population of strangers Appreciable level of infrastructure Poor sanitation and drainage system
Abrepo	Engulfed by Kumasi Growing rapidly Farming on the decline Most people now engaged in secondary occupations Rapid loss of farmlands to housing Large population of strangers Easy access to Kumasi Appreciable level of infrastructure Poor sanitation and drainage system

Source: field surveys, Ghana, 1999–2000

Environmental degradation in the Kumasi PUI, with particular reference to water resources

Water quality in the Kumasi PUI

The principal factors influencing water quality in the Kumasi PUI are:

- river water pollution, especially within and downstream from urban Kumasi, attributed to untreated sewage and other domestic waste; hospital waste; industrial waste (including an assortment of chemicals and, possibly, heavy metals; oils from informal motor repair businesses; and runoff from sawmills, brewing and formal and informal abattoirs – see Simon et al, 2001); urban and rural runoff (including agricultural chemicals and residues); and leachate from groundwater into the river system of any of the above pollutants;

- contamination of boreholes and wells situated close to polluted water courses through seepage;
- contamination of boreholes and wells by leachate from pit latrines and refuse dumps located upslope from them;
- unplanned and unregulated waste tipping, both by villagers and by urban dwellers, with inadequate (if any) management and mitigation measures;
- localized heavy resource exploitation – for example, sand winning (local term for sand quarrying, usually in floodplain sites), deforestation for agriculture and wood use – and new urban and peri-urban housing and industrial/commercial premises.

In terms of the summary of views expressed by local people and observations made by the research team, the major environmental problems in descending order of importance were river pollution, contamination of boreholes, unplanned waste tipping and sand winning. It is recognized, however, that the particular problem or problems perceived as most important vary with particular site conditions – for example, with proximity to a major source of pollution such as a factory or workshop.

The results of a two-year investigation of water quality, together with related short-term studies, are reported elsewhere (Thompson et al, 2001a; McGregor et al, 2002; project website, www.gg.rhul.ac.uk/kumasi.html).

Community perceptions

Interviews, focus group discussions and participatory appraisal activities were carried out in each village with different categories of residents (chiefs and elders, teachers and random samples of local men, women and farmers) in order to examine community perceptions of land-use and environmental change, principal local problems, drinking water supply, wastewater disposal, sanitation and refuse disposal.

For some topics, responses were consistent across the different groups within each village. However, in other cases, people's perceptions or rankings differ, no doubt as a reflection of the importance of each to the livelihood activities and daily routines of each category of participant and respondent in a particular village. As explained earlier, one of the characteristics of the PUI is that it spans a spectrum of rapidly changing conditions and challenges, from rural to essentially urban, with 'urbanness' increasing over time, albeit unevenly across space.

In all villages, people were aware of growing levels of pollution in streams and rivers, and the health problems that this could cause. Perceptions of community environmental problems are implicit in Table 19.1. The approximate correlation of rapid growth; population change and diversity; infrastructural provision (even if inadequate); and land-use and occupational change with relative proximity and ease of access to Kumasi is evident. Conversely, poor sanitation and drainage, and inadequate or discontinuous access to good-quality drinking water are ubiquitous problems.

Water treatment and environmental management infrastructure

Water from pipes and boreholes is not treated by villagers before use. The commercialized parastatal Ghana Water Company (GWC) does monitor the quality and provides chemicals for borehole treatment. The only other treatment methods reported by villagers were leaving the water so that the sediment settled out and (in Asago) filtering the water through a cloth. Respondents in Asago knew that water could be boiled in order to purify it, but said that no one did this.

Management of water and sanitation was said to be the responsibility of the elected unit committees (UCs) in all the villages as part of their general responsibility for village development and communal labour. Their main role was in contacting GWC (sometimes through their district assembly member) to fix and maintain the piped water supply and boreholes, and organizing communal labour to clean the toilet areas, maintain the rubbish dumps and collect fees. UCs do have a limited role in enforcing local rules – for example, about washing vehicles in the river or cultivating on riverbanks. Only in one village (Sepetinpom) did respondents say that the UC protected rivers, while in other villages people said that it was difficult to enforce local rules. In Maase, there were regulations over use of the spring during the dry season in order to prevent it from drying up. One village had a sanitation committee which organized communal labour for waste management, and four villages had water and sanitation (WATSAN) committees. The division of responsibilities between UC and WATSAN was unclear and varied between villages (see Table 19.2). One specific role of the WATSAN committee was to educate the villagers about water and hygiene.

Table 19.2 *Stakeholders in water management*

Stakeholder	Issues
Unit committee (UC)	Responsible for: • organizing community labour • waste management • contacting GWC to repair piped water supply • political affliations
Water and sanitation (WATSAN) committee	Operates in four villages; organizes community labour for water and sanitation management Split of responsibility with UC often unclear
Traditional authority	Many of their functions are being taken over by UC or WATSANs
Assemblyman/woman	Contact GWC regarding piped water issues where village is connected
Women	Often reponsible for maintenance of refuse sites and day-to-day water management
Ghana Water Company (GWC)	Provide/maintain piped water, mainly within metropolitan area
Community Water and Sanitation Agency (CWSA)	Responsible for water and sanitation at community level, mainly outside metropolitan area
Kumasi Metropolitan Assembly (KMA)	Responsible for waste collection within city boundary
Poor households	Frequently cannot afford local or GWC water charges, where made – hence, resort to drinking/washing with river water

A summary of water-related issues commonly raised by respondents is given in Table 19.3.

Table 19.3 *Summary of perceived water-related issues*

Issue	Community concerns
Access to water	Insufficient boreholes/standpipes – hence, resort to rivers Use of springs as an alternative to queueing for borehole/standpipe Absence of funds for boreholes
Market for water	Charging for water is common practice Ghana Water Company (GWC) charges for piped water People are willing to pay for better water, especially if alternatives are percieved to be polluted – for example, at Asago and Abrepo The poor cannot afford piped water or contribution to private borehole supply
Perceptions of water potability	Villagers are aware of an increase in water pollution They are less concerned about pollution if they have an alternative water supply Many use streams if there are no obvious sources of pollution Question of how people assess water potability for themselves
Water/waste management	Unit Committees (UCs), in many, cases are not functioning; yet, women and children are responsible for household water collection and refuse site maintenance Little evidence of district-wide planning for water and waste management Many communities have lobbied Kumasi Metropolitan Assembly (KMA) unsuccessfully

Peri-urban pollution

It is clear that, apart from pollution originating in Kumasi City, some pollution arises within the peri-urban villages themselves. Even Maase, on the top of the watershed, experienced some pollution problems caused by the siting of, and runoff from, its refuse tip into the springs. Residential development continues in the villages; but there is no provision for better waste management or drainage systems. These systems, which may have been adequate for a rural village, are no longer adequate for the growing peri-urban settlement. Outside the KMA boundary, the districts covering most of the PUI have no effective provision for waste collection. This is but one instance of the problems of urbanizing transition and fragmented governance (see also Chapter 14 in this volume). While it is evident that the pollution problems are most severe for villages downstream of Kumasi (Abrepo and Asago), locally generated pollution should not be overlooked. Asago has the worst of both worlds, suffering extrinsic sources of pollution, as well as increasing 'peri-urban' activities among the population, but without the urban waste infrastructure and waste-removal services.

Dissemination of good practice: Schoolchildren and water quality

In fostering sustainable and equitable watershed management practice, the involvement of all stakeholders is essential. In this respect, a key step towards ensuring that communities participate in decision-making and have access to ownership of the process of watershed management is raising awareness within the community of the necessity to monitor (and, if necessary, to control) resource use within their environment.

Schoolchildren and teachers are key potential adopters and disseminators of awareness and 'good practice' in relation to daily behaviour affecting the local environment, in general, and water quality, in particular.

In order to test the feasibility of a possible system of environmental self-monitoring, a pilot scheme was initiated in September 1999 by placing relatively simple water quality test kits (the *Catchment Action Starter Kit*, manufactured in South Africa and the UK), in five junior secondary schools (JSSs) and one high school. These kits are designed for use by children, youth and community groups as part of their formal education (where this relates to their syllabus) or as part of broader community education and awareness of the state of their local environment (Hill et al, 1997; Nel and Hill, 1997). Details of the results obtained and problems encountered appear in McGregor et al (2001).

Dissemination to the community was undertaken by most of the schools in the form of mimed plays relating to water protection and the dangers of pollution, performed by the pupils at community gatherings. These plays proved very popular with pupils and the wider community alike, and gave the children a sense of ownership of the new knowledge engendered on water quality, linkages through bad practice to hygiene and disease, and the need to protect water resources.

The test kit project was increasingly seen by project staff as an important element in not only helping to educate the children themselves, but also in taking this knowledge into the communities in a positive way. This is seen as an important generation of environmental awareness for a range of stakeholders, and the potential is underlined by the impact that even this small experiment has made. The strong interest shown by the Ghana Environmental Protection Agency (EPA) and the local office of the International Water Management Institute (IWMI) in taking this forward underlines the potential.

The WMF was one response to these issues. It was recognized that, if the kits provided communities with information, empowerment to change their environments would come not only from improving practice locally, but by encouraging communities to make use of governance structures and agencies which could act on their behalf. Hence, an important element of the WMF must be to disseminate to all groups within the community the chain of responsibility at the governmental level to which representations can be made, as well as the role of institutions such as the EPA and GWC. This is particularly relevant to the issue of extrinsic pollution sources. Organizing best practice and environmental monitoring at the local or community level requires information on what is best practice and also requires accessible structures for implementation – for example, the UCs and WATSANs.

The Watershed Management Framework (WMF)

Consideration of community responses and the issues raised by the school test kits, as well as discussions with local partners and interested institutions, along with our own reading of the literature on participatory and other approaches to tackling the manifest problems of peri-urban Kumasi, led to the development of a participatory framework for sustainable co-management of the environment and natural resources at the watershed scale. Co-management is the joint and participatory management of a resource, facility or particular area by all of the relevant stakeholders, but especially by those who live on/at and use the resource, land or facility.

This WMF is an integrated and flexible set of mechanisms and activities that can be undertaken in appropriate combinations in order to promote sustainable utilization of the villages' environment and its resources. It is not a formal plan or rigid blueprint. The basic purpose of the WMF is to promote better watershed management by involving all willing stakeholders in a structured approach to protecting the local environment, in general, and its land and water resources, in particular.

Each stakeholder, or group of stakeholders, has different priorities (for example, protection of agricultural land for the farmer and protection of unpolluted water supply for the villagers). These priorities have to be recognized and balanced against the necessity to use resources to provide sustenance or income (for instance, use of water for irrigation or for cooling machinery).

Structure of the WMF

The WMF comprises a systematic framework of mechanisms and activities at different scales within the catchment, designed to achieve the objective stated above. These scales are:

- the whole catchment or sub-catchment;
- individual villages or communities within the (sub-)catchment;
- micro-projects and other activities within villages that serve as catalysts for collaborative organization, action and maintenance.

Although distinct, these nested elements should be interdependent in a well-functioning framework. The different scales of mechanism and activity should not be thought of as hierarchical in a top-down sense. Co-responsibility and joint management is important in all of them, although the precise set of partners and partnership relationships varies. In general, the roles of professionals and officials are likely to be more pronounced at the strategic level of the (sub-)catchment, where liaison and integration across several communities is necessary. However, villagers and their representatives must be, and must feel themselves to be, central participants in decision-making and in control of the outcomes. This is the concept now often referred to as 'ownership' in development terminology.

WMF management at the community level

At this level, the WMF is intended to be managed through a spirit of participation and community ownership of the process in order to maximize its chances of promoting sustainability. *The underlying principle should be the co-management of the environment and environmental resources with the relevant institutional stakeholders.* It requires responsible individuals or committees to initiate and to drive the WMF forward within the community. In villages where community level facilitators (CLFs) are active, they may be willing to assume a lead role, with community agreement. Resident CLFs have been elected and trained in all eight villages where this project was active and in several others, under related DFID NRSP Projects R7995 and R8090 to formulate and then implement sustainable natural resource-based livelihood strategies for the poor (NRSP, 2003; CEDEP, 2004).

However, following experience with community-based programmes in different countries, the guiding principle in this respect must be to minimize the additional burden of new committee structures on the community. In other words, wherever possible, the relevant responsibilities should be given to appropriate committees that already exist and function reasonably well at the grassroots level. The most likely candidates in peri-urban Kumasi will usually be the UC and/or the WATSAN committee. The precise outcome will reflect the situation in each village and the focus of planned WMF activities there. In some cases, a joint sub-committee of both committees might be appropriate.

Only in cases where there is no effective committee structure, or conflicts within the community preclude effective operation of relevant committees and appropriate liaison between them and their traditional leaders and/or assembly representative, is it likely to be appropriate to establish a new committee with a specific brief to implement the WMF. In all participating villages, it would be sensible to try to establish a WATSAN or UC if no functioning one exists. Naturally, though, even grassroots committees tend to reflect existing power relations and can therefore not be assumed to operate in the interests of the poor or of all sections of the community. Trained CLFs therefore have a key mediating and awareness-raising role. In addition, our pilot activities and some of the livelihood activities implemented by the related project R8090 have already demonstrated to the poor, women and other potentially marginalized people that there is scope to address their own needs and priorities. This would help the community's institutional development in broader terms than simply this project and the WMF by facilitating liaison with relevant local institutions and integrating the village within statutory structures, thus enhancing the prospects of sustaining the WMF for the future.

Successful operation of the WMF will require one or two (sub-)committee members, as well as the CLFs if they are not committee members, to assume ultimate responsibility for the process. The individual(s) should have relevant skills (for example, science teachers), experience, interest and time, and thus not necessarily be the chair and/or secretary of the committee. The individual(s) will act as 'environment officer(s)' (or other suitable job title) for the community. It is likely that some training by a relevant authority (such as the EPA) would be required.

WMF management at the institutional level

Strategically, an overview of the progress and relative efficiency of individual community WMFs is required. Clear lines of communication must be established between the communities and higher-level institutions, such as area committee, district assembly or the KMA. There should be careful consideration of whether existing channels of communication are adequate and effective, or whether an appropriate (and specifically designated) officer in each of these bodies should be assigned to act as liaison person with the communities over WMF issues. Either way, a record of concerns raised by communities and the action taken would need to be kept by the respective bodies.

The overview of WMF activities and the degree to which the process is working to the benefit of all stakeholders require careful monitoring. This needs, if at all possible, to be undertaken by an agency which is seen to be both supportive of the general process and impartial in assessing its degree of efficiency. This points to the involvement of an impartial non-governmental organization (NGO), such as our research partner, the Centre for the Development of People (CEDEP), as the 'watchdog'. The involvement of the regional office of the EPA with regard to environmental matters is seen as highly desirable, although it is recognized that there is potential for conflict with polluting stakeholders.

Elements of the WMF

In its present form, the Watershed Management Framework is a bound document with separate ('stand-alone' but integrated) ancillary illustrative and other support materials. The full WMF is available for interrogation on the project website (www.gg.rhul.ac.uk/kumasi.html). There are five main elements of the WMF: land-use criteria; land allocation procedures; natural resource protection; community information structures; and community self-help. These are outlined in the following sections.

Land-use criteria

This is largely in written form and consists of a synopsis of the principal land-use problems encountered in peri-urban Kumasi, and what needs to be done about them in the local context (see Table 19.4).

Table 19.4 *Land-use criteria*

Problems	• Conflict of interest among chiefs and other stakeholders • Litigation over landownership • Unequal access to land for many • Unauthorized use of land; encroachment of reserve areas • Sale of land on floodplains and adjoining water courses • Resource exploitation (for example, sand winning) without proper rehabilitation • Weak enforcement of existing legislation
Solutions	• Chiefs to involve communities and other stakeholders in land management • Ownership of land to be well determined and respected by all • Access to land by community members to be ensured • Land-use rules strengthened to protect water bodies and reserved lands • Approach news media to get newspaper/radio coverage of disputes • Proper enforcement of legislation with agreement of stakeholders

Land allocation procedures

A basic understanding of the criteria applied by landowners when land is developed is essential in managing the process of land conversion. The main development control mechanism is the preparation of a layout plan for each village or community area. Plots are then, in theory, allocated to specific uses and, again theoretically, made available for sale for those specific uses, where appropriate. This section of the WMF sets out the principal problems of land allocation and suggests ways of resolving them (see Table 19.5). Table 19.5 also considers the problems associated with layout plans and suggests ways of resolving these.

Natural resource protection

The main sections of this part of the WMF comprise low-cost or no-cost methods of achieving natural resource protection through:

- catchment surface protection;
- water resource protection;
- waste disposal management;
- water harvesting;
- environmental self-monitoring.

This is achieved largely through practical illustrations of concepts and through diagrams (for example, Figure 19.2 illustrates a simple method of soil erosion control, Figure 19.3 illustrates basic rules for water resource protection and Figure 19.4 illustrates basic concepts for waste management). These diagrams are supplemented by tables indicating what specific key stakeholders can do to protect water resources (see Table 19.6).

Water harvesting is included here as a practical method for not only reducing the pressure on community wells and boreholes, but for reducing labour demands on women and children, who inevitably have the responsibility for household water collection. Environmental self-monitoring is encouraged by

Table 19.5 *Land allocation procedures*

Problems	• Increased land speculative activities • Multiple land sales of the same plots by landowners • Conflict of interest over land use • Loss of farm lands to the poor or no compensation • Loss of indigenous community land to migrants • Cumbersome procedures of land allocation • High fees charged by landowners
What needs to be done?	• Chiefs and stakeholders to prevent multiple sale of land plots • Adequate provision should be made for different uses of land to avoid conflict of use • Interests of those who depend on land for livelihood should be taken account of in layout plans • Streamline procedures to ensure transparency of land allocation
Problems with 'layout plans'	• Poor interaction between community and district assemblies • Lack of consultation between chief and community • Inadequate data on areas to be zoned and poor knowledge of communities by planning officers • Involvement of unqualified or unregistered planners in preparation of layout plans • Inadequate briefing of chiefs by planners • Lack of education to sensitize chiefs to procedures for preparing layout plans
What needs to be done?	• District assemblies to establish good communication links with traditional authorities in preparing layout plans • Traditional rulers should consult with communities on layout plan details • District assembly should allocate part of 'common' fund to support community preparation of layout plans • Adequate data and good knowledge of areas to be zoned necessary for layout plans • Qualified surveyors and planners must be engaged to prepare layout plans • District assemblies should mount educational programmes to educate chiefs on importance of good layout plans

hints on how to recognize the signs of polluted water and notes on the use of water quality test kits (as were used in the JSS project). Simple methods of noting the onset of land degradation (including soil erosion) are also used.

Community information structures

A crucial part of the WMF is communication with all stakeholders. This requires effective communication of environmental principles and restorative practice. Awareness-raising is central to this; as part of the WMF process, this has been approached using the following methods of dissemination:

A simple method of controlling soil erosion
Wooden stakes and twigs can form a barrier

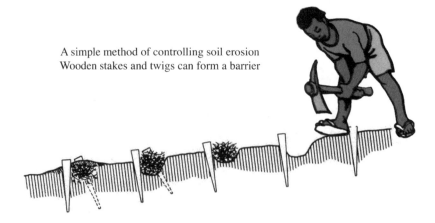

Figure 19.2 Cartoon to illustrate simple soil erosion control

Don't build your KVIP or pit latrine less than 100 feet (30 m)
from the borehole or well.

The KVIP or pit latrine **must** be downhill from the borehole or well

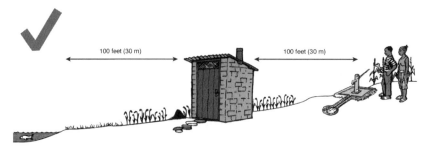

Figure 19.3 Illustration for basic water resource protection

Don't dump your rubbish uphill from a borehole or a well

It should be at least 100 feet (30 m) away from any water source

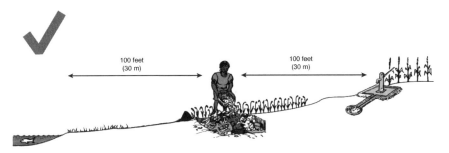

Figure 19.4 Illustration of basic waste management concepts

- liaison with relevant agencies and authorities;
- project workshops and field trips attracting all relevant stakeholders;
- a 'best practice' manual for community use;
- WATSAN manual;
- community posters;
- an environment directory;
- leaflets;
- the schools water-testing project;
- radio broadcasts.

Community 'best practice' manual

This consists of a series of drawings, cartoons and captioned photographs from the communities, illustrating the range of environmental problems and what to do about them. Examples include advice on the siting of pit latrines (see Figure 19.3) and the location of rubbish tips (see Figure 19.4). Photographs showing good and bad practices found in the project communities help to provide a very 'local' context. The full community handbook can be found on the project website (www.gg.rhul.ac.uk/kumasi.html).

Table 19.6 *Example of basic rules for protecting water quality*

Activities	Washing and toilet	Waste disposal	Cultivating the land
What bad substances come from this activity?	Bacteria, viruses and disease; detergent, soap and phosphates; nitrates and ammonia	Detergents, bacteria, phosphates, nitrates, oils, metals	Clearing the land can cause erosion of the soil during the wet season. Nitrates from fertilizer may enter rivers/water sources.
How can I avoid this bad effect?	1 Always use the latrine when you go to the toilet. Do not defecate in rivers or near water sources. Encourage your children to do likewise. 2 Do not wash yourself or your children near water sources. Try to use an agreed washroom/area if there is one in the village. 3 Wash your hands after going to the toilet. 4 Try to have an agreed area for washing clothes – away from the vicinity of the water source.	1 Try to use a communal rubbish tip – do not let waste accumulate around your house. 2 Try to sort your waste and compost organics and recycle paper. 3 Do not throw batteries/similar items on to the land surface where dangerous chemicals might leak into local water. 4 Discuss with unit committee (UC) and water and sanitation (WATSAN) committee members.	1 Locate your plot in a position to minimize runoff into the river when the land is bare/fallow. 2 Try not to cultivate right up to the riverbank. 3 If your plot is near the river, have a vegetated border to reduce the amount of runoff draining from plot to the river. 4 Do not cultivate immediately upslope of water sources. 5 Fill in gullies before they grow too big.
Are there areas where I should not do this activity?	On river banks; upslope from rivers or other water source; in the vicinity of a borehole/hand-dug well	Do not locate waste tips near or upslope from rivers, boreholes or wells; they should also be sited as far as possible from all water sources.	Depends whether you use a large amount of fertilizer. If you do – see above.
Are there other things I can do to protect individuals from polluted water from this activity?	Encourage other members of the community to follow your example.	1 Try to reduce the amount of material going to the waste tip by composting organics and recycling. 2 Plant grassed strips around waste tips to slow down runoff from the tip and to encourage it to percolate into the soil.	Do not use fertilizer indiscriminately.

WATSAN manual

This handbook was produced by Ingenieurgesellschaft fuer Internationale Planungsaufgaben (IGIP) consultants for CWSA, but was not disseminated in this area. It is specifically designed to enable WATSAN committees to be set up and organized, and to illustrate basic hygiene rules; how water-borne diseases are picked up and how to prevent spreading them; basic sanitation rules and procedures; and the dangers of drinking polluted water (see Figure 19.5). We therefore purchased copies for local distribution.

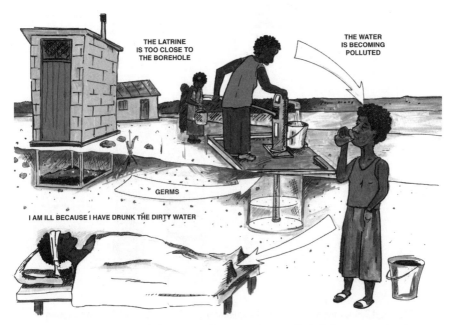

THE LATRINE IS TOO CLOSE TO THE BOREHOLE

THE WATER IS BECOMING POLLUTED

GERMS

I AM ILL BECAUSE I HAVE DRUNK THE DIRTY WATER

Figure 19.5 Example of illustrations from Ingenieurgesellschaft fuer Internationale Planungsaufgaben (IGIP) water and sanitation (WATSAN) committee manual

Community posters

A set of A1-sized laminated posters were designed to be prominently displayed and have been produced in English with Twi subtitles. They are designed to disseminate good practice, to be seen by all social groupings and to encourage the sense of community enterprise. They are based on the theme of 'a visitor to the community', with the local chief showing the guest around the village (see Figures 19.6 and 19.7).

Environment directory

This directory was accompanied by a section in the main WMF document detailing how communities can contact appropriate personnel and raise funds for environmental projects. It lists government agencies, NGOs, firms, academic departments and consultants with environmental remits or interests.

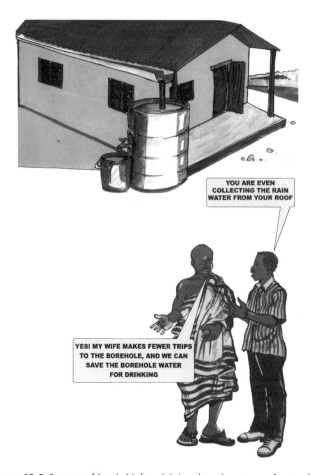

Figure 19.6 Cartoon of local chief explaining the advantages of water harvesting

Source: Dan Bradford

Supporting activities

These included leaflets, based on the theme of 'Water is life; conserve it', and were distributed in the communities. Team members had explained the objective of the leaflets to communities and schools before dissemination.

The schools' water-testing project was an integral part of information dissemination, and radio broadcasts by local project collaborators on two popular Kumasi FM stations were used to promote community-scale environmental issues.

Community self-help

Micro-projects were set up in project communities. These included screening and improving the appearance of waste tips using tree planting; roof water harvesting demonstrations located at the relevant JSSs, where possible, and on prominent community buildings where not; and gully amelioration demonstrations.

Figure 19.7 Cartoon of chief showing community erosion control strategies

Source: Dan Bradford

The emphasis here was on low-cost methods of environmental protection. In order to back this up, the WMF contains brief sections on community mobilization and participatory natural resource co-management, on stakeholders' roles and responsibilities, and on assisting community fund-raising for micro-projects (perhaps via sources identified in the environment directory).

Feedback from communities on WMF activities

During the development of the WMF, four successive rounds of evaluation interviews were held at approximately two-month intervals towards the end of the project. The research design was intended to:

- assess whether, and to what extent, perceptions and behaviour in relation to the environment within the eight study villages were changing as the project progressed and as different activities and micro-projects were implemented;
- ascertain whether there were any particular problems pertaining to project activities that we could address during the remaining life of the project.

Since the principal focus varied from round to round, slightly different methodologies were adopted by the team. The evaluations were undertaken by means of group discussions held with chiefs and elders, women, farmers and youth on the basis of who turned up to the previously arranged meetings;

follow-up meetings also occurred, when necessary, if attendance at the original meeting was not sufficiently representative – for example, with respect to inclusion of the poorest segments of the community.

The earlier evaluations focused on whether perceptions of environmental management were changing as a result of project activities, which activities had had positive effects and which had not. Environmental priorities identified by communities at an early stage in the research were revisited and were found, by and large, to have remained the same. Shortages of good-quality drinking water remained a much cited problem. It proved difficult to separate this from perceptions of the project as one that was going to provide funds for boreholes.

Leaflets and the schools project had made an impact, although this was not quantifiable. Some communities discussed the leaflets at village meetings; but there was a general feeling that project team members should have acted as facilitators for community discussions at dissemination in order to fully appreciate their significance. However, we had specifically decided not to facilitate actively in order not to bias the process.

Interest had been engendered, and awareness raised, by presenting drafts of cartoons, diagrams and captioned photographs to community groups.

The micro-projects were a focus of later evaluations, and here interest and enthusiasm was significant, if unevenly distributed. The more rural communities were willing to a greater extent than the more urban communities to undertake tree planting when provided with seedlings, and were more assiduous in protecting and watering the seedlings.

The water harvesting demonstrations were enthusiastically received by all to the extent that the schools reported water from the tanks being stolen at night (although reprehensible, a clear indication of impact). Some communities were using the water for drinking, despite a warning not to do so, and even reported that they found the water more potable than from other sources, such as rivers and hand-dug wells. Warnings had to be underlined, and the necessity for regular cleaning and flushing of tanks had to be emphasized (Thompson et al, 2001b).

Most villages reported that refuse dump-related diseases had reduced due to appropriate relocations and remediation of refuse dumps. In particular, Maase residents noted that the hitherto annual epidemic of typhoid had diminished since they relocated their dump. Adagya had also relocated its dump, with reportedly positive results on health, while the community at Atafua had made representations to an upstream village about their dumping of rubbish in the stream. These early signs indicate a positive impact upon peoples' behaviour and environmental perceptions.

Conclusions

The output from evaluations is variable; but the overall impact of the project's activities is significant.

The uptake of, and response to, the various WMF activities, especially the participatory micro-intervention demonstrations, was positive overall, although it was also variable both within and between villages. In Adagya, Asago and Maase, the most rural communities, a consistent level of widespread interest was evident. Elsewhere, it was more variable and in the most urban villages of Abrepo and Sepetinpom only a few villagers engaged with the project.

It is clear that a committed chief (*odikro*) UC or WATSAN chair or secretary would make a substantial difference; for example, particular CLFs were able to stimulate commitment when appointed towards the end of the project.

Overall, experience suggests clearly that responsiveness and uptake were generally most pronounced in the more rural villages – namely, Adagya, Asago and Maase – where communal spirit and identity, and the role of traditional leaders, were still most evident. Conversely, the most urban villages – Abrepo and Sepetinpom – had lost much of that ethos, and people were more concerned for their own families and households. Hence, any communal activities were far harder to organize or sustain. Even getting a reasonable attendance at research or awareness-raising meetings was difficult, with project staff having to make repeated and often frustrating visits. This experience is entirely consistent with those of PUIs elsewhere, where increasing urbanization is quite rapidly reflected in more urban lifestyles and behaviour, even if the village retains traditional leadership and aspects of its identity and territory.

The leaflets were generally felt to be appropriate, and many respondents appreciated the bilingual production. Children were particularly enthusiastic about the message of water quality protection.

The schools' water test kits project clearly fulfilled an important role and served not only to raise the awareness of the children directly involved and some of their peers, but was also reported as enlivening and making more relevant part of their school syllabus. The extent to which this testing contributed to wider community awareness also varied among the villages, but plays and poetry readings undertaken by the JSS pupils certainly had an impact at community meetings. The role of dynamic head teachers and/or science teachers was clearly central, both to the way in which JSS pupils were involved and enthused, and in terms of wider community dissemination. Variation was only to be expected, since we did not prescribe any specific activities; rather, we provided initial demonstrations and made some pertinent suggestions. This enabled us to observe how different staff and groups of pupils responded. Occasional problems of pupil selection and teacher continuity did arise; but overall the results were most encouraging. Furthermore, there is no doubt that regular visits by the EPA and project staff to the villages for liaison and other project activities raised the profile of these activities and, more generally, of local environmental problems.

By late 2004, copies of the WMF and ancillary material had been in the communities for up to two years. Feedback in late 2004 confirms that best uptake remains within the more rural communities. Of course, it is difficult to attempt to measure changes in public awareness, let alone behaviour, from single actions and interventions. These are longer-term and complex processes, with behavioural change often resulting from cumulative exposure to consistent messages. Even seeking to measure such changes at the end of the project is premature. It would be instructive to conduct a follow-up evaluation in a further year or two in order to see whether the participatory activities and the role of the CLFs have actually become sustainable once support inputs by the NRSP projects have ended.

The WMF is designed to be an active, rather than a static, set of procedures. Villagers and other stakeholders are encouraged to adapt the content to their particular situation and to lay more emphasis on the sections that will repay greater dividends in improving their environment. Critically, communities are encouraged by the WMF to be proactive and to help themselves, rather than relying on outside financial, material or labour assistance. An example of this is better use of the water resources already available, rather than simply sinking yet more boreholes to provide potable water.

It is also important to stress that community priorities will change over time with increasing urbanization and increasing land-use pressures, particularly on the remaining agricultural land. Individual stakeholders may themselves undertake a wider range of agricultural and micro-industrial/micro-enterprise activities, and these will alter their perceptions of environmental management. WATSAN committees or other appropriate community groups might be encouraged to list these activities and to develop strategies to minimize the environmental consequences within a holistic 'watershed' approach.

Acknowledgements

This chapter is an output from a project funded by the UK Department for International Development (DFID) for the benefit of developing countries. The views expressed are not necessarily those of DFID.

We acknowledge the support and participation of many people in Kumasi, notably Kwame Omane Poku, Vesta Adu-Gyamfi, Bright Asare Boade, Nana Ama Asare, Nii O Kotei, Daniel Benefor, Diana Ampofo, Michael O'Neal Campbell and Donna Alexander.

References

Project papers cited can be accessed through the project website, www.gg.rhul.ac.uk/kumasi.html

Brook, R. M. and Dávila, J. D. (eds) (2000) *The Peri-Urban Interface: A Tale of Two Cities*, School of Agricultural and Forest Sciences, University of Wales, Bangor and Development Planning Unit, University College London
CEDEP (Centre for the Development of People) (2004) *DFID Project R8090. Research Report 1: Community Level Facilitators*, CEDEP, Kumasi
Government of Ghana (2002) *Development Plan for Kumasi Metropolitan Area (2002–2004)*, Kumasi Metropolitan Assembly (KMA), Ministry of Local Government and Rural Development, Government of Ghana, Kumasi
Hill, T., Nel, E. and Papalouzia, G. (1997) 'Water test kits: Helping schoolchildren identify safe drinking water in the Eastern Cape', *On Stream*, February 1997, issue 8, pp4–5

Mbiba, B. and Huchzermeyer, M. (2002) 'Contentious development: Peri-urban studies in sub-Saharan Africa', *Progress in Development Studies*, vol 2, no 2, pp113–131

McGregor, D. F. M., Thompson, D. A., Kotei, N. O. and Poku, K. O. (2001) *Testing a Method of Environmental Self-Monitoring: Water Quality Test Kit Project, Peri-urban Kumasi*, CEDAR/IRNR Research Paper 2, Department of Geography, Royal Holloway, Egham

McGregor, D. F. M., Thompson, D. A. and Simon, D. (2002) 'Water quality and management in peri-urban Kumasi, Ghana', in *Land-Water Linkages in Rural Watersheds*, FAO Land and Water Bulletin 9, abstract p66, full paper on CD-ROM, FAO, Rome

Nel, E. and Hill, T. (1997) 'Development of available resources', *Conserva*, October–December 1997, pp22–23

NRSP (Natural Resources Systems Programme) (2003) *Natural Resources Systems Programme Research Highlights, 2001–2002*, NRSP, Hemel Hempstead

Simon, D., Nsiah-Gyabaah, K. and McGregor, D. F. M. (2004) 'The changing urban-rural interface of African cities: Conceptual issues and an application to Kumasi, Ghana', *Environment and Urbanization*, vol 16, no 2, pp235–247

Simon, D., Poku, K. O. and Nsiah-Gyabaah, K. (2001) *Survey of Large Industries in Kumasi: Water Use and Environmental Impacts*, CEDAR/IRNR Research Paper 6, Department of Geography, Royal Holloway, Egham

Thompson, D. A., McGregor, D. F. M., Kotei, N. O. and Poku, K. O. (2001a) *Water Quality in Peri-Urban Kumasi: Preliminary Results and their Significance*, CEDAR/IRNR Research Paper 3, Department of Geography, Royal Holloway, Egham

Thompson, D. A., Quashie-Sam, J. and McGregor, D. F. M. (2001b) *Testing the Feasibility of Water Harvesting as a Supplement to Clean Water Supply in Peri-Urban Kumasi*, CEDAR/IRNR Research Paper 8, Department of Geography, Royal Holloway, Egham

Part 5

Synthesis

20

The Peri-Urban Interface in Developing Areas: The Research Agenda

Duncan McGregor, David Simon and Donald Thompson

Introduction

This chapter seeks to identify and draw out the key themes that recur in the individual chapters of this volume. It is not intended as a comprehensive review of these chapters, nor does it purport to be a comprehensive definition of, or statement on, the peri-urban interface (PUI) (for which see Chapter 1). Nor is it a literature review (for which, again, see Chapter 1). It presents and discusses the research agenda, as identified within the individual contributions, for further work into the dynamics of the PUI.

The overviews in Chapters 2 to 4 have set out the background to broad human–environmental PUI research problems. These include the need for an applied scientific approach to inform social and economic studies. In Chapter 2, Douglas points out, for example, that the implications for human activity of land-use/land cover changes in the PUI should be informed by accurate mapping of the nature and rates of change, as, for example, through the use of aerial digital photography. This forms an accurate baseline resource from which the pressures on land can be identified and the urbanizing, degrading and polluting consequences quantified. Impacts upon water and ecological/biophysical resources and the generation of waste, in particular, require careful monitoring, which will assist in planning the sustainable use of natural resources. The medium of geographical information systems (GIS) can be utilized to bring order to these observations and can provide a framework for decision-making (see Chapter 17).

A recurring theme in this book is how, as set out by Allen in Chapter 3, the use of peri-urban environmental resources might be driven by local, sub-national and national, or even international, pressures. Individual livelihoods may be affected in different ways by these respective pressures. Access to land and natural resources is critical, which points to the need for detailed consideration of land tenure and regulatory systems for access to land. Several chapters demonstrate that inadequate controls on access to, and alienation of, land will inevitably lead to marginalization of some groups within the community, particularly farmers and the poor. Allen notes, however, that opportunity may arise from the progressive transfer of land from rural to urban uses, such as nutrient recycling in the form of peri-urban waste management (see, for example, Chapter 16).

A central theme throughout the book is that a focus on livelihood strategies is essential to identify sustainable pro-poor interventions. This implies the urgent need for research not only into peri-urban production systems (see below), but on the political capacity of peri-urban groups, as this relates to resource management.

A major problem exists for the PUI in terms of environmental planning and interventionist policy. The PUI is neither purely urban nor solely rural, yet much public policy is designed to apply either to urban areas or to rural areas. Institutional responsibilities are seldom defined specifically for the PUI, and urban forces are often dominant in shaping change in the PUI. In Chapter 4, Dávila notes that sectoral policies such as transport, energy and agriculture impinge upon the PUI, but are seldom designed with its particular problems in mind. The net effect of these policies has frequently been to hasten the degradation of the resource capital of the PUI, and thus inevitably to further marginalize the poor. Dávila concludes that specific concern with environmental sustainability of the PUI does not figure in the policy interventions of government, the private sector, non-governmental organizations (NGOs) or international agencies. Dávila does not, however, advocate the creation of policies specifically designed for the PUI, as this is dynamic in space and time; instead, he identifies a need to create awareness among policy-makers of the effects of sectoral policies on the PUI. This indicates a need to research the effects of specific sectoral policies on the social groups found within the PUI and, in particular, to examine how these policies affect their livelihoods. The linkages between policy, the environment and livelihoods are particularly critical in the PUI, and holistic research is also imperative.

Definitional considerations

Little importance is now placed by researchers on attempting to measure the precise width of the PUI. Indeed, this would be a futile exercise in the context of rapid expansion of the PUI, as illustrated in, for example, Harare (see Chapter 11), Accra (see Chapter 14) and Kumasi (see Chapters 16 and 19). As a generalization, there is a gradient between more urban and more rural segments within the zone. This gradient slopes away from the city, but is not spatially uniform, and it is possible (as in peri-urban Kumasi) to find relatively rural communities close to the city limits, often but not always a function of poor transport links. Urban 'outliers' are also the consequence of the incorporation of formerly distinctive towns within the growing PUI. We have found that for many (but not all) purposes, it is important to consider the inner PUI as an extension of the city rather than as an entirely separate area or zone. This is because the city region functions as an integrated whole in terms not only of its ecological footprint, but also of its economic and demographic processes (Simon et al, 2004). Conversely, however, in political and administrative terms, a large city such as Hubli-Dharwad (see Chapters 7 and 13) or Kumasi, and even its inner peri-urban hinterland, is fragmented, exacerbating many of the well-known problems regarding a lack of integrated planning, service delivery and management.

Peri-urban production systems

The chapters in Part 2 illustrate the nature of the pressures on livelihoods in the ever expanding PUI. Principal among these is ubiquitous pressure on agricultural land, usually through the transfer of agricultural land to building land. This is exacerbated by problems of access to land, of control by indigenous inhabitants on their own lands, of intensification of use of the remaining land, and of infrastructural problems arising from the land conversion process from agriculture to non-agricultural uses.

The expansion of urbanization does, however, provide opportunities in terms of jobs within the PUI itself, and of growing urban and peri-urban markets for agricultural produce. Such opportunities have been taken up in a variety of ways illustrated here. For the local market, intensification of production is possible through the use of a variety of strategies, such as dry season irrigation, hiring of labour, use of urban bio-wastes to effect soil nutrient improvements, as shown in the case of Jos (see Chapter 5). In the case of the Kolkata wetlands, aquaculture, a non-traditional variant of a traditional activity, is providing a growing output of food for urban use, based on recycling the nutrients present in human wastes (see Chapter 8).

Provision of services is a further way in which peri-urban inhabitants can create and diversify livelihood opportunities, though these may sometimes be problematic. In Chapter 9, Aberra shows how landless pastoralists who are settling in the PUI of Yabello (southern Ethiopia) have turned to firewood collection and sale, although this is regarded socially as a demeaning task for pastoralists to take up and it is a financially precarious livelihood with significant environmental consequences. In a more materially 'advanced' society, the shortage of labour opportunities in peri-urban St Lucia has been, to an extent, addressed by regular events specifically aimed at tourists – here, a weekly 'Fish Fry' at Anse La Raye, a suburb of the primate city Castries (see Chapter 10).

Both of these examples illustrate that turning away from traditional livelihoods, however enforced this may be, gives rise to social and financial problems. In the Anse La Raye case, infrastructural development has lagged and this is holding back progressive and sustainable development of the Fish Fry activities.

Infrastructural difficulties are another recurring theme. For example, in Chapter 7, Brook et al show how milk production and sale have provided a growing livelihood opportunity in peri-urban Hubli-Dharwad, but that this is progressively less profitable with increasing distance outwards from the urban centre. Farmers at a distance from Hubli-Dharwad not only receive a smaller payment for their milk due to marketing and transport costs, but the milk itself is less favourably perceived by city inhabitants compared with milk produced in the inner PUI on the grounds of 'freshness'. Dairy farmers in the inner PUI, with immediate access to sales (most are reported to sell their milk door-to-door) are progressively producing more milk, even those who do not own plots of land. These landless farmers rely heavily on acquiring fodder for stall feeding or on common land grazing.

Another frequent theme is the important role of markets in the PUI. Where road infrastructure permits, the supply of agricultural produce to regional markets is also seen as an opportunity for local producers. Farmers in the Jos, Nigeria, PUI (see Chapter 5) and in Tanzania (Chapter 6) are able to market their produce regionally. In Chapter 6, Lynch and Poole point to the research need for a better understanding of precisely how farmers and traders interact, and how better degrees of organization and of information among farmers would improve their profitability. Key to this is the proper assessment of the risks for farmers associated with the current marketing system, which would inform better marketing information structures. Lynch and Poole point to the potential of radio broadcasts and telecommunications, although this requires trialled research at present.

The principal generic research and implementation need which emerges from these examinations of a diverse set of livelihoods is the importance of designing holistic resource management structures. Perhaps Mukherjee's designs for the Kolkata wetlands in Chapter 8 comes closest to this in that all aspects of resource use and management have been focused on a design for balanced, sustainable but maximal resource use, even including opportunities for leisure activities.

Parts of the individual livelihood systems reported here work well, but parts do not. Marginalization is exacerbated by road and other infrastructural issues. Information flows are also often a source of inefficiency. The unsustainable use of common property or open-access resources such as firewood needs to be urgently addressed, particularly as this often affects the livelihoods of the poorest sectors of peri-urban society.

There are clear linkages in these studies between changing livelihoods and pressures on the natural environment. This is, in turn, linked to increasing population pressures on resources as brought about by the process of urban expansion. The need to research more sustainable production systems for the PUI must pay due regard to the natural and built environments alike. Further research issues which affect the success or failure of peri-urban production systems include land tenure, communications and the potential need in particular cases of elements of environmental impact assessment.

Peri-urban planning and development

The five chapters in Part 3 exemplify the common theme of how livelihoods and sustainability are often radically affected by active (and sometimes inactive or inefficient) processes of governance. Careful research on the process of peri-urbanization as it affects land speculation and shortages of land for traditional livelihoods such as agriculture can identify conflicts within communities, and between people and the planning/governance process. Such conflicts also underscore the need for research into appropriate forms of proactive and integrated development planning.

Issues of conflict between formal and informal governance are identified in peri-urban Harare (see Chapter 11) with regard to cultivation of vlei (*dambo*) lands within the expanding urban and peri-urban zones. Bowyer-Bower argues that the core characteristic of a PUI may occur where urban and rural land uses coexist, and where the impacts of the interactions of these are most felt. Bringing together formal and informal governance will be a critical step in managing the PUI sustainably, and this requires research in a variety of situations.

In the drylands case of peri-urban Kano, as examined by Binns and Maconachie in Chapter 15, the critical planning interface is the need for planning sustainability of the natural resource base in the face of increasing population pressures. Here, there is a long history of settlement densification and cultivation, with attendant governance challenges. Administrative boundaries are more or less irrelevant, and accessibility has changed in terms of distance from the city and the road network.

Binns and Maconachie argue that substantial investment and community action are urgently needed in the Kano case, and it might be instructive to consider the Machakos case (Tiffen et al, 1994), where careful holistic planning has reduced land degradation despite a significant increase in population. Although doubts have been cast recently on some of the precepts of the Machakos case, the basic principle of holistic planning – in effect, forms of integrated rural development planning – forms the focus for research.

Elements of community-level planning are required to avoid prejudicing livelihoods, as illustrated by Shindhe in the case of the Hubli-Dharwad bypass (see Chapter 13). The research lessons from this study are that significant impacts on livelihoods and social fabric could have been reduced with appropriate planning effort, taking into account local community fabric and customary activities. Necessary infrastructural projects, such as the Hubli-Dharwad bypass, are bound to affect local patterns of farming and other livelihood activities. Improper planning and, in this particular case, improper execution of construction activities caused significant dislocation in local community life. Further generic issues are the need for proper compensation to be paid (as opposed to promised) and properly planned action to avoid planning blight, such as the provision of sufficient and well-located access roads beneath or above the roadway.

Such issues of the need for planning to be effective at the community level also link through to the peri-urban Accra case (see Chapter 14), where poor planning has led directly to conflict within and between communities, and between communities and government authorities. As elsewhere in Ghana, the issue of planning the layout of building plots in the PUI highlights the need for improved governance, including closer liaison between officials and communities. Here, development control through the imposition of surveyed and 'thematically zoned' plot layouts, while sensible in theory, has proved to be less satisfactory in practice as the surveyed layouts frequently take little account of local topography and hydrology, and inevitably lead to dislocation of traditional livelihoods such as farming.

The very rapid nature of change in the PUI is emphasized throughout this volume, and in Chapter 12, Dangalle and Närman highlight how rapid industrialization in Colombo's PUI has led to planning dislocation. Social, economic and infrastructural capacities have lagged behind industrial development, with knock-on effects on land access, land values and a range of environmental problems. Once again, the research imperative is for focused study of the development process in order to inform proactive planning strategies.

Generically, these chapters illustrate the need for peri-urban planning and management to take account of both the physical and human environments, and to take due account of community-level livelihood and land-use patterns.

Strategies for sustainable development in the peri-urban interface (PUI)

How can the research themes identified above be taken forward? Chapters 16 to 19 in Part 4 illustrate some potential initiatives and structured solutions. Generically, these (and earlier) chapters inform the following issues:

- Strategies for development of the PUI should be community focused and informed, where practicable, by Participatory Action Research (PAR).
- Strategies at community level should be affordable and based, where practicable, upon self-help.
- Participatory technology development works best in promoting the interests of the poor and the marginalized in the PUI.
- Promoting sustainability is a prime requirement, including environmental sustainability.
- With different scales of research focus, different data requirements will be required to inform the way forward.
- Interventionist and pro-poor strategies must be carefully researched.

In this scenario, these issues are not particularly distinctive to the PUI, and more generic research strategies can be drawn upon.

The advantages of PAR are illustrated here by Adam-Bradford et al in Chapter 16 (community-based waste management strategies) and Stevens et al in Chapter 18 (promoting the interests of the peri-urban poor). Waste composting offers an opportunity not only to boost crop production and, potentially, to provide a source of income, but to help in cleaning up the PUI, where the responsibility for refuse collection often falls into a gap between the limits of the city collection services and those of the surrounding districts (as in the case of peri-urban Kumasi; see Chapter 16). Adam-Bradford et al also illustrate how participatory and affordable self-help approaches are essential underpinnings of PAR strategies.

Natural resources suffer severe degradation in many peri-urban zones.

This is illustrated in most chapters in this book – for example, the PUIs of Jos, Yabello, Castries/Anse La Raye, Harare, Accra, Kano and Kumasi. But the approach of the Intermediate Technology Development Group (ITDG), reported for peri-urban Nakuru, Kenya (see Chapter 18), shows graphically how improving livelihoods, particularly for the poor, requires research into the interests and asset base of the poor. In illustrating this through case studies of sand extraction and peri-urban agriculture, the ITDG process of participatory technology development mirrors that of Adam-Bradford et al in terms of action research, which is participatory and pro-poor, with due attention paid to conserving natural resources as far as is practicable.

Such strategies promote sustainability within an environmental context. Experience suggests, however, that the commitment of communities can only be ensured if environmental management strategies are based on low-cost or no-cost interventions and self-help strategies. This is illustrated by the Watershed Management Framework (WMF) discussed in Chapter 19, which is an output of research into ways of putting across environmental and resource management information (here focusing on water resource use and management) at the community level. The nature and effectiveness of information strategies (see also Chapter 6) and interventions are the two critical research imperatives here. The importance of careful research into promotional pathways is evident.

A critical linkage, common to many of the chapters, is of the dependence of PUI inhabitants upon natural resources, but with insecure tenure or access. This leads to increasing vulnerability of the poor (Chapters 9, 14, 15 and 18), exacerbated by lack or weakness of regulatory frameworks (Chapter 11), and to unsustainable exploitation.

It was noted above that with different scales of research focus, different data requirements will be required to inform the way forward. At the community level, information and intervention must be affordable; but this does not apply to the creation of frameworks for strategic planning and governance. The use of GIS for strategic planning is illustrated by the approach of Diaz-Chavez for the PUI of Mexico City (see Chapter 17). The development of indicators suitable for measuring progress towards sustainable development illustrates the generic benefits of information organization available through the medium of GIS. This has also been recognised by the UK Department for International Development (DFID), who have fostered the use of GIS in their Natural Resources Systems Programme (NRSP) research in Hubli-Dharwad and Kumasi (see Brook and Dávila, 2000; McGregor et al, 2002). Thus far, however, the use of GIS has not proved to be easily applicable at the community level, due principally to hardware, software and training costs, though the potential at the institutional planning level is clearly seen.

Conclusions: Directions for research and the dissemination of new knowledge

The key to successful research into the PUI lies in the recognition of the high temporal dynamism of the zone. In this rapidly changing area, research into the linkages between human activities, whether agricultural, urban, residential or industrial, and the natural environment is of critical importance. As the discussion above shows, the concerns with peri-urban production systems and peri-urban planning and management give key pointers to structuring of research. Critical to this is the need for close attention to community practices and dynamics, and generic, concluding questions will now be addressed.

Towards an integrated approach to research in the PUI

The significant consequence of an integrated approach in practical research terms is to shift attention away from studying or verifying peri-urban natural resources management and livelihood strategies as somehow distinct (or unique), and towards a more nuanced and holistic understanding of peri-urban resource use and management as part of the livelihoods/survival strategies, and the perceptions and priorities, of peri-urban residents. These strategies may well involve urban and, perhaps, even rural areas in addition to the peri-urban zone. Stated differently, the approach reorients the principal focus away from a spatially defined zone (the PUI) per se towards a more holistic focus on livelihoods and natural resource use and management of/by peri-urban residents, on the one hand, and on the peri-urban consequences of actions by peri-urban, urban and, perhaps also, rural actors, on the other. A key dimension of the research required to parameterize this approach would be to examine the scope for meaningful action at the community level to address natural resource and environmental problems, and to improve the quality of life, especially for poor and marginalized groups.

In doing so, we should seek to avoid the pitfalls in participatory projects identified by Rhoades (1997). Thus, particular attention should be devoted to:

- local 'ownership' by working through and with community leaders and village committees;
- acknowledging, understanding and seeking to accommodate the diversity of stakeholders and their respective positions and priorities, even at the village level;
- genuine interdisciplinary collaboration in all aspects of the research or intervention, rather than following traditional disciplinary divisions in a manner inimical to holistic integration;
- integrating research, perceptions and awareness-raising at different geographical scales.

Intervention

A key research bottleneck remains the identification of effective mechanisms for transferring new knowledge into widespread changing policy and practice – in effect, how best to target 'intervention'. PAR/Participatory Rural Appraisal (PRA) are very useful in this respect (see, for example, Chapters 16 and 18); but interface with communities (for instance, via community-level facilitators (CLFs)) and engaging officials on a sustained basis are crucial.

The DFID sustainable livelihoods approach is illustrated here through research funded by the NRSP, which ran from 1995 to 2005, and research influenced by the NRSP ethos (see Chapters 4, 7, 10, 16, 18, 19). The 1997 UK government's commitment to poverty reduction led to a revision, in 1998, of DFID's strategy for research on natural resources. The principal focus of NRSP-related research changed then from natural resources-related production increases to the delivery of new knowledge that enables poor and marginalized people who are largely dependent on the natural resource base to improve their livelihoods sustainably. Interventions are therefore focused on the community level, although due attention is paid to dissemination to decision-makers in what might loosely be considered a 'bottom-up' strategy.

In contrast, the Scientific Committee on Problems of the Environment (SCOPE) Peri-Urban Environmental Change Project (PU-ECH) programme (see Chapter 2) focuses on bringing together scientists in order to develop communication with decision-makers and to develop an appropriate research data base with which to inform this interaction. This has some elements of a 'top-down' strategy, though emphasis is placed on work at different scales and on many fronts, on both science and advocacy, with a view to intervening in the most effective way.

In research terms, either approach can be used usefully to structure the research effort. The NRSP focus on capacity-building and the SCOPE PU-ECH approach of providing accurate information to underline advocacy contribute in different ways to a holistic understanding of physical and human conditions within the PUI. The critical issue is one of communication, balancing the needs and aspirations of the community with the economics and logistics of putting practicable solutions in train. The *level* of intervention is less important than researching the full context of the intervention. Thus, an amalgam of the NRSP and PU-ECH approaches would be desirable.

Knowledge gaps

In terms of current natural resource use and management, and environmental quality in the PUI of developing areas, the chapters in this volume point to several generic knowledge gaps. The most important of these gaps relate to:

- the changing nature of agriculture in the PUI as progressive urbanization takes place;
- the extent and precise nature of natural resource quality and degradation/pollution in peri-urban areas, including the contribution of different sources and types of pollutant to the overall degradation/pollution;
- the natural resource-based and other activities of urban industries and peri-urban micro-enterprises that might impact upon peri-urban environmental quality;
- current natural resource use and environmental management practices by peri-urban communities;

- the diverse nature of livelihoods – especially in relation to natural resource use – of people in villages experiencing different degrees of urbanization-driven pressures in the PUI, and how these livelihoods and conditions in the villages have changed due to absorption within the built-up area;
- the generally low levels of awareness among all stakeholders about the state of the peri-urban environment and the exploitation of natural resources; and
- the perceptions and priorities of peri-urban villagers, in particular, in relation to current natural resource use and environmental conditions, as well as potential improvements, including their willingness and ability to adopt low- or no-cost strategies to address natural resource problems.

Addressing community priorities: Research versus technical assistance

In keeping with 'best practice' in development work, any strategy for engaging with communities should be based on the principle of working with and through the existing community structures, rather than simply putting in a borehole, for example, without involving the community in meaningful interaction. Most research shows quite clearly that a small core of involved people tend to be active in a multitude of local fora, and the establishment of a new structure would only add to their loads without necessarily engaging a wider range of people. The appointment of community-level facilitators has been shown to be effective elsewhere (CEDEP, 2004, 2005).

Although technical assistance is clearly essential, raising community awareness of their actual and potential environmental problems empowers communities in ways that 'straight' technical assistance may not. Strategies include:

- raising awareness of existing problems through participatory methods such as the use of basic water testing kits by junior secondary school (JSS) pupils (see Chapter 19), through local radio broadcasts (see Chapter 6) and through production of widely distributed leaflets and posters (see Chapter 19);
- bringing the various stakeholders together to discuss these problems and to explore ways forward by means of community meetings, focus group and roundtable discussions (see Chapters 6, 9, 13 and 14), and field visits to familiarize stakeholders with the variety of conditions in the PUI;
- facilitating self-help and mutual help, through the compilation of resources such as a contact list of agencies who could be of assistance, and through the production of guidelines for community-based diagnosis of problems and appropriate actions to address them (Chapter 19);
- finding some appropriate mechanism for demonstrating these principles and remedial actions to villagers and other stakeholders in the manner of pilot or demonstration projects (Chapter 16).

The rural–urban transect of 'willingness to participate' in interventions

Overall, the experience of interventions suggests clearly that responsiveness and uptake is generally most pronounced in more rural villages, where communal spirit and identity, and the role of traditional leaders are still most evident. Conversely, the more urban communities may have lost much of that ethos, and people tend to be more concerned for their own families and households. This experience is entirely consistent with the notion of the PUI elaborated elsewhere in this volume, where increasing urbanization is quite rapidly reflected in more urban lifestyles and behaviour, even if the village retains traditional leadership and aspects of its identity and territory.

Depending on their specific nature, evaluation of individual one-off events or products in terms of their impact (as distinct from quality) often proves problematic in practice. Relevant examples include cartoon leaflets and radio broadcasts. It is very difficult to attempt to measure changes in public awareness, let alone behaviour, from single actions and interventions. These are longer-term and complex processes, with behavioural change often resulting from cumulative exposure to consistent messages. Post-project evaluation is indicated.

Prioritizing the poor

It is inadequate simply to regard all peri-urban villages and villagers as poor – a view often proposed by local collaborators who tend to be professionals or academics. Even smaller villages may contain significant group and socio-economic differences (see, for example, Chapters 5 and 9). Analysis should also be sensitive to recent poverty discourses (Burnell, 1998; Rakodi, 2002) that highlight wider dimensions of poverty than income and material assets. In particular, relative access to power is an important differentiator even at this level – for instance, in terms of social distance from the chief or elders, or membership of the political party in power.

Discussions with villagers on the subject of 'who are the poor' often prove difficult as the issue is sensitive and perceptions of poverty vary widely. Certainly, chiefs and elders, and other wealthier individuals are generally not very reliable on this. Teachers, nurses and midwives, by contrast, often have good appreciations of the nature and extent of local poverty.

Inclusion of a wide spectrum of people in focus groups and participatory appraisals, ensuring that poor villagers benefit from awareness-raising activities and interventions, is desirable. Although some of the poor may be available during the day on account of their unemployed status, others may be too preoccupied with day-to-day survival to participate. Research outcomes will thus be biased away from the needs of the poor. In addition, factors such as literacy may act to exclude the poor from access to help.

Distinctiveness of the PUI and natural resource issues within it

The research reported in this volume leads us to the conclusion that the PUI is most appropriately conceived of as something of a continuum (although not necessarily with a simple linear form) between the poles of urban and rural. The width and nature, and even particular boundaries, of the PUI are dynamic and subject to rapid change according to the pace of urban growth and related processes. The distinctiveness of the PUI is therefore twofold:

1   the spectrum of conditions from de facto 'urban' to 'rural', with the most intensive impacts of urban influence occurring in the 'inner' zone closest to the growing city; and
2   the rapid change in conditions, with a changing balance between essentially urban and rural features.

The implications of this for natural resource use, environmental quality and natural resource-based livelihoods follow fairly logically. In essence, there are no unique or distinctive natural resource uses and livelihood activities associated with the PUI that do not occur elsewhere. Rather, as villages begin to experience urban influences – in terms of improved access; changing pressures on land use and natural resources; increasing pollution; arrival of outsiders seeking affordable accommodation; reduced prices for manufactured goods; and so on – their rural character starts to change, with a progressive shift towards combinations of rural and urban features, activities and facilities. Ultimately, when urbanization is complete, such areas are no longer peri-urban.

In terms of natural resources, there is a progressive shift from agricultural and pastoral land use towards residential, commercial or industrial use. This is almost invariably associated with increases in land values but losses of entitlement on the part of some farmers if appropriate compensation is not forthcoming and, hence, a sometimes dramatic impact on their livelihoods. Similarly, pressure on woody biomass for fuelwood or through land clearance intensifies, leading to scarcity and, perhaps, commoditization as its collection and sale become livelihood activities for some people (see, for example, Chapter 9). Sand winning commonly also increases in floodplain areas, with environmental (Chapters 5 and 18) as well as health impacts if rehabilitation is not undertaken to prevent the breeding of disease vectors in water-filled borrow pits or windblown erosion of exposed soil. Available land for other purposes also declines. Water and air pollution from the city commonly increase, while intensive agriculture or livestock/poultry rearing for urban markets, along with inappropriate disposal of the growing volumes of human waste and refuse (Chapter 16), may contaminate the groundwater and rivers.

In terms of livelihood strategies, the increase of urban pressures therefore leads to adaptation and diversification for most people, particularly the relatively and absolutely poor. Where possible, this may result in a combination of rural and urban livelihood activities – for example, wage labour and cultivation. Otherwise, different non-urban activities may become necessary, using traditional skills (for instance, craft production for urban or tourist markets) or new ones (such as food and other commodity provision; see Chapter 10). Certain environmentally harmful activities that use natural resources do tend to concentrate in peri-urban areas, where the land or other resources are still available. Examples include car washing adjacent to rivers or streams and stone crushing for the road-building and construction industries. However, even these are not distinctively peri-urban, and not all those who carry them out are peri-urban residents.

The sense of environmental dynamism and human pressures on natural resources does distinguish the PUI from the rural or the urban. Investigating the interaction between humans and their natural resource base remains the generic research key in approaches to sustainable natural and human resource use in the PUI.

References

Brook, R. M. and Dávila, J. D. (2000) *The Peri-Urban Interface: A Tale of Two Cities*, School of Agricultural and Forest Sciences, University of Wales, Bangor and Development Planning Unit, University College London

Burnell, P. (1998) 'Britain's new government, new White Paper, new aid? Eliminating world poverty: a challenge for the 21st century', *Third World Quarterly*, vol 19, no 4, pp787–802

CEDEP (Centre for the Development of People) (2004) *DFID Project R8090. Research Report 1: Community Level Facilitators*, CEDEP, Kumasi, Ghana

CEDEP (2005) *Final Technical Report of R8090, Boafe ye Na*, CEDEP, Kumasi

McGregor, D. F. M., Simon, D. and Thompson, D. A. (2002) *Project R7330 Peri-Urban Natural Resources Management at the Watershed Level, Kumasi, Ghana*, Centre for Developing Areas Research, Royal Holloway, University of London, www.gg.rhul.ac.uk/kumasi.html

Rakodi, C. with Lloyd-Jones, T. (eds) (2002) *Urban Livelihoods: A People-Centred Approach to Reducing Poverty*, Earthscan, London

Rhoades, R. E. (1997) *The Participatory Multipurpose Watershed Project: Nature's Salvation or Schumacher's Nightmare?*, Keynote address, Conference on Global Challenges in Ecosystem Management in a Watershed Context, Toronto, Canada, 25–26 July

Simon D., McGregor, D. and Nsiah-Gyabaah, K. (2004) 'The changing urban–rural interface of African cities: Definitional issues and an application to Kumasi, Ghana', *Environment and Urbanization*, vol 16, no 2, pp235–247

Tiffen, M., Mortimore, M. and Gichuki, F. (1994) *More People, Less Erosion: Environmental Recovery in Kenya*, John Wiley and Sons, Chichester

Index